Ethnocentrism:

THEORIES OF CONFLICT, ETHNIC ATTITUDES, AND GROUP BEHAVIOR

ETHNOCENTRISM:
Theories of Conflict, Ethnic Attitudes, and Group Behavior

Robert A. LeVine
University of Chicago

Donald T. Campbell
Northwestern University

John Wiley & Sons, Inc., New York · London · Sydney · Toronto

Library of Congress Cataloging in Publication Data

LeVine, Robert Alan, 1932–
    Ethnocentrism: theories of conflict, ethnic attitudes, and group behavior.

    Bibliography: p.
    1. Ethnocentrism. 2. Social conflict. I. Campbell, Donald Thomas, 1916– joint author.

HT1521.L43   301.6'36   72-39130

ISBN 0-471-53117-0

Printed in the United States of America

10 9 8 7 6 5 4 3 2 1

PREFACE

This book originated in 1958 when we, an anthropologist (R.A.L.) and a psychologist (D.T.C.), participated in a faculty seminar on international relations at Northwestern University, organized by the political scientist Richard C. Snyder. As we discussed the possible universality of political scientists' hypotheses about international relations and attempted to bring cross-cultural evidence to bear on this problem, we realized that modern social and cultural anthropology has seriously neglected interethnic relations, warlike and peaceful, as a topic for data collection. The relevant cross-cultural facts are not available in publications or archives and, furthermore, may never be recorded, since the precolonial (or prenational) period in which ethnic groups were not controlled by European authority is receding from the memories of living men. This urgent situation induced us to draft a "Proposal for Cooperative Cross-Cultural Research on Ethnocentrism," which was circulated among specialists on intergroup relations. The proposal was revised and published in a special issue of the *Journal of Conflict Resolution* (1961) on the anthropology of conflict (the issue being edited by R.A.L.). In the proposal we suggested, in detail, topical areas and interview questions for ethnographic data collection on interethnic behavior, attitudes, and hypothetical correlates of such behavior and attitudes. (Our efforts in this regard were supported by Richard C. Snyder's Programs in International Relations and Comparative Politics, and by Melville J. Herskovits' Program of African Studies.)

Our proposal put the methodological cart before the theoretical horse: the research instrument had been designed, even though in preliminary form, before the systematic survey of the questions that it was supposed to answer. We then made an inventory of the varied and contradictory social science theoretical literature for the propositions about ethnocentrism that were testable in cross-cultural research. We did this in the manner of other propositional inventories, that is, by extracting from complex theoretical formulations their empirical implications and stating them as testable propositions in a common operational terminology. The researcher armed with this inventory could go to the field or do his comparative analysis not as a partisan of one theory or another but in the spirit of discovering which of several contradictory propositions survived the confrontation with the facts. In 1962, the Carnegie Corporation of New York made a five-year grant to Northwestern University to allow us to carry out our "Proposal" as a project involving the cooperation of dozens of anthropologists, and the inventory assumed the highest priority on our work schedule.

Four or five versions of the theory survey were written between 1962 and 1969. The early versions informed the first groups of cooperating anthropological field workers on the Cross-Cultural Study of Ethnocentrism (CCSE) about the theoretical interests of the study. Investigators often try to eliminate bias in research by keeping the data collectors ignorant of the hypotheses being tested; we reversed this strategy, asking the cooperating anthropologists to acquaint themselves with the range of competing predictions and contradictory implications of social science theories for their field research. A semifinal version of the survey was mimeographed in 1965 and was distributed to the CCSE field workers before they began collecting data.

As the research project developed, our original goal of a systematic inventory of propositions about ethnocentrism seemed less attainable and less desirable — less attainable because, properly defined, the task appeared endlessly perfectible; less desirable because the rigid style of a propositional inventory would detract from its readability for dubious research benefits. In any event, in transforming this survey from a project working paper into a book, we have been acutely aware of its less than complete accomplishment of the original goals: it is neither as comprehensive nor as systematic as we had intended. Moreover, it bears our personal stamp; we do not believe that anyone else surveying theories in this field would extract the same propositions and arrive at the same conclusions about their relations to one another, despite our initially objective intent. (The survey did turn out, however, to be as interdisciplinary as we intended: some chapters are jointly written, with little internal discontinuity; some of the anthropological chapters have been written by the psychologist and vice versa.) As a book, the survey retains some of the limitations imposed by its role in the cross-cultural study of ethnocentrism, primarily its comparative, anthropological focus on cross-cultural variation across the full spectrum of human societies.

Whatever its limitations of scope and purpose, this book identifies some theoretically crucial problems for comparative research on war and peace and ethnic relations. Also, for the student of intergroup behavior and related topics, it is an introduction to diverse bodies of theory that make predictions about a single subject matter of prime importance to the human species. Finally, we hope that it will contribute to the current discussions of how the social science disciplines can be made relevant to policy problems that face the world's peoples.

For the support of the writing of this book we thank not only the Carnegie Corporation and Northwestern University but also the National Institute of

Mental Health (for Research Scientist Development Award K-502-MH18444-10 to R.A.L.) and the Center for Advanced Study in the Behavioral Sciences. Many of those who worked with us on the CCSE contributed to the book. They include Marilynn B. Brewer (whose coauthorship of Chapters 11 to 13 and general editorial management are acknowledged), George Roth (who contributed the term "ethnic community" and other ideas to Chapter 7), Paul C. Rosenblatt, Daniel Druckman, and Jerome Barkow. We are also indebted to the many social science colleagues who responded to earlier versions of this work with critical and supportive comments.

Grateful acknowledgment is made to the following publishers and authors for permission to quote copyrighted material:

American Anthropological Association, American Psychological Association, M. K. Bacon, M. H. Fried, J. R. Goody, International African Institute, London. Institute of Psycho-Analysis, E. R. Leach, London School of Economics Monographs on Social Anthropology, I. D. Mac Crone, The MacMillan Company, R. K. Merton, M. Moerman, C. S. Otterbein, K. F. Otterbein, Oxford University Press, Princeton University Press, Mrs. Alix Strachey, H. U. E. Thoden van Velzen, University of Washington Press, A. P. Vayda, G. A. Zegwaard. Finally, we thank Sarah E. LeVine for assistance with the index.

Robert A. LeVine
Donald T. Campbell

CONTENTS

INTRODUCTION

Ethnocentrism has become a familiar word most generally understood, in parallel with "egocentrism," as an attitude or outlook in which values derived from one's own cultural background are applied to other cultural contexts where different values are operative. In the most naive form of ethnocentrism, termed "phenomenal absolutism" by Segall, Campbell, and Herskovits (1965), a person unreflectively takes his own culture's values as objective reality and automatically uses them as the context within which he judges less familiar objects and events. As in Piaget's stage of egocentric thought, it does not occur to such a person that there is more than one point of view. At a more complex level is the ethnocentric attitude or outlook that takes account of multiple points of view but regards those of other cultures as incorrect, inferior or immoral.

Even as generally understood, however, ethnocentrism is not simply a matter of intellectual functioning but involves emotions that are positive and negative. Symbols of one's own ethnic or national group or of the values shared by that group (or both) become objects of attachment, pride, and veneration; symbols of other groups or their values become objects of contempt and hatred. Furthermore, groups develop collective symbol systems that arouse the ethnocentric emotions shared by individuals in a population.

Thus the term "ethnocentrism" in common usage indicates individual attitudes and emotions, cultural symbols, and ideologies. Social scientists since Sumner (1906), however, have been primarily interested in collective actions and institutions that could be termed ethnocentric — actions and institutions augmenting order, solidarity and cooperation within a group or violence and antagonism between groups — and in the connections between such actions and the ethnocentrism of attitude and ideology. Concerned with relations among nations, "tribes," and groups defined by race, religion, language, and ethnicity, social scientists have debated questions such as: Are ethnocentric attitudes and ideologies autonomous forces that can lead to war and discrimination or are they merely mobilized to support warlike and discriminatory policies that have been

1

caused by other factors? Can nations and "tribes" achieve stable boundaries and internal cohesion without engaging other nations and "tribes" in conflict? If not, must the conflict be violent?

In introducing the concept of ethnocentrism into the comparative sociology of his day, William Graham Sumner offered a view that answered these questions in no uncertain terms: the ethnocentrisms of attitude, ideology, and action were inextricably linked together, mutually reinforcing, universal, and necessary for survival. Some subsequent social scientists have shared his certainty, but others have not. More important, they have developed conceptions of group behavior that are consistent in detail neither with Sumner's views nor with each other. The result is an extensive literature on topics related to ethnocentrism – in anthropology, economics, political science, psychology, and sociology – without substantial agreement about what it is or how it works.

The specialized social science disciplines are largely a product of the twentieth century, in which world events have brought the phenomena of war and peace, nationalism, and ethnic relations to the forefront of public awareness and concern. Developed in this milieu, most theories of man and society have something to say about cohesion and conflict in human groups. Even theories about the individual rather than the group have been extrapolated to the level of groups and their interaction. As each deterministic or reductive school of thought has claimed sovereignty over the domain of ethnocentrism, more complex explanatory systems have proliferated to dispute those claims. The conceptual territory of ethnocentrism cuts across the analytic boundaries of the social, cultural, and personality systems; it is thus a natural field for the clash of diverse social science theories, expressing their more general opposition in terms of explaining war, ethnic relations, and nationalism. But the combat has seldom been direct, and each camp has tended to put a barrage from its armamentarium of terminology and has declared an easy victory. The field has thus been obscured by the smoke of battle without a decisive conflict. At this point the positions must be clarified before the outlines of a settlement can be imagined.

In this book we have undertaken this task of clarification. Our goal is to restate social science theories about ethnocentrism in terms that expose both their contradictions, implicit and explicit, and their agreements, latent as well as manifest. Sumner is our point of departure, not because we endorse his view or even credit him with theoretical invention, but because in his concept of ethnocentrism he brought together the social, cultural, and psychological aspects of the phenomenon in a comparative perspective of broad relevance to the sciences of man, and because he did so early enough to influence in one way or another most important formulations on the subject. We share Sumner's comparative perspective and his interest in peoples at all levels of socioeconomic and technological development, and we seek to bring that interest in the diversity of humankind to the specialized theorizing of the last 60 years.

This survey of social science theories begins without our attempting to define ethnocentrism. We discuss, instead, Sumner's early conceptualization in detail and explicate its social and psychological implications as fully as possible. We then examine a variety of social and psychological theories for their implications on the same subjects, always focusing on cross-cultural variations in ethnocentric actions, institutions, ideologies and attitudes. Finally we compare these theories with respect to their agreements and disagreements, highlighting contradictory propositions about the shape of future evidence.

The appendix presents our field manual for ethnographic research on the propositions uncovered by our survey.

Nov. 1, 90

Crystal,

I ~~would~~ wish to
speak to you ~~I~~
won't be home Allday
but I'll be in school
tommorow at 11:00 Am

Gwen

PART 1

The Concept of Ethnocentrism

Chapter 1

SUMNER AND THE UNIVERSAL SYNDROME
OF ETHNOCENTRISM

In his *Folkways* of 1906, William Graham Sumner contributed to modern social science the widely used concepts of *ingroup, outgroup,* and *ethnocentrism.* Considering the elaboration of these concepts today, it is surprising that his formal presentation of them takes only a page and a half, and that his total presentation, which includes 18 one-sentence illustrations plus an extension of the concept to cover chauvinism and patriotism, comprises only four pages. Because of its historical importance in establishing the problem area, the basic one and one half page selection is given here in full:

"13. *The concept of 'primitive society;' we-group and others-group.* The conception of 'primitive society' which we ought to form is that of small groups scattered over a territory. The size of the groups is determined by the conditions of the struggle for existence. The internal organization of each group corresponds to its size. A group of groups may have some relation to each other (kin, neighborhood, alliance, connubium and commercium) which draws them together and differentiates them from others. Thus a differentiation arises between ourselves, the we-group, or in-group, and everybody else, or the others-group, out-groups. The insiders in a we-group are in a relation of peace, order, law, government, and industry, to each other. Their relation to all outsiders, or others-groups, is one of war and plunder, except so far as agreements have modified it. If a group is exogamic, the women in it were born abroad somewhere. Other foreigners who might be found in it are adopted persons, guest friends, and slaves.

"14. *Sentiments in the in-group and towards the out-group.* The relation of comradeship and peace in the we-group and that of hostility and war towards others-groups are correlative to each other. The exigencies of war with outsiders are what make peace inside, lest internal discord should weaken the we-group for war. These exigencies also make government and law in the in-group, in order to prevent quarrels and enforce discipline. Thus war and peace have reacted on each other and developed each other, one within the group, the other in the intergroup relation. The closer the neighbors, and the stronger they are, the intenser is the warfare, and then the intenser is the internal organization and discipline of each. Sentiments are produced to correspond. Loyalty to the group, sacrifice for it, hatred and contempt for outsiders, brotherhood within, warlikeness without — all group together, common products of the same situation. These relations and sentiments constitute a social philosophy. It is sanctified by connection with religion. Men of an others-group are outsiders with whose ancestors the ancestors of the we-group waged war. The ghosts of the latter will see with pleasure their descendants keep up the fight, and will help them. Virtue consists in killing, plundering, and enslaving outsiders.

"15. *Ethnocentrism* is the technical name for this view of things in which one's own group is the center of everything, and all others are scaled and rated with reference to it. Folkways correspond to it to cover both the inner and the outer relation. Each group nourishes its own pride and vanity, boasts itself superior, exalts its own divinities, and looks with contempt on outsiders. Each group thinks its own folkways the only right ones, and if it observes that other groups have other folkways, these excite its scorn. Opprobrious epithets are derived from these differences. 'Pig-eater,' 'cow-eater,' 'uncircumcised,' 'jabberers,' are epithets of contempt and abomination. The Tupis called the Portuguese by a derisive epithet descriptive of birds which have feathers around their feet, on account of trousers (Martius, *Ethnog. Brasil.*, 51). For our present purpose the most important fact is that ethnocentrism leads a people to exaggerate and intensify everything in their own folkways which is peculiar and which differentiates them from others. It therefore strengthens the folkways" (Sumner, 1906, pp. 12-13).

These paragraphs set the general problem area and touch on most of the major variables of this book. We are using the term ethnocentrism to cover both the ingroup-outgroup polarization of hostility and the self-centered scaling of all values in terms of the ingroup folkways. Ambiguity of usage is possible here, since some have taken the first sentence of Sumner's paragraph 15 as a complete definition. We, on the contrary, take the phrase "this view of things," to refer back to his preceding paragraphs 13 and 14, and thus utilize the broader connotation, that is, the "relations" as well as the "sentiments."

Sumner's theory, if it may be called that, has these three facets: he points to a number of attributes of social life and hypothesizes that these go together as a syndrome; he posits that this syndrome of ethnocentrism is functionally related to group formation and intergroup competition; he generalizes that all groups show this syndrome. In this chapter we focus primarily on the first and third of them; the second is dealt with subsequently in Chapter 3's discussion of realistic-group-conflict theories.

Before elaborating the facets of the ethnocentric syndrome, some methodological explanation is needed. We enumerate the components of the syndrome, not only as explicitly stated by Sumner but also as implied by him. We make more explicit and subdivide such terms of Sumner as "peace group" and "contempt." We also include a few features not identifiable in Sumner's presentation but that are a part of the syndrome as used by social scientists today. For the syndrome, even if not the explanation of it, is a widely shared common property of the social sciences, not necessarily because of the influence of Sumner, but rather because of the recurrent encountering of it by scholars starting from quite divergent backgrounds, as from the historical and political study of modern nationalism, or from the individual psychology of prejudice.

In the course of enumerating the features of the syndrome, we attempt to separate where possible the ingroup orientation variables from the outgroup orientation variables, to make more testable Sumner's most important insight that the two are functionally related. For many topics this cannot be done because the essential variable is a contrast or comparison, the two sides of the contrast being essential to any statement of it, and the two separate statements of it being redundant. In fact, in certain instances, we have probably pushed the separation to an untenable degree.

Two other preoccupations are present. First is the effort to state each variable in such form that groups could be described as differing on it. This done, Sumner's posited ethnocentric syndrome becomes the general hypothesis that all of these dimensions of group difference will show positive correlation with each other, will represent a general factor, and will scale as a unidimensional scale. Thus groups with the most ingroup peace should show the greatest outgroup hostility, and the like. A little of this attention to correlated group differences is explicitly present in Sumner, as in these sentences: "The size of the groups is determined by the conditions of the struggle for existence. The internal organization of each group corresponds to its size." And still more relevantly, "The closer the neighbors, and the stronger they are, the intenser is the warfare and then the intenser is the internal organization and discipline of each." This is essentially the form of the modern interest — more interested in laws of relationship among variables than in statements of universals in categorical form. It lends itself to simple graphic and quantitative description, as in the correlation coefficient. It is the most general form in which the competing theories can be translated into testable predictions. We thus begin here the list of variables with which more formal theories will repeatedly deal.

Second and more difficult is an effort to explicate Sumner's propositions so that the allegation of universality can be tested. That such propositions are occasionally testable can be noted by a consideration of the problem of the universality of warfare and warlikeness. The data reject this universal. Sumner himself notes exceptions (Sumner et al., 1927). However, on ethnocentrism he cites no exceptions to contrast with his numerous positive instances. In *Folkways* (1906) he cites 18 cases. In *The Science of Society* (Sumner et. al,

1927), under the topic "group hostility" in Volumes 1 and 4, he cites 75 positive illustrations. That he cites no negative instances is presumably because in his wide-range reading he found none. However, with a multiple-faceted syndrome and the freedom to cite a different aspect for each different tribe, this is perhaps less surprising, and certainly calls for a trait-by-trait examination of the proposition of universality. Equally problematic is how to interpret the hundreds of ethnographies that he read which presumably failed to touch on the subject. For this data quality problem (cf Naroll, 1962) the theory of ethnocentrism is itself reflexively relevant. We must assume that the very great preponderance of the ethnographers available for Sumner to read were themselves unconsciously ethnocentric (see Boas, 1904; 1905; 1911; Sapir, 1928). We must further assume that these ethnographers were subject to a very universal law of stimulus strength or strikingness, in which the more unexpected, the less usual, and the farthest from the ethnographer's adaptation level on any given dimension, the greater the stimulus intensity (Helson, 1959; Campbell, 1961). Thus, for example, when an ethnographer who himself regarded the people he studied as obviously inferior found in them a self-adulation and pride comparable to that of a European, this was highly noteworthy, surprising, and humorous. Whereas if a group had a demeaning self-image in agreement with the ethnographer's view of them, it might well have gone unnoticed. And even an ethnographer whose negative cathexis of his own culture and its ethnocentrism led him in the manner of Swift's *Gulliver's Travels* to use the ethnocentrism he found abroad to provide perspective on the ethnocentrism of his own culture would be more apt to notice positive instances than negative ones.

Relevant background to this problem is a minor study done preparatory to the present inquiry (reported in Campbell and LeVine, 1961, p. 84). A sample of 55 groups from the Human Relations Area Files were examined under the topics of Ethnocentrism, Behavior towards Nonrelatives, International Relations, Ethnic Stratification, and Ingroup Antagonisms. *Some* information on ethnocentrism was judged to be present in 36 of the 55, but with no more possibility of systematic topic coverage than in Sumner. Of the 36, 35 were judged to be ethnocentric. The one negative instance, if it be that, were the Lepchas (Gorer, 1938). The Lepchas are reported to have a fundamental acceptance of other groups as equals with customs which, while unacceptable for Lepchas' use, are perfectly moral for the group in question. Nevertheless, these differences in custom are a frequent topic of Lepcha conversation, and are noted with both amusement and personal disgust. Taken as a whole, the data do not seem significantly to invalidate Sumner's bold universal generalization.

We retain, therefore, an interest, albeit quixotic and archaic, in testing and elaborating the universal proposition. We would like to render it testable facet by facet, and to describe the minimum contents of the syndrome that can be regarded as universal. Two types of problems are encountered in this. First, some of the features are so obviously true, so inextricably tied up with the designation of group qua group as to make incongruous or insulting an attempt to collect data on them. Thus ingroup members universally show greater obedience to ingroup authorities than to outgroup authorities, show retention of ingroup membership rather than conversion to outgroups, and show greater willingness to fight and die for ingroup preservation than for outgroup causes. These are important empirical hypotheses only if group membership can be designated independently of them. Even if this is possible, the empirical verification of them might be feasible only through long-term observation. Such propositions will be touched on however, if only for completeness and in recognition of the protean role of tautologies in empirical science. What at a pretheoretical level are nontautological empirical regularities (such as the fact that the sum of the angles of a triangle is 180°) become analytic tautologies (for example, implied in the definition of triangle) when a theory successfully relating them has become accepted.

Another problem in the testing of universals comes from the fact that what are stated as categorical qualities, present or absent, are, in fact, dimensions on which the present-absent dichotomization boundary is arbitrarily drawn. Thus potentially we can affirm or infirm the hypothesis of universality by where we draw the line. The edge of this criticism is, in practice, blunted by the availability of points of dichotomization for bipolar pairs of terms that are established by referents separate from the comparison of groups; and by creative imaginations that can conjure up nonactualized possibilities against which to contrast the actual — to show that the actual is distributed in only a narrow range of the dimension of the conceivable. In any event, even when examined more closely, some facets of the syndrome hypothesized as universal attributes of groups still seem to us worth empirical investigation with resulting infirming or affirmation. Such a facet is, perhaps, contained in Points 1.1[1] and 1.2 that follow.

Facets of the Syndrome of Ethnocentrism

As an initial overview, a listing of 23 facets of the syndrome of ethnocentrism is offered (see Table 1.1). This is followed by an expanded treatment of each. The last three are definitely not present in Sumner, but are widely included in

---

[1] Throughout this chapter and the subsequent expositions of theories, a number system is used to designate variables or propositions. The portion to the left of the decimal indicates the chapter, and therefore the theory, in which the variable or proposition receives its major presentation; the portion to the right indicates the ordinal position of treatment within the chapter. Such numbers are used for cross referencing. Where the same variable or proposition is an integral part of two theories, it may receive a separate number in each. A convenient mode of abbreviation and cross reference has been sought, rather than a logical notation of analytic consistency. In some instances a generic concept and its component parts are numbered seriatum, without the number system indicating this part-whole relationship. Propositions needed in the exposition of the theory have been numbered without distinction from the derived propositions stated at a potentially testable level.

Table 1.1

Attitudes and Behaviors Toward Ingroup	Attitudes and Behaviors Toward Outgroup
1.1 See selves as virtuous and superior	1.2 See outgroup as contemptible, immoral, and inferior
1.3 See own standards of value as universal, intrinsically true. See own customs as original, centrally human	
1.4 See selves as strong	1.5 See outgroups as weak
	1.6 Social distance
	1.7 Outgroup hate
1.8 Sanctions against ingroup theft	1.9 Sanctions for outgroup theft, or absence of sanctions against.
1.10 Sanctions against ingroup murder	1.11 Sanctions for outgroup murder or absence of sanctions against outgroup murder
1.12 Cooperative relations with ingroups members	1.13 Absence of cooperation with outgroup members
1.14 Obedience to ingroup authorities	1.15 Absence of obedience to outgroup authorities
1.16 Willingness to remain an ingroup member	1.17 Absence of conversion to outgroup membership
1.18 Willingness to fight and die for ingroup	1.19 Absence of willingness to fight and die for outgroups
	1.20 Virtue in killing outgroup members in warfare
	1.21 Use of outgroups as bad examples in the training of children
	1.22 Blaming of outgroup for ingroup troubles
	1.23 Distrust and fear of the outgroup

other discussions. Sumner's concept of "contempt" has been split into superior morality, which is clearly intended, and superior strength, which is more problematic both as to Sumner's meaning and as an empirical generalization. Similar expansion has been given Sumner's concepts of "peace group" and "loyalty."

1.1   *See selves as virtuous and superior.*
1.2   *See outgroup as contemptible, immoral, and inferior.*

Although these two facets are obviously related, we believe it is possible to measure them independently enough to make their concomitance problematic. In fact, Sullivan and Adelson (1954) found that favorable attitudes toward the ingroup go with favorable attitudes toward outgroups. Their setting was, of course, highly different, representing individual differences within a single ingroup instead of differences between groups, and representing attitudes toward internal minorities instead of discrete outgroups.

If ingroup members describe ingroup characteristics and outgroup characteristics in such a way that the number of good and bad characteristics attributed to each can be computed, then the proportion of good characteristics (in terms of the ingroup's evaluation) should be more than one half for the ingroup and less than one half for the outgroup, and the higher is the self-adulation index, the more disparaging should be the net image of any outgroups. Similarly, if groups are compared on morality, the ingroup should be judged more moral and virtuous than the outgroup.

Sumner's claim of universality might be judged to be confirmed at any of these different levels: (a) *all* outgroups receive a net unfavorable index and all ingroups receive a favorable balance; (b) the *average* outgroup described by each ingroup receives a net description that is unfavorable and all ingroups receive a favorable balance; (c) all outgroups receive a less favorable description than does the ingroup in question; (d) the average outgroup described by one ingroup receives a less favorable description than does the ingroup for all ingroups studied. Levels *c* and *d* do not achieve the independent confirmation of the two aspects, and do not make possible the correlation confirmation utilizing group differences. However, even the confirmation at level *d* would be an impressive confirmation of the claimed universality.

In dealing with ethnographic data in the confirmation of correlational hypotheses like this, one should be alert to the possibility of systematic relationships emerging from differences in data quality (Naroll, 1962). In the present content area, these dangers seem likely: the less rapport the ethnographer has with the informant, the more defensive and less self-critical the informant is apt to be, and this might result in a greater net ingroup-favorability, and in that way more ethnocentrism. On the other hand, outgroup deprecation might be suppressed by informants who are concerned with the development of modern nationalism, for which traditional tribalism has been such a recurrent obstacle and available tool for colonialist control. Again, it may minimize the reported ethnocentrism that the "best" informants are often local social science types, semi-alienated and negatively ethnocentric, and more apt to be critical of their own society than would be the typical ingroup member.

1.3   *See own standards of value as universal, intrinsically true. See own customs as original, centrally human.*

One core meaning of ethnocentrism is "This view of things in which one's own group is the center of everything, and all others are scaled and rated with reference to it . . . Each group thinks its own folkways the only right ones" (Sumner, 1906, p. 13). Six of the 18 illustrations provided in *Folkways* are instances of peoples whose name for their own tribe means *men* or real *people*, and others illustrate ethnocentric value absolutism. This usage has been preserved in current anthropological discussions, particularly in regard to cultural relativism (for example, Herskovits, 1948; Segall, Campbell, and Herskovits, 1966), as when one is criticizing the ethnocentrism of the modern Western citizen who assumes that his own values are the universally correct ones. In ethnographic data this aspect of ethnocentrism is manifest when ingroup informants provide disparaging or negative moral evaluations of the customs of neighboring tribes in such a way as to imply a belief in the universal moral rightness of their own customs, a belief that all persons "ought" in some absolute God-given sense live up to and be judged by the values of the ingroup culture. This aspect of ethnocentrism is related to the more general naive "phenomenal absolutism" (Segall, Campbell, and Herskovits, 1966), the tendency to assume that the world is exactly as one sees it, and that all other persons (other groups, other cultures) really perceive it in the same way but behave the way they do out of a perverse wickedness or incompetence. The naive confidence lying behind these views makes it sometimes difficult to get them into the ethnographic record. Thus an informant may describe in objective terms the customs of a neighboring tribe which are actually extremely offensive to him, without making this moral judgment explicit because of the assumption that the ethnographer as a sensible man will have the same moral reaction, a sort of "need I say more" assurance of a common evaluative base. The fact that the basic conversation is usually between informant and interpreter (as Phillips, 1960, has effectively described), and the fact that the interpreter is a fellow tribesman for whom less explanation is actually needed, accentuates this difficulty.

1.4   *See selves as strong.*
1.5   *See outgroups as weak.*

The concept of strength and weakness is certainly a part of the more general idea of ingroup superiority and of contempt for outgroups. Yet unlike moral superiority, it is one on which a transcultural standard of judgment is apt to exist, and for which the objective realities are apt to be so compelling as to lead some of the weakest groups to concede the superior strength of the most obviously strongest outgroups. For this reason, it seems best to treat it separately. What is referred to is the collective strength and power of the group, rather than the physical strength of individual men, insofar as these are independent. Strength in warfare is the major referent. The image of the ingroup as brave and the outgroup as cowardly in warfare is relevant.

The hypothesis of universality might be confirmed at these levels: At one extreme, *each* ingroup might describe itself as strong, and all of its outgroups as weak, or might rank itself as the strongest of local groups. At an intermediate level, each ingroup might rank itself as stronger than the average of its outgroups. Where the study of each of a group of neighboring tribes makes possible a pooled consensus as to relative strengths which may be treated as "correct," then a minimal test is made available, in which each ingroup should exaggerate its own strength relative to that of its outgroups.

1.6   *Social distance.*

Although the notion that an ingroup restricts outgroups from certain degrees of intimacy allowed to ingroup members is not quite explicit in Sumner's presentation, it seems in keeping with it, and has represented a part of many other uses of the term ethnocentrism (for example, Adorno et al., 1950). This content area taps an enormous independent research area initiated by Bogardus around 1923 (Bogardus, 1925; 1928). This research area has been primarily focused on the comparative degree of social distance at which specific outgroups are held by a given ingroup, and it has been utilized primarily for such specific descriptive purposes. In Bogardus' form and in variations, it has been used throughout the world (for example, Dodd, 1935; Adinarayaniah, 1941; Prothro and Melikian, 1952; Mukerjee, 1951; Lambert, 1952; Smythe and Kono, 1954; Catapusan, 1954; Mitchell, 1956; Berreman, 1958; Mehar, 1959, 1960; Triandis and Triandis, 1962). This literature supports some universal generalizations: that all ingroups, as judged by the average member, hold most outgroups at some degree of social distance, even if not that all ingroups hold all outgroups at some social distance. Over and above these universals, perusal of the literature shows large differences among ingroups in the degree of social distance at which outgroups are held, and for any ingroup, highly stable differences in the distance to which different outgroups are held. These dimensions of variation are among the most important of those on which social science theories offer predictions.

Another dimension of possible universals lies in the rank ordering of social-distance steps. Although Bogardus' steps are somewhat specific to a multi-ethnic, industrialized national state (visitor to nation, co-national, local co-resident, co-professional, friend, marriage), some of the stages might be universally appropriate and rank ordered in the same way. Other steps need to be added, and each local setting may have its own. Thus Mukerjee (1951) and

Mahar (1959, 1960) used special caste-related steps, such as touching metal pots, touching earthen pots, and admittance to the kitchen. Steps that might prove of wide relevance would include admission to homes and meals, the rights of immigrants to own land, the rights to till land, and the rights of access to leadership roles.

1.7   *Hatred of outgroups.*

Although closely allied, hate and disrespect (as represented in 1.2) are occasionally separable, hate and respect for specific qualities occasionally going together. Perhaps even more certainly universal than unfavorable stereotypes of outgroups is dislike of outgroups. From the standpoint of testing theories, predicting which outgroup is most disliked by the ingroup is of particular utility.

1.8   *Sanctions against ingroup theft.*
1.9   *Sanctions favoring theft from outgroups, or absence of sanctions against.*

Central to Sumner's conception is the ingroup as a peace group and the outgroup as one against which plunder is sanctioned. Recurrent in the writings of others is the observation of the double standard in traditional morality, one set of ethics for ingroup members, a lower set or no restraints for outgroup members (for example, Rosenblatt, 1964; Cooley, 1902, p. 240; Gilbert, 1950, pp. 28-30; Goffman, 1959, pp. 214, 215; Green, 1956, p. 425; Katz, 1940; Lasswell, 1927; Murdock, 1931; Westermarck, 1926). Theft may be used as one symptom of "peace group" versus "plunder." Killing and rape are others.

At the level of sanctions, Sumner may turn out to be right about the universal presence of ingroup theft prohibitions, although he probably exaggerated the universality of sanctions that encourage the plunder of outgroups. At the level of actual frequency, greater opportunity and temptation might make ingroup theft more frequent than outgroup theft.

1.10   *Sanctions against ingroup murder.*
1.11   *Sanctions favoring murder of outgroup members or absence of sanctions against outgroup murder.*

It is hardly problematic that all groups have some sanctions against murder among the ingroup, although groups such as the Eskimo may rank this crime as less serious than some others. More problematic is the universality of sanctions in favor of isolated killing of outgroup members independent of war.

1.12   *Cooperative relations with ingroup members.*
1.13   *Absence of cooperation with outgroup members.*

In this facet we connote Summer's concepts such as "draws them together," "order," "government," "comradeship," "internal organization," and "brotherhood." In his concept of *antagonistic cooperation* (1906, p. 16) he recognizes that this ingroup cooperation is achieved in spite of competing interests and frictions within the ingroup. That such cooperative relationships are greater between members of the same ingroup than between ingroup member and outgroup member is so obviously true as to need no documentation. However, the degree to which there is such collaborative effort versus individualistic ingroup activity and the degree to which collaborative efforts transcend group boundaries differ so much from area as to be worth treating as variables. In this, Sumner might be read as predicting that the greater the ingroup collaboration, the less the cooperative activity between groups.

1.14 *Obedience to ingroup authorities.*
1.15 *Absence of obedience to outgroup authorities.*

These facets concretize such phrases of Sumner as "internal organization," "law," "government," and "discipline." On this dimension he clearly made correlational predictions: for example, the more hostile the neighboring groups and the greater the internal discipline and organization, the more authoritarian the political structure. At the level of universals, this is one of the most obviously true. Yet modern anthropologists are finding stateless societies much more common than had been previously recognized (see Chapters 4 and 7), and the existence of deference patterns in which the nobility of outgroups receive obeisance from ingroup members is not entirely unknown. For these reasons, it seems well to retain these two dimensions for the study of group differences.

1.16 *Willingness to remain an ingroup member.*
1.17 *Absence of conversion to outgroup membership.*

This facet is specified as one aspect of Sumner's concepts of "loyalty" and "solidarity." While it is obviously a universal of those aggregates of persons we call groups, it is nonetheless an important dimension of group variation. Furthermore, it seems certain that the ethnographies available to Sumner grossly underestimated the amount of intertribal migration that took place even in precolonial days, over and above that achieved through exogamy and slavery. Escape from punishment and marital bonds, available free land, and ostracism, all contributed migrants. Where flexible institutions of adoption existed, newly incorporated captives might fight against their birth-group. In some areas, famines were the occasion of selling children of both sexes and of women in exchange for grain and cattle, even in the absence of normal exogamous relationships. Also frequent were bilingual border communities with opportunistic identification with the larger ethnic groups (see Chapter 7). The older tradition of wishing to study a homogeneous isolated group and of neglecting the heterogeneity actually found was probably accentuated by the informant's similar tendencies to think in pure category, group-identity terms. Certainly ethnic groups differ in the extent to which their members could be alienated in these several ways, and as well in the degree to which they were attractive to the alienated of neighboring groups (see Chapter 5). An index of birth-group adherence might be possible which would express the number of emigrees as a proportion of the total ingroup population. A comparable index of attractiveness might simply state the proportion of all current ingroup members born as outgroupers, although the population supply of outgroups would also have to be considered.

1.18   *Willingness to fight and die for ingroup.*
1.19   *Absence of willingness to fight and die for outgroups.*

This is a specification of aspects of Sumner's concepts of "loyalty," "sacrifice," and "warlikeness." It is obviously an important dimension of group differences, manifest in the eagerness with which groups initiate wars, the degree of provocation required, the unwillingness of soldiers to be taken captive or to serve in novel ingroups, the severity of sanctions against cowardice, and the sorts of self-preservatory acts regarded as cowardly.

The issue of universality seems also important. If this is an obvious universal, it is one that is being seriously neglected in modern social science discussions of the causes of war. Wars may not be born in the minds of men, but the minds of men, the nature of man, make wars possible. And among the many aspects of that nature, the altruistic willingness for self-sacrificial death in group causes may be more significant than the tendency for covetous hostility toward outgroup members. This altruistic aspect of man's warlike nature seems unduly neglected in modern individualistic psychologies, sociologies, and decision theories (Campbell, 1965; 1972).

1.20   *Virtue in killing outgroup members in warfare.*

This aspect of Sumner's syndrome is clearly more universal than the sanction of killing outgroupers under conditions that parallel individual murder. Yet just as traditions of warfare are not quite universal, so this may not be. And as a dimension of group difference, it no doubt shows important variations, as in whether overwhelmed enemies are killed, taken captive for exchange, or disarmed and set free. Taboos on the conditions under which enemy soldiers may be honorably killed show marked differences, as do restraints on the killing of enemy women, children, and old men. Furthermore, while in some groups the killer of an enemy has only honors, in others the rituals he must undergo have aspects of purification and parallels to the sacrifices and restitutions required for the murder of an ingrouper. Even if they are expressed in terms of fears of vengeance from the spirit of the dead man, they show an extension to the outgroup of the social control devices preserving ingroup peace.

1.21   *Use of outgroups as bad examples in the training of children.*

Although not explicit in Sumner, one of the most frequent occasions for the expression of opprobium toward outgroup customs is in the teaching of children. This aspect of ethnocentrism may well be universal but also varies in degree from ingroup to ingroup. The image of the outgroup may be invoked as a bad example in the training of children almost as much as the ideal ingroup model is invoked as a good example. This is sometimes done in such a manner as to implicitly threaten the child with loss of ingroup membership or with treatment as an outgrouper if he misbehaves. Such aspects of the ethnocentric syndrome have been given prominence in Levinson's concept of contra-identification (Adorno et al, 1950, p. 146), in which a focused but negative emotional involvement is developed toward a specific outgroup. Similar, too, are older psychoanalytic concepts of the splitting of the father image into the good father and the bad father, the latter with its paternal origin repressed being projected onto the outgroup, the former being generalized into the overidealized ingroup image.

1.22   *Blaming of outgroup for ingroup troubles.*

Ubiquitous in modern discussions of ethnocentrism is the attention to the tendency for the ingroup to blame the outgroup for the troubles and deprivations of ingroup members. This tendency thus deserves a place in any description of the universal syndrome of ethnocentrism as utilized in contemporary social science. It is no doubt implied in Sumner's concept of hostility.

1.23   *Distrust and fear of the outgroup*

When Murdock (1931) attempted to state the then current meaning of Sumner's concept of ethnocentrism for the *Encyclopedia of the Social Sciences*, he included this aspect. It is likewise widely described even as an aspect of the attitudes of powerful dominant majority groups toward minority groups. Dollard (1938) relates it to the image of the outgrouper as immoral: "These images usually denote men who are to some degree released from the moral order which binds us and are feared because 'anything' may be expected of them." Ichheiser (1944; 1949) selected this as epitomizing prejudiced intergroup attitudes and insightfully separated out fear of fraud and fear of violence as two major types. As the tendency to regard outgroups as treacherous, untrustworthy, aggressive, self-seeking, using differing moral standards in dealing with the ingroup than in dealings among themselves, and desirous of the ingroup's destruction, these attitudes may be both universal and "valid" in that they essentially accuse the outgroup of being ethnocentric. When the focus is on fear, the attitude may be lacking for those highly ethnocentric and locally dominant ingroups whose ideology justifies aggression against outgroups without a defensive posture (for example, Murphy, 1957). The fear of outgroups also contradicts the attitude of ingroup superiority.

At this point another problem of ethnographic data quality should be noted, pertinent to all group solidarity or intragroup conflict variables, and again reflexively invoking the theory of ethnocentrism. The ethnographer is inevitably an outgroup member and, in the modern day, not even a member of an outgroup so novel that no traditional attitudes toward him exist. In the face of an outgroup member, the closing-of-ranks among ingroup members takes place, making the ingroup informants less likely to disclose intragroup factionalism. Thus the shorter the period of the ethnographer's stay and the poorer his rapport, the less ingroup factionalism he is apt to report. Leach, for example, states: "Although the factionalism inside the community was often intense, the populace usually presented a solid front to outsiders . . . indeed, I had lived in Hapalong for over four months before I realized that the feuds so lovingly described to me were not, as everyone pretended, matters of past history but bitter issues of the present day situation" (1954, p. 70). Pitt-Rivers (1955, p. 8 footnote) comments similarly:

"Casual conversation does not always reveal the animosities between pueblos, for the educated tend to laugh at it, while the informant may feel the solidarity of the area in face of a foreigner and give an account in which each pueblo seems more marvelous than the last. While travelling, one day, up the valley of the Rio Genal with a local man, I was amazed at the praises which he bestowed on each pueblo in turn. Coming finally to the most miserable of them all, I asked whether this was not a rotten place. 'This one?' he replied. 'No, indeed, a fine pueblo. A very rich pueblo. It has many acorns.' "

The Syndrome as Correlational Propositions

As previously mentioned, the word *syndrome* contains the implication or hypothesis that each aspect correlates positively with each other aspect. Sumner was at times quite explicit on this and his major emphasis — the more ingroup peace, the more outgroup hostility — is one of his most striking and valuable assertions. Stating this as a general correlational syndrome or as a general factor in the sense of statistical factor analysis, saves the tedium of specifying the innumerable specific correlations between pairs of variables that are involved. If there are 23 separately specifiable variables in the syndrome, then there are 23 x 22/2 such pairs, 253 particular hypotheses.

It is, of course, an empirical question whether or not all 253 are true, and in the long run it needs to be answered — at least, to the level of ascertaining whether all variables belong to the general factor, if it exists, or whether or not they break up into several semi-independent clusters (for example, the contempt, social-distance, sanctions of outgroup theft, and use as bad examples variables might separate out from a fear, distrust, and hate cluster).

On some of the 253 correlations, evidence has already been accumulated. Some of it will be presented herein when the correlation reappears as a part of one of the theoretical analyses reviewed in the subsequent chapters. We cannot aspire to more than a sampling of this voluminous literature, since the identification of this syndrome of ethnocentrism is a collective achievement of the social sciences, reappearing in sociology, anthropology, political science, and social psychology.

Rosenblatt (1964) has attempted to pull together some of the recurrent propositions of this dispersed literature. Among those relevant to the simple hypothesis of syndrome are the following.

"The greater the group nationalism and ethnocentrism, the greater is the group homogeneity of attitudes, beliefs, language spoken, and ways of behaving, the greater is the group cohesiveness, and the greater are the pressures for homogeneity and cohesiveness" (Blake and Mouton, 1961; Coser, 1956, p. 31 ff.; K. Deutsch, 1953b, pp. 73 ff.; Hayes, 1926, Ch. I; Kohn, 1944, p. 11; Likert, 1959; Murdock, 1931; Riecken and Homans. 1954, pp. 817–1818; Royal Institute of International Affairs, 1939).

"Nationalism and ethnocentrism tend to produce reductions in intragroup social disorganization" (deGrazia, 1948, pp. xi-xvii; Hertz, 1944, p. 227; Murdock, 1931).

"Intragroup hostilities, crime rates, and suicide rates drop following an increase in ethnocentrism or nationalism (Williams, 1947, p. 58). Groups with greater ethnocentrism or nationalism have lower crime rates and lower suicide rates (Alexander, 1951, p. 208; Murdock, 1931) and less internal conflict" (Hertz, 1944, p. 37; Phillsbury, 1919; Sulzbach, 1943, p. 9; Turney-High, 1949, pp. 231–232).

Chapter 2

CROSS-CULTURAL VARIATIONS IN ETHNOCENTRISM

Sumner's concept of ethnocentrism has been presented as a descriptive syndrome, one widely noted also by other social scientists. The explanatory theory offered by Sumner has thus far been neglected. In the following sections, we shall continue to discuss the same syndrome of ethnocentrism, essentially the same variables, but now in the context of social science theories that attempt to explain their occurrence, and in the context of other variables that are a part of the explanation. A wide range of theories will be sampled, some of which are centered on other problems and only tangentially make predictions about intergroup relations and attitudes. What is attempted is a brief and modest propositional inventory, limited to propositions falling in the domain of ethnocentrism that might be testable by comparative ethnographic data on human populations.

The optimal role of data in the development of scientific theory is to make possible choices between competing theories. Theories are not usually accepted or rejected as they stand alone. Social science will progress best if there can be assembled competing theories making discrepant predictions into areas where data are available. Our effort in the following sections is to interpret available theories in this light. Our abbreviated versions of various theories are deliberately biased in the direction of making them as different as possible from each other, and of generating discrepant predictions. To accomplish this goal, we have often divested these theories of the many hedges and concessions by which their original authors made their statements more "realistic" and thereby softened and blurred the distinction between their theory and that of others.

At the present state of the social sciences we do not usually have theories in the sense of rigidly articulated explicit models with a parsimony of parameters, each parameter being multiply used. What we call theories are, instead, often close to being aggregated descriptions in which the full range of terms in our ordinary language is available for the parameters, with most such parameters entering only once, as enumerated features rather than as underlying factors with multiple manifestations. This state of affairs is inevitably the result when we aim to describe completely any single natural situation. And even where, as in this book, we aspire to an abstracted description of the recurrent aspects of a syndrome, complex multiple determination is likely to be the case to such an extent that any rigid formal theory will be incomplete, and the complete description of even the abstracted syndrome will be too complex, enumerative, and aggregative, to qualify as formal theory. In spite of this foreboding, it seems desirable to probe available theoretical formulations to see to what extent they will generate testable propositions that differ from those of other theories.

In considering the range of relevant theories, remember that the setting under consideration is that of the relationships among autonomous territorial groups and the typical intergroup attitudes of their members. Theories focusing on explaining why one person is more prejudiced than another within a single ingroup are not relevant except as they also offer predictions as to why one ingroup would be more ethnocentric than another. Similarly, analyses specific to minority-majority group relations within a single organized society are not relevant unless they have implications for the relationships between politically autonomous groups.

Types of Correlational Analyses

Ethnocentrism can be studied comparatively at several levels of variation: (1) across the cultural groups of the world, (2) among the groups of a given region, and then across regional units, (3) among the diverse outgroup attitudes and relations of a given ingroup, and (4) across dyadic units of intergroup relationship, that is, two groups considered in relation to each other. Since some of the propositions in the following chapters are relevant to each of these levels, it will be helpful to outline the diverse types of correlational analysis that are involved in testing them.

First, are what we will call *cross-cultural* correlations. This is the commonly encountered type of relationship found in cross-cultural studies, for instance, those of Murdock (1949), and Whiting and Child (1953). In them a pool of groups widely distributed and ideally noncontiguous are each given scores or assigned to ranked categories or classified dichotomously, on two or more variables. The association between such variables taken two at a time is then expressed in terms of some index of correlation or association. Thus one might compute a correlation between the tendency for great ingroup peace and the tendency to have contemptuous attitudes toward outgroups, pooling data from groups scattered all over the world.

The second type, *intracluster correlations,* can be used for the same purposes, but occasionally tests distinctive propositions. For them, data are required for sets of clusters of adjacent groups. For each such cluster, the relationship is computed separately and these indexes are then averaged across clusters. Where these show the same type of relationship shown in the cross-cultural, then it can be regarded as reflecting functional instead of diffusional associations (Naroll,

1961). If it is frequent that all groups in a cluster have been studied by the same person or school, then the intracluster approach controls possible spurious correlations that might appear in a cross-cultural correlation caused by differences in method and emphasis of the ethnographers rather than by actual differences in the groups (Campbell, 1961, p. 348). Where the measures employed provide interpretable comparisons within a cluster but not "absolute" measures universally comparable across clusters, the intracluster approach is to be preferred. Reputational data (LeVine, 1966a) are a prime instance of this.

The third type of correlation could overlap in use with the first two, but is uniquely applicable for certain hypotheses. It may be called the *ingroup-based correlation.* In such analyses, correlations are computed separately from the standpoint of each ingroup. (Thus in a cluster of five groups, any particular pair of variables would be correlated five separate times, from the standpoint of each ingroup in turn). The ingroup is typically the source of the data, but the comparisons are only among the outgroups for that ingroup. Hence, in the cluster of five groups, each correlation would be based on the four outgroups of each ingroup). Thus one could compute for each ingroup the correlation between the hostility it felt toward each outgroup and the social distance that it kept toward each outgroup, or the nearness of each outgroup, or the cultural similarity with each outgroup, or the military strength of each outgroup. These uses do not lend themselves to the cross-cultural correlation or to the intracluster correlation. Instead of asking the question as to what kinds of groups are most ethnocentric, the ingroup-based correlation asks questions such as: for the average group, toward what kind of an outgroup will it show most ethnocentrism? In this typical use, the ingroup-based correlation lacks the "objective" character of the other relationships, indicating rather how these attributes go together in the minds of ingroup observers. To test empirical generalizations, these coefficients would be averaged over ingroups. Notice that although some of these require data from other members of a cluster, many interesting ones can be computed entirely from data collected within a single ingroup, and could employ all of the outgroups on which the ingroup had usable imagery.

A fourth type is the *dyadic correlation.* In this, attributes or scores are assigned to the dyad, expressing an attribute of their relationship rather than referring to either separately. Thus it might be proposed that each group observes a real difference between it and the other member of a dyad and represents this difference in the stereotyped imagery of the other, although reporting it with opposed evaluative connotations (Campbell and LeVine, 1961, pp. 85–86). If such dyadic stereotype sets were to be scored for complementarity, contrast, or similarity, such scores would be dyadic. Dyadic scores could likewise be generated on things such as intensity of past warfare, nearness, linguistic similarity, mutual social distance, and the like. Correlations could then be computed between these dyadic trait scores over a population of dyads.

PART 2

Societal Theories

A major portion of the following theoretical exposition involves psychological considerations, considerations of man's individual and biological nature, and the processes of individual learning, perception, cognition, and motivation. These psychological factors (albeit in conjunction with social-organization factors) will be employed to predict social-level phenomena such as intergroup relations and common stereotypes of neighboring outgroups, rather than being used for the prediction of individual differences in such reactions.

There have been numerous social science reactions against both psychologizing and the mixing of societal and individual levels of analysis. Abel (1941), White (1949), Bernard (1957), Newcomb (1960), and Faris (1962), among others, have explicitly affirmed the inadequacy and irrelevancy of psychological-level explanations, usually with the frustration-aggression-displacement theory as an example. Some quotations will illustrate this point of view:
"Warfare is a struggle between social organisms, not individuals. Its explanation is therefore social or cultural, not psychological" (White, 1949, p. 132). "To attempt to explain war by appeal to an innate pugnacity would be like explaining Egyptian, Gothic, and Mayan architecture by citing the physical properties of stone" (White, 1949, p. 131). "Explaining the forces which lead a particular individual to become a warrior or a soldier to be pugnacious and aggressive no more explains why that individual's tribe or nation is fighting another nation than a knowledge of the chemical composition of a boulder reveals the reasons why it rolls down hill when pushed" (Newcomb, 1960, p. 321). ". . . many prominent and influential investigators of intergroup interaction made an early choice of the wrong path in seeking the explanations in the processes of individual psychology and psychoanalysis . . . Part of the difficulty appears to lie in defects of knowledge and theory in the above fields, but the more important part stems from failure to recognize the nature of collective processes" (Faris, 1962, p. 43).

Without implying agreement with these statements, and while recognizing that societal-level theories regularly invoke psychological processes, we begin our treatment of theories with the societal-level theories.

Devons and Gluckman's (1964) extensive analysis of the problem of interdisciplinary relations in social science research requires special consideration here. We accept, as inevitable their emphasis on the necessity of delimitation in any empirical research, and we find appropriate their distinctions among circumscription, incorporation, abridgment, compression, and naivety. Particularly useful are their detailed discussions of instances of overstepping the limits of naivete on the social-psychological boundary in the work of Freud, Malinowski, and Kluckhohn. And on this boundary we would endorse, in part, the objections, cited above (White, Faris, etc.), to psychologists overreaching themselves in the study of intergroup conflict when they give unquestioned causal priolty to the psychological, describing intergroup conflict as only a projective symptom of internal psychological problems.

What we disagree with in the quotations from White et al. is the implications that in science each level of analysis must be studied in isolation from others, and that the appropriate theory for each must involve only concepts stated at that one level. This is not Devons and Gluckman's position, but their emphasis on the necessity of each scholar's keeping his nose out of other scientists' business may support such a doctrine of isolationism. Actually, however, Devons and Gluckman's detailed bad examples of overstepping the limitations of naivete are accompanied by specific calls for cross-disciplinary research, as, for example, psychological data that compares people living in a witchcraft society and those not, as indicting Malinowski and Kluckhohn for not collecting the relevant psychological data their analyses assumed, etc. Their position is one of rejecting efforts where naivety about the neighboring field has led to naive error in presumptuous excursions into that field. They do not seem to reject those studies in which there is a competent cross-disciplinary relating that pays attention to the facts and laws of each.

Our own point of view may be epitomized by the phrase *nonreductive congruence.* It is assumed that there are delineable multiple levels of analysis at which the collation of empirical regularities and the proposing of laws might take place. No one of these levels has a priori status as the optimal starting point. Thus if we take molecule, cell, organism, and social organization as levels, inquiry can start at any level, and this inquiry can proceed independently of other levels. In particular, no level need wait on the perfection of a lower one. Thus statistical genetics could proceed without waiting for biochemistry; learning theory could develop without waiting on neurophysiology; and a chemistry of combinatorial laws among elements need not wait on an adequate science of subtomic particles. Especially we emphasize that sociology need not be postponed until an adequate psychology is achieved. Thus there exists among the achieved and potential sciences an *optional autonomy.*

But it is also our position that theories at any one level will have inexorable implications for the other levels. In the asymptotic perfection of the theories, there will be a *congruence* among theories, so that the "true" theories at any one level have no implications contradictory of the "true" theories at any other level. For example, although learning theory is developed quite independently of neurophysiology, any learning theory sets limits on the possible neuro-physiologies, broad and nonspecific though these limits may be. The "true" neurophysiology must be capable of sustaining the kind of memory and elicitation processes required in the "true" learning theory. Although the day is not yet here, we can imagine one learning theory being rejected in favor of another on the grounds of compatibility with the facts of neurophysiology, and vice versa for neurological theories.

Similarly, we argue that each sociological theory sets limits on possible psychologies — it implies the psychological processes that sustain it. Thus realistic-group-conflict theory in predicting certain group reactions to group threats, predicts the psychological or individual reactions concomitant to sustaining that group reaction. Thus a psychological theory implies the collective group effects concomitant with it. The restraints of cross-level implication may be very loose. There may, for example, be many neurophysiological models congruent with even the most complex set of laws of learning. Many psychological theories may be compatible with the most refined data on group reaction to group threat. But some restraint is nonetheless there.

The autonomy of levels mentioned above is *optional*. Just because a level can be investigated in isolation is no reason for thus restricting investigation. On the contrary, in the successful sciences, those achievements that we think of as explanatory theory most regularly involve a crossing of levels, relating laws at one level to those of another. Thus currently, the relating of structural biochemistry to genetics is a field of exciting scientific advance, and the relating of cellular neurophysiology to memory and learning promises similar advances for the future.

One model for such interrelationships is already with us and must be rejected — this is the reductionist view that there is a hierarchy of the levels of analysis, and that within this hierarchy, the "more basic" levels explain the higher ones. Under this program one expects eventually the laws of sociology to be subsumed under laws of psychology, the laws of psychology to be subsumed under the laws of physiology, and these to be subsumed under chemistry, and the laws of chemistry to be subsumed under subatomic physics. Thus it has been proposed that laws of sociology might be stated in terms of the laws of subatomic physics. This we reject in principle, particularly as it implies a causal priority to the "more basic" level, defining "more basic" as more molecular. One of the long-standing observations of biology, and one of the theoretical achievements of cybernetics, is the observation that larger-system parameters can control subsystem variables, can "cause" them in the same sense that a change in the setting of a thermostat can "cause" a change in room temperature. This kind of systems-theory perspective, most relevant to the study of human group behavior, makes traditional psychological reductionism untenable.

Another aspect of our emphasis on quasi-autonomous levels of analysis is that the existence of each level is a factual matter, rather than an arbitrary level of analysis. We are hypothesizing the existence of real systems at each level (Miller, 1965). In particular, the justification of a social group level of analysis and the rejection of methodological individualism depends on factual criteria for the existence of social systems or social entities (Chapter 7 and Campbell, 1958).

Having stated our position on this fundamental issue, we begin our survey of societal-level theories with what is probably the most antipsychological one: what we term "realistic-group-conflict theory."

Chapter 3

REALISTIC GROUP CONFLICT THEORY

Most who have rejected psychological explanations have espoused a point of view that is here called the realistic-group-conflict theory. This theory assumes that group conflicts are rational in the sense that groups do have incompatible goals and are in competition for scarce resources. Such "realistic" sources of group conflict are contrasted with the psychological theories that consider intergroup conflicts as displacements or projective expressions of problems that are essentially intragroup or intraindividual in origin. Among those who have articulated such a point of view are Sumner (1906), Davie (1929), White (1949; 1959), Sherif (1953; 1961), Coser (1957), Bernard (1957), Newcomb (1960), and Boulding (1962). Not all of them eschew psychological explanations; for example, Coser and Boulding do not, nor does Sherif except for the displacement-projective ones. But for all, realistic sources oт group conflict are a primary emphasis. Much of the elegant elaboration of the theory has to do with the course of conflicts, with the formation of coalitions, with the optimal strategies in conflict, with relative payoffs, and with other features not transferable to the present setting (see, Bernard, 1957; Boulding, 1962). Many other features, more descriptive than deductive, perhaps, are highly relevant and are enumerated below. This enumeration is not completely parsimonious, in that some principles are simply more explicit spellings-out of other more general ones.

3.1   *Real conflict of group-interests causes intergroup conflict.*

Intergroup conflict is most intense where the real conflict of interests is greatest and where the conflicting parties have the most to gain by victory. Since reasonable a priori statements can be made about the real conflict of interests between the groups in any area, this can be spelled out in terms of a number of more specific propositions. However, this will not be done immediately because more economy oт presentation will be achieved if some intermediate proposi-tions linking threat and conflict to ethnocentrism are presented first.

3.2   *Real conflict of interests, overt, active or past intergroup conflict,
and/or presence of hostile, threatening, and competitive outgroup neighbors,
which collectively may be called real threat, cause perception of threat.*

This proposition is usually implicit but is needed for the inclusion of Sherif
and much of Coser and, more generally, for the prediction from group level
phenomena to the corresponding sentiments of individual ingroup members.
With this causal sequence in mind, the subsequent principles could be stated
either in terms of real threat or in terms of perceived threat, or stated as separate
principles in both terms. As most characteristic of the literature being surveyed,
the real threat statement has been employed, with perceived threat implicit,
except in those instances where perceived threat has other sources than real
threat.

Notice that while the variables of the previous chapter, 1.1 to 1.23, all dealt
with ingroup customs, attitudes, beliefs, or behavior, the new real threat
variables deal with the environment of the ingroup. Whereas the ingroup's
perception of the outgroup has already entered as symptoms of ethnocentrism,
as in 1.2, 1.5, 1.22, 1.23, here the "real" character of the outgroup enters as a
cause of ethnocentrism. The operationalizing of these real threat variables thus
obviously requires data ascertained independently of the ingroup sources. For
real conflict of interest, independent ethnographic data on the economies of the
groups, the extent to which they exploit the same natural resources, the scarcity
of these resources, and population pressures, are all relevant. For the virulence of
previous warfare, historical records and oral traditions would be needed. Data
from each outgroup on the amount of time devoted to preparing for war, the
degree of professionalization and the prestige of soldiers, the presence of an
ideology advocating war for aggrandizement, and attitudes of belligerency
focused on the outgroup of theirs that is the ingroup for the particular analysis,
all could be utilized in ascertaining the presence of hostile, threatening, and
competitive outgroup neighbors. These considerations point to the importance
of parallel studies in adjacent groups. If a number of adjacent peoples were
studied in parallel, the pooled perception of outgroups by the several ingroups
could achieve a quasi-objective status as an index of real threat, whereas a single
ingroup's perceptions must retain the status of ethnocentric imagery to be
treated as an ingroup attribute. For certain predictions to be enumerated, these
data should be kept separate by particular outgroup; for other predictions, the
pooled threateningness of total environment would be invoked.

The variable, perceived threat, is well enough represented in the discussion of
1.23, "distrust and fear of outgroup," and will be treated as a symptom of
ethnocentrism, a part of the large and complex dependent variable of the present
study.

3.3   *Real threat causes hostility to the source of threat*

Although often left implicit as too obvious to need stating, this is a
characteristic proposition of realistic-group-conflict theory. Sherif (1953; 1961,

p. 45) states it in terms of the dislike of an outgroup emerging as a result of perceived threat or the perception of the outgroup as in conflict with the ingroup. The proposition implies a correlational relationship between degrees of threat and degrees of hostility. Sherif (1961, p. 45) makes this explicit, in stating that the more important the goal competed for, the greater the value that is being threatened, and the greater the perceived interference with goal attainment, the greater the hostility.

3.4   *Real threat causes ingroup solidarity.*

This is the most recurrent explicit proposition of the theory. White gives a typical expression of it: "An international event at Pearl Harbor transformed a listless, disgruntled mass of conscripts into a spirited fighting force. It would make more sense to say that it is war that breeds martial spirit than to argue that pugnacious instincts cause wars" (1949, p. 133). Sumner becomes a realistic-group-conflict theorist on this point: "The exigencies of war with outsiders are what make peace inside, lest internal discord should weaken the we-group for war. These exigencies also make government and law in the ingroup, in order to prevent quarrels and enforce discipline" (1906, p. 12). This is one of Sherif's most emphasized points (1953, p. 196; 1961, p. 21) stated as the principle that the presence of a negatively related outgroup increases ingroup solidarity. This is likewise Coser's strongest theme among the many well-articulated principles he presents (Coser, 1957, pp. 87-95). On this point he is able to cite Simmel (for example, 1956), Sorel, Marx, Sumner, and many others. Other theorists who state this principle are Lewis (1961), Murphy and Kasdan (1959), Boulding (1962, pp. 162-163), and Mack and Snyder (1957, Proposition 9). We can make no pretense to comprehensive citation of this most ubiquitous principle. For example, Dahrendorf (1964, p. 58) makes this application of it:

"It appears to be a general law that human groups react to external pressure by increased internal coherence. In the East-West conflict, each society finds itself in such a position of pressure from without . . . [which] may lead the liberal societies of the West to restrict internal liberties in the name of resistance to totalitarian pressure . . . [resulting in] the paradoxical possibility that democracy can be destroyed while it is being protected."

The mechanism whereby external threat produces greater internal peace and solidarity is not explained. That it is functional in surviving inter-group conflict is obvious and may be regarded as explanation enough. Perhaps the general theory of functionalism has this specific application: groups in conflict will have the characteristics that make them function most adequately in intergroup conflict. The teleological character of such a blatant statement is characteristic of functionalist theory in general. To get beyond this teleology, one needs a selective-survival model of sociocultural evolution: in a long social history in which certain organizational forms and cultural attitudes have dropped out while others have been perpetuated, the surviving groups, institutions, and attitudes will be those that further survival in intergroup conflict. The general implications of selective-retention theory in sociocultural evolution will be treated separately in other sections of this volume.

Whatever the mechanisms at the societal level, there are also counterpart processes at the individual level, whether carried by indoctrinated emotional attitudes and modes of reaction, or by accumulated innate predispositions. It can be noted that such response tendencies will undoubtedly persist in social man long after historical developments have made wars disfunctional even for victors. One of the implications of this principle and the preceding one is that the increased terror of modern war (and of the educational campaigns emphasizing that terror) may, by increasing the perception of threat, actually increase citizen attitudes of bellicose intransigency at the national level, and may actually increase ethnocentric solidarity instead of increasing international conciliatoriness (as the educational campaigners might have hoped).

3.5   *Real threat causes increased awareness of own ingroup identity.*

This is stated in Coser's (1957, pp. 104-110) terms, but can for convenience be used also to cover the accentuation of the distinctness and superiority of ingroup customs (1.1, 1.2, 1.3). Sherif emphasizes that threat and intergroup competition causes the exaggeration of ingroup virtues and the magnification of outgroup vices (1961, pp. 143, 21, 38, 45, 46). Leach (1954) has illustrated in great detail how factional conflict can lead to the otherwise dysfunctional and artificial preservation and exaggeration of (linguistic) differences quite inconsistent with historical, racial, residential, or cultural antecedents. The reactivation of traditional languages under conditions of conflict, as in the Irish effort to reestablish Gaelic, are symptoms of this same principle. Sumner seems also to have this in mind, although he uses ethnocentrism rather than external threat to represent the causal forces involved: ". . . ethnocentrism leads a people to exaggerate and intensify everything in their own folkways which is peculiar and which differentiates them from others. It therefore strengthens the folkways" (1906, p. 13). Yinger (1961) provides other illustrations.

3.6   *Real threat increases the tightness of group boundaries.*

This principle is elucidated by Coser (1957, pp. 95-104). For convenience we shall interpret tightness of group boundaries to refer not only to actual boundary marking, wall building, guard posting, traveler stopping, shibboleth usage, and the like, but also, in a more figurative sense, to social distance maintenance. Sherif has observed the effect of group competition on social distance (1961, p. 46). See also Mack and Snyder (1957, Proposition 32.)

3.7   *Real threat reduces defection from the group.*

This point of Coser's (1957, pp. 95-104) specifies one aspect of 3.4, ingroup solidarity, the particular aspect also treated under 1.17.

3.8   *Real threat increases punishment and rejection of defectors.*

This specific solidarity maintaining mechanism of vengeance against renegades and apostates is noted by Coser (1957, pp. 67-72).

3.9   *Read threat creates punishment and rejection of deviants.*

This solidarity mechanism of reduced tolerance for loyal innovators, revisionists, and heretics has been noted by both Coser (1957, pp. 70-71; 100-101) and Sherif (1961). (See also Singer, Radloff, and Work, 1963.) Rokeach (1960) provides an extensive theoretical and empirical study of the effects of threat on dogmatism. At the level of threat to ingroup (in contrast to threat to individual persons), his most relevant evidence comes from a historical analysis of the degree of dogmatism found in Papal Encyclicals over a 1200-year period. The more real the threat, the greater the dogmatism, expressed both by the severity of punishment specified for deviators and in the degree of absolutism of the threat (1960, pp. 378-388). It seems convenient, therefore, to assimilate dogmatism to this principle, although it also partakes of 3.8 and 3.5 above.

3.10   *Real threat increases ethnocentrism.*

The above points may be summarized by saying that the realistic-group-conflict theorists generate the whole syndrome of ethnocentrism from the reaction to conflict and threat from outgroups. In the last two principles, new aspects of the ethnocentric syndrome have been introduced, in points 3.8 and 3.9, but these obviously belong. It will be economical in the following points to use the term ethnocentrism for variables covered in 3.3 to 3.9 instead of multiplying the number of principles by specifying each aspect separately. Rosenblatt (1964) has provided a number of citations to this point, most of which could also be used to support 3.3 and 3.4 (Alexander, 1951, p. 208; Berkowitz, 1962, pp. 188-191; Clark, 1938; Hayes, 1926, Chapter VII; Murdock, 1931; Myers, 1962; Pillsbury, 1919, Chapter III; Royal Institute of International Affairs, 1939; Simpson and Yinger, 1958, pp. 114, 339; Williams, 1947, p. 58).

3.11.1   *The weakest group in a local cluster should be the most ethnocentric.*

Since the weakest group is under the most threat from stronger neighbors, it should, following the above principles of this theory, be the most hostile, have the greatest solidarity and, in general, be the most ethnocentric. Although this conclusion lacks descriptive plausibility, it seems to follow directly. While it is the sort of prediction that a social scientist might try to avoid by hedges, the introduction of qualifying variables, and the like, it is treasured here as one of the few predictions from realistic-group-conflict theory that is different from those of other major theories. For example, evolutionary theory and frustration-aggression-displacement theory would both predict that the neighboring group with the most military power would be the most ethnocentric in terms of ingroup solidarity, as well as outgroup hostility. Murphy's (1957) case of the Mundurucú, and Ray's (1963) description of the Modoc provide instances where the militarily powerful neighboring group is apparently the most ethnocentric, although in neither case were ingroup data collected from the surrounding peoples. Nor do two contradictory cases destroy a hypothesis if the general run of the data are in favor of it, and the data are not yet available to decide the issue. Also contradictory is Guetzkow's (1955) finding for nine large modern nations that the larger and more economically strong the nation, the more loyal the attitudes of the citizens. A consideration of minority groups may support the argument: the more powerful majority group may have less ethnocentric solidarity than the more threatened minority group, and where this is not true, it may turn out to be the rule that the minority group is one in spite of itself, that is, for reasons such as skin color it may be given no opportunity of converting or assimilating into the majority group. Realistic-group-conflict theory should certainly be allowed the exception to the prediction where the weakest group is so weak as to have lost stability and to be in the process of dissolution (Yinger, 1961).

3.11.2   *However, in cross-cultural correlations, the weakest groups should be the least ethnocentric.*

Because of the difference in the mode of computation of the intracluster correlations and the cross-cultural correlations, this prediction does not necessarily contradict the previous one—although, in most cases, the two types of correlation would be expected to be the same.

3.12.   *The groups within regional clusters will tend to be homogeneous in ethnocentrism and strength.*

Considerations of homogeneity due to shared culture areas and diffusion support this prediction. A further process is that weaker groups will tend to be incorporated into the stronger, although balance of power coalition formation complicates this. More important, perhaps, is the fact that realistic-group-conflict theory predicts it, since it states that the degree of ethnocentrism and the degree of military preparedness, war strength, and the like, will be determined by external threat, a process which tends to bring neighbors up to comparable levels of war effectiveness and belligerency. This "vicious circle" in which the defensive moves of one group are perceived as hostile, aggressive, and expansionist by the other, has been often noticed. Richardson Process Models (Boulding, 1962, pp. 19-40) provide formal models for arms-race spirals, escalation effects, a positive feedback system restrained only by the costs of the resulting war, war weariness (Boulding, 1962, pp. 141-144), and the depression of internal standards of living. This whole set of mathematical models can be regarded as elaborations of certain aspects of the realistic-group-conflict theory.

Thus all members of a regional cluster will tend to be similar on the two variables of ethnocentrism and military strength: all low, or all intermediate, or all high; and when correlations are plotted pooling groups from the world over, all members of a cluster will tend to be plotted near each other on the scatter diagram, producing the overall positive relationship. When, however, the plot for each cluster is examined separately, the opposite trend results. (The mode of wording of the 3.11.1 proposition in terms of weakness should not be allowed to be a source of confusion here—for verbal convenience it is frequently convenient to state a corelation of variables in terms of a single polar term from one extreme of each variable.)

The relationships of the two laws can be diagramed in the following pure case. In this A, B, . . Z are individual groups from three regional clusters. For the total plot of all twelve groups, the correlation is positive, although not perfect, the general slope being from lower left to upper right. Within each cluster, the slope is negative, from upper left to lower right. The correlation computed for the average of the three intracluster correlations would be highly negative (see Figure 3.1).

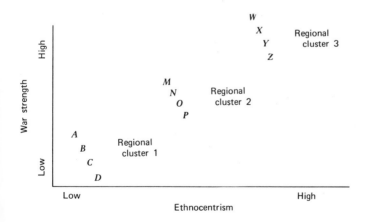

FIGURE 3.1

3.13.1   *The more dissimilar an ingroup's economy from that of its outgroups collectively, the less ethnocentric.*

In general, the more dissimilar the ingroup's economy from that of its neighbors, the fewer common resources they will be competing for. Thus a fisherfolk surrounded by tillers of the land should be under less competitive threat and, hence, less ethnocentric than if surrounded by other tribes of fishermen. The dimension can go beyond simple dissimilarity to complementarity where the different products produced lead to economic ties, further reducing ethnocentric hostility between the groups. Similarly,

3.13.2   *Of all of its outgroups, the ingroup will show the least ethnocentric hostility toward the outgroup with the least similar economy.*

This is, of course, a *ceteris paribus* prediction; thus it might well be qualified by limiting the prediction to *adjacent* outgroups. Principles that relate similarity and liking, predicted by other theories (for example, Rokeach, 1960; Homans, 1950; Newcomb, 1959) are so prominent, and economic similarity is so apt to go together with linguistic and general cultural similarity, that even if true, this principle may be covered over in most empirical situations.

3.14   *Groups exploiting natural resources in short supply will be more ethnocentric than groups economically dependent upon abundant resources.*

Thus population pressure, shortage of free land, scarcity of water holes, and the like, should make groups more ethnocentric. Famines and plagues should result in temporary increases of ethnocentrism. Although the prediction is clear, the data may turn out to be quite complex. For example, we found that the Kenya rinderpest epidemic which destroyed the cattle herds in 1890 increased conflict and real threat among adjacent groups, resulting in increased outgroup hostility and ingroup solidarity for a group such as the Gusii, under pressure from neighboring Kipsigis and Masai, who had been struck earlier by the epidemic. On the other hand, famines due to grain crop failures in the same area were traditionally times of formal peacemaking, increased trade, sharing across ethnic group lines, and the peaceable transfer of children and women from the group with most famine to others more fortunate, in exchange for grain. (See Mack and Snyder, 1957, Proposition 48.)

3.15   *Those groups with the most movable wealth will be most ethnocentric.*

The greater the supply of wealth and the more conveniently movable the wealth, the more gain for a predatory outgroup and, hence, the more real threat to an ingroup. Lowest in temptation are those hunting, gathering, and agricultural peoples whose food stuffs are perishable. Stored dry grains are much more tempting movable wealth, but cattle seem regularly even more tempting because they transport and reproduce themselves. Where economies utilize slaves, the presence of enslavable populations represent movable wealth.

The considerations overlap evolutionary theories (see, White, 1949; 1959; Newcomb, 1960) as summarized in Chapter 6. Steward (1955a) has particularly pointed to the granaries of early irrigation civilizations as generating the predation from neighboring nomads that led the irrigation civilizations to develop a professional soldiery.

3.16   *Those groups most isolated from their outgroups will be least ethnocentric.*

Isolated groups, groups protected by natural barriers to communication and invasion such as mountains, deserts, swamps, forests, oceans, or rivers, should be under less threat and, hence, less ethnocentric. Sumner has made this prediction: "The closer the neighbors . . . the intenser is the warfare, and then the intenser is the internal organization and discipline of each" (1906, p. 123). This might seem to be confirmed in the low-ethnocentric, highly isolated Lepchas (Gorer, 1938) and Eskimos. However, from both realistic-group-conflict theory and frustration-aggression-displacement theory (to be treated later), such isolated peoples, lacking the external threats necessary to create a one-group solidarity, would be split by factionalism, would thus not be single isolated groups but would be divided locally into several opposed groups (for instance, the Big Endians and the Little Endians of Swift's *Gulliver's Travels*). These local groups would no longer be isolated; each would have near at hand competing outgroups. A study of isolated islands might be instructive here.

3.17   *The further an island is from its nearest neighbor island, the more likely it should be to be divided into two or more separate political entities.*

Easter Island, at least as reported by Heyerdahl (1958), provides an example of great isolation and destructive division. Nonetheless, if isolated singular groups are found, they should be less ethnocentric. Their internal dissension and near-fractionation would be a sympton of this at one level.

3.18   *The nearer outgroups should be the targets of the most ethnocentric hostility.*

In particular, adjacent outgroups should be hated more than nonadjacent outgroups, as the practical threat, the opportunities to compete for scarce resources are greater. Sumner may seem to imply this principle in his statement cited just above, although he seems in general to be considering only the immediate neighbors, the first level of adjacency, and to say that the closer the adjacent neighbors, the more ethnocentrism. The very fact that he neglects nonadjacent groups implies the endorsement of this theory. Traditional Hindu political theory of a Machiavellian kind predicts that one's neighbors are one's natural enemies, while *their* neighbors — outgroups in the second level of adjacency — are one's natural allies (Zimmer, 1951, pp. 114–115, quoted in more detail in Chapter 11 in this book).

Similarly, Lewis Richardson's mathematical model of warfare posits a positive relationship between extent of common territorial boundaries and the frequency and magnitude of conflict between social groups (Richardson, 1960; Wesley, 1962).

However clearly deduced and "obviously" true, many of the facts to date fail to support this proposition, although they, perhaps, cover only limited aspects of the syndrome, aspects that might on this point show different effects from the bulk of the syndrome. Mitchell (1956) studied social distance on a tribal basis among migratory workers in the Zambian copperbelt from 20 tribes. He found, as one of three emerging principles, that there was *less* social distance for nearer tribes. His reporting of the data do not make possible an analysis in terms of immediate adjacency versus the second level of adjacency, but this analysis was made among 30 tribes in East Africa by Brewer (1968) and confirmed the finding of a direct relationship between physical distance and social distance (that is, the nearer the outgroup the lower the social distance). It should also be remembered that Mitchell's respondents were hundreds of miles away from home, thrown together with total strangers. Under these conditions a familiar former enemy who knew one's own locale and customs might well become one's friend in coexile, However, Brewer's data were obtained from respondents in their native locale and still confirmed the positive effect of nearness on social relations between groups.[1]

In many areas adjacency co-occurs with cultural similarity which, on the grounds of other theories, strongly predicts amity. The joint operation of

[1] One other body of relevant data comes from Wilson (1961) as a biproduct of our reanalysis of his data, reported more extensively in Chapter 11. Respondents from 12 tribal areas in East Africa answered questions in which they had opportunities to name the other tribes favorably in three items and unfavorably in three others. From these data a matrix of intertribal likings has been prepared (see Table 11-1). This has been examined for the effects of proximity, holding similarity constant since, as Chapter 11 shows, similarity is a powerful source of liking. The results show no clearcut trend, certainly no confirmation of the proximity-hostility hypothesis. Insofar as there are trends, the groups one-removed are least liked, those most remote are best liked, but the sign tallies show these trends to be utterly inconsistent.

		Mean		Sign Frequencies		
	Adjacent	One-Removed	Remote	$A > O$	$A > R$	$O > R$
Net favorability	−5	−11	−2	$9/16$	$8/16$	$7/16$
Received votes	4	− 5	−1	$8/16$	$11/16$	$9/16$

In these data, highly similar outgroups do not enter, as no ingroup had such an outgroup for more than one level of remoteness. A given ingroup could enter into these tallies twice, once tor comparisons of *dissimilar* outgroups at various levels of adjacency, and once for comparisons involving outgroups of intermediate degrees of similarity. (The net favorability row reports the analysis in terms of votes given, the Received votes in terms of votes received, the analyses having different strengths and weaknesses, as discussed in Chapter 11).

adjacency and similarity may lead to inconsistent data that should not be interpreted as contradicting either as general principles. They both can be true and still mutually canceling in specific instances. In Mitchell's data the two effects are to a considerable degree separable, and he does find nearness operating to produce *low* social distance independently of similarity. Brewer's (1968) survey of 30 tribes of Kenya, Uganda, and Tanzania confirmed this finding, with cultural similarity emerging as the most powerful determinant of low social distance.

Middleton (1960) also reports a contrary instance. Among the Lugbara, the more remote the outgroup, the more horrible it is believed to be. Thus the most remote are cannibals who walk on their heads and have powerful sorcery. Immediate but still essentially unknown groups are believed to walk on their heads, too, and to eat decayed flesh — even though not human flesh — an image slightly less terrifying. Nearest groups are recognized as human. Swartz (1961, p. 77) reports that the Trukese regard the remote people of New Guinea as unregenerate cannibals and group them together with sharks and other fearsome and hateful animals. Nearer people are given more human stereotypes. We found a minor parallel to this pattern among the Gusii in which the only group stereotyped as animal rather than human and the group most frequently used to connote poverty and lack of civilization are the Dorobo, known only indirectly and conceptualized as very remote or of unknown location. In this case, however, the specific characteristics attributed to them are quite accurate, for example, lack of livestock or cultivation, solitary forest living, absence of warfare, the use of honey and wild animals, extreme shyness on approach of outsiders, and use of poisoned arrows. Meggitt (1962, p. 43) reports that the Walbiri attribute cannibalism and large genitals to a remote group with which they have no contact. No nearby groups receive such unfavorable stereotypes.

The power of an immediate neighbor to overhear and to retaliate may be one factor working against the predicted outcome (for example, Coser, 1957) and also that:

3.19   *The strongest and most threatening outgroup should be the target of the most ethnocentric hostility from the ingroup.*

This prediction follows directly from 3.3 above, and seems implied if not explicit in Sherif's (1953; 1961) presentation, although his specific data are limited to two-group situations. Coser might well make this prediction, although he also recognizes the inhibition of aggression because of anticipated retaliation from the target group (Coser, 1957). Presumably, the stronger the group, the greater the realistic fear of this retaliation. Such inhibition on aggression might generalize to verbal expressions within the ingroup of hostility toward the strongest outgroup. This qualification undermines many other aspects of realistic-group-conflict theory. Psychoanalytic concepts of identification with the aggressor elaborate this theme.

As to the data, Mitchell (1956) in the study cited above, found a very definite pattern for those groups who were most famous for aggressive military power to be held at the least social distance. In much of the data supporting this, however, these famous warriors were not near enough to represent a real threat. The hypothesis would be better tested by utilizing adjacent outgroups only. Studies of the "favorite" outgroups for minority groups within polyethnic states should throw light on the problem. The minority group should show the most ethnocentric hostility toward the dominant and powerful majority group instead of toward other small and weak minority groups. In the attitudes of the Irish toward the English, this would seem to be confirmed. The attitudes within conquered, occupied, and colonial countries toward the occupying forces and other outgroups could provide a valuable empirical confirmation.

Realistic-group-conflict theory also makes predictions about the content of ethnocentric stereotypes about outgroups:

3.20   *The more ethnocentric the ingroup, the more it should perceive outgroups as strong, aggressive and effective, rather than despising them as weak, cowardly, stupid and lazy.*

In pulling together here a recurrent common set of related propositions described by numerous observers, we have inevitably trimmed and distorted the complete views of any one of these observers. Where these scholars have, like ourselves, attempted a general survey of principles of intergroup conflict, some comments on the amendments seem appropriate.

Sherif and Sherif's *Groups in Harmony and Tension* (1953) is a classic in this area, particularly when combined with the later experimental replication and extension (Sherif et al., 1961). Although the realistic-group-conflict emphasis covers the largest part of his propositions and, in particular, is what he emphasizes when protesting the falsity of frustration-aggression-displacement theory, it is by no means all that he has to offer. Even within the scope of realistic-group-conflict theory he offers one additional principle:

3.21   *Intergroup conflict and mutual ethnocentric hostility can only be removed by superordinate common goals or shared threats.*

The capacity of such superordinate goals to remove well-developed experimental intergroup hostility he has experimentally demonstrated in his classic boy's camp studies (especially Sherif et al., 1961). Another major type of theory utilized by Sherif is reference group theory, treated separately below, and the grounds on which Mitchell's finding of less social distance toward more powerful outgroups is anticipated.

As stated previously, this chapter borrows heavily from Coser's brilliant and conscientious survey, *The Functions of Social Conflict* (1956). Particularly helpful for a secondary analyses like the present one is his organization of the material into clearly stated propositions. Many of his most valuable formulations from a general social-science point of view have been omitted here because he focuses primarily upon the functions of social conflict within a social system, rather than between social systems.

Unlike many of the realistic group-conflict-theorists, Coser has no quarrel with Freudian dynamics and, indeed, in one place or another, presents most of the frustration-aggression-displacement mechanism. But his major emphasis is on rational sources of conflict and on the useful functions of conflict. Although he recognizes that hostility causes conflict, he more strongly emphasizes that conflict causes hostility. He notes in agreement with cognitive dissonance theory that sacrifice and suffering for the group creates increased loyalty to the ingroup. He observes the increased cruelty of altruistic conflict done in the group's name, as compared with the selfish conflict between individuals.

One of his points that makes external conflict and hostility a projective symptom of internal problems, rather than a product of intergroup problems, will be enumerated here:

3.22   *False perceptions of threat from outgroups cause increased ingroup solidarity and outgroup hostility* (in consistency with the 3.1 to 3.4 sequence above).

He notes that leaders may seek out an enemy or create a fictitious one just to preserve or to achieve ingroup solidarity (Coser, 1956, p. 105-106). This is certainly one of the most ubiquitous observations on the exploitative opportunism of nationalistic politics. White has stated it thus:

"Hostility toward a foreign power or toward a minority group within a society is often an effective means of unifying a nation. In times of national emergency or crisis, therefore, a nation may attempt to achieve inner unity and solidarity by fomenting hostility towards a foreign power — an old trick — or against a minority group within its gates – also an old trick" (1949, p. 137).

Boulding (1962, p. 162) notes the principle. Rosenblatt, (1964, p. 133) in a review of parallel principles in ethnocentrism and nationalism, provides these citations to this principle: Alexander (1951, p. 281), Allport (1933, Ch. VII), Bay et al. (1950, p. 8, 93 ff.), Braunthal (1946, Ch. IV); Gilbert (1950, pp. 28–30), Hayes (1926, Ch. III), Hertz (1944, p. 218), Machiavelli (1947, p. 65); Murdock (1931); Pillsbury (1919, Ch. III); Royal Institute of International Affairs (1939); Simpson and Yinger (1958, p. 114): Skinner (1959, p. 8); and Znaniecki (1952, pp. xiv-xv).

While this principle does not involve real threat, it does involve an opportunistic exploitation of the major principle of Realistic-group-conflict theory and, hence, is retained in this section as the final proposition. Its utilization in the internal competition of individuals for political control needs attention. White, in the citation above, neglects this in reifying the group as actor deciding to unify itself. A further point worth noticing is that this internal solidarity mechanism plays a role in the escalation of conflict because the outgroup is an eavesdropper on internal communication and takes such mobilization activities as a threat against itself. Furthering this "arms-race" effect are those external words and acts of belligerent intransigency that an insecure leader says and does for the benefit of his internal ingroup audience and his political acceptance by them.

Thus the major proposition of realistic-group-conflict, extended to its "artificial" exploitation in the solution of internal problems, brings us around to a position in which intergroup conflict becomes a "projective" product of internal problems — intrasocietal if not intrapsychic.

Chapter 4

SOCIAL-STRUCTURAL THEORIES OF CONFLICT IN ANTHROPOLOGY[1]

There are several theoretical formulations that might be included under the heading of realistic-group-conflict theories but which have a special structural premise: that most individuals in most societies regard themselves as members of more than one ingroup, and that the ordering of their loyalties to the several ingroups of which they are members has important consequences for the solidarity of the total ethnic group, particularly where the ethnic group is politically uncentralized. Where the ethnic or linguistic group is politically centralized, the structuring of subgroup loyalties among its members can be viewed as contributing to or hindering the national solidarity — as political sociologists have repeatedly pointed out — but in the uncentralized, acephalous, segmentary, or multicentric systems common among folk societies, the structure of group loyalties within the ethnic community may be critical in determining something as fundamental as the boundaries across which military conflict occurs and within which peace is maintained.

Two basic types of loyalty structures have been described by social anthropologists such as Evans-Pritchard, Fortes, Colson, Gluckman, and Murphy: (1) the pyramidal-segmentary type, and (2) the cross-cutting type.

The pyramidal-segmentary type is based on a virtually universal characteristic of societies: the membership of the individual in groups that are, in turn, segments of larger collectivities, so that each individual can correctly regard himself as a member of several units increasing in scope and inclusiveness up to the "total society" itself. In any such pyramid of membership units, the individual must have a way of organizing the several claims that multiple membership makes on him, and he usually has a way of ranking his loyalties to groups at different levels. If the demands made by the groups to which he belongs are mutually compatible (for example, by being diversely specialized and

[1] See chapter addendum.

nonsimultaneous), then he may not have to rank his multiple loyalties. If they are not entirely compatible, so that conflicting demands can be made simultaneously, then a ranking of loyalties is inevitable. Numerous alternative rankings are available in a pyramidal system, depending on the nature and diversity of the demands made by the several groups. A *parochial* ranking of loyalties would be one in which the individual conformed to the demands made by the small, low-level groups to which he belonged but ignored those made by the larger units of which the small groups are segments. A more *universalistic* ranking of loyalties would be one in which he put the demands of wider groupings before the demands peculiar to their smaller segments. Societies can be organized so as to favor parochial or universalistic rankings of loyalties by the degree to which they weight demands on the individual at low or high levels in his pyramid of memberships.

As a distinctive structure of loyalties, the pyramidal-segmentary type originally presented by Evans-Pritchard (1940) and Fortes and Evans-Pritchard (1940), and later discussed by Fortes (1945, 1953), Mayer (1949), Southall (1952, 1956), Smith (1956), Middleton and Tait (1958), Murphy and Kasdan (1959), and Sahlins (1962), among others, has the following properties: (1) No single level of grouping has a monopoly on the use of violence in the society, and group combat occurs sporadically at several levels; (2) Groups at several levels in the pyramid demand military loyalty of the individual; (3) Loyalties are ranked so that the claims of higher-level groups are recognized as prior whenever they coincide temporally with those of lower level segments. This situation permits what Evans-Pritchard has called the fission and fusion of segments, that is, the temporary alliance of two hostile groups when a higher-level unit of which they are both segments demands their military allegiance in combat against an equivalent higher-level unit. It must be noted that such fusion (as an actuality rather than as a potentiality) is temporary and strictly military, so that it should be thought of as *alliance* or *threat-dependent solidarity* instead of as a stable form of integration of the segments. Another distinctive feature of this system (as compared with some other stateless systems) is that segments of the same higher-order unit are only disloyal to one another — in the sense of engaging in mutual combat — when neither of them is faced with threat by an outside group. When there is an outside threat to one of the warring segments, the others help defend it rather than allying with its outside enemy. In defending their "internal" enemies against "external" enemies, they recognize their loyalty to the higher-level unit as prior to the segmental loyalty, which would, after all, be best served by taking *any* ally against the other segment.

This "closing of ranks" in the face of outside threat is a prominent feature of many political entities and has often been remarked by political scientists. The notion that outside threat acts to submerge subgroup loyalties and to increase overall ingroup solidarity is a central tenet of the realistic-group-conflict theory of ethnocentrism and is discussed under that heading in the previous chapter. However, the distinctiveness of the pyramidal-segmentary type described by Evans-Pritchard et al., inheres in the frequent occurrence of military combat between subgroups when higher-order loyalties are not called into action and in the failure to establish permanent solidary units at any but the lowest levels. The gains in solidarity from outside threat are more temporary and specifically military than in any other known type of threat-dependent solidarity. Individual participants in these segmentary societies are always aware of the dual potentialities for alliance and conflict institutionalized in their social structure; although their feuding between low-level segments is often bound by stricter rules and less lethal than at higher levels, they do not allow themselves to indulge in dreams of permanent intersegmental unions involving the abolition of feuds and the formation of joint decision-making agencies. This institutionalized capacity to "forget" higher-order alliance as soon as it is no longer demanded by the military situation and to resume local feuding makes this type of society, which seems to have been unknown to Sumner, an apparent exception to evolutionary theories which assume that outside military threats produce socioeconomic development through the cooperation required to survive. Comparative study might show, however, that the ethnic community in this type of society was never faced with the kind of massive external threat that promotes the development of centralized institutions.

In examining the pyramidal type of loyalty structure, we are confronted with another universal attribute of group membership: that persons define themselves as group members by opposition or contrast to other groups, so that in order to identify himself to another, a person selects from his multiple memberships a group that will serve to distinguish him from members of other coeval groups at the level in the pyramid that he believes the person he is addressing has in mind. Evans-Pritchard illustrates this:

"If one meets an Englishman in Germany and asks him where his home is, he may reply that it is England. If one meets the same man in London and asks him the same question, he will tell one that his home is in Oxfordshire, whereas if one meets him in that county, he will tell one the name of the town or village in which he lives. If questioned in his town or village, he will mention his particular street, and if questioned in his street, he will indicate his house. So it is with the Nuer" (Evans-Pritchard, 1940, p. 136).

The difference between the pyramidal-segmentary type of stateless political system discussed here and the structural relativity of self-reference in a modern nation-state is that in the former, each level of segmentation involves not simply an ill-defined or variably defined group loyalty, but specifically a military loyalty in combat against other segments of that level. (The genealogical framework for equating structural levels provided by a lineage system is another major difference but not essential to this discussion.) Opposition nonetheless appears to be a fundamental ordering principle in defining boundaries for group action in any pyramidal hierarchy of group membership and loyalties.

A final distinctive characteristic of the pyramidal-segmentary structure of group loyalties, especially as discussed by Fortes and Evans-Pritchard (1940), is the "balanced opposition of segments." According to their analysis, the system of military alliance given above results in a situation in which conflict always occurs between groups that are roughly equivalent in power. Even if a larger group attacks a smaller, the latter can call its coeval segments with the same high-order loyalty as military allies, and they form a coalition of groups equivalent in size and power (as well as structural level) to that of the attacker. This potential balance of power acts to deter attack, since any group initiating military action anticipates being faced with a coalition of defenders that has equal or possibly greater military power. The balance or "equilibrium" makes the stateless segmentary society an "ordered anarchy" rather than an unstable, self-destroying population. This system in its abstract properties closely parallels that of the classical eighteenth and nineteenth-century European balance of power as analyzed by students of international politics (Kaplan, 1957).

The consideration of the pyramidal-segmentary type in isolation from other types of group loyalty structures generates the following propositions:

4.1   *Where military loyalty is demanded by territorially discrete segments at several levels in a stateless pyramid of such segments:*
4.1.1   *Intersegment military conflict at one level will alternate temporally with intersegment conflict at higher levels, lower-level segments of the same group ceasing to fight each other when one of them is attacked by a segment of a different group.*
4.1.2   *Segments of one level engaging in mutual combat will not take outside allies to fight one another.*
4.1.3   *The more frequent the military conflict at any structural level (for example, between the total ethnic community and other ethnic communities or between major segments of the total ethnic community), the less frequent is military conflict at lower levels (that is, among the segments whose higher-order loyalties make them temporary military allies).*
4.1.4   *Adjacent groups are the most frequent allies in common defense against remote groups and are, therefore, less likely to be targets of ethnocentrism than are groups at some further remove.*

The first proposition, 4.1.1, is a statement of the basic military situation in a society of this type, and 4.1.2 and 4.1.3 spell out explicitly some of the distinctive implications of this situation. The last proposition, 4.1.4, needs some explanation, particularly as it directly contradicts proposition 3.18 from realistic-group-conflict theory, which states that adjacent groups should be in greatest conflict. The pyramidal-segmentary type of loyalty structure as territorially organized assumes that proximity in space is a basis for military alliance when higher-order units are involved and, therefore, that adjacent groups cannot maintain the highest degree of social distance, enmity, and negative stereotyping of each other, since to do so would endanger their frequently called-on alliance against outsiders. On the other hand, very remote groups are so infrequently contacted that they, too, are not the optimal groups to serve as targets for aggression and hatred. The structure seems to encourage most frequent military conflict at some medium range of proximity in which, for the majority of participants, the groups they are fighting are well-known enough to have provoked disputes (over property, water resources, etc.) and to be perceived as sources of grievance, but are remote enough not to be needed in the most frequent defense of the area. If we think of two curves sloping negatively with distance from the ingroup — one for intergroup competition for resources, the other for the frequency of needing a group as a military ally — it would seem that the latter gradient is steeper, leaving some medium-range groups who are more clearly competitors than frequently needed allies. These groups, then, are the most likely targets of ethnocentrism, as contrasted with the adjacent groups who might be stronger competitors but are more needed as allies, and the more remote groups, who are less needed as allies but are not competing for the same resources. It should be noticed, however, that this paradigm is presented in the literature as applying to culturally homogeneous groups that recognize common ancestry rather than to the interaction of ethnically distinct groups within a region. Nevertheless, in those regions where distinct ethnic units are small — that is, as small in population and area as culturally homogeneous groups elsewhere — it would be interesting to see if the same system of alliance and conflict holds true. Insofar as it does not, we may detect the effect of cultural boundaries on conflict patterns when other factors are held constant.

The crosscutting type of loyalty structure has these distinctive properties:

1. Each male individual in the society owes military loyalty, or a more vaguely defined primary loyalty that involves defense under emergency conditions, to more than one group.

2. One of the groups to which he owes loyalty is his local group, to which he is bound not only by common residence but also by the common interests and cooperative activities which result from common residence; the other is a group (based on common descent or age) whose members are dispersed over several local groups, each of which is a possible autonomous military unit.

3. No clear ranking of these two or more loyalties exists, so that when they make contradictory demands on the individual, he is disposed to find a novel way of satisfying the two or more groups instead of being disloyal to one of them.

When the contradictory demands arise in a situation of possible military combat between two groups to which the individual belongs, he is likely to press for a peaceful solution in which both demands are relinquished rather than having to, for example, join his kinsmen to fight his neighbors or vice versa. If a large enough proportion of the male population is in this position for a long enough period of time, their individual multiple-loyalty dilemmas may aggregate at the societal level as a pacifying network of crosscutting ties. The network can become self-multiplying as group members take advantage of the initial security that is afforded by crosscutting ties to disperse themselves even further, thus increasing the pacifying effect. The anticipation that many persons will suffer contradictory motivations and, therefore, will desire peaceful solutions may itself become institutionalized, so that combat disappears as an alternative in situations of intergroup conflict — *without* the establishment of central decision-making institutions. The reasoning involved in the analysis of this type of group-loyalty structure resembles the premises on which the proponents of an organized exchange of hostages between the United States and the Soviet Union and the proponents of an increased intermigration among modern nations base their arguments.

The distinctions between pyramidal-segmentary and crosscutting loyalty structures leads to the general proposition:

4.2   *Less intersegment conflict will occur in crosscutting than in pyramidal-segmentary loyalty structures.*

The implications for other aspects of ethnocentrism are elaborated in what follows.

The preventive effect of crosscutting loyalties on overt conflict between groups in a society is well represented in the literature of political sociology and political science (Simmel, 1956; Coser, 1957; Lipset, 1959; Guetzkow, 1955). In social anthropology, social structures that exhibit some of these properties were described by L. H. Morgan (1901) for the Iroquois Indians and W. L. Warner (1937) for the Murngin of Australia. However, the most explicit analyses of this phenomenon are to be found in the ethnography of Africa and South America. Evans-Pritchard (in Peristiany, 1939) pointed out that among the Kipsigis of Kenya, regiments, clans, and age-sets crosscut localities to make internecine warfare virtually impossible. The Kipsigis, are a particularly good example of the snowballing effect of this overlap, since individuals among them took advantage of internal peace to move wherever land was available and, by thus dispersing, reinforced the peace that allowed their movement. Colson's (1953) analysis of the effects of multiple loyalties on the peaceful settlement of disputes among the Plateau Tonga of Northern Rhodesia is particularly persuasive because she shows in a specific case how "displaced persons" acted as mediators to mitigate conflict between their clansmen and their neighbors when retaliation for a murder seemed imminent. Since the dispersion process was less advanced among the Plateau Tonga than among the Kipsigis, it was easier to detect the hypothesized functional relationship as a temporal (presumably causal) sequence in which intergroup conflict was threatened, persons with multiple loyalties were both endangered and put in a loyalty dilemma, and such persons acted to propose peaceful alternatives. Gluckman (1955), reanalyzing Evans-Pritchard's (1940) data on the Nuer of the Sudan, concluded that a similar situation obtained there, despite Evans-Pritchard's emphasis on balance of power through segmental opposition rather than crosscutting ties as having a deterrent effect on intergroup violence. Gluckman argues that the Nuer vengeance group is sufficiently scattered so that retaliation in a case of intergroup homicide may involve a displaced person's either having to fight with his neighbors against his kinsmen or being threatened by his neighbors as a representative of the offending group — in either case making him favor peaceful settlement through compensation instead of blood vengeance. Whether or not Gluckman is right about the Nuer, both he and Colson have presented a strong case for the possibility of peace through divided loyalties in stateless segmentary societies, including those societies Fortes and Evans-Pritchard believe to fit the pyramidal-segmentary model of power balance discussed above.

In Murphy's (1957) analysis of the Mundurucu of the Brazilian rain forest, the crosscutting type of group loyalty structure emerges as a fullblown testable hypothesis explicitly relevant to ethnic relations and ethnocentrism. First, he takes matrilocality as a specific indicator of the multiple primary loyalties of males, since it necessarily disperses men at marriage from the kinsmen with whom they grew up. It is presumed that a man remains loyal not only to his mother's brothers remaining in his childhood home but also to his brothers, living at the homes of their respective wives, while also acquiring loyalty to his wife's kinsmen, who are his neighbors. When the central political situation allows the male populations of these various home areas to operate as autonomous military entities, the crosscutting loyalties of the dispersed males become critical in the prevention of violence. Murphy hypothesizes that matrilocal societies of this type are less likely to exhibit internecine violence than patrilocal societies, in which men bound together by descent remain living together and are thus not faced with the dilemma of siding with neighbors or kinsmen. He reports that the patrilocal societies of Brazil manifest more internecine violence than the matrilocal societies. In this connection, it is interesting that matrilocality (or uxorilocality) is a factor in the crosscutting ties of the Iroquois Indians and the Plateau Tonga.

Murphy further proposes that in the matrilocal societies the males must "repress open aggression in order to insure cohesion and continuity"; the psychoanalytic assumption is made that there *is* some aggression to repress and that it is likely to find an outlet by displacement onto a more remote target. In his analysis of the Mundurucú, Murphy asserts that the aggression that is forbidden intrasocietal expression is displaced onto surrounding tribes, who are attacked not for material gain but to release the aggressive tension built up within the society by the inhibition of violence.

On this basis it is now possible to represent the crosscutting type of loyalty structure by a series of propositions, of which the following apply only to stateless societies.

4.3.1   *The greater the proportion of the adult male population that owes military loyalty to groups whose members are located outside their own local defense units, the less the likelihood of violence between such local defense units.* This can be spelled out in more specific terms:

4.3.2   *The more actual residence patterns involve a man's moving from one local community (village, band, homestead cluster) to another, at adolescence or later (when he may be presumed to have been socialized into loyalty to his natal group), the less the likelihood of violence between local communities.* Such residence patterns are indicated by (a) uxorilocal marriage with community exogamy; (b) avunculocality where brothers and sisters reside in different communities; (c) neolocality with shift of residence out of community occasioned by marriage rules, permanent age-villages, or the dispersion of families in the settlement of new land or other migratory situations.

To this basic hypothesis can be appended Murphy's discussion of warfare:

4.3.3   *The less violence between component local segments of the ethnic community, the greater the propensity of that ethnic community to attack others around it.*

By simple deduction we arrive at the following proposition:

4.3.4   *The greater the proportion of the adult male population that owes military loyalty to groups whose members are located outside their own defense units* (either because of residential mobility or from other causes), *the greater the propensity of the ethnic community to attack other ethnic communities.*

This last proposition, unlike the others that preceded it, is highly relevant to unicentric societies, that is to those with a central political organization in which violence is not possible between component local segments of the ethnic community. Since military loyalty in a unicentric society is unequivocally that demanded by the central state, the proposition is better recast in residential terms, as follows:

4.3.5   *The greater the intercommunity residential mobility of the male population at or after adolescence, the greater the propensity of the society (ethnic community) to attack other ethnic communities.*

van Velzen and Van Wetering (1960) give extended theoretical attention at the comparative level to the Murphy hypothesis, offer a somewhat different alternative analysis, and test the hypothesis in a cross-cultural sample of societies. The following excerpts convey most of their central argument:

"We use the term *power group* to denote a group which resorts to aggression when the interests of one of its members are threatened. Such power groups are part of the patrilocal Crow society, but are not found in the matrilocal Cheyenne society.

" . . . On the evidence of the above we are inclined to claim that, *ceteris paribus*, societies without power groups are peaceful ones."

". . . Our considerations of the Cheyenne and Crow societies gives rise to the following causal hypotheses:

(1) In societies with power groups every act of violence elicits a chain reaction and there is danger of any individual deed of aggression leading to group conflict Much intra-societal aggression can be attributed to the existence of power groups. Where they are not present, there will be no struggle for power at the group level.

(2) Violence can be more effectively suppressed if the individual concerned is not part of a power group which is ready to support him through thick and thin. Bystanders who separate and restrain combatants can curb a great deal of potential aggression. The individual lacks the psychological assurance of a reliable stronghold behind him.

(3) In societies where there are no power groups, differences in power will merely consist of differences in muscular strength and personality."

". . . The *fraternal interest* group forms the basis of a power group."

"Power groups need not remain limited to brothers; their size may vary from a few brothers to an entire lineage or sib."

"Brothers form an interest group when they share primary interests and cooperate in promoting them."

"There will be no interest group among brothers where the principal economic interests are shared with others."

"Fraternal interest groups will exist in all patrilocal societies" (pp. 179—180).

"The peacefulness that is characteristic of some matrilocal societies is not due to the fact that adult males inhibit their aggressiveness on any large scale as a result of conflicting loyalties, but is more likely to be attributable to the absence of sufficiently strong interests which might lead to group conflict" (p. 185).

This last statement is a significant departure from Murphy's analysis and from the crosscutting loyalty model altogether. According to van Velzen and Van Wetering, the territorial dispersal of patrilineally linked males does not result in conflicting loyalties but, instead, in the prevention of nonterritorial loyalties. They point out, with ethnographic illustration, that there are means of resolving intrapersonal loyalty conflicts — for example, allowing those most affected to be noncombatants — without avoiding group violence. They also argue that it is rarely the case that loyalties are so multiple and widespread as to conflict between every dyad of potentially opposing groups. They formulate their hypotheses as follows:

Hypothesis 1.   Violence occurs less frequently in matrilocal than in patrilocal societies.

Hypothesis 2.   In matrilocal societies, in contrast to patrilocal societies, everything possible is done to prevent violence.

Hypothesis 3.   In contrast to partilocal societies, peacefulness in social relations is a principal value in matrilocal societies (p. 196).

They selected a sample of 51 unstratified societies, fairly evenly split between matrilocal and partilocal groups, and rated each one on the frequency of fighting, murder, blood feuds, sexual revenge homicide, the separation of combatants in fights, and on the value set on aversion to intrasocietal bloodshed. A combined index of (internal) peacefulness (with the emphasis on frequency of fighting and murder) showed a strong association with matrilocal as opposed to patrilocal residence (χ^2 = 26.5; p < .001). van Velzen and Van Wetering interpret this finding as a confirmation of Murphy's hypothesis that relates matrilocality to intrasocietal peacefulness, which indeed it is, but their divergent interpretation of the intervening mechanism leads to a different expectation concerning ethnocentric behavior. Murphy views the incompatible loyalties in terms of a quantity of aggression which "normally" develops from the opposition of groups and which must, in the matrilocal situation, be displaced onto other societies. van Velzen and Van Wetering, however, see most matrilocal societies as lacking "power groups" and, hence, as lacking the opposition-caused quantum of aggression. On the contrary, in their view it is the patrilocal societies with their opposed fraternal interest groups that magnify what could be minor interpersonal quarrels and homicides into group violence that affects many individuals in the society. According to them, the patrilocal structure generates aggression that never develops in the matrilocal societies rather than the matrilocal groups' having to repress it. Their position is more purely structural than Murphy's, eliminating any psychoanalytic assumptions concerning the channeling of aggression. We must emphasize, therefore, that van Velzen and Van Wetering would agree with proposition 4.3.2 but not with 4.3.3 and 4.3.4, since the latter propositions assume that internal peacefulness requires the inhibition and consequent displacement onto outgroup targets of intrasocietal aggression; they would presumably tend to expect confirmation of the null hypothesis for 4.3.3 and 4.3.4.

Noberini (1966) has provided data on this very point by testing a version of proposition 4.3.4 in which matrilocal societies should exhibit more outgroup hostility than patrilocal ones. She rated the 40 societies from van Velzen and Van Wetering's sample on which information was available on a scale of external warfare frequency devised by Naroll, and found an association between matrilocality and warfare (χ^2 = 3.88; p < .05) supporting Murphy's hypothesis that the crosscutting ties of matrilocal societies cause a displacement of aggression from the ethnic ingroup onto foreigners.

Otterbein and Otterbein (1965) in a cross-cultural study of 50 societies found a relation between the frequency of the blood feud and patrilocal residence. This lends additional support to van Velzen and Van Wetering's hypothesis concerning fraternal interest groups, but it is also consistent with Murphy's formulation (and proposition 4.3.2 extracted from it). The Otterbeins went on to measure the presence of fraternal interest groups in another way as well — through polygyny, on the assumption that it creates a situation in which half brothers live near each other and in which men are less likely to have marital ties competing affectively with fraternal ones. Thus:

4.3.6   *The presence of polygyny makes internal feuding more likely.* The greater the frequency of polygyny the greater the frequency of intergroup feuding within the ethnic community.

This hypothesis, since it is based, in part, on the assumption that the absence of polygyny allows the territorial dispersal of males, is also consistent with Murphy's reasoning as to the mediating mechanism involved. The Otterbeins found that polygyny is positively related to the frequency of feuding and that polygyny and patrilocality together constitute a better predictive index of feuding than either alone.

LeVine (1965) has attempted to generate hypotheses linking social structure and stereotypes by recasting the dichotomy between pyramidal-segmentary and crosscutting loyalty structures as "socially divisive" and "socially integrated" societies. The former type of society has structural features such as patrilocality or local group endogamy that foster the development of a *parochial* loyalty structure; small local groups form solidary units with few primary bonds between these units. In the socially integrated type, the dispersion of males through the means discussed above fosters the development of loyalties to wider groupings or prevents the formation of rigid cleavages between local groups. Since the socially divisive societies have warfare among segments of the ethnic community, and the socially integrated societies do not, the social structures are seen as favoring different norms of conduct concerning social intercourse within the ethnic community. In the socially divisive type, there is suspicion, malicious gossip, and witchcraft accusation; while in the socially integrated type, these behaviors are both less adaptive and less prevalent, with cooperation and sociability being more pronounced.

This divergence between internal structure and behavior is hypothesized as having outcomes in behavior toward other ethnic communities. Socially divisive societies: (a) do not develop images of other peoples as being drastically inferior or immoral as compared to themselves, their images being largely contingent on the current state of military alliances and oppositions or on whether or not the other people had ever attacked them; (b) adopt a defensive rather than offensive military posture; (c) regard membership in their ethnic community as purely hereditary and are unreceptive to immigration. Socially integrated societies: (a) regard alien peoples and particularly their ways of life as drastically inferior or immoral; (b) adopt an offensive, courageous, even foolhardy military posture; (c) regard membership in their ethnic community as a prerogative of their superior way of life and accept immigrants who acquire the behavioral traits that they value.

Some of the reasoning involved in this typological model is that the divisive-social-organization society makes boundaries and group relationships unstable: today's friends are tomorrow's enemy. One must be as ready to fight members of one's own ethnic community as members of alien groups; hence, the latter are not viewed as worse people in an absolute sense but only judged in terms of the past and present state of military encounters and alignments. The situation of intrasocietal violence encourages a defensive military posture, since there is continual danger of attack at the local level and alliances are based on considerations of vengeance and mutual defense. This defensiveness is assumed to be extended to the intersocietal level, since the boundaries are not very sharp in military terms. The strong local groups based on consanguineal descent, combined with the generalized suspicion of others, makes immigration seem undesirable to them. The integrated society, on the other hand, has stable boundaries that divide the permanent peace group or security community from the alien ethnic communities, who are then seen as drastically discontinuous from the ingroup. Since segments of the ethnic community are never military enemies, the entire society can be exalted vis-a-vis other societies, and the latter are remote enough to be targets for nondisruptive aggression through offensive attack. Since the acceptance of strangers by local groups is an institutionalized part of their social structure, and since the ethnic community through its internal peacefulness and self-exaltation is a moral community, immigrants from foreign ethnic groups will be admitted if they demonstrate the capacity to acquire ingroup norms.

These propositions are generated by this speculative typological analysis:

4.4   *The more internally divisive (as indicated by frequency of intersegmental violence) a stateless society or ethnic community:*
4.4.1   *The less it is likely to maintain institutionalized images of outgroups as inferior and immoral.*
4.4.2   *The more likely it is to organize itself for military defense rather than attacking outgroups without provocation.*
4.4.3   *The fewer outgroup immigrants will it allow in and the more difficult will acceptance of an outgroup immigrant as an ingroup member be.*

Noberini's above-mentioned study (1966) provides some evidence supporting these propositions: in a sample of 31 societies rated on general ethnocentric attitude, high ethnocentrism was related to low internal warfare (χ^2 = 4.18; p < .05) and to matrilocality as opposed to patrilocality (χ^2 = 5.52; p < .02).

The theoretical formulations surveyed so far in this chapter have been based exclusively on data concerning societies lacking a centralized political organization. In their study, however, the Otterbeins were interested in testing hypotheses relating political development to internal feuding. They state three basic propositions:

4.5.1   *The higher the level of political complexity the less frequent is internal feuding.*

4.5.2   *Correlations of the strength of fraternal interest groups* (as indexed by patrilocality and polygyny) *with the frequency of internal feuding are significantly larger among stateless societies, taken by themselves, than among politically centralized societies taken by themselves.*

4.5.3   *Societies that frequently engage in war with their neighbors are less likely to have feuding than societies that have peaceful external relations.* (This is an operational form of the proposition "Real threat causes ingroup solidarity" stated on page 31).

Using Murdock's levels of political integration (based on the size of politically integrated population units), the Otterbeins divided their sample into societies high and low on political integration. They found:

For 4.5.1, no support, with Otterbein measure of feuding or van Velzen-Van Wetering measure of internal peace.

For 4.5.2, mild support; the relations of patrilocality and polygyny were somewhat stronger among societies low on political integration than among societies high on it, but the difference in coefficients were not significant.

For 4.5.3, no support (ϕ = .04) when the whole sample was used, but strong support (ϕ = −.48) when societies high on political integration are taken separately, and a relation inverse of that predicted (ϕ = +.44) when societies of low political integration are taken by themselves.

These findings contain several surprises. First, feuding is not significantly less frequent among the societies of larger-scale political integration, so that a simple relation between widening of political units and the suppression of internal feuding is not confirmed. Of course, much hinges on the definition of "political unit"; it could be defined so as to entail necessarily the control of feuding. Of importance here is the fact that if it is defined independently of the control of feuding, the two are not related. This leads one to ask what conditions must obtain for societies high on political integration to control feuding; the Otterbeins answer on the basis of their data that they must be engaged in external warfare.

Another important surprise is that the "Real-threat-causes-ingroup-solidarity" paradigm works for "states" but not "stateless" societies; among the latter, it is the more war, the more feuding. This gives rise to a new proposition:

4.5.4   *Frequency of interethnic warfare and frequency of intraethnic feuding are positively related in stateless societies and negatively related in politically centralized societies.*

The Otterbeins explain this by stating (in effect) that in stateless societies the threat of warfare from outside cannot be translated into a cessation of feuding because there are no superordinate officials to intervene effectively to stop feuding. If this explanation is correct, then the pyramidal-segmentary loyalty structure, in which segments are assumed to close ranks automatically (that is, without superordinate intervention) when faced with outside threat, is to be seen comparatively as a rather ineffective mechanism for the long-term control of internal violence; it allows only temporary cessation of ingroup feuding.

Proposition 4.5.4 and the data supporting it suggest that there might be different laws relating ingroup and outgroup relations in stateless societies, on the one hand, and centralized polities, on the other. The familiar external-hostility-ingroup-solidarity mechanism and the displacement of hostility generated within the ethnic community onto other ethnic communities (proposition 8.14 in Chapter 8) might be operating in centralized polities, where political boundaries at the ethnic level are sharper and more important, but not in stateless societies where ethnic boundaries have less political salience because they are not associated with a superordinate structure. In the latter case, external-threat-internal-solidarity and displacement-onto-outgroup mechanisms might be operating in the short run (as the pyramidal-segmentary model implies), while generalization mechanisms (based on greater stimulus equivalence between all groups boundaries) guide the long-term pattern of action — hence the more war, the more feuding. This resembles LeVine's conception of socially divisive societies and is congruent with proposition 12.2 in the chapter on transfer theories. The finding on stateless societies could also be predicted on a realistic-group-conflict basis, with no psychological assumptions, as in the following proposition:

4.5.5   *In societies lacking a superordinate political authority, situations of scarce resources cause intergroup conflict both within and between ethnic communities;* thus internal feuding and external warfare covary with scarcity of resources and are positively correlated with each other. Where there is a superordinate authority, the group competition resulting from scarce resources manifests itself only between ethnic communities, as in warfare, since each ethnic community has the means available to suppress internal feuding in the service of external warfare; hence, scarcity of resources is correlated positively with external warfare but negatively with internal feuding, the latter being a luxury permissible only in situations of abundance.

Regardless of the theoretical position adopted, it is clear that hypotheses relating ingroup and outgroup aggression should be tested separately in samples of centralized and stateless societies. In subsequent publications (1968a, 1968b) reporting a study of "internal war" in a different sample of 50 societies, Otterbein gives results that differ from but do not contradict the ones reported above. War between political communities is defined as "internal" when the outgroup is culturally similar and "external" when it is not; "feuding" is armed combat within a political community. The results show no association between internal and external war, thus defined, for centralized or uncentralized political systems. In other words, when the ingroup is defined in terms of cultural similarity rather than political community, the syndrome of internal-solidarity-external-hostility in centralized political systems does not hold up. This suggests that political boundaries are more salient than ethnic or cultural boundaries as organizers of military activity; and that proposition 4.5.4 and the discussion following it might only apply where ethnic and political boundaries are congruent. Where they are not congruent, and particularly where there are culturally similar but politically autonomous groups in a region, it is combat within and between *political* communities, not ethnic communities, that is likely to exhibit the inverse correlated posited by Sumner.

ADDENDUM

We omit from this chapter the extensive anthropological literature on factionalism, which deals restrictively with conflict between subgroups of communities that are not themselves autonomous but are units in colonial or national systems. The theoretical analyses of Siegel and Beals (1960a), however, deserves attention here. Siegel and Beals (Siegel and Beals, 1960a; 1960b; Beals, 1961; Beals, 1962; French, 1962; Chance, 1962) have presented a theory of intragroup dissension which, although not explicitly related to ethnocentrism and intergroup conflict, makes contact at all points with theories and variables that are. It contrasts with the realistic-group-conflict theory in that external stress is predicted to reduce group solidarity under certain conditions. This presentation is most dependent on Siegel and Beals (1960a) and, as a brief condensation, is necessarily overclarified and oversimplified. The dogmatic statement of ceteris paribus propositions is foreign to the aims of Siegel and Beals, who aspire to a more context-dependent analysis, attending to complex interactions among variables.

Factionalism is overt, unregulated, disapproved of conflict between transient or stable factions within the group which interferes with the achievement of group goals that are recognized by members of the factions as desirable. Such factionalism is made more likely when there are strains within the social structure and when external stresses of certain types occur. The nature of these stresses and strains is made more explicit in the listing of propositions, the first group introducing different classes of strains, the second group introducing different classes of stress.

Sources of Strain

4.6.1   *The more ambiguities and incompatibilities in obligations, obedience lines, and duties, the more prone is the society to factionalism* (the lower is ingroup solidarity).

4.6.2   *The more uneven the distribution of rewards within the group, the more likely is factionalism.*

4.6.3   *The more oppressive, ranked, and arbitrary the power structure* (the greater are social-distance norms and prescribed discriminations, the less the opportunity for upward mobility, the longer sons must remain under the domination of fathers, etc.) *the more likely is factionalism.*

4.6.4   *The more incongruity between traditional beliefs or practices and external reality, the more factionalism.*

4.6.5   *The more generalized the authority and leadership pattern* (in that the same persons exercise religious, economic, and political control) *the more pervasive factionalism, although not more schismatic factionalism.*

The above principles are based on sources of strain. The following ones are based on the sources of stress that predispose factionalism. (Not all types of stress have this effect.)

Sources of Stress

4.7.1   *The more covert or hidden the external stress, the more likely is it to produce factionalism.*

4.7.2   *The more novel and unprecedented the stress the more likely is factionalism.*

4.7.3   *Of recurrent stresses, the less regular, more random the stress, the more likely is factionalism.*

4.7.4   *The more complex is the stress, the more numerous the stages and subproblems in any solution to it, the more likely is factionalism.*

4.7.5   *The longer the stress persists, the more likely is factionalism.*

4.7.6   *The more the stress curtails the alternatives available, the more likely is factionalism.*

4.7.7   *The more the stress impinges unevenly on subgroups, the more selectivity with which it affects particular subgroups, the more likely is factionalism.*

4.7.8   *The more the stress disrupts traditional modes of social control, the more likely is factionalism.*

In relating this set of propositions to others, a number of complications arise. First, Siegel and Beals recognize, as do the realistic-group-conflict theorists and the frustration-aggression-displacement theorists, that stress in the form of focal

HT 1521 L43

LeVine, Robert
Alan 1932

Ethnocentrism: theories of conflict, ethnic attitudes

1. What is the title of Sa

    Just a country 1

2. Who published the book

    Oxford Universit

3. What is the title of E

    Edie, an America

4. What is the call numbe
   England?

    SH 383.2 S76

5. What is the call numbe

    PR 6033 U4 S5

1. On what page did the o
   appear?

   B. 21

2. What periodical publis

   B. Science and

3. What is the name of th
   racing

   B. Glass

4. In 1985 the article "I
   SCIENCE DIGEST?

   A. 16

5. In what volume of ESS
   overcome shyness" pub

   C. 14

threat by an outgroup tends to reduce factionalism. In their terms, such a stress is overt (rather covert), and is an expected threat, for which culturally established responses are available. Furthermore, they accept parts of the frustration-aggression-displacement theory, in particular, the frustratingness of coordinated social cooperation. Misunderstandings can arise from their tendency to define as stress *any* change in external contacts or environment. Thus threat and stress are not always to be identified. For example, they speak of the past solidarity of the two principal illustrative groups as being "threat-dependent." *Removal* of the threat of invasion by neighbors or the removal of the threat of starvation are classified as stresses. It should also be observed that their instances of stress all involve acculturation pressures and domination by alien social systems that contradict or render useless the traditional exercise of authority.

Chapter 5

REFERENCE GROUP THEORY AND THE ANTHROPOLOGICAL CRITIQUE OF SUMNER

In the contemporary sociological theory of reference groups, Sumner's concepts of ingroup and outgroup are credited with their greatest influence, and his ethnocentrism syndrome is subject to its most explicit criticism. Concerning this influence, Merton and Rossi (1957, pp. 276-277) state:

"There have been several lines of development in sociology and social psychology which now give promise of merging in a functional theory of reference group behavior. Each of these has, after its own fashion, made major contributions, but in retrospect, the impressive fact is that, in large measure, their mutual implications have not yet been consolidated. As is generally known, these are the conceptions of in- and out-groups set forth by Sumner, the ideas regarding the social self developed by James, Cooley and Mead, the more recent systematic researches on reference group behavior represented by the work of Hyman, Sherif, and Newcomb. . . .

"The general and, in this truncated form, uninstructive fact that men are variously oriented to groups besides their own was captured in the terminology invented by Sumner to distinguish between 'ourselves, the we-group, or in-group and everybody else, or the other-groups, out-groups.' Sumner proceeded to describe the relations between these types of groups. Essentially, these somewhat premature observations held that conditions of amity and order obtain in the in-group whereas the relation to out-groups is that of hostility, plunder, and exploitation. That this is the case (under unspecified conditions) Sumner was able to show through numerous *illustrations* drawn from history and ethnology. But in adopting a descriptive, rather than analytical, outlook on the facts of the case, he inevitably blurred and obscured the otherwise conspicuous fact that, under certain conditions, the out-group becomes a basis of *positive*, not merely hostile reference and that the science of sociology is thereby committed to determine the conditions under which one or the other orientation to out-groups obtained. In short, the initial distinction put Sumner well on the way toward opening up a series of problems regarding reference group behavior. But this avenue to the development of a theory of reference group behavior, open in principle to those who would explore it since the appearance of *Folkways* in 1906, was not followed up by systematic research."

Merton (1957, pp. 297-299) has elaborated on his criticism of Sumner's ethnocentrism hypothesis:

"It is evident that membership groups are not coterminous with in-groups, nor non-membership groups with out-groups, although the contrary may seem to be implied by William Graham Sumner in the famous passage which first introduced the concepts of in-group and out-group. At the outset, Sumner is speaking primarily of 'primitive society' but, before he is through, he has much the same to say about more complex societies. . . .

"Following this lead, we sociologists have been wont to repeat, rather than to test in its many implications, the thesis advanced by Sumner. Rather than regarding the in-group as that special kind of membership group which is characterized by inner-cohesion-and-outer-hostility, we have tended to develop the practice, encouraged by Sumner's own ambiguous formulations, of assuming that all membership groups exhibit the characteristics of the in-group. Nor are sociologists alone in this practice. On every side, it is taken for granted that solidarity within the group promotes hostility toward those outside the group, and conversely, in a cumulative spiral of inner-cohesion-and-outer-hostility. At first glance, and in its largest reaches, there is much to support this view.

"Intense nationalism, as the historical record shows and as contemporary life makes abundantly clear, is typically accompanied by hostility toward other nationalist societies. Attacks or threats of attack by each only strengthens the cohesion of the other and sets the stage for even greater hostility toward the outsider. The identifiable cases conforming to this pattern of group interaction are too numerous and too notorious to allow one to deny the existence of the pattern. What can be questioned, however, and indeed is being questioned here, is whether this is the *only* pattern that connects up the inner cohesion of groups and their external relations, whether in effect, all membership groups operate in the fashion described by Sumner.

"This turns out to be not a matter of logic, but a matter of fact. For, as has been indicated, there is a tendency to assume that, from the standpoint of their members, all groups are 'in-groups,' and consequently, it is inferred that membership groups generally exhibit Sumner's syndrome of behaviors. Yet inquiry shows that this is not the case.

"Lacking any but the most primitive conceptions of psychology, Sumner too soon and without warrant concluded that deep allegiance to one group generates antipathy (or, at the least, indifference) toward other groups. Coming out of the evolutionary tradition of social thought, with its emphasis on society as well as nature being red in tooth and claw, Sumner described an important but special case as though it were the general case. He assumed, and his assumption has been echoed as established truth on numerous occasions since his day, that intense loyalty to a group necessarily generates hostility toward those outside the group.

"Reference group theory which *systematically* takes account of *positive* orientations toward non-membership groups can serve as a corrective of this prematurely restricted conclusion. In-groups and out-groups are often sub-groups within a larger social organization, and are always potentially so, since a new social integration can encompass previously separated groups."

As developed by Merton, Hyman (1942), Shibutani (1955), Sherif (1953, 1955), Newcomb (1960), and others, reference-group theory is a general formulation of wide-ranging applicability that is particularly relevant to the analysis of large-scale complex societies and situations of great social mobility. Its application to ethnic interaction among folk societies, although perhaps not immediately apparent, can begin with Merton's critique of Sumner and his injunction to examine empirical cases rather than granting a priori validity to the ethnocentrism hypothesis. First and foremost, reference-group theorists argue that the groups to which persons actually belong are not always the ones they would like to belong to, feel loyalty to, or — most important — whose standards they adopt, hence a noncongruence of membership groups with reference groups. There are individuals who are disloyal to their membership groups (turncoats) or who reject the standards of their own group (alienated rebels); there are those who aspire to membership in groups to which they do not belong (for example, social climbers) or who accept the evaluative standards of an external group (for example, members of subordinate castes). These exceptions to the Sumnerian equivalence of membership-loyalty-exaltation-of-ingroup-standards with rejection-and-hostility-to-outgroups are so familiar in modern societies that the noncongruence is virtually self-evident. But what is the situation in the nonindustrial regions of the world where social life is more stable and less differentiated?

There are several anthropological studies that suggest the relevance of reference-group concepts. As the political organization of stateless societies in Africa and elsewhere has come under ethnographic scrutiny, it has become apparent that individuals in these societies regard themselves as members of several groups simultaneously, that multiple membership involves loyalties and norms of conduct that are not always compatible, and that situations occur in which persons must choose between groups in varying scope, between kinship and territorial groups, between agnatic and cognatic kin, and between lineage and paramount chief. Some of these types of recurrent multiple-loyalty arrangements are reviewed in Chapter 4; others are described in Gluckman (1955) and Fallers (1956). The problem of deciding which of the several groups he belongs to will be reference groups with respect to particular kinds of behavior is a problem that the person in these societies shares with members of modern societies, and reference-group theory is equally relevant in both situations to the question of which properties of groups make them more or less likely to be selected.

Some of these societies that have been analyzed in functionalist and equilibrium terms seem to have such traditional and rigidly organized principles for selecting reference groups in particular multiple-loyalty situations that individuals acting alone or collectively have no choice, which makes a reference-group analysis considerably less interesting. As investigations have become more detailed concerning what actually happens (as opposed to principles or rules concerning what should happen), it becomes clear that reference-group selection is not always the automatic process it seems. For example, Brown (1964) shows that in the Chimbu region of the New Guinea Highland, groups will take external allies to fight other segments of their own higher-order group, contrary to the implications of the pyramidal-segmentary loyalty structure described in Chapter 4 (see Chapter 7 for more detail on this point). At this writing it seems likely that these alliances, not based on genealogical or other traditional or automatic determinants of selection, are much more frequent than the ethnographic record to date would suggest. Factors of population size, propinquity, wealth, power, prestige, and success in warfare may turn out to be sufficiently important in the creation of alliances to make turncoats of formally linked groups (or groups linked by primordial ties).

In more striking discord with Sumner's concept of ethnocentrism are the documented cases of peoples who are territorially, economically, and politically autonomous but who have taken another people as their positive reference group. Many of the smaller Bantu peoples of northern Tanzania and western Kenya have emulated in dress, warfare patterns, age-set organization and other aspects of culture the Masai and other pastoral Nilo-Hamitic peoples such as the Nandi. For example, Beidelman (1964) reports that it is an insult for an outsider to tell someone of the Baraguyu tribe that he is *not* like a Masai; the same is true of the Arusha (Gulliver, 1964) and some of the Gogo Rigby (1969). Although the history of the region is far from clear, LeVine and Sangree (1962) have speculated that the conspicuous success of the Nilo-Hamites in warfare led those Bantu groups that were smaller and less geographically protected from military raids to adopt their enemies as positive reference groups and attempt to become like them.

This example of group imitation in the borrowing of culture traits brings us to the topic of culture change. In Sumner's view, change was internal, "primarily due to changes in life conditions" (1906, p. 36); the literate classes of stratified societies might transcend their ingroup prejudices and attempt to impose on the masses foreign customs that they perceived as advantageous, but "primitive society" was too dominated by ethnocentrism to borrow consciously, and it ruthlessly suppressed dissenters from ancestral mores. In the main, "each ingroup forms its own ways, and looks with contempt and abhorrence on the ways of any out-group" (1906, p. 116). Even in stratified societies, the literate minority was usually unable to reform the mores of the masses. This is the Sumner familiar to intellectual historians (Hofstadter, 1959), the pessimistic Social Darwinist who stated, "Stateways can't change folkways" in an essay entitled, "The Absurd Effort to Make the World Over." On the other hand, Sumner showed a peripheral awareness that his view might not cover all of the facts concerning "primitive society":

"Contiguity, neighborhood, or even literature may suffice to bring about syncretism of the mores. One group learns that the people of another group regard some one of its ways or notions as base. This knowledge may produce shame and an effort to breed out the custom. Thus whenever two groups are brought into contact and contagion, there is, by syncretism, a selection of the folkways which is destructive to some of them. This is the process by which folkways are rendered obsolete" (1906, p. 116).

His examples, however, suggest that he had in mind conquest situations in which the subjugated imitated the "superior" mores of the conquerors, and the intermixing of culturally diverse populations, in which mores of less adaptive value would fail to survive.

Sumner comes close to a significant admission of factual ignorance in the following passage:

"Groups select, consciously and unconsciously, standards of group well living. . . . The historical classes adopt the decision which constitute these group plans and acts, and they impose them on the group. . . . In a lower civilization group interest and purposes are less definite. *We must believe* that barbarous tribes often form notions of their group interests, and adopt group policies, especially in their relations with neighboring groups" (1906, pp. 62-63, italics added).

Here his only examples are of concerted efforts by American Indians to make war. Sumner's evolutionary position did not allow him to view the empirical facts of cultural borrowing and diffusion as inconsistent with, or indeed relevant to, his postulation of ethnocentrism as universal.

Anthropological studies of diffusion, borrowing, and acculturation have almost always been based on the assumption that one culturally distinct population could take another as a positive reference group, at least, to the extent of emulating its customs. The works of Boas, Dixon, and their students are full of documented cases of this phenomenon, among autonomous groups at the same level of socioeconomic development. Hence the study of cultural diffusion and its successor, the study of acculturation and culture change — insofar as they have demonstrated that diffusion and acculturation can take place consciously and without conquest and coercion — have produced a body of evidence inconsistent with the assumption of ethnocentrism as universal. The phenomenon is so well established as to need no extensive review here. It is worthwhile, however, to mention the work of recent investigators of culture change who emphasize that nonethnocentric behavior, far from being a rare event, is a recurrent feature of sociocultural processes in non-Western societies alike.

Wallace (1956) defines a revitalization movement as a "deliberate, organized, conscious effort by members of a society to construct a more satisfying culture" (1956, p. 265). He includes in this category cases that have been termed "nativistic movements," "cargo cults," and "messianic movements," among others. Some of the criterial attributes are as follows:

"Revitalization is thus from a cultural standpoint, a special kind of culture change phenomenon: the persons involved in the process of revitalization must perceive their culture, or some major areas of it, as a system (whether accurately or not); *they must feel that this cultural system is unsatisfactory*; and they must innovate not merely discrete items, but a new cultural system, specifying new relationships as well as, in some cases, new traits" (1956, p. 265, italics added).

The recurrent nature of revitalization is indicated in the following statements:

"The formulations are based in major part on documentary data, mostly published. . . . Our files now contain references to several hundred religious revitalization movements, among both western and non western peoples, on five continents. These represent only a small portion, gathered in a quick preliminary survey of anthropological literature. An earnest attempt to collect all revitalization movements described in historical, anthropological, and other sorts of documents, would without question gather in thousands" (Wallace, 1956, p. 264).

If Wallace's estimate is correct, there may turn out to be on record almost as many revitalization movements as there are "cultures" in Murdock's (1953) listing! Regardless of actual numbers, conscious and organized dissatisfaction with ingroup culture has a widespread occurrence and cannot be dismissed in considering the universality of the ethnocentrism syndrome. In societies at various levels of socioeconomic development the world over, persons have rejected their own societies as reference groups and have attempted, sometimes with success, to alter drastically the normative order inherited from their ancestors.

As anthropologists have extended their field investigations to regions of considerable social stratification, social mobility, and political hierarchy, they have increasingly discovered cases of noncongruence between membership groups and reference groups, particularly in historical perspective. The best known case is that of the Kachins of Highland Burma as described by Leach (1954):

"The *gumsa* conceive of themselves as being ruled by chiefs who are members of an hereditary aristocracy; the *gumlao* repudiate all notions of hereditary class difference. *Gumsa* regard *gumlao* as commoner serfs who have revolted against their lawful masters; *gumlao* regard *gumsa* as tyrants and snobs. But while the two terms represent in Kachin thinking two fundamentally opposed modes of organization, both are consistent with the same general set of cultural trappings which we recognize as Kachin. Of two lineages of the same clan one may be *gumsa* and another *gumlao;* *gumsa* and *gumlao* speak the same languages; both in mythological and historical time *gumsa* communities have been converted into *gumlao* communities and vice versa" (1954, p. 198).

Leach recognizes this situation as exemplifying certain recurrent social processes:

"*Gumsa* organization as developed in the Hkamti Long area was, I insist, a kind of imitation of the Shan political order. There is nothing very mysterious about this. In our own age we are familiar with the phenomenon of subject colonial peoples who, in achieving independence, carry on with a political system imitated and modified from that of their former rulers" (1954, p. 252).

Leach's critique of ethnographic method suggests that persistence of the Sumner ingroup-peace-external-hostility paradigm in anthropological evidence may be due to persistent bias in the collection and analysis of data:

"Finally let me make the plea that the general type of analysis which I have attempted in this book may have value in other contexts besides that of the Kachin Hills Area. The cultural situation in the Kachin Hills, as I have described it, is both confused and confusing but it is not exceptional. On the contrary I would claim that it is largely an academic fiction to suppose that in a 'normal' ethnographic situation one ordinarily finds distinct 'tribes' distributed about the map in orderly fashion with clear-cut boundaries between them. I agree of course that ethnographic monographs frequently suggest that this is the case, but are the facts proved? My own view is that the ethnographer has often only managed to discern the existence of "*a* tribe" because he took it as axiomatic that this kind of cultural entity must exist. Many tribes are, in a sense, ethnographic fictions" (1954, pp. 290-291).

Leach's work in Highland Burma has a particularly important implication for comparative study. It is that, taken at one point in time, groups may exhibit a high degree of ethnocentrism and may lead the investigator to think that they are perpetuating ancient cultural divisions, inherited from their ancestors. Looked at historically, however, the same groups may be found to have fluctuated greatly over time in their allegiances, their alliances, and their norms, suggesting much less rigidity in the ethnocentrism syndrome than Sumner and others have suggested. The ethnographer and the comparativist must beware of building models of discrete social or cultural systems based on purely synchronic data concerning ethnic relations, when diachronic data may show a system of interethnic transactions and transformations to be operative.

In dealing with the integration of tribal groups into political orders of wider scope, social anthropologists have come closer to the perspective of reference-group theory. Kopytoff (1966) has analyzed the ethnopolitical history of the southwestern Congo from the precolonial period to independence explicitly in terms of the reference groups involved; he shows how "tribalism," far from being "traditional," emerged as the result of policies altering the reference-group structure. Mitchell, whose Central African research was cited by Merton (1957, p. 306) in his elaboration of reference-group theory, shows how urban Africans manage their multiple reference groups in differing interactive situations:

"I have tried to show in this essay that one of the features of the social structure of the African population on the Copperbelt is that except in these dancing teams, tribalism does not form the basis for the organization of corporate groups. It remains essentially a category of interaction in casual social intercourse. Similarly the prestige ranking system does not serve to organize Africans into corporately acting groups. It operates as a category of interaction together with tribalism in mediating social relationships in what is predomi- nantly a transient society. These two principles of association determine the behavior of comparative strangers to one another mainly in day-to-day relationships. . . . I have presented evidence to show that in their opposition to the Europeans, Africans ignore both their "class" and tribal differences. . . . The same people who stand together in one situation may be bitterly opposed in another" (1956, pp. 42-43).

Thus recent anthropological studies have produced a number of cases that are not consistent with the assumption that the ethnocentrism syndrome, as Sumner described it, is universal. These are cases in which (a) the traditional social structure provided each individual with multiple memberships, to be selected among in particular situations; (b) segments of groups are militarily disloyal to their coeval segments by taking "outgroup" allies against "ingroup" enemies; (c) autonomous folk societies take one of their military enemies as a positive reference group, consciously attempting to become like them; (d) communities and individuals in folk societies adopt the political and social norms of outside groups; (e) organized rebellious and innovative religious movements occur, based on conscious dissatisfaction with ingroup culture; (f) sentiments of ingroup loyalty were not associated with ethnic, cultural, or linguistic boundaries until colonial policies endowed those boundaries with political importance; (g) "tribal" feeling is manifest only in certain interactive contexts, and the tribe or ethnic group coexists with groups defined by race and occupational status in the individual's repertoire of reference groups.

These empirical cases are of great importance for theory, and bring us back to the problem posed by Merton and Rossi, namely, to determine the conditions under which one or the other (that is, positive or negative) orientation to outgroups obtained" (1957, p. 277). In terms of our present task of generating propositions for cross-cultural research, we are particularly concerned to make some statements about the conditions under which ethnically distinct outgroups can become positive reference groups among folk societies. Of the conditions mentioned in reference-group theory as favoring this state of affairs, the ones that seem most relevant are those that involve group reward or advantage and group visibility. The following propositions can be tested:

5.1   *Of the groups in a region those most likely to be taken as models for emulation are those that have a conspicuous advantage over the others in terms of survival or adaptation in the environment that all the groups share.*

5.1.1   *Where there is much intergroup warfare, the group perceived as most successful in warfare will be most admired and emulated, even though it may be a military aggressor.*

5.1.2   *Where some groups have a superordinate political hierarchy and others do not, those groups having it will be most admired and emulated, although they may be resented as well.*

5.1.3   *Where there are conspicuous differences in the wealth of groups, wealthier groups will be admired and emulated, although perhaps resented as well.*

5.1.4   *Where there is an occupational ranking system prevailing across the region, those groups recognized as higher in it will be admired and emulated, although perhaps resented as well.*

5.2   *Where intergroup warfare is prevalent and alliances are not auto-matically assigned on a genealogical or other traditional basis, groups chosen as allies will be those perceived as most likely to be successful in warfare. Specifically, groups chosen will be those having a conspicuous advantage in:*

5.2.1   *Population size.*

5.2.2   *Military record or reputation for warlikeness.*

Other conditions that determine how the ingroup relates to its various outgroups are suggested by Sherif (Sherif and Sherif, 1953; Sherif et al., 1961) who defines a reference group in terms of the acceptance of the outgroup's social distance scale, that is by evaluating other groups, including the ingroup, by the outgroup's standards. According to Sherif's analysis, this acceptance of outgroup standards is negatively related to ingroup unification and solidarity.

5.3.1   *The more internally unified an ingroup the more outgroups will be rejected and the fewer outgroups will be used as positive reference groups.*

5.3.2   *The more internally unified an ingroup, the more similar the outgroup must be to the ingroup to be used as a positive reference group.*

The motivational and standard-of-comparison functions attributed to reference groups (Kelly, 1952; Shibutani, 1955; Turner, 1956) do not necessarily imply membership in the reference group nor aspiration to membership. However, Turner (1956) and Sherif and Sherif (1964) emphasize the importance of the desire to be accepted as a determinant of the selection of reference groups.

5.4   *The more closed to membership an outgroup, the less likely it is to be used as a positive reference group.*
5.4.1   *The more closed to membership all outgroups are, the more ethnocentric the ingroup.*

On the other hand, lack of availability or visibility of an outgroup has effects on the ingroup's perception which could affect its selection as a reference group. For instance, a lack of familiarity with the norms and customary behavior of the outgroup may lead to greater perceived homogeneity (Hyman, 1960).

5.5   *The less contact with outgroup members, the greater the opportunity for overidealizing (or underevaluating the outgroup's performance and values and the more likely its adoption as a positive (or negative) reference group.*

The concept of "negative ethnocentrism" proposed by Swartz (1961) is also relevant to a discussion of reference groups. This involves attributing ingroup values to an outgroup and evaluating the outgroup as higher in the performance of them.

It should be observed that all of these hypotheses thus far, although departing from Sumner's concept of the ethnocentrism syndrome, are consistent with his commitment to the more general theory that culture traits of greater adaptive values are more likely to survive, and could be generated as correlational propositions from his theory.

The following hypotheses follow from reference-group theory and are also consistent with an application of behavioristic learning theory notions (see Chapter 11) to the achievement of ingroup loyalty through positive reinforcement of that loyalty. In this form, they are derived primarily from Guetzkow (1955).

5.6   *Groups offering their members greater rewards for membership will exhibit more ingroup loyalty and solidarity and less tendency to emulate other groups.*

The members will be more likely to prefer ingroup membership, values, customs, to outgroup membership, values, and customs. Consistent with the behavioristic emphasis on reinforcement and the Freudian analysis of ambivalence, there will be greater attraction (k in Hull-Spence theory, *valence* in Lewin) where there has, in the past, been the greatest reward.

5.6.1   *Where there is intergroup warfare, a group whose members perceive it as successful in warfare will exhibit more ethnocentrism than groups whose members perceive their membership groups to be unsuccessful in warfare.*
5.6.2   *Where some groups have a superordinate political hierarchy and others do not, those groups having it will exhibit more ethnocentrism than those who do not.* (The assumption here is that such a hierarchy gives members benefits in the form of safety, security, and ingroup order.)
5.6.3   *Where there are conspicuous differences in the wealth of groups, wealthier groups will be more ethnocentric than poor ones.*
5.6.4   *Where there is an occupational ranking system prevailing across the region, those groups recognized as higher in it will be more ethnocentric than those that are lower in it.*

It should be noted that these four hypotheses are parallel to 5.1.1 to 5.1.4, but on the ingroup side. The two sets of hypotheses taken together predict that differences in conspicuous advantage within a region generate asymmetrical patterns of interethnic attitudes such that successful or advantaged groups are most admired by others but do not reciprocate — they also prefer themselves to others. If these hypotheses were validated it would mean that social attitudes usually associated with social strata in a single social system also operate across autonomous groups.

Again, there is some consideration of the role of visibility in the selection of reference groups. Apart from the importance assigned to visibility in reference-group theory, international relations theory has produced a concordant prediction: Corbett (1953, cited by Guetzkow, 1955) emphasizes that it is the perceived concomitance of nation and reward that is essential (see Chapter 8 for our parallel analysis for frustration concomitance). Thus anything that sharpens the boundaries of the ethnic group and makes it more salient as a perceptual entity to its members should facilitate perceiving the rewards accruing to group membership (presumably there are always some rewards) as associated with the ethnic group. This reasoning would predict proposition 5.6.2 (above), since political centralization sharpens ethnic boundaries. Other propositions based on visibility are as follows:

5.7.1   *Those groups in which items of major value* (for example, property, consumable subsistence goods, prestige emblems, high status positions) *are awarded on a basis that perceptibly involves ethnic group membership,* (for example, as rewards distributed publicly by leaders of the ethnic group to good warriors or faithful followers) *will exhibit more ethnocentrism than groups in which such items are distributed otherwise.*
5.7.2   *Among those groups perceived as having an equivalent degree of*

advantage, the one most likely to be emulated will be the one most distinctively different, on the basis of visible symbols of ethnicity, particularly material culture.

5.7.3 *In the absence of conspicuous advantages among the groups of a region, the nearer a group (and, hence, the more visible) the more likely it will be to serve as a military ally and model for emulation.*

5.7.4 *Those segments of an ethnic group that are closer to boundaries with other groups or which in other ways have more contact with outgroups* (which are, hence, more visible to them) *will show more tendency to imitate the customs of other groups than more central or otherwise isolated segments;* this will be more true in stateless than in centralized ethnic groups.

Chapter 6

EVOLUTIONARY THEORIES

In Chapter 3 we created the category of realistic-group-conflict theory and mentioned, along with many others, theorists like Leslie White (1949; 1959), W. W. Newcomb (1960), and Sumner himself, who are more familiarly (and with a greater sense of intellectual history) identified with evolutionary thinking in the social sciences. If realistic-group-conflict theory is the set of all theories that generate the ethnocentrism syndrome from the competitive struggle of groups with incompatible interests, evolutionary theories comprise the subset that provides a particular type of account of the source (environmental adaptation for survival) and consequence (development of more efficient adaptive forms) of that struggle. From an evolutionary viewpoint, however, realistic group conflict can be viewed as merely one of many adaptive mechanisms that promote group survival. Thus each category of theory can subsume the other. Since our aim is not to establish a hierarchy of theories but to explicate the diverse perspectives they create for viewing comparative data, we need not worry about which is more general but shall be concerned with giving an adequate propositional account of each. Evolutionary theories, reflecting (however, unevenly and imperfectly) a common Darwinian heritage, are sufficiently distinctive in their empirical implications to warrant separate review.

Evolutionary views of social and cultural phenomena are quite diverse. (See Campbell 1965b for a description of this diversity). With regard to ethnocentrism, evolutionary theorists fall roughly into four classes: (1) the survival-of-the-warlike school, including social Darwinists like Herbert Spencer (1898) and (to a lesser degree) Sumner (1906) and modern anthropologists like Goldschmidt (1959), Naroll (n.d.), and Otterbein (1970), who view the evolution from primitive to industrial societies as having occurred mainly through war, with those societies most successful in warfare surviving; (2) the so-called neoevolutionists in anthropology such as White (1959), Newcomb (1960), and Fried (1961), who see the evolution from primitive to industrial societies as having occurred through technological, economic, and organizational stages of development – not necessarily involving war – and who emphasize the developmental prerequisites for different predatory goals and types of warfare; (3) the cultural ecologists, typified by Vayda (1961), who show by ethnographic instance that particular types of warfare are adaptive for societies in particular ecological niches; (4) the ethologists and primatologists who investigate the biological basis of human aggression through the consideration of continuities and analogues between nonhuman and human aggression and social organization. In this chapter we discuss the first three classes, the social and cultural evolutionists, considering the last category beyond the scope of this book.

Naroll presents the case of the survival-of-the warlike school in a most explicit propositional form: "A number of traits, many associated with social evolution, make for success in warfare; societies with traits making for success in warfare tend for this reason to displace those which lack such traits" (n.d., p. 1). Narroll argues that if this hypothesis is valid, "higher civilizations" should be more warlike than primitive societies, and he finds evidence supporting this expectation in the works of Wright (1942) and Turney-High (1949). He goes on to hypothesize that those culture traits that could plausibly be thought to bolster the military capability of a society will be found positively related to actual military expansion in a comparative study of societies. These traits include the high status of warriors, the punishment of cowards (in military situations), cultural values favoring numerous progeny, the accumulation of material wealth and obedience to political officials, and socioeconomic differentiation and complexity (occupational specialization, organizational ramification, and urbanization). His other major hypotheses are that the presence of these culture traits is directly related to higher developmental levels of forms of warfare itself (in terms of conquest as a goal and the use of surprise and missiles plus contact weapons in military tactics), and that higher developmental levels of warfare tend to displace lower levels. Societies at the highest developmental levels of warfare have conquest as a goal so that the realization of this goal would make them more militarily expansive.

Although Naroll does not assume warfare to be the only selective mechanism through which societies and cultures have evolved, his hypotheses, if all validated, would show that societies with socioeconomic and cultural characteristics that improved their military potential had realized this potential in a parallel development of warfare institutions, and that this military development had been translated into successful expansion at the expense of societies less advanced in both warfare and in general military capability or potential. The less advanced societies, being less effective in their manner of conducting warfare as well as less developed in terms of societal scale, coordination, and discipline, would have had to imitate their more warlike neighbors or be conquered and absorbed by them. Thus surviving societies would be more warlike on the average than their predecessors, and the ethnocentrism syndrome in its ingroup solidarity and outgroup hostility components would represent the product of social evolution and its inexorable direction. The cross-cultural study by Otterbein (1970) lends empirical support to several aspects of this position.

Naroll's statement of the survival-of-the-warlike hypothesis contains, explicitly or implicitly, these propositions, testable in comparative study:

6.1   *Groups at higher levels of societal complexity or social development are:*

6.1.1   *More ethnocentric and bellicose.*

6.1.2   *More developed in warfare institutions, giving warriors high status, ranking conquest over prestige, plunder and revenge as military goals, and using surprise (as opposed to prearrangement) and missiles together with contact weapons (as opposed to either separately) in their military tactics.*

6.1.3   *More predatory and expansive militarily.*

6.1.4   *More successful in warfare and military expansion.*

Otterbein's (1970) study provides evidence in support of 6.1.2, 6.1.3, 6.1.4.

There should be a positive relation between the apparent or estimated directness of the contribution of a cultural feature to military effectiveness and the relative strength of its relation to ethnocentrism, warfare development, and expansion, across societies, such that:

6.2.1   *Among the cultural features usually regarded as developmental, those contributing more directly to military effectiveness (for example, obedience to leaders, organizational ramification) should be more strongly related to ethnocentrism than those less directly contributing (for example, development of the arts).*

6.2.2   *Those cultural features that are not usually regarded as developmental but which contribute directly to military effectiveness (high status of warriors, punishment of cowards) should be more strongly related to ethnocentrism than developmental traits not contributing to military effectiveness.*

6.3   *There should be a positive relation between the military history of a region and its social development and complexity, such that:*

6.3.1   *Regions with a longer history of intergroup warfare should have more complex and developed societies.*

6.3.2   *Societies low on ethnocentrism and societal complexity should be found only in regions with relatively peaceful histories.*

Except for recent immigrants, the societies of a region should be similar in the level of development and ethnocentrism or should be moving toward similarity at the highest locally available level of development (since if there were inequalities, the more developed groups would conquer or absorb the others or would forcibly diffuse their way of life to them).

The neoevolutionist school of Leslie White has adopted an opposite (although not necessarily contradictory) emphasis: namely the amount of socioeconomic development necessary before organized warfare can be conducted. Thus they view warfare not as the selective process through which evolution takes place but as one of many capabilities characterizing societies at higher levels of development, in which energy is more efficiently controlled, a surplus is produced, and subsistence tasks require a smaller proportion of man's time and effort. For war in its more organized forms to be conducted by a society, it must be able to divert men from subsistence activity, to coordinate their military activities, and to make use of the fruits of predatory warfare. Societies at lower levels of technological development have such inefficient means of harnessing energy that they can do none of these things; for them, large-scale warfare would be maladaptive if not suicidal.

The emphasis on warfare as a consequence rather than a cause of evolutionary development can be seen in statements of Leslie White like the following:

"Peoples will not fight over grazing lands, fertile valleys, oil reserves, and uranium mines until culture has advanced to such levels of development" (1949, p. 132).

"As agriculture developed and industries flourished, wealth accumulated, and this incited nations to attack one another" (1959, p. 297).

Newcomb (1960) has organized and expanded this orientation, and it is primarily from his presentation that the following principles are abstracted. Whereas the propositions in Newcomb are about warfare alone, accepting the realistic-group-conflict theory that White presents concomitantly, they can be extended to predictions of ethnocentrism more generally.

6.4   *The more fully food gathering occupies all persons' time, the less warfare and the less ethnocentrism in general.*

6.5   *The more the economy makes slaves useful, the more warfare and the more ethnocentrism.*

6.6   *The more stored and transportable wealth* (granaries, livestock, tools, precious metals, and cloth), *the more warfare* (in that predation is rewarded) *and ethnocentrism.*

6.7   *The more politically organized the people, the more warfare and ethnocentrism.*

6.8   *The more able a society is to exploit natural resources* (fields for tillage, mineral resources, etc.), *the more warfare. The higher the technological level, the more warfare and ethnocentrism.*

6.9   *The more complex the division of labor, the more warfare and ethnocentrism.*

6.10   *The more dense the population, the more warfare and ethnocentrism.*

6.11   *The less self-contained and self-sufficient the economy (the greater its need for imports), the more warfare and ethnocentrism.*

Hobhouse, Wheeler, and Ginsberg (1915, p. 228 ff) present data supporting similar relationships between war-related behavior and the level of social development:

6.12   *The higher the level of social development, the more prevalent is war, the more elaborate is war, the more frequent is slavery, the more frequent is human sacrifice, and the less frequent is the killing of prisoners* (that is, the more frequently they are enslaved, adopted, or exchanged).

Gorer (1938) has also offered similar social-evolutionary hypotheses. In particular, he argues for 6.4, 6.6, and 6.7. On the basis of the greater utilization of stolen animals over stolen land, he argues, with respect to 6.6, that for a common subsistence level, pastoralists and hunters will be more warlike than agriculturalists and gatherers of vegetable food. This prediction he also supports in the manner of 6.4 with consideration of the amount of leisure time available.

Fried (1961) has presented what is, perhaps, the most sophisticated general theory of warfare from this general viewpoint. He states its major theses in propositional form:

"First: The evolution of complex politically organized society has entailed two major and generally distinct steps prior to the invention or emergence of the state considered as a political mechanism. In this evolution the development of ranking tends to precede the development of stratification but it is possible, at least theoretically, for both to develop concomitantly.

"Second: Warfare serves to institutionalize rank differences only when these are already manifest, or at least implicit, in the society in question. I do not believe that pristine developments in the formulation of rank can be normally attributed to even grave military necessity.

"Third: Warfare serves to institutionalize stratification only when the social orders of one or more parties to the warfare have already become stratified.

"Fourth: The state can be precipitated by warfare but only in the presence of certain conditions. On possibility is that two stratified but non-state-organized societies clash and remain in active contact after the period of violence. Another possibility is that a non-state-organized society is conquered by a state society and either appended to or absorbed by the victorious state; it is also possible that the victorious society will withdraw but having left behind a stimulus that impells the defeated society to crystallize its own state apparatus" (1961, pp. 134-135).

Fried is here arguing against the view that the development of the central state and social classes can be *simply* attributed to a threat-induced military organization carried over into peacetime life. War *can* lead to political development, as envisioned by Naroll, but only if certain social-structural prerequisites have already been fulfilled; otherwise wartime mobilization can be quickly abandoned after peace is resumed, as Fried illustrates ethnographically. In essence, Fried uses the requisite analysis of the neoevolutionists to attack the problem posed by the survival-of-the-warlike school of thought. He distinguishes three levels of social development: egalitarian societies, which lack ranked statuses, ranked societies, which have status differentiation but no differentiated access to strategic resources of the society, and stratified societies, in which different statuses give differential access to strategic resources. The intensity and severity of warfare increase from one level to another, but it is only in the last level that the economic motive for warfare becomes predominant because of the internal differentiation between those who have access to strategic resources and those who do not: "Such societies can be made to feel the need for expansion long before a ranked society under similar environmental circumstances" (1961, p. 146). The implicit reason appears to be that stratified societies generate feelings of relative deprivation that cannot be produced in ranked or egalitarian societies where all have roughly similar access to strategic resources. Among the stratified societies, Fried believes that war does play an essential role in the development of the state and "superstratification," but not in the egalitarian and ranked societies; except that in the more complex ranked societies, warfare institutionalizes ranked statuses.

From the viewpoint of nonhistorical comparative study, Fried's formulation adds few testable hypotheses to those of Newcomb and Naroll; his main contribution is in bringing together the limits set by social development on warfare and the effects of war on development in a single, more sophisticated conceptualization of historical process. Careful ethnohistorical studies are needed to test its validity. For present purposes, the major novel proposition is:

6.13   *At any given level of economic scarcity, those groups in which the status structure institutionalizes subgroup differences in the degree of deprivation experienced* (for example, a poor majority with an affluent elite) *will be more warlike and ethnocentric, and more oriented to economic warfare goals, than groups in which deprivation is more evenly diffused through the population.*

At the level of more specific studies of cultural ecology, Vayda (1961) has challenged Murphy's (1957) view of warfare as a "safety-valve institution" and has argued that the adaptive value of warfare is not limited to the promotion of ingroup solidarity.

"It may of course be argued that a group's survival and prosperity depend *inter alia* upon the group's solidarity (cf. White, 1959:103) and therefore anything that maintains or promotes solidarity does indirectly have economic or ecological consequences. However, we know that the solidarity of peoples throughout the world has been achieved by many means other than warfare. It has been achieved through ceremonies, through games — through a very large variety of customs (cf. White, 1959:215). Therefore it seems doubtful that the solidarity of any particular people should be attainable only through warfare, which is a means of having such maladaptive or dysfunctional effects as the loss of life, the considerable diversion of time and effort from productive activities, etc. On the assumption that culture tends to be adaptive in the sense of providing people with the means of adjustment to the geographical environment and to the other basic conditions of life . . ., we should expect warfare to serve people in more ways than merely through providing them with solidarity or cohesion and we should expect, furthermore, that the other functions of warfare will tend to offset the maladaptive consequences of fighting. In other words, we have grounds for expecting the primitive hostilities of the types discussed by Steward, Murphy, Wedgwood, and Wright to have more direct ecological functions or consequences than those derived from the attainment of social solidarity" (Vayda, 1961, pp. 346-347).

In accordance with this expectation several evolutionary anthropologists have sought and found ecological functions for warfare in populations that occupy certain types of ecological niches. Vayda (1961) suggests that different predictions must be made for expanding (that is, demographically growing) and nonexpanding populations. For expanding populations the basic problem is the redistribution of basic subsistence resources across groups differing in population density. In other words, if some groups expand to the limits of their available resources while others have more than they need, a peaceful mechanism must exist for redistributing resources in accordance with need, or intergroup warfare will result. The warfare, it should be noted, is hypothesized to serve the function not only of reallocating resources but of killing enough people to reduce population pressure on resources.

Vayda illustrates the warfare patterns of expanding populations with two ethnographic cases of populations practicing swidden (slash-and-burn) agriculture. This shifting cultivation pattern he argues, poses special adaptive problems for peoples who lack iron or are surrounded by hardwood rain forests, because it is extremely difficult for them to clear virgin forest when they have used all the available fertile land that is already cleared; this increases the likelihood of their attempting to seize land from their neighbors by warfare. The Maori, with largely endogamous villages separated from one another by topographical obstacles to travel, and with no permanent peace above the "subtribe" level, were unable to expand peacefully beyond subtribe boundaries and, hence, conducted predatory and lethal warfare at the subtribe level, thus reestablishing a balance between population and locally available land. The Iban, a riverain people who were able to travel easily and settle new land within the "tribe," a unit that also represented the limit of permissible endogamy, did not conduct warfare at the intratribal level but, instead, across Iban tribes and with non-Iban peoples, with whom their greater mobility brought them into greater contact than was the case with the Maori. Thus Vayda suggests that the same process is operating among Maori and Iban and that the farthest boundary within which peaceful redistribution of people onto cleared land can take place is the boundary across which predatory and lethal warfare is conducted; this boundary defined smaller units among the Maori than among the Iban.

Vayda's analysis involves the following conditions: (1) a system of cultivation that continually requires new land, (2) inadequate technology to clear virgin forests or to make fallow cultivable quickly (that is, fertilizer), (3) population growth, with varying densities among groups occupying the ecological niche, (4) sociopolitical boundaries that limit the peaceful redistribution of people on land among the groups, (5) a lack of central political organizations able to prevent warfare across the boundaries. Where all of these conditions are present, there will be warfare across those boundaries that mark the outer limits of peaceful mobility and resettlement, and the warfare will involve territorial aggrandizement and large-scale killing. Successful instances of warfare will help the adaptation of the region by giving the predators more land for their population and by simultaneously reducing the population of the defeated so that they can subsist adequately on less land.

Vayda speculates that in populations that are not expanding, warfare might serve other purposes no less important ecologically, for example, the dispersed spacing of groups in finite territories so as to exploit the ecological niche more fully (as in subhuman populations), the capture of women and children in small populations with unbalanced sex ratios. Most of these other adaptive functions do not require large-scale killing or even particularly lethal warfare, as might be expected for the survival of stable or declining populations; they are attained through dramatic displays of force, token killing or injury, raiding for movable goods, or the capture of persons.

Sweet (1965) has described such a pattern of warfare for the North Arabian Bedouin and has argued that it (camel raiding) is a mechanism of ecological adaptation, supporting not only the Bedouin economy (camel-based) but also Bedouin political dominance over other peoples in the region and even "the whole network of social and ideological relations of Bedouin life" (Sweet, 1965, p. 1148). Bedouin camel raiding, hedged about with a myriad of rules that attentuate its violence (particularly against other Bedouins), is predominantly nonlethal and is aimed directly at economic aggrandizement. It fulfills the latter purpose to some extent, as "an effective measure for recovering herd strength in local groups" suffering from the effects of local drought and disease not affecting their neighbors, but Sweet stresses that raiding is not merely a response to economic pressures. It is the major male occupation throughout the year and results in a wide-ranging exchange of camels among Bedouin tribes. Sweet suggests two adaptive functions, apart from economic distribution, for this extensive raiding pattern: (1) it maintains active Bedouin control over the subordinate peoples of the region, by fostering raids on them as a by-product of long-distance intertribal raiding among Bedouins ("raiders . . . are easily deflected to action against any passing party") and by keeping the Bedouins militarily prepared at all times; (2) it maintains, through the constant negotiation of truces and alliances, and through the highly conventionalized nonlethal raid itself, continuous communication and some minimum degree of solidarity among all the Bedouin camel breeders of the ecological zone in the absence of any superordinate political organization. In the light of a comparative study by Salzman (1967) which concludes that only in areas of predictable climate and relatively great resources do pastoral nomads have "political authority roles and stable group parameters," it is not surprising that the Bedouins, under unpredictable and severe climatic conditions, are not able to achieve a solidarity greater than that involved in raiding and alliance relations. From this comparative perspective, Bedouin camel raiding is remarkably adaptive; as Sweet (1965, p. 1148) points out, "The two or three thousand year time span which we can allot to Bedouin occupation of the North Arabian desert as camel breeding specialists seems to demonstrate quite adequately the success of this system."

Ekvall (1961) has pointed out that pastoral nomadism as found among the Amdo Tibetans involves the rapid mobilization, knowledge of terrain, and other subsistence patterns useful in warfare.

These ecological analyses of warfare generate, directly or by implication, the following propositions:

6.14   *Groups in regions having more population pressure on resources, because of faster population growth or higher population densities, are more likely to engage in lethal warfare involving large-scale killing, and less likely to engage in highly restrained forms of warfare involving elaborate rules and etiquette.*

6.15   *Stateless groups whose territorial segments suffer unequal amounts of economic scarcity* (through microclimatic variation or unequal population growth) *will have intersegmental warfare with frankly economic objectives* (territorial conquest or animal raiding).

6.16   *Stateless, slash-and-burn agricultural peoples with population pressure, without the opportunity to clear virgin forest* (through unavailability or inadequate technology), *and without manuring or fertilizer techniques to restore the fertility of fallow fields, will manifest predatory warfare activities across those boundaries that mark the outer limit of peaceful mobility and resettlement on unused land.*

6.17   *Where nomads have a purely pastoral economy but inhabit an area with an unpredictable and severe climate, they are more likely to manifest intrasocietal feuding, raiding or warfare, but with rules limiting intersegmental homicide and with associated negotiations and alliances that promote the solidarity of their total ethnic community vis-a-vis other ethnic groups in the ecological zone.*

6.18   *The nomadic peoples of a region, being better prepared for warfare by their mode of subsistence, are more likely to be warlike and more effective in warfare than other peoples of the region.*

Chapter 7

THE PROBLEM OF ETHNIC BOUNDARIES

Rather than generating propositions from one more societal level theory, this chapter has a metatheoretical focus. It reviews the recent anthropological literature that criticizes the prevailing assumption in traditional ethnography concerning the universality of ethnic units with clear-cut boundaries. This literature is, of course, highly relevant to the societal-level theories we have just reviewed. Each of them also makes such assumptions, with the exception of the crosscutting loyalty structure described in Chapter 4. Even there, although there might be conflicting loyalties, it was assumed that within each crosscutting type of organization there were clear-cut group boundaries. Moreover, from our perspective on levels of analysis, this recent critique can be viewed as challenging the appropriateness of employing the societal level of analysis for many of the peoples studied by anthropologists. In the material that follows, we first review the relevant anthropological literature, and then offer a theoretical perspective in which social groups as systems can be conceived of as having varying degrees of social-system discreteness as a matter of the frequency of coincidence of numerous specific functional-organizational boundaries.

ANTHROPOLOGICAL ASSUMPTIONS ABOUT ETHNIC BOUNDARIES

Anthropologists, like other observers of human behavior, make simplifying assumptions about their subject matter. However useful and convenient these assumptions may be as standards of relevance in data collection, their plausibility must be reexamined periodically in light of the available evidence. Over the last 15 years the accepted assumptions about ethnic groups and their boundaries have been challenged by an increasing number of social anthropologists with the support of an accumulating body of evidence. They claim that these assumptions are presumptive oversimplifications, like group stereotypes in popular belief, which lead to the neglect of the relevant intercultural context of social action and, therefore, to falsely secure conclusions about social and cultural processes. In this chapter we review some of the issues and evidence involved in this challenge and offer a view of ethnicity that takes account of the new evidence and the potential for bias in ethnographic observation.

The standard anthropological position on ethnic groups and their boundaries is closely tied to the accepted procedures of field research in modern social anthropology, which had their origins in the work of Bronislaw Malinowski (1922) on the Trobriand Islanders. Before Malinowski, most anthropologists of sound empirical outlook used the interviewing of informants as their primary research procedure, with the aims of making an inventory of customs in an area and reconstructing the history of contacts among peoples in the area to account for the distribution of customs among them. When functional interpretations of customs were made, they were largely based on reconstructions of past social life drawn from the accounts of elderly informants. Malinowksi showed that customs could be more completely understood through the direct observation of the ongoing social life of a community to uncover the contexts of interaction and belief in which the customs normally function. This demonstration was very impressive and eventually won complete acceptance in the anthropology of the English-speaking world.

The ethnographic method initiated by Malinowski demanded much of the anthropologist: he had to spend a long time in the field, learn the language, participate to some degree in the community life of the people being studied, attempt exhaustive descriptions of institutions from the point of view of the people themselves, and use interview, observation, and anecdote critically and synthetically in pursuing the functional connections among institutional patterns. This method meant that the anthropological fieldworker had to spend much more time than before in a single local community or set of closely related communities, and much more of his scholarly career in attempting to understand a single set of institutional patterns. In contrast with the previous more superficial ethnography which often involved sampling the cultures of a variety of peoples in a region, the Malinowskian method was inward-looking: it focused on the functional interdependencies among the institutions of "a culture" rather than the interdependencies among peoples in a region. Ethnographers following this method in its several versions of divergent theoretical emphasis (which is to say, most ethnographers since about 1935) could afford little time to collect data on intercultural or intersocietal relations, and they tended to treat the culture or society studied as if it were a discrete and even isolated entity (see Cohen and Middleton, 1970, p. 4). One consequence has been that in the period of greatest increase in our detailed knowledge of peoples of the world, available data on their relations with and attitudes toward each other (outside of the colonial situation) has not increased concomitantly.

Malinowski's field method was logically embedded in his functional theory of culture. In that theory, the view of cultures as bounded systems played a prominent part, as this statement illustrates:

"An ethnographic map of the world shows, on every continent, well-defined boundaries which separate one tribe from the other. The unity of such a tribe consists *de facto* in the homogeneity—at times, identity—of culture. . . . The tribe in this sense, therefore, is a group of people who conjointly exercise a type of culture. . . .

". . . One tribe . . . differs from the other in the organization of the family, the local groups, the clan, as well as economic, magical and religious terms. The identity of institutions; their potential cooperation due to community of language, tradition and law; the interchange of services; and the possibility of joint enterprise on a large scale—these are the factors which make for the unity of a primitive, culturally homogeneous group. This, I submit, is the prototype of what we define today as nationality: a large group, unified by language, tradition and culture. To the division as we find it between primitive culturally differentiated tribes there correspond today such divisions as between Germans and Poles, Swedes and Norwegians, Italians and French" (Malinowski, 1941, in Bramson and Goethals, 1964, pp. 255-256).

The majority of social anthropologists adopted Malinowski's field method without accepting his entire theoretical system, but they were strongly influenced by it. The following assumptions about ethnicity and group boundaries represent a widespread form of the Malinowskian influence, as modified and revised by subsequent theorists. (1) There exist named units which are readily perceived as units by their members, their neighbors, and anthropological observers alike. (2) Such a unit, called a society or a culture, is in its typical concrete embodiment a population with territorial boundaries that represent discontinuities in breeding, language, economy, sociopolitical structure, and culture. (3) In a unit so distinguished from its neighbors, each of the institutionalized aspects of social action has the properties of an organized entity, like a biological system, with interdependent parts and a normally high degree of stability.

These three assumptions could be regarded as hypotheses to be tested in empirical research but they have been most frequently adopted as articles of faith or as postulates of convenience to enable the fieldworker to collect data for a structural-functional analysis of "a society" or "culture."

An anthropologist who makes these assumptions, whether he regards them as ontological truths or heuristic devices, is likely to have his initial perceptions in the field structured in terms of them. He will seek named territorial units and discontinuities associated with their boundaries. Once he has identified a unit he will use it to set limits on the extent of his investigations into institutions and their functional properties, thus overlooking continuities and interdependencies across the boundaries of named units. Furthnermore, he may begin thinking, however tentatively, of the "pure" or "intact" culture of the X, represented in one part of their territory, as opposed to their "mixed" or "acculturated" areas, and will decide to work primarily in the "pure" area, thus shielding himself from exposure to the more complicated situations available.

As the field work so initiated progresses, the data themselves tend to convince the anthropologist that he is, indeed, dealing with a sharply bounded entity constituting a functioning system; he may not recognize that it has been, at least in part, a self-fulfilling prophecy. The cognitive processes involved include sharpening and leveling, as in rumor communication (Allport and Postman, 1947), and selection and accentuation, as in the formation of group stereotypes (Allport, 1954). The idea of the ethnic entity and its bounded attributes is so salient to the ethnographer that consistency with the idea becomes inadvertently a primary criterion for noticing, recording, and (later) emphasizing data. Inconsistent data are less frequently noticed, recorded, or emphasized and/or they are reinterpreted as consistent, thus yielding a final image of a smoothly functioning entity without rough edges. If the ethnographer does not recognize the part his arbitrary decisions have played in creating the image, he is likely to claim it as an aspect of reality, confirming his general assumptions about the nature of society and culture.

Many careful ethnographers from Malinowski onward have, in fact, acknowledged the arbitrariness of their decisions and the hypothetical character of the entities and systems that they have described, and they have not ignored continuities and interdependencies that lie beyond the boundaries of their fieldwork. Until recently, however, acknowledgments of this kind have been mainly parenthetical tributes to a complexity that is not itself an object of investigation. In the mainstream of anthropological discourse and conceptualization it has been taken for granted that social interaction and culture patterns come in sufficiently convenient and durable territorial packages to be suitable for both standard fieldwork (by a single ethnographer) and comparative study. This type of assumption has been shared by those who have produced ethnographic case studies of limited scope and the comparativists who have used their data for cross-cultural hypothesis-testing. (See Murdock's, 1953, *Outline of World Cultures* for an attempt to list all the cultural entities known to ethnography.) But a countermovement has developed among social anthropologists who refuse to accept limitations of convenience and who insist on taking ethnic complexity and "irregularity" as objects of field investigation in themselves. Their findings have important theoretical and methodological implications that require close examination.

THE NEW EVIDENCE

The challenge to the accepted presumption of an ethnic community was launched by Edmund Leach (1954) in his book *Political Systems of Highland Burma*, which presented evidence inconsistent with the presumption and a polemical attack on the ethnographic limitations of those who accept it. Some of Leach's most relevant arguments have been incorporated in the foregoing discussion of the anthropological approach to ethnic groups and boundaries. Since the publication of Leach's book, Frederik Barth, Jack Goody, Michael Moerman, and many others have produced evidence from different parts of the world which is equally problematic for social anthropology. As Southall (1970, p. 71) has stated, "The studies of the last few decades, in particular, have indicated that very many traditional societies are of a much more ambiguous nature than had been supposed from the earlier idea of the tribe as a simple and clearly bounded entity." In the following overview of this evidence the term "ethnic community" designates the ideal type of named, bounded, culture-sharing entity conventionally referred to as "a society" or "a culture."

There are, at least, five documented phenomena that cast doubt on standard anthropological assumptions concerning sociocultural entities and their boundaries.

1. Territorial Interpenetration of Ethnic Communities.   This refers to a situation in which ethnic communities are interspersed as multiple enclaves in a region, so that it is not possible to draw a single continuous territorial boundary that separates them but in which they maintain an ethnic ideology that differentiates them, as well as *conspicuous* differences in, at least, one (and usually more) of the following characteristics: language, ecology, (mode of subsistence), material culture, social organization, religion, and life-style. The ethnic ideology consists of group names, and beliefs in diverse origins and stereotypes of distinctive attributes. Members of the same ethnic community tend to reside together at the primary group level and to marry each other; they are *frequently* semiautonomous politically and are treated as local political units by officials at higher levels in the governmental hierarchy. The variations of integration and interrelationship (some of which are dealt with below) are endless, and range from those resembling the familiar religious pluralism of Western industrial nations to those involving groups of extremely contrasting ecologies and life-styles, the latter being of more obvious theoretical interest to social anthropology. At one time it was possible to assume that such situations were aberrant, products of violent upheavals and disruptions of well-bounded social and cultural entities, found in "cultural shatterbelts," "refuge areas," and other "marginal" regions. It now appears that they are too numerous and widespread to be considered exceptional or relegated to marginal status.

The most dramatic examples of territorial interpretation are those of Southeast Asia, particularly the hill regions of Burma and Thailand which have been described by Leach (1954), Moerman (1965; 1968), Lehman (1967), and others. The local geographical contrasts between hills and valleys have been combined in complex, variable, and surprising ways with cultural, linguistic, and historical-political characteristics, giving rise to an ethnic "mosaic" to which no map can do justice. In fact, the Burmese and Thai cases are so rich in their complexity, and illustrate so many of the phenomena reviewed here, that they can blind us to the generality of territorial interpretation itself. The drastic local variations in altitude found across the mountain regions of Southwest Asia have given rise to ethnically interspersed regions. Barth (1956) has shown that in Swat, North Pakistan, ethnic groups differing along a pastoral-agricultural dimension tend to occupy ecological niches defined by elevation rather than by continuous territory. He generates ecological and political principles concerning their relations and states:

"Where such principles are operative to the extent they are in much of West and South Asia, the concept of 'culture areas,' as developed for native North America, becomes inapplicable. Different ethnic groups and culture types will have overlapping distributions and disconforming borders, and will be socially related to a variable degree" (p. 1088).

Nor is such a situation limited to regions of varying altitude (see Barth, 1969b). In Africa, throughout the savannahs of the Western Sudan and along the edge of the Sahara Desert, the Fulani and other cattle nomads live among a myriad of sedentary peoples from whom they differ in language, social structure, and life-style as well as ecology. Similar situations are found throughout the areas of the Old World where pastoralism is well established and agriculture is also possible, in a swath ranging from West and North Africa through the Middle East to the Indian subcontinent. (See Cohen and Middleton, 1970, p. 11, for a discussion in more general terms of the ecological basis of ethnic interpenetration in Africa.) It must not be thought, however, that ethnic interpenetration is exclusively an Old World phenomenon. Even among North American Indians, noted for their sharply bounded cultures, there were areas of ethnic complexity without clear group boundaries, particularly in the Columbia River Plateau and certain other parts of the Pacific Northwest where what French (1963) calls "unbounded organization" prevailed.

The assumed territorial discreteness of ethnic communities has often implied or even been based on an assumed territorial discreteness of speech-communities (languages or dialect groups), at least, among nonliterate peoples. Hymes (1968) has recently reviewed the evidence that shows how frequently this assumption is incorrect. There is no part of the world for which one can make this assumption with impunity. Multilingualism is found even within local communities among certain groups of Australian aborigines, South American Indian peoples, Indians of the Pacific Northwest, as well as in the Burmese villages portrayed by Leach (1954). In territories larger than local communities, linguistic heterogeneity or interspersal is even more frequently encountered.

Ethnic mosaics seem to be associated with mobility — in nomadism of various types, in small-scale and large-scale migrations, and in conquests and the expulsion of peoples. The dispersal of groups and subgroups — to seek specialized economic opportunities, flee from war and revolution, and in response to other environmental pressures — is a familiar fact of modern world history and contemporary events. There is reason to believe that similar pressures and opportunities have dispersed peoples, without homogenizing them, throughout human history, and that when the ethnographic and ethnohistorical records are complete we shall have many more instances of ethnic interpenetration.

The incompleteness of the ethnographic record on ethnic mosaics is well illustrated by Africa, where the coherent cultural entities of familiar ethnographies have been more fully documented than complex regions of ethnic interspersal. The latter are quite widespread and fall into at least four classes, of which only the first have been well described. (a) First are polyethnic conquest states such as the Tswana (Schapera, 1940) and the Nupe (Nadel, 1942), or somewhat weaker but also polyethnic "segmentary states" like the Alur (Southall, 1956; 1970). In this type of situation one ethnic community subjugates all or parts of other ethnic communities and allows them to retain a measure of local territorial integrity and autonomy under the sovereignty of the central authority. (b) Second are residues of former polyethnic empires, found in many parts of the Western Sudan (for example, Mali). During the period of empire there had been freer movements of persons and the spread of a lingua franca, resulting in the permanent interspersal of certain groups and a blurring of group boundaries. (c) Third are so-called refuge areas, like the Nuba Hills (Nadel, 1947), in which political units are small, linguistic, and cultural variation are great, and the territorial boundaries of the political units fail to coincide with the cultural and linguistic boundaries that might be plotted on a map. Parts of the Jos Plateau and adjacent regions of Nigeria and Cameroun exhibit this pattern. It is not, however, confined to inaccessible rockbound areas; for example, the southern (coastal) part of Ghana, near Accra and other cities, contains an ethnic and linguistic complexity of considerable proportions, with interspersed villages of Ga, Akan, and Guang origins, differing in language, political traditions, and kinship systems. (d) Fourth are economically specialized ethnic communities (or members thereof) who have dispersed in pursuit of their speciality, or who live in enclaves among many other peoples. Some are very large ethnic-linguistic communities like the Fulani pastoralists, mentioned above, who herd their cattle in every West African country from Senegal to Cameroun (and some in central Africa), usually in close contact with sedentary peoples. The Hausa and Dioula are examples of dispersed trading groups. Hausa traders are found throughout West Africa and, less numerously, in parts of North and Central Africa; the Dioula are limited to one region of West Africa, but they are more completely dispersed in pursuit of trade. More recently, of course, many ethnic communities have developed "overseas colonies" of traders, laborers, craftsmen — for example, the Yoruba of Nigeria in Ghana and other West African countries, the Luo of Western Kenya in Mombasa, Uganda, and Tanzania — and there is no sign that these groups or dozens of other like them will lose their ethnic distinctiveness.

The examples given of African ethnic mosaics represent but a fraction of the total. Few have been adequately described, particularly in their more traditional contexts, although the recent volume by Cohen and Middleton (1970) is an important step toward filling in this gap in the ethnography of Africa. From the standpoint of present knowledge these cases seem to be not exceptional, but the products of recurrent processes of political and socioeconomic adaptation operating in a variety of historical circumstances. The historical circumstances in which ethnic interpenetration occurs may turn out to be more frequent than previously imagined, in Africa and elsewhere.

2.   **Continuous Variation in Cultural and Linguistic Characteristics.**   If interpenetration involves too many boundaries for ethnographic convenience, continuous variation means in effect no boundaries at all — at least, none that can be easily discerned by the investigator. The phenomenon is a familiar one in language, with dialects varying widely but gradually over an area so that adjacent groups seem hardly to differ at all whereas distance groups are obviously different. It is now clear that this type of distribution is not uncommon for nonlinguistic cultural characteristics too, particularly in regions without large-scale centralized polities. Goody (1956) called attention to the phenomenon and documented it in detail for one part of West Africa:

"In the Northwest of the Gold Coast, there are few marked discontinuities. Unilineal descent groups are widely dispersed among peoples of different language and social organization. Compounds are scattered unevenly across the countryside in such a way that it is difficult to tell where one settlement ends and another begins. There was no crystallized political system before the advent of the British, nor does any group crystallize around a cohesive ritual institution such as the Great Festivals of the Tallensi. Cultural changes take place imperceptibly like dialects merging into one another" (1956), p. 17).

"The interlocking of social relationships is parallelled by a gradual and continuous change of culture over the whole area; there are no distinct 'cultures,' but a slow merging as of linguistic dialects" (1956, p. 19).

Goody illustrated this cultural variation by showing the distribution of four types of xylophones, decreasing in size, across six groups located along an east-west dimension; eastern groups lacked the smallest xylophones, western groups lacked the largest ones, and the central groups fell in between — but there was considerable overlap in distribution, particularly between adjacent groups. Similarly graded variations are indicated for marriage and inheritance practices, language, and other social characteristics. This extreme type of continuous variation is typical of large areas of indigenous Australia, New Guinea, and Melanesia, and it seems to have occurred in other parts of precolonial Africa as well, although it is less well described there in the ethnographic literature. Moerman (1965) goes so far as to suggest:

"The delimitation of ethnic entities is especially problematic in all parts of the world which are continuously inhabited but not divided into either sharp ecological zones or strong and durable states" (Moerman, 1965, p. 1215).

Where continuous variation is found, there is frequently a related phenomenon, noncongruent variation, which creates special ethnographic difficulties. The problem is that several cultural characteristics do not covary in the region, so that the distribution of each one yields a mapping not matched by the others. Goody (1956) shows this in detail for Northern Ghana, and it is true not only of most regions with continuous variation but also for some regions with pronounced discontinuities. This means that if one observer decides to divide the region into ethnic communities on the basis of social-structural dissimilarities, another on the basis of religious patterns, a third along linguistic lines, and a fourth by the distribution of xylophones, they will produce different ethnic divisions, each appearing arbitrary and unreal from the viewpoint of the other.

This kind of arbitrariness has long been recognized by anthropologists, and there have been numerous attempts to provide definitive solutions (see Naroll, 1964; Moerman, 1965; and Dole, 1968, for reviews) by identifying critical features for the establishment of ethnic boundaries. One feature heavily relied on in the ethnographic division of a region has been mutual intelligibility of language. The assumptions are made (a) that ability to communicate (and, hence, to interact and transmit culture) is dependent on mutually intelligible speech, and (b) that the world is divisible into clearly demarcated zones of linguistic intelligibility. Hymes (1968) argues with great cogency that no such zones are possible. Like so many other features, intelligibility is not absolute or even finite; there are degrees and kinds of inter-intelligibility, not easily predictable from objective similarities between the languages. "Social attitudes towards such differences as exist" (Hymes, 1968, p. 35) constitute one class of factors determining mutual intelligibility of languages. Furthermore, multi-lingualism, common to many regions of the world, permits communication (and, hence, interaction and cultural transmission) across boundaries established on the basis of mutual intelligibility of first or native languages. Language boundaries, as usually defined, often fail to coincide with boundaries based on social or cultural characteristics, and since they are not necessarily communication boundaries, there seems to be no good reason for granting them priority in ethnic division.

   3.   **Disagreement about Ethnic Community Boundaries or Labels.**   This refers to inconsistency among peoples in a region in their assignment of ethnic labels to themselves and in their use of these labels to mark off one group from another.

   Where inconsistencies of this sort are pronounced, it is impossible to obtain a set of definitive boundaries based on the conceptions of the people themselves, although this approach is favored by many ethnographers. Ethnic divisions conceptualized and labeled by the people of the region are part of the culture of the region and are used by its inhabitants; in this sense they are less arbitrary than groupings based on cultural and linguistic variations identified by outside observers, which may be meaningless to the local inhabitants. But the indigenous conceptions of ethnic boundaries may reflect (and be part of) the cultural complexity and overlap of the region and, therefore, may fail to provide a basis for the identification of discrete ethnic entities. Mounting evidence indicates that when these indigenous conceptions are seriously investigated this is frequently the case. (See Goody, 1956; Moerman, 1965; 1968, for a discussion of issues and evidence.)

Peoples may disagree about the ethnic names themselves (that is, whether they are applicable in the region), about the inclusiveness of the groupings they designate, and about the criteria by which inclusion and exclusion are determined; these disagreements can exist as continuous variations between small-scale groupings throughout the region or discontinuously, between clearly demarcated groupings of "insiders" and "outsiders." In Goody's (1956) classic example from Northern Ghana, there is agreement about the use of two names, Lo and Dagaa, throughout the region; but they are used to designate different groupings based on different criteria.

"The group, unable to visualize its unity from within, defines itself in opposition to the surrounding peoples, who are considered in relation to the two cultural poles, *Lo* and *Dagaa*. This conceptual mechanism resembles our employment of the directional terms, North and South, for their use is determined by the speaker's situation in relation to two poles; indeed, the words were once translated as West and East by an educated person from the area, whose attention I had drawn to this phenomenon. This view corresponds to the sociological reality, for their polar cultures have inevitably a spatial aspect and the groups are strung out on the East-West axis. But there is a closer parallel to the use of directional terms. If we employ the term westerners to refer to all those living to the west of us, we automatically include ourselves among the easterners. This is how the cluster of peoples in this area use *Lo* and *Dagaa* in relation to their own institutions and to those of their neighbors" (Goody, 1956, pp. 24-25).

This is a very high degree of disagreement, but it is probably common to most areas of continuous variation without political centralization.

Another type of conceptual disagreement is illustrated by the Lue of Northern Thailand (Moerman, 1968) who agree with their immediate neighbors about the names to be used in their region, and about who is included and excluded by the designation "Lue," but apparently disagree about the criteria for inclusion. To put it more accurately, Lue offer as criteria marking them off from surrounding groups cultural characteristics some of which they, in fact, share with those groups. In some cases the Lue claim that the other groups borrowed the traits from them, but since most of the traits are in any event trivial, it seems that the division is created largely by a historically derived ideology of ethnic distinction associated with endogamy and differential association despite prolonged contact. Such traits as objectively differentiate Lue and non-Lue — like dialect — are emphatically recognized, but so are many others that are spurious, presumably to exaggerate the Lue's distinctiveness. This kind of disagreement about the criterial attributes of strongly emphasized ethnic boundaries is found in other parts of Southeast Asia (see Leach, 1954).

In a third type there occurs disagreement about names, their inclusiveness and criterial attributes, between insiders and outsiders. Here are two examples from West Africa:

"The term Yoruba is sometimes said to have been derived from a foreign nickname, meaning cunning, given to the subjects of the Alafin of Oyo by the Fulani and Hausa . . . Yoruba has been commonly applied to a large group, united more by language than by culture, whose members speak of themselves as Oyo, Egba, Ijebu, Ife, Ilesha and other names of various tribes" (Forde, 1951, p. 1).

"Some contend that the whole people should properly be called 'Ife' rather than 'Yoruba', a name which originally applied to the powerful Oyo alone and only in the nineteenth century was given, apparently by Christian missionaries, to the subjects of all the kingdoms and to their common language" (Smith, 1969, p. 15).

"Before the advent of Europeans the Ibo had no common name and village groups were generally referred to by the name of a putative ancestral founder. The word *Ibo* has been used among the peoples themselves as a term of contempt by the Riverain Ibo (Oru) for their hinterland congeners . . . Its use by Europeans in the form Heebo or Ibo appears early in the slave trade to refer to any Ibo-speaking groups" (Forde and Jones, 1950, p. 9).

Similarly in Northern Thailand:

"Burmese, Chinese, Siamese and Northern Thai do not use the same labels. Moreover, translation of these labels is not always a matter of merely finding a convenient gloss, for not everyone recognizes the same categories. The Chinese *Pai-i*, for example, includes some, but not all, of China's Thai people. The term *Yang* is used by the Siamese for the Karen, by the Eastern Lao for the Lue, and by the Lue of Ban Ping for non-Buddhist Thai in China . . ." (Moerman, 1965, p. 1223).

In cases of this kind ethnic communities outside a region but in contact with some of its peoples develop their own terminology for groups in the region, often creating on the basis of externally perceived similarities in language, customs, or behavior, larger groupings than have been recognized locally — or groupings based on the peculiar nature of their contacts with the region. If these foreign ethnic communities (or others associated with them) penetrate the region and come to dominate it by trade or conquest, their labels may replace the indigenous ones. At an early stage in this process the foreign ethnic label, like Yoruba or Ibo, may be used to differentiate groups within the region, but later the excluded groups become included themselves (for reasons described below). At most points in this development there are inconsistencies in ethnic designation between group members oriented to foreign innovations and those oriented to local tradition and between groups located near areas of outside influence and more distant groups. New ethnic identities with new names become superimposed on older ones, but the latter are not eliminated and remain salient for significant segments of the population. This phenomenon is by no means limited to European colonial rule or political modernization: it has repeatedly occurred where outside groups have come to exercise political or economic dominion over an area of somewhat similar but previously independent groups. When the domination has not lasted long enough to complete the process of forming large-scale ethnic entities, the region is often left permanently with several inconsistent sets of ethnic terms, boundaries, and criteria.

Several points about indigenous ethnic concepts and their inconsistencies are relevant here. First, several writers have mentioned (for example, Goody, 1956; Moerman, 1965) that such concepts are often contrastive and seem to be cognitively satisfactory so long as they exclude other groups that are felt to be remote or different; beyond that no need may be experienced for definitional consistency or discreteness of boundaries. Second, multiplicity of group memberships and identities is ubiquitous (see Moerman, 1968); therefore, bases for overlapping and shifting ethnic designations are usually available and can lead to group disagreements. Finally, it appears that the more intensively indigenous ethnic concepts are studied, from semantic and historical points of view, the less likely they are to yield well-bounded ethnic communities for a region.

4.   **Interaction across Ethnic Communities.**   The conventional concept of an ethnic group implies discontinuities in interaction such that members have more frequent and intense contacts with each other than they do with outsiders. Social anthropologists have nonetheless recognized for a long time that ethnic communities or "societies" are rarely social isolates and that their members engage in formal and informal interaction across the boundaries that separate them. Malinowski himself described the institutionalized interethnic economic transactions of the *kula* ring (1922), but ironically a major influence of his methodology on ethnography has been the neglect of interethnic behavior mentioned above. This failure of ethnographic description has contributed heavily to the reification of ethnic entities in anthropological thought. As data become available, it is possible to construct a more balanced view of the social context in which ethnic communities are embedded.

There are as many varieties of interaction across ethnic boundaries as there are of social interaction in general, but we shall mention a few that have come to light which seem to be of particular significance for the concept of an ethnic community.

a. *Military alliance.* The issue here concerns the generality of the model of military alliance in stateless societies (particularly those with localized patrilineages) constructed by Evans-Pritchard (1940) in his account of the Nuer of the Upper Nile region. The tendency has been to assume that stateless groups in which the primary organizational form is that of patrilineages with corporate territorial and other interests, and which are linked through recognition of genealogical connections, cultural and linguistic similarity, and territorial contiguity, will — despite the persistence of feuding among themselves — not only have means for resolving their "internal" conflicts (see Middleton and Tait, 1958, for the concept of "jural community") but also will close ranks in the face of military threat from groups more distant in genealogical connection, culture, and territory. In other words, it is assumed that segments in a pyramidal structure of potential alliances may feud with each other but not betray each other in alliances with outsiders against their congeners (see Chapter 4).

The evidence to date seems to indicate that this kind of military boundary situation does, indeed, occur in a variety of places but that it is by no means the only situation among stateless peoples with localized patrilineages. What needs most emphasis, because it is contrary to the prevalent expectation, is that in some cases segments ally with "foreigners" against their own kind.

Here is an example from the Chimbu people of the Highlands of West New Guinea:

"In inter-tribal warfare the common interest of the tribe in defending its personnel and property was not always sufficient to ensure continued support after a death. The initiators of the fight, usually the sub-clans whose land bordered the enemy tribe, were considered responsible for any losses. When a member of a supporting clan was killed, and the initiators did not immediately offer compensation, the bereaved group sometimes turned against the initiators. As our informants put it, 'We blamed the N for the war, and the enemy had killed one of our men, so we killed one of the Ns'. At some stage in a conflict parts of a tribe were often found on opposing sides, each with extra-tribal allies. Sometimes part of a tribe fought with the outside enemy against its own fellow tribesmen" (Brown, 1964, p. 351).

"Instances of increased vigor in fighting the external enemy as the result of a loss are rare in our accounts; anger was more often turned against the internal instigators of the war. Loyalties shifted readily." (Brown, 1964, p. 352).

Brown states that the Chimbu are not entirely satisfactory for her theoretical argument (only part of which is relevant here) because they have continuous variation in social distance between groups, that is, "a gradation in closeness of ties from neighboring clans within the tribe, to other tribesmen, to adjacent tribes, and to distant groups. Sometimes ties to adjacent groups in other tribes are closer than to separated clans within the tribe" (p. 354). She speculates that the "perfect case" (for a study of affinal relations, that is, social ties established by marriage, and intergroup conflict) might be found among the Gusii of south-western Kenya, "where the clan is the main political and military unit and alignments are definitive" (p. 354). Our fieldwork among the Gusii in 1964 suggests that alignments were not as definitive as they have seemed. Since the Gusii inhabit a region of sharp discontinuities in language and social structure in which ethnic boundaries are often spoken of as if they were impermeable, it is worth examining this case in some detail.

The Gusii, a stateless, Bantu-speaking people with a segmentary structure of localized patrilineages and rituals of circumcision and clitoridectomy, were adjacent to two peoples speaking distinct and reciprocally unintelligible Nilotic languages: the Luo, who resembled the Gusii in social structure but lacked genital operations and initiation ceremonies, and the Kipsigis, who had the operations and initiation ceremonies but a social structure based on age groups rather than lineages. The Gusii despised the Luo and raided them for cattle (in between friendly contacts), but they regarded the Kipsigis as dangerous enemies. Armed combat nevertheless took place most frequently within the Gusii ethnic community, that is, between patrilineal clans and between "tribes" (territorial alliances of clans, some with genealogical connections); intra-ethnic combat, although conducted according to rules, involved the killing of considerable numbers of men. In the 1890's, when the rinderpest epidemic reduced the cattle herds of the Kipsigis, they intensified their raiding of the Gusii to such a degree that many of the bordering Gusii of North Mugirango (where fieldwork was conducted) built earthen-walled settlements (*chindoaki*) to protect themselves. Eventually, a large-scale alliance of Gusii groups (and some Luo as well) ambushed and massacred a substantial force of Kipsigis warriors in a memorable battle that caused a military reorganization of the Kipsigis (see Peristiany, 1939). A few years later, in 1907, the area came under British control.

In 1964, we interviewed a number of men aged 77 to 93 who remembered some of these events and recounted them to us. One significant fact that emerged was that, despite the state of Gusii-Kipsigis hostilities, one Gusii clan in North Mugirango, located at the boundary, occasionally allied itself with the Kipsigis in battles with other Gusii clans. Furthermore, one of our informants, a man of about 88, had been captured by the Kipsigis and had fought on their side against the Gusii, before escaping to his own people where he was taken back with no trouble. Other informants, aware of his activities at the time, considered it quite natural that a man would fight side by side with those among whom he was living, even if they were an enemy ethnic group attacking his own people. They did not regard him as a traitor or turncoat and, in fact, their vocabulary did not include equivalent terms. Loyalty did not seem to be conceived of in terms that transcended current residence and strategic advantage, although for most persons at most times these would coincide with membership in the Gusii ethnic group and maximal lineage.

This surprising state of affairs along a tense boundary between two sharply differentiated peoples, one of them a classic case of a patrilineal segmentary society with "definitive alignments," suggests that such boundaries may not have received adequate attention in anthropological research. In fact, neither the Chimbu nor the Gusii are isolated examples in their respective regions. The New Guinea Highlands are full of patrilineal groups with shifting loyalties and ambiguous boundaries of military alliance, (see Watson, 1965). The Kenya-Tanzania border region just south of the Gusii contains other ethnic communities in which segments at the boundary made common cause with their culturally distinct neighbors against their own congeners, particularly in cattle raids. Although more data are needed for comparative analysis, it is already clear that patrilineal segments do not always close ranks against outsiders in the neat way described for the Nuer, and that military alliances can and do violate genealogical and cultural affinities in segmentary societies.

b.   *Joking relationships.* This type of institutionalized social relationship, familiar in the study of kinship, is widespread at the interethnic level in tropical Africa. Mitchell (1956) brought it to theoretical attention in his study of interethnic relations on the Zambian copperbelt and discussed the earlier accounts of the phenomenon in Tanzania by Scrivenor (1937) and Moreau (1941; 1944). In Swahili it is known as *"utani."* Moreau states:

"The *utani* bond is one of extraordinary power, so that in some respects *watani* are closer than relatives by blood; they have the most far-reaching mutual obligations of hospitality and the sharing of property; they perform special functions at each other's funerals, they have certain quasi-magical powers between themselves, and finally, their mutual abuse and horseplay are not merely permissive but almost ritual and are linked with a remarkable system of forfeits" (1944, p. 387).

Moreau found a network of *utani* relations among 15 ethnic groups in Tanzania, including most of the major groups there, as well as overlapping into Zambia and Malawi. Mitchell (1956, pp. 36—42) documents its existence among other groups of Zambia and Malawi. Beidelman has discussed in detail the connections between "internal *utani*," as Moreau called the interpersonal and intergroup joking relationship and associated obligations within the ethnic community, and "external *utani*," the acknowledgment of which between two tribes means that "every member of each tribe is, by birth and irrespective of age or sex, the *mtani* of every member of the other," (Moreau, p. 387). A theoretical analysis of this phenomenon is provided in Beidelman (1966).

Mitchell (1956) has argued that "tribal joking relationships came into being mainly *after* the establishment of European law and government, and that in fact they are most viable in townships where erstwhile hostile tribesmen were thrown together under conditions in which peace was enjoined on them" (p. 37). This may be true in eastern Africa, but the phenomenon was not limited to areas of European control. In writing of the Hausa of the Western Sudan, Smith (1955) says:

"Joking relationships are not confined to kin and affines, but also hold on set occasions between categories of persons of different occupation, affiliation with an ethnic group, or state, thus: butchers and blacksmiths: mallams and hunters; barber-doctors and blacksmiths; Kanuri and Fulani; men of Zaria and Kano; men of Zamfara and Katsina, and others. Joking relations also hold between ethnic and occupational groups, such as Buzaye (serfs of the Asben people, Touareg) and blacksmiths (p. 43). . . . Joking relationships between states or racial groups are said to have been accompanied by a permanent peace; they were regarded as the expression of linkages between such states or groups which stabilized the wider framework within which the Seven Hausa States . . . . maintained their existence, by drawing sharp boundaries to the spread of war and by providing warring groups with the means of ending hostilities through the good offices of neutral groups linked by these ties to the parties concerned" (p. 45).

Goody (1956), reporting from a different part of the Western Sudan, the region of the Volta River, writes:

"One of the most remarkable features of the political structure, in establishing a community which recognizes certain rights and duties between members and provides an alternative to armed conflict in the settlement of disputes, is the extensive development of the joking partnership and cathartic alliance. The maximum range of these institutions . . . is very wide. All 'Dagarti' (that is, Western Mossi-speakers) and all 'Farafara' (that is, Eastern Mossi-speakers) are said to be joking partners. Joking partnerships in fact tend to operate where the recognition of unilineal descent ends and before armed conflict begins. However these partnerships are also characterized by the exchange of reciprocal ritual services and therefore partake of the nature of cathartic alliances" (p. 112).

The interethnic joking relationship is a good example of a pattern of group interaction which can be understood properly only by the examination of an entire region, and which, once understood, might alter our conception of conflict and cohesion not only in the region as a whole but in each of its constituent ethnic and political communities. That there are other such patterns of group interaction can hardly be doubted, although the ethnographic evidence is fragmentary. Beidelman's (1961) assessment of East Africa could be applied to many other parts of the world:

"I do not suggest that Baraguyu-Kaguru relations in Ukaguru are wholly typical of intertribal relations in East Africa. However, they do represent a problem concerning a large area and over a dozen tribes in Tanganyika. The Baraguyu and

Masai have often been described as classic examples of warlike peoples, predatory upon neighboring tribes. Writers on East Africa often tend to minimize or even ignore, the dependence of the Masai upon the Dorobo, Kikuyu, Nguu, Kamba, Sonjo and other tribes for necessities, such as metal and grain, as well as tobacco, honey and women. The case was similar with the Baraguyu. If traditional enemies such as the Nilo-Hamitic tribes and the Bantu are dependent, upon each other, we may suppose that there may also be comparable relations between many other less hostile people who are neighbors. Anthropologists in Africa frequently neglect such relations, and this has distorted, it seems to me, their descriptions of economic and political systems of certain African peoples" (p. 548).

Even on the basis of presently available evidence it would be possible to examine interethnic economic transactions regionally and thereby gain a more accurate picture of the interdependencies among ethnic communities.

The migration and absorption of groups or segments into alien ethnic communities, intermarriage, and the assimilation of individuals are hitherto neglected topics on which fuller data are needed to correct our view of ethnic boundaries. (See Cohen and Middleton, 1970, and especially the chapters by Abrahams, Colson, and Goody.) For example, the region of Kenya inhabited by the Gusii (described above) is often thought of as one of sharp and relatively impermeable ethnic boundaries between peoples who differ in language, culture, and social structure, but the oral traditions in the area suggest permeability: one of the Gusii tribes is said to be comprised largely of immigrant Nilotic Luo who were assimilated, while Gusii groups are reported to have settled among the Luo of Central Nyanza and the Kipsigis of the Sotik area with subsequent assimilation. To the West, along Lake Victoria, are the Suba, a Luo-speaking people of Bantu origin. Farther North, there are examples of Bantu-speaking groups' becoming culturally assimilated by their Nilotic neighbors, while they retained their territorial and political autonomy: the Tiriki by the Nandi (LeVine and Sangree, 1962); the Vukusu by the Masai (Wagner, 1949), and the Bunyore by the Luo (Wagner, 1949). These events occurred before the colonial period, and the historical account by Were (1967) yields a different view of the permeability of ethnic boundaries in the area than the one obtained through observation of the current state of affairs. As for intermarriage, it is found that, although most Gusii say that marriage with the uncircumcized Luo is unthinkable, there are border regions in which it occurred, possibly on a substantial scale. Over and over again, it appears that the boundedness and permanence of ethnic entities is an illusion produced by the neglect of boundaries and transactions across them as objects of study in themselves.

5.   Shifts of Ethnic Identity and Culturally Defined Life-Styles.   For highland Burma and the Pakistan-Afghanistan border region, Leach (1954) and Barth (1969), respectively, have shown that individuals and groups change their ethnic affiliations on the basis of calculations of strategic advantage and that such change is a recurrent part of social process in those regions. In some of the situations they have described, the visible attributes of cultural difference have become symbols to be manipulated in a struggle for social mobility or political power rather than indications of stable groupings or objects of permanent attachment. Their case studies show such drastic shifts in ethnic identity and life-style, and such dramatic reversals, that they may appear exceptional rather than of general import. But the question is not whether these extreme cases can be duplicated elsewhere but whether there are other situations in which ethnic identities and/or the life-styles associated with them can be readily changed as part of the normal functioning of social and cultural processes. There is, at least, some evidence that they can, particularly in regions where ethnic interpenetration exists. Relations between the (originally) pastoral, Niger-Congo-speaking Fulani and the sedentary, Chadic-speaking Hausa of Northern Nigeria serve as a case in point:

"Ethnic classifications in Zaria remain fluid according to the social context; *Fulanin gida* (sedentary Fulani) sometimes describe themselves as "Hausawa" (that is, Hausa) to the European, but in fact, though they have lost most of their independent culture, all their language but the greetings, most of their cattle and, through intermarriage and concubinage some of the Fulani physical traits, among themselves they draw sharper distinctions not only between the dominant Fulani and subject Hausa, but between Fulani members of ruling families and other settled Fulani" (Smith, 1955, p. 3).

"There is little doubt that semi-sedentarism arises principally through losses of cattle by disease . . . . Semi-sedentary communities have been viewed as transitional communities in which the erstwhile Pastoral Fulani are moving toward absorption in the cattleless agricultural communities which surround them. This transition is marked by the abandonment, in the home area, of one of the traditional types of Pastoral Fulani shelter in favor of the hut type common among the sedentary population. The pressures involved in maintaining this dual economy, as well as the attractions of sedentary life, are largely responsible for this. There is, however, evidence that Pastoral Fulani who engage in agricultural pursuits as a consequence of cattle losses do succeed in re-establishing herds capable of supporting them completely, and then take up the nomadic life once more" (Stenning, 1959, pp. 7–8.)

In other words, some Fulani have remained entirely distinct from the sedentary Hausa, others have merged with them in most ways except self-concept, and still others are in between, having to decide whether to move one way or the other, or remain where they are. Although relatively few may effect a complete ethnic transformation in one generation, they can move a considerable distance from semisedentarism toward Hausa urbanism or Fulani nomadic pastoralism. We suspect that similar situations exist wherever incentives for acculturative change vary according to local circumstances instead of being overwhelmingly unidirectional for an entire region.

CONCLUSIONS FROM THE ETHNOGRAPHIC EVIDENCE

The evidence reviewed above, however fragmentary, indicates that the ideal-typical ethnic community, in which boundaries, loyalties, and labels coincide in a single order of precedence, is not the general case for nonindustrial peoples but a special phenomenon that requires explanation. This gives rise to the questions: (a) What explains the development of well-bounded ethnic entities where they do occur and their absence elsewhere? (b) What accounts for the widespread assumption among social anthropologists that such ethnic entities are the general rule?

Although any answer to the first question is bound to be partly speculative at this point, it is possible on the basis of available evidence to make some assumptions about nonindustrial societies to replace the traditional ones:

1. The well-bounded ethnic entity is associated with a rather advanced stage of political development and a relatively high degree of stability at that stage. Where political development has not reached that stage, that is, among those peoples variously termed stateless, segmentary, acephalous, or multicentric, boundaries are unlikely to be sharp or mutually congruent with each other, with loyalties or with labels. Among such peoples, groups located in boundary areas are likely to exhibit "opportunism" in their alliances, interaction patterns, and cultural borrowings, as they seek personal and group advantage unhampered by border restrictions or rigid loyalties. In regions of continuous variation this type of behavior may be found throughout the region. Where boundaries, loyalties, and labels have become sharper, more congruent, and less variable in a region *without* the usually associated political development, this should be considered an exceptional condition that requires explanation through geographical and ethnohistorical inquiry.

2. The well-bounded ethnic entity is more likely to emerge indigenously where there has developed the small-scale state, that is, a specialized central leadership capable of making decisions (concerning social control, common defense, and administration) that are regarded as binding by a set of coordinate territorial segments. This is because the state makes novel demands on the population (for obedience to its decisions, taxpaying, and conscription) and, therefore, needs to define publicly who is subject to the state's demands and who is not, and to make those who are amenable to the demands.

3. Making the population amenable to the demands of the state requires making the state and membership in it salient public objects of awareness and attachment. An ideology develops, along the usual lines of group stereotype formation, in which (a) the political entity is sharply differentiated from outsiders by name, territory, and a variety of other attributes, (b) membership is endowed with a positive value, nonmembership with negative value, (c) the positive and negative values are extended to attributes — geographical, racial, social, cultural, linguistic — that happen to coincide, however roughly, with the territorial boundaries of state rule. This official ideology provides a cognitive and affective basis for the demands the state makes on the people and prepares them to engage in collective and coordinated action with other members of the same state.

4. The official ideology operates as a new set of norms for the regulation of social interaction across the political boundaries of the state, increasing social distance between members and nonmembers. If it operates long enough and consistently enough, its net effect is that of a self-fulfilling prophecy (Myrdal's 1944 principle of "cumulation"), creating a culturally homogeneous and loyal ingroup surrounded by alien and unfriendly outgroups.

5. If the state collapses without being replaced by an equally demanding superordinate structure with an equally salient ideology, and fragmentation follows, the ideology of former statehood and state membership survives as a cognitive basis for group nomenclature and stereotypes after the state organization has ceased to function. In these cases, however, the ideology loses much of its force as a regulator of intergroup behavior, and boundaries defined by different criteria lose their former congruence as groups and individuals shift ethnic identities and loyalties to gain advantage. The situation that results is even more complicated if the former state did not operate long enough or with sufficient stability to achieve ethnic coherence in its own realm. Some of the more confusing ethnic situations known to ethnography are of this type.

6. By contrast with the relatively small-scale preindustrial evolution discussed above, the development of large-scale national units on a polyethnic basis (particularly in postcolonial Africa and Asia) entails the building of ethnic identities and loyalties at a level of grouping intermediate between the indigenous political units and the national state, namely in regions or ethnic-linguistic blocs that engage in communal competition for newly available resources (see Geertz, 1963; Melson and Wolpe, 1971). In this case the ethnic ideology has its origins not in the demands of the state but in the processes of social

comparison among groups in the novel context of economic expansion and differentiation initiated during the colonial period. First, colonial administrative divisions are created that are larger than the indigenous units, and there are often different policies in different divisions, laying a basis for differential group perception and comparison. Later, apparent group differences in capacity to take advantage of new opportunities are observed by the more literate people in the cities, and they react by developing the ideology of an ethnic bloc as an interest group within the national society. This ideology broadens and redefines group loyalties, creating sharper boundaries between regions and blocs that may have had no contact before and reducing social distance and perceived cultural differentiation among groups of the same bloc that were formerly hostile. Under these conditions, ethnic blocs can be formed so rapidly that they often appear to be indigenous, "traditional" groupings to the outside observer.

In all of these developments, traditional and contemporary, the roles of ideology, cognition, and social comparison processes are crucial. Persons in groups observe and generalize about themselves and others and communicate their generalizations and judgments as programs of action that become norms and affect the establishment of social and cultural boundaries. Errors of observation and generalization in the original process of stereotyping may be determined by the economic and political interests of those making them, but the resultant ideology can become a normative force of its own, creating or augmenting boundaries and loyalties.

We consider now the second question: What led social anthropologists to take the existence of ethnic entities for granted in their ethnographic research? The influence of the assumptions in the Malinowskian method, with its emphasis on the intensive study of interdependencies within a presumed system, was discussed at the beginning of this chapter. The self-fulfilling prophecy occasioned by these assumptions has recently been illustrated by Moerman (1968):

"By his very presence as someone interested in culture and cultures, the social scientist establishes the primary relevance to him of ethnic (or kinship, or class, or political) categorization schemes as ways of reporting, recording and analyzing human occurrences. He thus pressures those who would talk to him to pay primary attention to these categorizations even when they would not otherwise do so. Consider, for example, the following field note recorded about a month after we arrived in Chiengkham, and before we had moved to Ban Ping. At a funeral, 'I was told . . . that the deceased was a Shan. Also that most of the guests were Lue or Shan. I think it safe to suppose that had we not been the specific strangers we were — foreigners interested in learning what the Lue were like — her categorization would not have been ethnic. Instead, she might have thought fit to tell us of kinship relations, relative wealth, official connections, or neighborhood. All of these category sets are, like the ethnic set, used by the people of Chiengkham. I do not believe that the ethnographic stranger can make people use category systems that are unavailable to them. But he can, and does, and in principle can never be sure that he has not altered the local priorities among the native category sets which it is his task to describe" (pp. 165–166).

". . . Most of what is called 'cultural anthropology' consists of reporting the folk predicates of folk ethnic identification labels, of assuming that all predicates are properly ascribable to such labels, and of hunting for human populations to which the labels can be pinned . . . . Anthropologists do not distinguish between native clichés about predicates and analyses of them . . . Anthropologists suppose that all of these imperfectly understood predicates can correctly be ascribed to a single category of subject: the ethnic identification" (Moerman, 1968, p. 166).

There is some overstatement here, but the basic point is apt. (See Cohen and Middleton, 1970, pp. 3–9.) Two other factors not mentioned by Moerman help account for the reification of ethnic groups and boundaries in social anthropology: the ahistorical approach and the peculiar historical conditions under which most ethnographic research has been conducted.

The rejection of history, or of the historical speculation once dominant in anthropology, was a major feature in Malinowski's methodological revolution. The anthropological fieldworker was to concentrate on the here and the now, which could be observed, instead of on historical origins, which were matters for conjecture. Radcliffe-Brown strongly supported this approach, inveighing against "conjectural history"; together, Malinowski and Radcliffe-Brown influenced several generations of anthropologists during the most important period of expansion in social anthropology. The ethnography of contemporaneous life became established as the dominant goal of fieldwork, and it remains so today, despite the development of interdisciplinary ethnohistorical investigations which use documents and archaeological evidence as well as oral tradition. Most fieldworkers gather so much data about the present and so little about the past that they tend to view the situations they confront as having a greater permanence than is demonstrable. This is particularly liable to happen with respect to ethnic entities and boundaries, since the people themselves are usually so emotionally involved in the current boundaries that they act as if they had always been there, forgetting, denying, or distorting past states of affairs. Detailed historical evidence, when available, often shows how impermanent contemporary ethnic alignments have been, but few social anthropologists seek this evidence or take it sufficiently into account. Thus they exaggerate the sharpness and impermeability of boundaries that have been transgressed and rearranged many times in the past, and the coherence and solidarity of recently formed ethnic groups.

The ethnographic record on nonliterate societies consists of data collected mostly by professional, Malinowskian anthropologists after 1930 and of earlier data collected by historical ethnologists and amateurs (missionaries and colonial officials), largely after 1880. With some exceptions, ethnographic investigation followed the imposition of European colonial administration, often after several decades. Thus, from the viewpoint of the sociology of knowledge, ethnography is predominantly information about colonial or otherwise subject populations gathered by Europeans and Americans in the last part of the nineteenth and the first half of the twentieth centuries. This was a period when nationalist ideologies were prominent in the intellectual and political climate of Europe, the United States, and Latin America, and they influenced the observations and judgment of colonial administrator and anthropologist alike. Colonial officials were predisposed to view "tribes" as sharply bounded entities displaying the internal solidarity, hostility toward outsiders, and centralized leadership characteristic of modern nation-states, not only because they believed the world was and should be that way but also because it made for more convenient administration. It is a cliché among anthropologists that colonial administrators often mistakenly assumed a tribe must have chiefs or overestimated the authority of such chiefs as there were, but it is less well known that ethnic boundaries were similarly misperceived or simply invented by the same officials. In some cases the officials or their successors were in a position to turn their errors into self-fulfilling prophecies, for if an aggregate of people is treated as a unit long enough by those who control its strategic resources, it will become a unit based on common interest and common fate (Campbell, 1958).

That social scientists were also affected by the nationalist temper of the times cannot be seriously doubted. The ethnocentrism syndrome as formulated by William Graham Sumner in his *Folkways* (1906) can be seen in retrospect as an intellectual application of nationalist ideology to "tribal" societies, and thus to all mankind. In going to the field, some anthropologists took with them the intellectual baggage of modern nationalism as tacit assumptions about ethnic boundaries. Whether or not they did, however, they were faced with a population that had been named, mapped, and administratively grouped by the colonial administration in accordance with its beliefs and its convenience. By the time the anthropologist arrived, groupings invented by Europeans or assembled in the period immediately preceding European control had already become self-recognized ethnic entities with clear-cut names, loyalties, and ideologized cultural and linguistic patterns. Many African examples come to mind: the Yoruba and Ibo of Nigeria, mentioned above as recent ethnic blocs, and the tribes of the Mount Kenya and Mount Kilimanjaro regions where neat ethnic divisions emerged from vague boundary situations and assemblages of diverse groups during the colonial period. Kenya has conspicuous cases of ethnic groups named, and to some extent created, late in the colonial period: the "Abaluyia," from ten Bantu groups in a continuous territory (Were, 1967) and the "Kalenjin" peoples, a radio broadcasting label to save saying, "the language spoken by the Kipsigis, Nandi, Tugen, and several other peoples," but which has achieved a certain measure of political reality. Such examples could be multiplied indefinitely. (See Cohen and Middleton, 1970, and Kopytoff, 1966, for other African cases.) The point is that most anthropological fieldwork in colonial and postcolonial regions was carried on at a time when boundaries, names, and common interests had been recently reorganized and made clearer and more mutually congruent than before.

In considering the problem of ethnic boundaries anew, the published ethnographic evidence must be reread as potentially reflecting the ethnic divisions that grew or were strengthened during the colonial period. The ethnographer has sometimes been the captive not only of his own assumptions and his own sharpening and leveling processes but also of the assumptions and cognitive distortions of colonial officials and their subject populations. Social anthropologists are becoming increasingly aware of their own cognitive processes and of the limitations and distortions imposed by their conventional procedures for obtaining knowledge; there is reason to believe that from this self-awareness will emerge a more accurate and refined view of ethnicity as a general human phenomenon.

BOUNDARIES, GROUPINGS AND SYSTEMS THEORY

Although this book is not intended as an attempt to build a unified theory, our task of clarification would not be complete without offering a unitary perspective within which to view theories of ethnocentrism and the anthropological data examined in this chapter. We argue that a relatively unbiased empirical approach to boundary phenomena fits best within the framework of systems theory and involves a revised but still recognizable concept of ethnocentrism.

Although initially our discussion focuses on anthropological facts, behind our conceptualization is a more formal analysis of the grounds for applying "thing" or "entity" conceptualizations to social groups (Campbell, 1958). This analysis makes "thinghood" or "entitativity" a matter of degree, rather than an absolute quantum, even for such things as stones and white rats: after all, they too are transient and only partially discrete entities, permeable to many probes, and with fuzzy boundaries at the microlevel. If the clues for diagnosing entitativity can be abstractly operationalized, it will be found to exist in degrees, and many social groups will be found to have considerable thinghood.

The human visual system is the preeminent device for diagnosing those middle range entities around which our thing language developed. It is visual evidence that initially makes us consider such low-entitative things as a candle's flame or a cloud as entities at all. The Gestalt principles of perceptual organization can be reinterpreted as clues for diagnosing entities demonstrable when the degree of entitativity is low. These principles each become grounds for use in diagnosing the entitativity of aggregates of persons:

1.   *Proximity.* Elements close together are more likely to be perceived as parts of the same organization.

2.   *Similarity.* Similar elements are more likely to be perceived as parts of the same organization.

3.   *Common fate.* Elements that move together in the same direction, and otherwise in successive temporal observations share a "common fate," are more likely to be perceived as parts of the same organization.

4.   *Pregnance, good continuation or good figure.* Elements forming a part of spatial organization or pattern, as a line or more complex form, tend to be perceived as a part of the same unit.

To these four Gestalt principles, Campbell adds two others, appropriate to stones and white rats as well as social groups:

5.   *Boundary impermeability, resistance to intrusion, and reflection of probes such as light and radar waves.*

6.   *Internal diffusion, transfer, and communication.*

Proximity enters in the initial and empirically well-justified decision to assume spatial contiguity for most of the social units to be described (see Campbell, 1958, p. 22, for exceptions). *Pregnance* is the closing and completing of a bounded figure. Since boundary is a spatial concept, and since humans usually organize themselves for warfare and many other intergroup activities on a territorial basis, this discussion first centers on the spatial distribution of people in a region and the congruence among bases for dividing them into meaningful segments or clusters. It is thus a discussion of the kinds of maps that might be drawn of peoples in a region, and of the effects that these maps might have on their ethnocentric behavior. We have found it convenient to classify the bases for drawing boundaries within a region into six types. The first four have been tentatively identified with principles 2, 3, 5, and 6 of the above classification. Although evidence of forcing remains, the degree of fit is noteworthy considering that the specific categories and the multiple boundaries conceptualization were developed independently of the above analysis, on the basis of anthropological experience.

Similarity: Objective Discontinuities in Morphological and Genetic Characteristics, Language, and Culture Traits or Patterns.   This basis consists of those objective measurements of similarity and dissimilarity made on individuals and groups in the region at one point in time. The "boundaries," never absolutely sharp, consist of contour lines dividing from one another peoples who manifest dissimilarities in characteristics such as phenotypical physical traits, gene frequencies, dialect or language (isoglosses), and culture traits such as subsistence economy (for example, agriculture versus fishing), dress and scarification, language, forms of sociopolitical organization, and kinship system. All of these characteristics have been occasionally so mapped by physical anthropologists, linguists, and ethnologists. When the physical anthropologist finds some stable differential in gene frequencies, he will infer that the lines at least partially divide *breeding populations* from one another. When the linguist detects lexical or syntactical divergence of communicative significance and historical depth, he will infer that the lines represent boundaries of *speech communities*. When the ethnologist finds discontinuities in complexes of culture traits he infers that his map shows distinct *cultures* or even *societies*. In each case there is inference from assessments of similarity-dissimilarity to a unit concept (breeding population, speech community, culture, and society) that involves interactional isolation. The maps drawn by one genetic feature may, of course, not coincide with the ones drawn by another, nor these maps with those drawn by various cultural attributes among each other. Yet the general finding is for much more than random coincidence among boundaries. The greater the coincidence of such boundaries, the more useful the boundary and, in some sense, the more "real" the group concept resulting (Campbell, 1958).

"Common Fate": Coaction, Cooperation, Decision-Making Groups.   It is interesting that Wertheimer borrowed a human social concept in labeling this aspect of the visual process. If we reanalogize the concept back to a social application, one aspect that it covers is the *acting together* of individual persons in collective enterprises, and the processes that make this possible. On this basis, one draws boundaries around those territories in which the people recognize a common leadership or other mechanism for making decisons that are binding on them but not on those outside the territory. This is sometimes called *political community* (Deutsch, 1954). In stateless societies, however, there may be many rather than a single political community; thus a different set of boundaries may be involved for different types of decisions — administrative, military, judicial, ritual — and on each for different occasions. The units so defined are typically related to one another if not congruent. Thus the widest judicial decision-making unit, sometimes called the *jural community* (Middleton and Tait, 1958), may operate on occasion as a military unit even though it may not be the most frequent grouping of military decision making. Generally speaking, three gross criteria distinguish what anthropologists think of as centralized or unicentric (Bohannon, 1963) political systems from uncentralized (multicentric, segmentary, acephalous) systems: (a) the number of units defined by decision-making boundaries, (b) the degree to which boundaries defined by different types of decisions are congruent, (c) the degree to which decision-making power is concentrated in a few leadership positions. Regions with centralized systems tend to have few units, a high degree of congruence between boundaries defined on various decision-making bases, and a concentration of power in the hands of a few; uncentralized systems deviate markedly on, at least, two of these points.

Restrictions on Spatial and Social Boundary-Crossing.   "Boundary impermeability and reflection" are most clearly shown in the military sentries who demand that the shibboleth be spoken, in customs and immigration officers who stop or slow people moving across national boundaries, and in the local mores that prevent too strange a stranger from building a house and farming locally, or hunting with, or marrying into, the local group, or even visiting or dining among them, that is, the social distance criteria. Frequently, if not always, these restrictions on permeability will produce distinct boundaries, but there also may be a continuous variation such as was discussed in the earlier part of this chapter.

Interactional Discontinuities.   In this category we identify the analogue to the diffusion, internal transport, and communication boundaries. It is theoretically possible to plot on a map all recurrent face-to-face contacts between persons in a region. This map would resemble a *sociogram*, with each person represented by a point or circle and each kind of contact represented by a line between persons. Contracts of a more binding nature (for example, marriage) or that are made more frequently could be represented by thicker lines than less intense or less frequent types of interaction. The parts of the map that turned out to have the densest concentration of overlapping lines would be taken as interaction units of some kind, whereas the thin or blank spaces between these concentrations would represent boundaries, dividing interactional isolates. For certain purposes, the mapping of one particular type of interaction or restriction of interaction might be taken as optimal. For example, mapping the widest spatial unit of actual or permissible endogamy might yield a set of boundaries that makes a good deal of sense in genetic terms, even though not entirely congruent with the boundaries defined by other criteria. This type of boundary has been discussed by Deutsch (for example, 1953).

Folk Concepts of Clusters of People.   This refers to the cognitive maps that the people living in a region produce as symbolic representations of their human environment in its spatial dimensions. The cognitive map includes the names or labels assigned to peoples in the regions, the territories seen as associated with them, the boundaries dividing the territories, and the distinctive characteristics attributed to each of the named peoples. An ethnographer can elicit such a map from an informant, and he can find out how much agreement there is between the cognitive maps of different informants. A crucial point is whether the maps differ systematically according to location in the region or whether people located in different places see the region as having approximately the same boundaries. Goody (1956, quoted above) has provided a classic case of location-specific, noncongruent boundary beliefs.

Folk Values Concerning Group Boundaries.   The cognitive maps described above involve boundaries that are simply seen as dividing one people and their territory from another, without reference to the "strength" of the boundaries or the values assigned to being on one side or another. If we take the associated values into account, we must distinguish between one kind of boundary and another and among several kinds of units. A boundary may be simply a river that is seen as fortuitously dividing one group from its neighbors without any further significance of desirable differentiation. Land boundaries may be seen by the people as permeable – that is, traversable in numerous peaceful interactions – or as impermeable, representing a valued barrier to peaceful intercourse between adjacent peoples. In other words, boundaries can be symbolic spatial representations of some desired degree of social distance between peoples, and a group may differentiate among the numerous boundaries in its cognitive map of the region, viewing some as self-imposed, rigid barriers and others as neutral markers of cultural, linguistic, or territorial difference.

Furthermore, the units or entities defined by the boundaries may be valued in different ways by the people in a region. They may regard a unit that includes themselves as an object of strong emotional attachment, superior to its neighbors and commanding their loyalty in warfare and other matters of intergroup relations. On the other hand, this type of reification of a group and emotional attachment may be lacking or present in lesser degree. Thus the indigenous cognitive map of a region, in order to indicate the group values operating there, would have to show boundaries of varying strength and units of varying salience.

Multiplicity and Noncongruence of Boundaries

Early ethnographic work tended to overlook the problem of boundaries and to lead to the implication that different types of boundaries coincided, as discussed above. Even making general-purpose decision rules for data analysis purposes has proved frustrating as the recent interchange surrounding Naroll's (1964) suggestions has shown.

But an emphasis on the fact that boundary maps based on different criteria often do not coincide should not lead us to the opposite conclusion that they never coincide, nor that group designations are entirely arbitrary. On the contrary, whether correct or incorrect in any given instance, the anthropologist's working assumption that "a society," that is, an ethnographically designated entity, is also a breeding population, a speech community, a social system, and an object of unique positive regard for its members – this assumption reflects a functional direction of social interaction and cultural development.

A principle of least effort operates to make groups drift in the direction of coinciding boundaries. For example, people who speak the same language are more likely to interact, and their interaction is likely to lead to marriage and reproduction and thus an increase in genetic and cultural homogeneity. Or, starting from another point, people who interact intensively over time are likely to find a common medium of communication, to become a breeding isolate through mate-selection based on propinquity, to socialize their young to a common set of norms, to regard these norms with positive affect, and to see people who differ in one of these many ways as somewhat dangerous or inferior.

Beyond this drift dictated by least effort, there are — as we shall argue below — positive advantages for group survival involved in having the various types of boundaries coincide. Group decision making and coordination are facilitated by swift and easy communication, consensus on group norms, a loyalty-inspiring concept of the group, and by the sharp definition of boundaries themselves. Thus ethnocentric norms of behavior (which, if followed, increase the genetic and cultural distinctiveness of the ingroup) may be perceived by group decision makers as having survival value and may thereafter operate in favor of boundary congruence. If these drift and survival-value phenomena are real selective processes, then a majority of societies may either exhibit a high degree of boundary congruence or be striving toward it in one way or another; this would help explain (and justify) the easy assumption of its universality by early anthropologists. And just as in political science the earlier model of the national state as coinciding with a race, a language, a culture, and an economy proved to be oversimplified, but nevertheless useful as a guide to the integrative difficulties of the newer states, so in anthropology the omnibus concept of the sharply defined society provides a background against which to diagnose the characteristics and functional problems of societies in which boundaries defined by different criteria are not congruent.

Systems Theory and Boundaries.

Numerous behavioral scientists have tried in the last decade or so to develop a body of theory that would cover *systems* generally. A system is a collective of units which function as a unit on a larger scale. A collective of cells functioning as an organism is an example. A machine is an example, more clearly so the more it embodies automatic self-steering. A human group or social organization is clearly a system. Major features of systems are the diversification of function among parts, coordination, exchange of products, and communication of information and command. These features may require that a system have boundaries and, perhaps, the more clear-cut the boundaries, the more systematic or organized the system is.

Presentations of systems theory are, for the most part, focused on single encompassing systems, and generate very few principles about the interaction of systems. The discussions of subsystem relations tend to be inappropriate inasmuch as the emphasis is on the complementarity of function, and the mechanisms of coordination, instead of on the competition of similar subsystems. Another weakness of the literature for the present purposes is the tendency to stipulate systemicity, so that it is assumed for any aggregate of elements, rather than to make it an empirical matter whether any degree of system is in fact present. An emphasis on "open systems," which never return to any prior state of equilibrium, is apt to end up so open that there is no justification for the word system, the phase "open aggregates" being more appropriate.

There are, however, several recent efforts to apply general systems theory to human social behavior that should be exempted from the full force of these criticisms. Buckley (1967) and especially Miller (1965a,b,c) pay attention to the problem of group boundaries (see also Platt, 1969). Berrien (1968) has a chapter specifically on conflicts between systems. In it he makes use of Boulding (1962), as we have done with regard to several principles given in the chapter on realistic-group-conflict theory. Both in its analysis of boundaries, and in its effort at making systemicity a matter of fact and of degree, our 1958 paper remains one of the best available examples of general systems analysis.

In the realm of animals and plants, clearly the more evolutionarily complex and locomotor they become, that is, the more one group of cells act as a unit separate from other cells and the medium in which they exist, the more definitely located the skin of the organism becomes, and the more the skin is made up of specialized cells whose adhesiveness toward the outside is much less than their adhesiveness on inwardly oriented sides. For simple human groups with a territorial division of labor it may be obvious that the network of reciprocal obligations and exchanges required is more easily achieved if the group is bounded, so that the circle of obligations can be closed. But we have enough examples of interactional networks that are not closed, or do not remain so very long, to prefer viewing this obvious advantage as an indication of a tendency rather than as a stable accomplished fact of human social life.

A number of social science theorists have emphasized the eufunctional qualities or adaptive advantages of social boundedness. For example, while Sherif's main emphasis is on the development of the ethnocentric syndrome as a result of competition between groups, he also emphasizes the relation between ingroup adulation and the intragroup coordination requirements. He says (1953, p. 299):

"Stabilization of a system of reciprocities implies the demarkation of ingroup structure from other ingroup structures. The ingroup thus delineated becomes endowed with positive qualities which tend to be praiseworthy, self-justifying, and even self-glorifying. Individual members develop these qualities through internalization of norms, and through example, verbal dictum, and a set of correctives standardized to deal with cases of deviation. Hence possession of these qualities, which reflect their particular brand of ethnocentrism, is not essentially a problem of deviate behavior, but a participation in ingroup values and trends on the part of good members who constitute the majority of membership as long as group solidarity and morale are maintained."

Parsons (for example, 1951 ad passim; Parsons and Shils, 1951, pp. 108-109) makes it clear again and again that the social system of which he speaks is a boundary-maintaining system, although his wording leaves open the possibility of other types of systems, and he recognizes that boundary-maintaining systems of both the biological and the social type require transboundary exchange activities.

Many exceptions to the functional view deserve consideration. Trade, the exchange of goods and services with or without the use of money, is an essential of the division of labor for both primitive and modern man, and can be achieved without clear-cut or stable system boundaries (and often in tolerated violation of group boundaries). Yet trading systems are obviously systems in an important sense. We suspect that complex unbounded (or unstably bounded) systems exist at many levels of biological as well as social organization. Also, our discussion of social groups as "real entities" (pp. 25–28 and Campbell, 1958) indicates that the concept of diagnosing boundary, of closed contour, underlies all of the other features. It is a boundary in common-fate coefficients, or a boundary in a similarity contour, and the like, that the diagnosing operations seek to generate. In this conceptual effort, groups were defined or diagnosed independently of reference to outgroups.

We propose the following formulation, in an attempt to do justice to what is known and to what is most plausible in available formulations: sharp and stable boundaries do not constitute a universal characteristic of human social systems. They are, however, a feature of more recent, more differentiated, and more centrally controlled political organizations, suggesting a social-evolutionary tendency toward boundedness, at least in political institutions. Sharply bounded political organizations displace ones with unstable or unclear boundaries through the selective propagation of adaptive forms (see Campbell, 1965b). That is, the advantages for survival of bounded groupings are perceived by the participants themselves, who act on this information to create sharper boundaries, or the advantages account for the differential survival of political organizations, with less-bounded ones being more liable to lose membership through death or defection or to be incorporated by more bounded organizations. In other words, drawn from systems theory, the disadvantages of less-bounded political organizations eventually become translated into negative feedback based on competition with sharply bounded forms. The competition can occur indirectly, in the differential survival of polities without contact between them, directly, in competitive interaction between groups; or vicariously, in the selective borrowing of political forms perceived to be most successful among neighboring groups.

What are the advantages of sharp political boundaries? In the foregoing discussion, we have suggested two that might hold true even for groups not located in a competitive intergroup environment: convenience or the principle of least effort, which is another way of saying that it is easier in terms of human information processing if boundaries of different types coincide rather than overlap, and functional efficiency of group coordination, which is improved when it is clear who belongs to the group and who does not. Insofar as these considerations of convenience and efficiency are perceived by members of a group and become salient to them, it is likely that they will move toward a bounded organization. Other advantages have to do with intergroup relations. Groups with more efficient coordination are likely to be more successful militarily, not only in terms of their military organization but because of more effective civilian mobilization in the support of military goals. Furthermore, the institutional means for achieving greater coordinative efficiency within the group constitute a capacity for adminstering larger groups, including foreign peoples of less military strength. Thus the advantages experienced by an ingroup from its own sharp political boundaries become translated, in action and cognition, into the experience of comparative disadvantages for less-bounded peoples in the same region. These patterns of group experience are the basis for the process of selective propagation outlined above. Its operation over time can account for the ethnocentric direction of political evolution in many places and periods in human history.

In the ethnocentrism of small-scale, homogeneous societies, the establishment of firm boundaries and more effective forms of coordination under central leadership proceeds in the context of a common culture and predominantly face-to-face social relations. There may be a religious element in leadership but the emphasis is on military and economic goals. In the development of large-scale polyethnic empires, military conquest is followed by an adminstration usually superimposed on indigenous groupings, the components being loosely integrated under an imperial leadership that is awe-inspiring and respected but exotic. Nationalism, that is, ethnocentrism in its most evolved, or perhaps only pure, form, entails the building of a large-scale political entity not only through adminstration but also through processes of social communication (Deutsch, 1953) that involve a common language and an ideology of historical unity and group distinctiveness, an ideology containing symbols of the state and its boundaries with which each individual can identify directly. In modern nationalism, which can be viewed as an attempt to restore through ideology the group solidarity and unquestioned identity of the small-scale homogeneous state, these symbols become objects of an emotional attachment so strong that they can be used to mobilize the population for military and other purposes more readily and fully than even before. Thus nationalism represents an advance over earlier forms of ethnocentrism, in the sense that it obtains the more intense and broad responsiveness of a large population to the state leadership.

If political boundedness is advantageous for survival and has been selectively propagated through evolutionary mechanisms operating over a long period of time, how is it that ethnocentrism and sharp political boundaries are not universal among human social systems? How could ethnocentrism remain an evolutionary tendency for so long without becoming an accomplished fact? Two answers are required. The first is that environmental pressures for survival were not the same everywhere. When a group can survive without creating sharp boundaries, it might not only find no need to create them but may even turn the flexibility of unbounded organization into an adaptive asset. The variety of physiographical environments in which human beings live and the variety of economies that have survived to the present makes it inevitable that some ecological niches would exist in which environmental pressures were not operating toward boundedness, or were operating too weakly to achieve sharp boundaries. If a group can survive at a stable level of efficiency and is protected by geography from direct competition with better coordinated, bounded groups, then its evolution toward sharp political boundaries could be very slow or nonexistent, and this was true in many isolated areas of low population density.

The second answer is that ethnocentrism destroys boundaries as well as creates them, and sometimes empires disintegrate under external attack and revolt from within without being fully replaced by stable political units. Examples of this in the Middle East, Southeast Asia, and the Western Sudan in Africa have provided anthropologists with some of the most complex ethnic situations reviewed earlier in this chapter. When a polyethnic empire is destroyed, and parts of it are reorganized as separate national states, there are often large areas that have only a tenuous political connection and hardly any cultural connection with the new nation. These areas are frequently geograph-ically isolated and heterogeneous linguistically and ethnically; for them, the demise of empire means a return to local organization but with the persistence of various status values and ethnic categories that had been introduced during imperial control and which present an unstable and confusing picture to the outside observer.

In the long run, these situations in the new nations of Asia and Africa may represent unstable vacuums of superordinate political integration, persisting only so long as they are free of overwhelming external pressure from more stably organized systems. Their existence indicates the unevenness of the evolution toward ethnocentrism but not its direction, at least up until recent times. In the present world situation, there appears to be a detachment of the outgroup-hostility component of ethnocentrism from its ingroup-solidarity component. National boundaries everywhere are presumed to be protected by tacit agreement among the superpowers and the political elites of most nations. On the other hand, ethnic divisions within nations thrive and threaten national unities. One way of viewing this paradox in evolutionary terms is to consider the superpower prohibition on decisive wars among weaker nations (the limits of which have been shown by the Indian-supported secession of East Pakistan) as preventing the stronger state in each region from conquering or otherwise absorbing its weaker neighbors, thereby freeing the latter of the competitive necessity to strengthen themselves internally in order to survive. This might allow the survival of nation-states that are weak not only militarily but politically, having failed to integrate their component ethnic groupings. What this means for the future is a matter for speculation, but at present it means continued unevenness in ethnocentrism among the world's peoples.

PART 3

Sociopsychological Theories

Our treatment of sociopsychological theories of ethnocentrism encompasses a wide variety of viewpoints — perhaps, wider than that of the societal theories — reflecting the divergence of psychoanalytic, behavioristic, and cognitive positions and their numerous descendants in social psychology. Our chapter divisions, instead of simply following the lines of psychological schools of thought, are based on what we regard as distinctive approaches to ethnocentrism and intergroup relations and attitudes. Thus Chapter 8 creates the category of frustration-aggression-displacement theory which, although hardly a separate general theoretical position, represents the most influential amalgam of Freudian and other psychologies in this area of study. Its importance in the literature on group prejudice and its large area of congruence and continuity with Sumner's concept of ethnocentrism seems to warrant an especially careful examination of its premises and predictions. Chapter 9 treats other theories of Freudian inspiration in a less extended fashion.

In Chapter 10 we present a formulation concerning the relations between group stereotypes and the objective realities of group characteristics and intergroup contacts. Although Allport (1954) dealt with this problem and our thinking owes much to his work on it, we do not claim it as a major tendency of theory in the field. Its prominence in this book results from its being a clear alternative or at least a major qualification, to the psychoanalytic inclination to view stereotypes as fantasies — and an alternative that can be plausibly generated from both sociological and psychological considerations.

The final two chapters in this section deal with two major theoretical influences in social psychology — cognitive consistency theories and the "purer" versions of behaviorism — in their implications for intergroup relations and attitudes. Although they may seem more strictly "psychological" than the foregoing chapters, they are straightforwardly relevant to group phenomena. This section as a whole, although entitled "Sociopsychological Theories," contains formulations that could have appeared in the preceding section, and vice versa. The division, however important for the theorists involved, is an arbitrary one as it relates to the subject matter of this book.

Chapter 8

FRUSTRATION-AGGRESSION-DISPLACEMENT THEORY

Under this heading we place the bulk of theories since 1930 that explain prejudice through *psychological* factors operating in a social context. Most of these theories are of Freudian inspiration, although Freudian theory also generates other theories of prejudice (for example, Jahoda, 1960; Alexander, 1941). The concept of scapegoating epitomizes these theories. We borrow primarily from the version developed by Dollard (Dollard et al., 1939; Dollard, 1938). Berkowitz (1962) reviews the present status of the theory as do McNeil (1959), Buss (1961), and Yates (1962). The theory has no doubt been independently invented, part by part, if not as a whole, elsewhere. The theory of the authoritarian personality (Adorno et al., 1950) overlaps when extrapolated from their context of individual differences into our context of group differences, although for convenience we treat it separately in the following chapter. MacCrone (1937, p. 251), drawing from Freudian theory along an independent line, states the theory concisely: "The greater the discipline of group life, its repressions, privations, and exactions either in the form of moral, religious, or economic sanction, the greater we can expect its aggressiveness to become at the expense of some other group or groups." This theory presents the biggest problem to the planners of peace insofar as it implies that the removal of external threat in the international scene would not be sufficient to remove threateningness and the perception of threat. To cite MacCrone (p. 252) again:

"The existence of the outgroup covers the ingroup against the risks of internal conflict and aggressiveness. If we could imagine a state of affairs in which such a group did not exist, it would become necessary to invent one, if only to enable members of the ingroup to deal with conflicts, internal and external, without wrecking their own group."

BACKGROUND PRINCIPLES

In presenting frustration-aggression-displacement theory, we first outline the principles that underly it, principles which, for the most part, are not at a level that can be directly tested by ethnographic data. Following this is a series of derived propositions at a level where testing with data from comparative study seems possible.

As this is the first of the psychological theories to be given, it seems important to notice that it is not a purely psychological theory, but that it makes assumptions about social structure and cultural traditions. Because of our interest in articulating the societal and the individual levels of theory development, the social-level propositions have been noted as such.

8.1   *Individuals are naturally narcissistic, self-centered, focused upon gratifying their own needs, except as socialization has modified these tendencies.*
8.2   (A sociological principle.) *Social life requires the partial restraint, inhibition, suppression, repression, or frustration of individual impulses and desires.*

This is true not only in infancy during the socialization process but also in adult cooperation and coordination. Ingroup discipline, self-denial, postponement of gratification, hard work, self-sacrifice, restraint on covetousness of one's neighbors' goods and women, all are frustrating. One of the remarkable features of this theory is that it posits that such "good" things as group life, ingroup peace, and cooperative coordination are frustrating to the individuals concerned. One of the probable reasons for the attractiveness of the theory is that people have found this so in specific instances but have tended to interpret them as specific deviations or wickedness in something that should be, in general, purely good and rewarding. It comes to them as a novel yet compelling insight that their specific troubled instances are samples of the general case rather than exceptions.

The sequence in anthropological interpretation of a peaceful people such as the Zuni shows a parallel development. Ruth Benedict's influential early description (1934) stressed the extreme ingroup peace, with the high level of cooperation and absence of competition promoting an exemplary kind of mental health that was worth imitating by those of us living in more competitive cultures. Later reports (summarized by Barnouw, 1963) have stressed the strong internal conflicts and interpersonal hostilities present in Zuni society.

8.3   *Restraint on impulse, frustration, pain, and the like, generates hostile, retaliatory, aggressive tendencies, normally directed at the perceived source of restraint.*

This is probably the best established of all of the principles (cf Berkowitz, 1962), although the experimental work with human subjects has generally involved insult rather than restraint on gratification. Kenneth Spence (personal communication) and other animal psychologists report that rats show more tendency to bite on extinction trials than on acquisition trials. Ulrich, Azrin, and associates (Ulrich and Azrin, 1962; Ulrich and Crane, 1964; Azrin, Ulrich, Hutchinson, and Norman, 1964) have demonstrated aggressive fighting responses as an unconditioned response to electric shock. Hamblin (Hamblin et al., 1963) shows a clear relationship between interference and aggression in a human simulation study. Common observation of children and adults supports the principle and there are probably no experiments attempting and failing to find it.

8.4   *Aggression itself is a goal-directed impulse and when aroused, its expression is gratifying.*

This gratification is usually assumed to result in a lowering of aggressive tendency (catharsis). The status of catharsis in experimental research is somewhat equivocal, Buss (1961) finding it generally supported, Berkowitz (1962) finding it uncertain (although the research issue is frequently the degree of hostility reduction from expression of hostility toward a displacement target). Another interpretation, compatible with the general modification of learning theory away from a drive-reduction principle to a pleasure-pain contiguity reinforcement theory, is to assume that the expression of aggression is enjoyable and reinforcing in this fashion. (Simmel, 1955, p. 19, says, "Opposition gives us inner satisfaction, direction, relief.") Aggressive impulses might be regarded as dissipating autonomously. Frustration of the impulse of aggression is itself aggression-generating, as a case of point 8.3 above. Aggressive impulses are assumed to cumulate over repeated frustrations, although some autonomous dissipation is also allowed.

8.5   *The normally perceived sources of frustration are the events and objects with greatest stimulus strength that are present in the immediate situation at the occasion of the restraint, inhibition, or frustration.*

This can be thought of as a contiguity conditioning principle. The recurrently present stimuli when impulse is blocked thus normally become the conditioned targets for retaliatory hostility. Expressing the conditioned response in subjective terms, these stimuli come to be "blamed" for the individual's deprivations; that is, to be perceived as the cause of the deprivation.

8.6   (A sociological principle.) *The stimulus objects most regularly contiguous when impulses are blocked and hopes are frustrated are other members of one's social group, particularly those in authority and those with whom one has to cooperate or coordinate the most.*

Most frustration comes from ingroup members. For the child, this will be his parents; for an adult, his spouse, supervisors, subordinates, and fellow workers.

LeVine (1962) has demonstrated that witchcraft accusations between co-wives (presumably a reaction to frustration) are more frequent the more contact the co-wives have with each other (see also Campbell, 1961, pp. 335-338).

8.7   *Learned anticipatory pain from aggressive acts can, if strong enough, inhibit the aggressive act.*

This principle refers to the "avoidance" component in the Miller and Dollard (Miller, 1944; Dollard and Miller, 1950) approach-avoidance conflict model.

8.8   (A sociological principle.) *The expression of aggression against the direct sources of restraint reduces societal coordination, interferes with collective action, and is incompatible with the complex division of labor and authority systems.*

It follows, therefore, that complex coordinated societal systems will occur only where there are restraints on this direct expression of retaliatory aggression. (The sanctions involved in doing this will generate more hostility as in point 8.3 above.) The presence of such complex, coordinated social systems thus presumes a functional social evolution of disciplinary mechanisms suppressing such expression.

8.9   *The hostility and aggressive tendencies generated by one stimulus object tends also to be expressed against other stimulus objects, the more so the more similar are these objects, i.e., the well-known principle of stimulus generalization.*
8.10   *The tendency to inhibit aggressive responses and hostility creates similar inhibitions for similar objects.*

However, the generalization gradient for the inhibition is steeper than for the aggression (Miller, 1944; Dollard and Miller, 1950; Whiting and Child, 1953). Hence the net aggressive tendency when inhibition has subtracted from aggression is greater toward some outgroups than toward the ingroup members, toward whom the inhibition is maximally learned. Such a shift of the point of maximum aggressiveness away from the instigating stimulus onto some other is called *displacement*. This maximum point will be intermediate between high similarity and total dissimilarity, since at the latter point the aggression tendency will be zero, as well as the inhibition tendency. However, this principle also points to the necessity of a clear distinction and dissimilarity between ingroup and outgroup. The best displacement outgroup has "visibility" (Young, 1932), and can readily be distinguished from the ingroup. Uniforms, costumes, body mutilations, and customs are functional for this purpose as well as skin color.

8.11   *Since guilt is painful, a person or group that one has aggressed against and, hence, a group that is contiguous with guilt arousal, becomes a target of hostility.*

Or, if guilt be conceived as hostility to self, this hostility is displaced onto others. Such guilt could also be due to one's own wishes and acts that are unrelated to the outgroup.

8.12 *Displacement is facilitated by provocation from the displacement stimulus.*

If the outgroup or displacement stimulus is also in its own right a source of frustration, the displacement mechanism is facilitated. Dollard (1938) says "Justifiable aggressive responses seem to break the way for irrational and unjustifiable hostilities." Berkowitz (1962, pp. 153-160) in experimental studies has found that displaced hostility is most expressed or only expressed where the displacement target has previously given grounds for dislike in his own right.

8.13 *Direct sources of inhibition affect displacement.*

A potential displacement target may inhibit the expression of displaced aggression through its own power to punish or retaliate.

8.14 (A sociological principle.) *Groups institutionalize the displacement of hostility and aggression onto outgroups.*

Presumably by a trial-and-error of customs over the ages of group development, there has been a selective retention of systems whereby groups specifically indoctrinate their young as to against which displacement targets to vent their hostility. Four lines of thought make these traditions understandable, and give different expectations for the content of such teachings. The first two represent traditionalized representations of the generalization-inhibition displacement model.

8.14.1 *If the expression of hostility toward a displacement target has a catharsis value, then this expression reduces the aggressive tendencies directed toward ingroup members, and has a functional selective value for this reason.*
8.14.2 *If the expression of hostility and aggression toward a displacement target is enjoyable, and if it does not lead to more frustration and pain, there would be a tendency to aggress against this particular target again when hostility was again generated, even if this did not reduce the inhibited hostility toward the initial hostility-generating stimulus.*

Such individual "learning" would lead to a kind of institutionalization, particularly when shared by others through imitation or conformity mechanisms.

Other cultural traditions exist that would further these two mechanisms. If there were genuine provocations (8.12) by outgroups, they would be shared in common by ingroup members. And through a traditional preservation or fabrication of such offenses, a cultural tradition relaying this displacement would develop (a related point is elaborated below). Remarked by Dollard

(1938), Coser (1956), MacCrone (1937), Murphy (1957), Faris (1962), and others is a tendency to portray the outgroup as animal or nonhuman. Erikson's concept of pseudospeciation makes this same point (Erikson, 1966; Lorenz, 1969). In similarity-generalization theory this would have the function of removing any generalized inhibitions to aggressive and exploitative actions, and is described as having such functions by these authors. The recurrent observation that outgroups are used as bad examples in the teaching of ingroup customs emphasizes their dissimilarity. (This is a different point from Levinson's, 1950, concept of *contra-identification* and MacCrone's similar ideas). Another way that custom can facilitate displacement is through manipulating the inhibition gradient by teaching that the outgroup is weak and unable to retaliate. Such cowardice can even be portrayed as justifying the aggression. The role of rationalization and justification in outgroup hostility must be recognized. If we take the concept of an inhibition gradient less abstractly, we can see that it becomes a matter of specifying the conditions under which aggression must be inhibited or may be expressed. Within the ingroup, aggression in the form of punishment is allowed against the child or adult who behaves immorally. An outgroup with differing customs is, indeed, behaving in ways that the ingroup member has been taught are immoral, and is therefore a target for legitimate, righteous aggression (Ranulf, 1938).

In principles 8.3 and 8.5, we have spoken of the "perceived cause" of frustration. This wording may seem evasive when compared to the usual behaviorist specification of stimuli, yet it was present in the initial formal presentation (Dollard et al., 1939, pp. 39-40). Miller (1948) and Berkowitz (1963, pp. 107-117) speak instead of "original stimulus," "instigating stimulus object," "frustrating object," "instigator," and "frustration source." These terms sound more objective, and yet for the restraints and frustrations of social life, the "true" source is often not available or perceptible to the frustrated person. He will often blame an "innocent" contiguous stimulus of conspicuous stimulus strength. The "true" frustrating object thus cannot directly enter as a parameter in our theory. Language must also be considered. The knowledge that he is being frustrated may often be delivered to an individual by language, as in a disappointing message, bad news, verbal punishment, and threat. And if this is true, it is equally true that he will often learn who or what the "instigating frustrator" was by verbal means. Verbally transmitted knowledge will affect the "perceived cause" of the frustration not only when the frustration is delivered verbally but also in many cases when it is a physical blocking or source of pain. Thus, since the *true* cause is often not available to the ingroup member, and since the effective stimulus object is verbally manipulable, it seems quite appropriate to use the word "perceived." We should, of course, specify the laws that govern which stimulus object will be thus perceived. We have done so, in part, in point 8.5 above, and for the nonverbal physical situation, the phrases "stimulus strength" and "immediate situation" or "temporally contiguous" can be further specified. Where language enters, less specificity is at present available. The general conditions of compatibility between perceptual-cognitive statements and behavioristic ones, extensively treated elsewhere (Campbell, 1963), make this mixture of scientific languages a tolerable one in this case.

With this background, we can state

8.14.3   *The socially institutionalized displacement target mechanism is a verbal tradition leading ingroup members to perceive outgroups as the cause of their frustrations.*

For a truly oppressed minority group, if such a tradition led to the perception of the majority group as to blame, it might actually increase the veridicality of the minority ingroup member's perception. Otherwise, it would be natural for him to perceive his fellow ingroup members who are temporally and spatially contiguous when frustration occurs as to blame. For a nation at war, there is also veridicality in such a verbally manipulated perception of the frustrator. But whether veridical or not, this verbal tradition would greatly serve the interests of group solidarity and coordination not so much through displacing hostility generated by the frustrations that ingroup members cause each other but, instead, by keeping such ingroup hostility from being generated in the first place, by making the initial conditioning of frustration-generated hostility to outgroup stimuli. The verbal tradition would act through manipulating the perceived cause of the frustration, that is, the "instigating stimulus object."

8.14.4   *A final way in which a traditionalized focus on an outgroup might control the otherwise disruptive effect of intragroup mutual frustration, would be to portray the outgroup as a threat and danger so great that the group dare not be weakened by internal strife.*

This is reminiscent of the basic principle of the "realistic-group-conflict" theories. However, here we are conceiving of it as a societally evolved invention or fiction, developed and maintained for its function in restraining the disruptive effects of intragroup conflict, that is, as unrealistic. Such a device is, of course, recognized by Coser (1956) and his sources in addition to his major emphasis on the results of realistic conflict. It belongs in this section as a displacement mechanism controlling frustration-generated aggression.

These mechanisms are no doubt all present, yet it may be convenient to conceive of them as rival alternative hypotheses rather than as joint determinants. Notice then that 8.14.1 and 8.14.2 lead to institutionalized stereotypes of the outgroup as dissimilar from the ingroup, immoral and weak or unable to retaliate; 8.14.3 leads to stereotypes of the outgroup as to blame for ingroup frustrations; 8.14.4 leads to stereotypes of ferocious strength, in contradiction to 8.14.1 and 8.14.2.

DERIVED PREDICTIONS

The frustration-aggression-displacement theory makes many predictions, most of them in agreement with the ethnocentrism syndrome as discussed in Chapter 1. It has, in fact, been developed so as to predict these features, and has accumulated complexities so as to make it fit reality better. We here enumerate the major ceteris paribus predictions. We first deal with the predictions of cross-cultural correlations.

8.15   *The more frustrating the environment, the more ethnocentric the group, holding ingroup peace and complexity constant.*

(Increased environmental frustration could, of course, lead to more interpersonal strife and, hence, could reduce societal complexity.) By the frustratingness of the environment, we should include its pain-producingness, as in extreme cold or heat, food shortages, and destructive weather. The time dimension is important here, because frustration is a product of expectations or of what one is used to. A lowering of conditions is frustrating no matter what the terminal level. Similarly, contrasts with neighbors can provide frustration. An impoverished tribe in isolation is less frustrated than one with rich neighbors. We would predict that could ingroup peace be held constant, the more culture stress, the more ethnocentrism. Selective retention may be a problem; if in the stressful environments it develops that for man to live there at all requires a great deal of coordination, one might not be able to vary culture stress and ingroup peace independently. One might be able to find a subset of environments of high stress but in which there is no advantage to social coordination. This prediction is a particularly valuable one because the other theories do not lead directly to it. If it fails of confirmation, it might be said that where nonhuman forces are the source of stress, there is too little similarity to lead to any generalization of aggression to human beings, ingroup or outgroup. The theory may be specific to human sources of frustration.

8.16   *The more ingroup coordination and discipline, the more outgroup hostility.*

This correlation has, of course, been predicted in the realistic conflict section and is the core part of the basic ethnocentrism syndrome. Viewed from this causal direction, however, different specific features may emerge. Here it would be predicted that the more hard work is required, the more complex the division of labor, and the like, the more ethnocentric the group. In consideration of the study by Barry, Child, and Bacon (1959) and in extrapolation from the authoritarian personality study (Adorno et al., 1950), the more domineering and autocratic the authorities and the more docile obedience required, the more ethnocentric the group should be. The more severe the punishments for violation of group norms, and the more restrictive the group norms, the more ethnocentric the group should be. (Although intragroup chaos and strife can be very productive of frustration, they are most apt to lead to direct expression of aggression in more ingroup strife).

8.17 *The more that ingroup norms place restraints on impulses, the more ethnocentric the group should be.*

Thus if the eating of food is prohibited under many occasions when food is present and people are hungry (as in the requirement to save up food for the winter, or seed for planting, or for ritual reasons), or if sexual urges are placed under narrow restrictions, the group should be more ethnocentric. These predictions are valuable in that they do not follow directly from the other theories.

The dominant moralities of our own ethnocentric culture idealize ingroup cooperation as purely good and rewarding. It is the renegade xenophiliac cynics among us who invent or discover the frustratingness of ingroup coordination and the covert hostility underlying much sweet cooperation. Adorno, Frenkel-Brunswik, Sanford, and Levinson (1950) have shown it is the more ethnocentric who most idealize the sweetness of ingroup relations, intrafamilial most specifically. Consistent with these observations and with the frustration-aggression-displacement theory, in general, it can be predicted that:

8.17.1 *The most ethnocentric groups will most idealize the rewards of ingroup coordination, will most deny its frustrating features.*
8.18 *The more restraints on expression of hostility within the group, especially against authority, the more ethnocentric the group will be.*

As we have pointed out above, if ethnocentric hostility and ingroup restraint are both products of outgroup threat, this principle is predicted by the realistic group conflict theory also. (See also Mack and Snyder, 1957; Proposition 39.)

8.19 *The fewer expressions of intragroup hostility, the fewer murders, drunken brawls, insubordinations, witchcraft accusations, and the like, the more ethnocentric the group.*

This is the behavioral counterpart of the restrictive norms of 8.18, and the joint predictions are similar.

8.20 *The more severe the socialization process, the more ethnocentric the group.*

This should include the use of severe disciplinary techniques, an absence of indulgence, and a severity of socialization (cf Whiting and Child, 1953). Whiting (personal communication) now would emphasize particularly the severity of sanctions against ingroup aggression, the severity of punishment for fighting in childhood, and the presumably resultant fear of expressing aggression.

8.21   *The strongest local group will be the most ethnocentric, since ingroup restraint and peace require outgroup hostility and make possible military effectiveness.*

This prediction has been discussed above (3.11.1), citing Murphy's (1957) case of Mundurucú. It is one on which realistic-group-conflict theory and frustration-aggression-displacement theory make opposing predictions.

8.22   *Removal of ethnocentric outlets, as through the suppression of wars, will lead to an increase in intragroup hostility of the varieties listed in 8.19.*

Thus witchcraft accusations have increased in parts of Africa and Oceania where European controls restricted intertribal warfare (LeVine, 1965). (Frustration may also have increased as aspirations increased through demeaning comparisons with European standards of living.) Goldfrank (1943) documented the pattern of ingroup hostility for the Teton Dakota during the nineteenth century and identified two periods of extensive ingroup violence separated by one period of "defensive solidarity" corresponding to a period of survival warfare against alien groups. If ingroup peace was sustained through outgroup danger, this is also predicted by the realistic group competition theory. On the other hand, the selective-retention model, which would regard ingroup peace and outgroup hostility as structurally separate, should not predict this shift. Data on witchcraft increases are often impressionistic, and it is not clear that retrospective memories that might now be collected would be interpretable, if it is true that the older generation always sees things as going to the dogs. Where there have been public trials of witches, retrospective accounts of specific occasions, past and recent, might be of value. Similar accounts of ingroup murders, and their causes, could be of similar value.

Proposition 8.22 implies a catharsis or hydraulic model rather than a dispositional model for aggressiveness. That is, it implies that there is for any culture a total pool of frustration-induced aggressiveness, due to external and intragroup sources, and a total set of aggression outlets of which outgroup aggression is only one. Any increase in the frustration pool would tend to increase outgroup hostility. (This is not necessarily dependent on catharsis; see 8.4, 8.14.1, and 8.14.2.) Any increase in ingroup hostility outlets will tend to decrease outgroup hostility, through reducing the pool (again, this does depend on catharsis). Not considered in these mechanisms is the amount of new punishment and frustration such aggressive expression generates. Various modes of expression (brawling, witchcraft accusations, scolding, and damning) may differ in the amount of this feedback, and other conditions, such as drunkenness at the time may likewise affect it. Where the hostility is verbally expressed within the ingroup, it no doubt generates pain in the listening targets and, hence, increases their frustration level and their hostile retaliation. Where the target for verbal hostility is a not-present outgroup, no such feedback of increased frustration may occur until aggressive expression reaches the level of warfare or of mutual pillaging, and the like. This is another way of approaching the functional value of displacement onto a group that is outside the main communication net, including the net of gossip and talebearing about what one group says of the other.

Related to this question is the finding of Naroll (1962) that indexes of intracultural aggressiveness (culture stress) do not correlate highly. This leaves open the possibility that the hydraulic model might work, and that a summation of his indexes of homicide, drunken brawling, witchcraft accusations, and suicide might correlate negatively with outgroup hostility, warfare, or societal complexity.

From premise 8.11, it should be predicted that:

8.23   *The group whose depredations on their outgroups and whose values provide the most cause for guilt would be the most ethnocentric.*

Although the comparison of the attitudes of Moslem and Christian conquist-adores at comparable periods of guilt-arousing mayhem would be interesting, this proposition may not be testable insofar as indexes of outgroup hostility may not be independent of overt aggressive depredations of a guilt-producing sort. The correlation of the verbal symptoms of the ethnocentric syndrome with overt outgroup aggression might be interpreted as relevant. In any event, this consideration makes it important to examine the taboos on murder and of theft from outgroup members. Turney-High (1949), for example, reports such for the Papago, a nonaggressive people.

8.24   *Those outgroups with more hostile, aggressive, and warlike neighbors will be more ethnocentric.*

This follows from several features of the model. First, neighbors of this kind are a direct source of frustration, pain, and anxiety. According to points 8.3 and 8.5 above, such neighbors should be the direct objects of retaliatory hostility. The more frustration, the more hostility directed toward them as outgroups, and through these contributions to the average, to outgroups in general. Generaliza-tion and catharsis (8.9, 8.4) can, of course, operate in all directions, and thus if only these points were to be considered, the prediction would also be that the more hostile, aggressive, and warlike the neighbors, the more ingroup expression of hostility. Certainly this occurs at times of ingroup demoralization. It is also furthered when overt conflict is involved and when the outgroup's power to retaliate creates an inhibition of overt, or even verbal, aggression toward it (8.13). Thus at this level, the prediction is that:

8.24.1   *Those outgroups with more hostilely aggressive and warlike neighbors will show the more outgroup-rejection aspects of ethnocentrism, and less ingroup peace and solidarity aspects of ethnocentrism.*

The group survival feedback aspects of 8.24.1, as seen through point 8.8, implies that if ingroup coordination disappears, the group will disintegrate and, short of complete disintegration, be so weakened that it is unable to resist conquest by competing tribes so that we shall only get transient instances of such cases or none at all.

Where the aggression involved is verbal, the communication feedback boundaries, discussed above, lead to much less retaliatory feedback from hostility toward outgroupers than toward ingroupers. Thus the direct inhibition of outgroup aggression (8.13) is less than the direct inhibition of ingroup aggression (8.8).

The present principle (8.24), in both its outgroup hostility and its ingroup peace aspects, is also predicted by invocation of point 8.12, that displacement is triggered or facilitated by provocation. In this, it joins the prediction (3.11.1) of the realistic-group-conflict theory, in implying that the weakest or most provoked of local groups should be the most ethnocentric, and is in disagreement with implications of 8.21 of the present section. Frustration-aggression-displacement theory thus seems to make contradictory predictions. However, this is not inappropriately true. Both outgroup and ingroup are sources of frustration and are appropriate targets for direct and displaced aggression. As in displacement theory per se, it becomes a matter of the relative strength of the instigations and inhibitions involved. Frustration-aggression-displacement theory remains unique in being able to predict 8.21 under certain conditions. Short of being able to quantitatively measure the separate parameters involved, we should consider more generally whether the present principle is likely to contradict 8.21 on the grounds contained within the frustration-aggression-displacement theory. We judge this not to be so. Just as each sibling in his normal interactions with other siblings provides enough direct provocation to legitimize displacement onto him of hostility generated in other siblings by frustrations provided by the father, so too each adjacent outgroup, no matter how weak, will have provided enough provocation to trigger displacement. Point 8.12 is extremely unlikely to go unfulfilled, and although it should be included, it is not likely to provide important variance across groups. Thus frustration-aggression-displacement theory's stronger commitment is to prediction 8.21 rather than to any contradictory aspects of the present principle.

8.25   *Those aggregates of people farthest removed from any outgroup will be the least ethnocentric and have the least social complexity.*

Consider first small islands of a uniform size, but varying in distance from neighboring islands. The more isolated such an island, the less effective are its neighboring islands as outgroups and, therefore, the less internal discipline it can achieve. On similar grounds, and holding societal complexity and island size constant, the more isolated an island, the more apt it is to be split into two separate political organizations. This prediction follows also from the realistic-group-conflict model. (For illustrative instances, see Murdock, 1949, p. 90.)

8.26   Holding distance from nearby outgroups constant, *those ingroups with a two-faction or moiety system providing a regularized internal competition and hostility focus will be less ethnocentric, and less warlike, than groups with singular focus.*

This is Murdock's hypothesis, which he states in frustration-aggression terms:

"So widespread are such functional divisions, so frequently is their number precisely two, so commonly do they oppose one another in games and other activities, and so often are their reciprocal relations marked by rivalry, boasting, and covert forms of aggression, that the phenomenon seems hardly accidental. Ethnocentrism suggests a possible common function. A dual organization of a community, or of a larger social group, may provide a sort of safety valve whereby aggression generated in the ingroup disciplines may be drained off internally in socially regulated and harmless ways instead of being translated into outgroup hostility and warfare. If this highly tentative hypothesis is valid, opposing factions should be more characteristic of peaceful than warlike communities. Perhaps herein lies the fundamental social justification of a two-party political system" (Murdock, 1949).

8.27   *The greater the population density, the greater the residential proximity and crowdedness, the greater the ethnocentrism* (holding ingroup peace and coordination constant).

This is predicted on the basis of the principle 8.2, assuming greater crowding requires more restraint, and on the basis of principle 8.6, greater frequency of contiguous other persons. These are essentially the same grounds by which LeVine (1962) predicts greater witchcraft accusations under greater co-wife proximity. Gulliver (1961) presents an illustrative case of this principle. Chinese Sampan dwellers with little floor space should be highly ethnocentric; Pueblo dwellers more so than dispersed Navaho herders; in Israel, Kibbutz dwellers should be more ethnocentric than Moshave farmers, and so forth (ceteris paribus).

8.28   *Those ingroups that most blame outgroups for their troubles and teach general outgroup hostility most extensively, will have the greatest outgroup hostility as otherwise measured, and the greatest ingroup peace and solidarity.*

(This follows from 8.14, above.) (The implications of the use of fear of outgroups to frighten children into good behavior are not clear.)

8.29   *Those ingroups that provide supernatural symbols (for example, Hopi use of Kachinas) contiguous with punishment may be able to achieve ingroup peace without hostility displaced onto outgroups,* in that the initial perceived instigating object is not the ingroup.

On the other hand, it is a venerated object against which retaliation is not allowed. In any event, from the conditioning point of view, the situation of punishment by Kachinas, shamans, and the like, is so special and interesting that inquiry should be made into its relation to ethnocentrism.

Predictions as to Choice of Outgroup

The frustration-aggression-displacement theory not only predicts which groups should be the most ethnocentric (as in points 8.15 to 8.29 above), it also predicts for each ingroup toward which of the available outgroups it will show the most ethnocentric hostility. From facets of the theory come the following predictions that are interesting and worth testing even where they are mutually contradictory.

8.30   *The outgroup perceived as most frustrating to the ingroup will be most hated.*

Assuming some veridicality to perception (plausibility and veridicality factors are treated in Chapter 10 on the perception of real differences):

8.30.1   *The nearer outgroups, insofar as they have more opportunity to frustrate, will be more hated.*
8.30.2   *The stronger outgroups, insofar as they have more capability to frustrate, will be more hated.*
8.30.3   *The outgroup with which warfare has been carried on most recently and severely will be most hated.*

Direct interference with biological needs, or physical injury, are not the only sources of pain for human beings. Verbal disparagement, insult, and abuse are also sources of pain and frustration. Thus we predict:

8.30.5   *The outgroup with the most disparaging images of this particular ingroup will be most hated.*
8.30.6   *The outgroup whose ethnocentrism the ingroup is most in a position to "overhear" will be most hated.*

This would include the nearer outgroups, outgroups sharing a common language with the ingroup, and outgroups sharing "talebearers," such as itinerant merchants, with the ingroup.

Contumely, self-love that implicitly disparages others, is also insulting:

8.30.7   *The most ethnocentric outgroup in terms of unwarranted self-esteem will be most hated.*

The fact that the self-esteem is unwarranted is significant, as for example, Parsons (1958, p. 318) states:

"The outgroup should be a group in relation to which one can feel a comfortably self-righteous sense of superiority (not at issue here) and at the same time a group which can plausibly be accused of arrogating to itself an illegitimate superiority of its own. Correspondingly it should be a group with strong claims to a position of high ethical standing of its own, which, however, can plausibly be made out to be essentially specious and to conceal a subtle deception."

There are a variety of reasons not necessarily all integrated with frustration-aggression-displacement theory, why the unwarrantedness of the self-esteem is important. It may be an aspect of that particular vindictiveness that one shows toward another who is engaging in self-indulgent behavior that one has denied oneself. In such a case, the outgroup is being scolded for behaviors also punished within the ingroup, generating a strong moral righteousness, a particularly virtuous hostility, as described by Ranulf (1938) in his analysis of moral indignation in middle-class psychology, and as noted incidentally in the discussion of 8.14 above. The more unwarranted the self-esteem, the more legitimate the criticism or hostile action, the less likely counter-criticism or guilt feelings for having thus aggressed. For reasons discussed under 8.12 and in Chapter 10 on social perception, there is a strong tendency to utilize realistic or justified criticisms where they are available to the ingroup or person motivated to be hostile.

8.31   *Those outgroups will be most hated which are intermediate in similarity to the ingroup sources of frustration and inhibition.*

This follows from principle 8.9, the generalization of aggression and hostility, with the assumption that inhibition generalizes less than aggression tendencies. It corresponds to the observations that the "favorite" outgroups for competitive middle-class businessmen are other competitive middle-class businessmen, for example, Jewish businessmen for Christian businessmen. If an outgroup is too similar, they tend to be perceived more or less as "one of us." If they are too dissimilar, it is not plausible to accuse them of one's own vices, and they become irrelevant as displacement targets.

The problem of the conditions of displacement are still unresolved (for example, Bush and Whiting, 1953). If the ingroup sources of frustration leading to hostility were differentiable from the ingroup sources of inhibition of hostility expression, then the differential similarity of various outgroups to one or the other of these ingroup stimulus sets would provide further specified predictions. This differential in sources of frustration and inhibition does not seem likely, however. Following Whiting and Child (1953) in their analysis of fear of human versus animal ghosts, and considering the effect of a general raising of the inhibition gradient, this prediction emerges:

8.31.1   *The more extreme the punishment for ingroup aggression, the more dissimilar will be the most hated outgroup.*

8.32   *Those outgroups will be least aggressed against who are perceived as having the greatest power to and likelihood of retaliating* (principles 8.7 and 8.13 above).

Through response generalization, the inhibition of overt physical aggression may generalize to the expression of verbal aggression, hence:

8.32.1   *The outgroup most capable of and likely to retaliate will be the object of the least unfavorable stereotypes.*

Since some retaliation may be elicited for verbal disparagement "overheard" by the outgroup:

8.32.2   *Among outgroups capable of retaliating, the one most able to "overhear" ingroup expressions of ethnocentrism will be least hated.*

Principles 8.30.6 and 8.32.2 are related to the ubiquitous ingroup use of hostile statements about the ingroup quoted from the foreign press in building ingroup ethnocentric loyalty. In the ethnographic setting, the analogue would be awareness by the ingroup members of the outgroup's stereotype of the ingroup. False beliefs about these stereotypes are, of course, equally relevant.

8.33   *Those outgroups will be most hated which the ingroup has most unfairly exploited,* has most infringed on, that is, toward which the ingroup should have the most guilt and, hence, toward which the most need to rationalize past actions.

This follows from principle 8.11 above. Evidence on this should be available from the history of warfare and from other intergroup relations. Relevant also are data on exploitative relations, serfdom, recurrent theft, and raiding.

8.34   *That outgroup will be most hated, most unfavorably stereotyped, and most aggressed against which is most used as a bad example in child training* (as in 8.14 above).

8.35   *That outgroup will be most hated, negatively stereotyped and aggressed against which practices the most acts tabooed within the ingroup* (as in 8.14 above).

Predictions about the Content of Stereotypes

In previous sections, we have made predictions first about which ingroup would be most ethnocentric, followed by predictions about which outgroup a given ingroup would most hate. In the present section, we predict the content of the stereotypes held.

The most characteristic predictions come from the analysis of the displacement mechanism. This states that the retaliatory aggression responses generated by the frustrations of the ingroup are generalized onto the outgroup. The behavioristic framework in which the theory is stated is silent as to the perceptions, images, or stereotypes that accompany these response tendencies. In accordance with a view presented elsewhere (Campbell, 1963, and Chapter 10 in this volume), this silence is interpreted not as a denial of such content, but simply as an absence of specification. Behavior theory presumably can be expanded to include this content, as long as it is done in a manner compatible with the concomitant stimulus-response laws. The advocated way of doing this is by incorporating the laws of the cognitive social psychologists that relate conscious experience, cognition, or perception to behavior. In general, the perceptions are predicted to be such as to make appropriate or to justify the actions. In the case of generalization, the model is more specific: the stimulus to which the response is generalized is perceived as similar to the stimulus to which the response was learned or which originally instigated the response tendency. Furthermore, for the original or instigating stimulus, a veridical component is assumed: for any given response tendency, the stimulus environment will be perceived as the type of environment that would produce such a response disposition.

8.36   The first prediction is thus that *the outgroup will be perceived as frustrating, inhibiting, depriving.*

Blaming the outgroup for one's troubles would be one form of this. However, the prediction is of a more specific similarity. Blaming the outgroup for one's troubles usually takes the form of blaming them for the interruptions, the interferences with the carrying out of ingroup plans. The outgroup tends to be blamed for the frustrations that result from the disruption of orderly ingroup coordination. This would follow from the emphasis on the triggering of displacement by direct frustration from outgroups, as in principles 8.12 and 8.24.

The frustration-aggression-displacement theory predicts, however, that the major source of frustration is from the regular, stable, coordinated restraints of ingroup life. Generalization of them leads to the prediction that:

8.37   *The outgroup will be stereotyped as order-demanding, law-enforcing, and work-demanding.*

Freud's theory of anti-Semitism (Bakan, 1958) is compatible with this, in that Freud believed that anti-Semitism was, at an unconscious level, at least, a revolt against the people who symbolized the oppressive weight of the moral law, the law of Moses. Bettelheim and Janowitz's (1950) concept of superego projection onto certain outgroups is also relevant.

8.37.1   *The more similar the outgroup is to ingroup sources of control, the more these stereotypes should be held.*

8.37.2   *The more controlled the ingroup, the more strongly these stereotypes should be attributed to outgroups in general.*

8.38   *The outgroup (or some outgroup) will be perceived as doing the things the ingroup members has guilt for having done or wished* (as in principle 8.11 above).

8.38.1   *The more similar the outgroup is to the ingroup or self in regard to these attributes, the more these stereotypes should be held about it.*

8.38.2   *The greater this guilt, the more these stereotypes should be held about outgroups in general.*

8.38.3   If indeed any outgroup indulges in gratifications tabooed within the ingroup, *these indulgences will be emphasized in stereotypes and will be used to justify hostility* (as in the discussion of principle 8.4 above).

These 8.38 principles correspond to Bettelheim and Janowitz's (1950) concept of id-projections in stereotypes.

Presumably the theory deals with objective stimulus similarity. But related better to it than to other theories is the observation of 8.39 *a tendency to exaggerate the dissimilarity of the outgroup* (Sumner, 1906, p. 13; Leach, 1954; Gregor, 1963; Wolfe, 1959) even to the point of seeing them as nonhuman, subhuman, animal (Dollard, 1938; Faris, 1962; Murphy, 1957; Coser, 1956; MacCrone, 1937; Erikson, 1966; Lorenz, 1969) so that the inhibitions on aggression learned to apply to ingroup members would not generalize to the outgroup members.

Retaliatory aggression is not directed toward the ingroup because of the inhibition gradient. Corresponding to this inhibition would be a perception of power to punish aggression. The hated outgroup is dissimilar enough so that this inhibition does not generalize to it. Correspondingly:

8.40   *There should be the perception of the hated outgroups as weak, unable to punish.*

8.41   *The more strong and threatening an outgroup is, the more plausibly it can be blamed for ingroup problems and thus the better a displacement target it becomes.*

This prediction, opposite to 8.40, is thus also reconcilable with frustration-aggression-displacement theory (when combined with trial-and-error adaptation processes). It is probably most characteristic of the realistic-group-conflict theories: however,

8.42   *Supernatural sanctions regarding inhibition of aggression within the ingroup, and justification of aggression against the outgroup should be found.*

Aggression within the ingroup should be perceived as supernaturally punished; aggression against the outgroup should be perceived as permitted. The more ethnocentric the ingroup, the more such sanctions should be found. (Frustration-aggression-displacement theory does not necessarily provide a prediction of supernatural rewards for aggression against the outgroup.)

Frustration-aggression-displacement theory as we have discussed it in this chapter is a theoretical integration of psychoanalytic and behavioristic premises with cognitive and sociological considerations. Its consistency with the Sumnerian concept of ethnocentrism and its richness in empirical implications, indicated above, have made it attractive to psychologically minded social scientists and, for some, virtually synonymous with a psychological approach to intergroup attitudes and relations. It has been so extensively used in research and theoretical discussion that an adequate review would require an entire book. The abundance of other sociopsychological viewpoints, however, is demonstrated in the next four chapters.

Chapter 9

OTHER THEORIES OF PSYCHOANALYTIC ORIGIN

Apart from the frustration-aggression hypothesis and the concept of the displacement of aggression (discussed at length in Chapter 8), which have their origins in psychoanalytic theory, there have been numerous theoretical developments by Freudian and neo-Freudian psychoanalysts and behavioral scientists in which psychoanalytic concepts have been applied to group phenomena or have been reformulated in interpersonal terms so that this application is facilitated. In this chapter, rather than reviewing these theoretical formulations in all their richness, we adhere fairly strictly to our purpose of stating propositions testable in the comparative study of intergroup relations, grouped under the following headings: group narcissism, self esteem, projection, authoritarian personality, and compensatory masculinity.

9.1   Group Narcissism.   Freud regarded ethnocentrism as a form of narcissism at the group level. In *Group Psychology and the Analysis of the Ego*, first published in 1921, he discussed the problem as follows:

"The evidence of psychoanalysis shows that almost every intimate emotional relation between two people which lasts for some time — marriage, friendship, the relations between parents and children — leaves a sediment of feelings of aversion and hostility, which only escapes perception as the result of repression. This is less disguised in the common wrangles between business partners or in the grumbles of a subordinate at his superior. The same thing happens when men come together in larger units. Every time two families become connected by a marriage, each of them thinks itself superior to or of better birth than the other. Of two neighboring towns each is the other's most jealous rival; every little canton looks down upon the others with contempt. Closely related races keep one another at arm's length; the South German cannot endure the North German, the Englishman casts every kind of aspersion upon the Scot, the Spaniard despises the Portuguese. We are no longer astonished that greater differences should lead to an almost insuperable repugnance, such as the Gallic people feel for the German, the Aryan for the Semite, and the white races for the colored.

"When this hostility is directed against people who are otherwise loved we describe is as ambivalence of feeling; and we explain the fact, in what is probably far too rational a manner, by means of the numerous occasions for conflicts of interest which arise precisely in such intimate relations. In the undisguised antipathies and aversions which people feel towards strangers with whom they have to do we may recognize the expression of self-love — of narcissism. This self-love works for the preservation of the individual, and behaves as though the occurrence of any divergence from his own particular line of development involved a criticism of them and a demand for their alteration. We do not know why such sensitiveness should have been directed to just these details of differentiation; but it is unmistakable that in this whole connection men give evidence of a readiness for hatred, an aggressiveness, the source of which is unknown, and to which one is tempted to ascribe an elementary character.

"But when a group is formed the whole of this intolerance vanishes, temporarily or permanently, within the group. So long as a group formation persists or so far as it extends, individuals in the group behave as though they were uniform, tolerate the peculiarities of its other members, equate themselves with them, and have no feeling of aversion towards them. Such a limitation of narcissism can, acccording to our theoretical views, only be produced by one factor, a libidinal tie with other people. Love for oneself knows only one barrier — love for others, love for objects" (Freud, 1955, pp. 101-102).

In this account the universality of the ethnocentrism syndrome is accepted without question and cast into the terms of individual psychology. Later, in *Civilization and Its Discontents* (first published in 1930), Freud stated explicitly that the social function of group narcissism lay in its facilitating the displacement of aggression from ingroup to outgroup.

"It is clearly not easy for men to give up the satisfaction of this inclination to aggression. They do not feel comfortable without it. The advantage which a comparatively small cultural group offers of allowing this instinct an outlet in the form of hostility against intruders is not to be despised. It is always possible to bind together a considerable number of people in love, so long as there are other people left over to receive the manifestations of their aggressiveness. I once discussed the phenomenon that it is precisely communities with adjoining territories, and related to each other in other ways as well, who are engaged in constant feuds and in ridiculing each other — like the Spaniards and Portuguese, for instance, the North Germans and South Germans, the English and Scotch, and so on. I gave this phenomenon the name of "the narcissism of minor differences," a name which does not do much to explain it. We can now see that it is a convenient and relatively harmless satisfaction of the inclination to aggression, by means of which cohesion between the members of the community is made easier. In this respect the Jewish people, scattered everywhere, have rendered most useful services to the civilizations of the countries that have been their hosts; but unfortunately all the massacres of the Jews in the Middle Ages did not suffice to make that period more peaceful and secure for their Christian fellows. When once the Apostle Paul had posited universal love between men as the foundation of his Christian community, extreme intolerance on the part of Christendom towards those who remained outside it became the inevitable consequence. To the Romans, who had not founded their communal life as a state upon love, religious intolerance was something foreign, although with them religion was a concern of the State and the State was permeated by religion. Neither was it an accountable chance that the dream of a Germanic world-dominion called for anti-Semitism as its complement; and it is intelligible that the attempt to establish a new communist civilization in Russia should find its psychological support in the persecution of the bourgeois. One only wonders, with concern, what the Soviets will do after they have wiped out their bourgeois" (Freud, 1961, pp. 114-115).

The very term ethnocentrism suggests a relationship of group centeredness to self-centeredness. Ethnocentrism is easily identified as the narcissism of the group. This identification can be, on the one hand, purely analogical. Ethnocentrism is thus a group level analogue to individual self-love. On the other hand, the relationship may be more intrinsic: ethnocentrism may be redirected expression of individual narcissism, and may provide individual group members with narcissistic gratification. MacCrone (1937), Alexander (1941, pp. 514-516), and Fromm (for example, 1964, pp. 62-94) and no doubt many others writing in the Freudian tradition have made the latter point in the discussions of the phenomena of group identification.

"In becoming a social being man at first must give up for the sake of the other members of the family some of his personal narcissism. Then he must abandon clan spirit (clan narcissism) and replace it with patriotism (national narcissism). Obviously the next step toward world-peace is overcoming nationalism and exchanging it for a kind of highly diluted narcissism: an all-encompassing humanism. In this progressive process of extension of self-love to object love, every step consists in the desperate struggle to overcome the previous stage" (Alexander, 1941, p. 514).

"From the standpoint of any organized group that wants to survive, it is important that the group be invested by its members with narcissistic energy. The survival of a group depends to some extent on the fact that its members consider its importance as great as or greater than that of their own lives, and furthermore that they believe in the righteousness or even superiority, of their group as compared with others. Without such narcissistic cathexis of the group, the energy necessary for serving the group, or even making severe sacrifices for it, would be greatly diminished" (Fromm, 1964, p. 78).

"Finally, the apparently paradoxical behavior of the individual who sacrifices his own interests for that of the group or who may even go so far as to offer up his own life so that his group may live, becomes less mysterious when we recall that the group itself has become part of the individual, through his identification with it. He dies that the group may live, that is, he dies for that which embodies his ideal self, whether in the abstract form of a social or moral ideal of a society, or in the mere concrete form of a tribe, community, or nation, fatherland, or a motherland. His own physical death, and the extinction of his own egoistic gratifications, is not too great a price to pay for gratifying the demands of the very real self which is the group ideal or the embodied and personified group, the father or mother surrogate" (MacCrone, 1937, p. 249).

As a description, the concept of group narcissism readily expands to cover the whole syndrome of ethnocentrism. As explanation, we limit ourselves to those predictions that seem to specifically derive from it and that go beyond the statement of co-occurrence of the symptoms of ethnocentrism per se. For example, propositions of the nature, "the more ingroup narcissism the more outgroup hostility," will not be specified, even though the theory implies them, just because they have been covered in very much the same language in Chapter 1 on the general syndrome.

One very general prediction emerging is:

9.1.0   *Groups will be more ethnocentric for whom group narcissism provides more narcissistic gratification than do other available narcissistic outlets.*

Thus Fromm (1964, p. 79) predicts that:

9.1.1   *Within a group, those who are economically and socially poor, or for other reasons lack individual narcissistic gratification will be more ethnocentric.*

Sherif and Sherif (1963) found lower-status boys, and those whose lack of skill at baseball had jeopardized group standing, to be more ethnocentric. Public opinion surveys regularly find lower classes more bellicose and internationally intransigent in attitudes (Almond, 1960, pp. 124-126). The more opportunities there are for such identification, the more ethnocentrism. Thus large nations, successful in warfare, with noble public buildings and highways, and the like should inspire more group indentification. For a sample of European nations, this is what Guetzkow (1955) found. See also Mack and Snyder (1957: Proposition 48).

However, Fromm also predicts (1963) that:

9.1.2   *The poorer the ingroup the more it indulges as compensation in group narcissism.*

This prediction is not obvious, since for members of weaker ingroups, individual narcissism might be relatively more gratifying. Be that as it may, Terhune (1964) found that, of students in America, those from the poorer and less-developed nations were the more nationalistic. However, wounded narcissism may have been involved, due to their confrontation as students in the United States with national differences in standards of living.

9.1.3   *The larger the ingroup, the more attenuated the narcissistic gratification and, hence, the more unstable the group identification and the more likely is reversion to a small ingroup cathexis.*

This principle is recurrent in the presentations of Alexander (1941, p. 515) and MacCrone (1937, p. 253). It is, of course, a ceteris-paribus prediction, and could no doubt, be overridden by great unevenness in gratification potential. Thus in the United States, group identification objects like counties and states are, for most, much less cathected than the nation as a whole, probably because these lesser units are less readily reified as independent actors, and less appropriately perceived as sources of causation. The illustrative use, as by Alexander, of the instability of polyethnic states, of course, confounds depth of historical roots of identification and homogeneity with smallness.

The theory has implications also for the relation of child-rearing practices to ethnocentrism.

9.1.4   *The more the society represses the expression of individualistic narcissism in childhood and adult life, the greater the narcissistic cathexis of the ingroup will be, that is, the greater the ethnocentrism.*

9.1.5   *The more child-rearing practices reward sublimation of narcissism in ingroup identification, the more ethnocentric the group will be.*

It is a moot point whether conditions in infancy can affect the total amount of narcissistic energy available to a person, or merely transform it. If the former:

9.1.6   *The more narcissism produced by the child-rearing practices the more ethnocentric the group* (ceteris paribus, with the degree of group cohesion controlled, recognizing that individual narcissism run rampant may reduce group cohesion).

From the standpoint of the full complexities of the Freudian theory of narcissism and identification, this section must remain grossly oversimplified and, perhaps, should be regarded more as a call for a thorough and systematic treatment than our grand tour of theories allows.

9.2   Self-esteem.   There is a substantial body of theoretical formulation stemming from neo-Freudian concepts of adaptation, defense mechanisms, and social character that we have chosen to call "self-esteem theory." Variations of this theory appear in the works of Karen Horney (1937), Harry Stack Sullivan

(1955), Carl Rogers (1951), Erich Fromm (1941), Daniel Miller (1959), and numerous other psychoanalysts and clinical psychologists. The most relevant tenets of this theory for our purposes are as follows:

1. Self-esteem is a prerequisite for mental health, in general, and for appropriate esteem of others in particular.
2. A low level of self-esteem leads to mental pathology, in general, and to negative attitudes (hostility, distrust, contempt) toward others in particular.
3. Low levels of unconscious self-esteem lead to the use of one or more distortions of information concerning the self that maintain the minimum of *conscious* self-esteem required for nonpsychotic functioning in most interpersonal environments.
4. Since conscious self-esteem is usually based on a comparative evaluation of the self with others, the distortions of information about the self (defense mechanisms) often involve distortions of information about others. Projection, the attribution to others of unacceptable behavior characteristic of one's own motives or action, is one example of such a comparative distortion. Another example is the conscious (and exaggerated) belief in one's own superiority to others with a concomitant tendency to belittle them; this is compensation for the low level of unconscious self-esteem. Both of these mechanisms involve enhancement of contrast between self and others.

Two problems arise in attempting to extract from this theory a set of testable hypotheses for cross-cultural research: (1) the defining of the boundaries of the "self" at the group level, in terms of ingroup and outgroup; (2) the operational-izing of "self-esteem" in such a way that its unconscious form and its compensatory conscious form — which have opposite hypothetical correlates — can be reliably distinguished from one another.

The solution we propose to the first problem is to take the ethnic community — defined in terms of language, territorial continuity, and political centralization (where the latter exists) — as the group counterpart of the self. The rationale for this is that such a unit involves not only boundaries that are likely to be perceived as most sharply differentiating members from nonmembers but also the maximal extension of opportunities for internal communication and a sense of interconnectedness.

The second problem — that of distinguishing conscious from unconscious self-esteem — is the one usually encountered in putting apparently double-edged psychoanalytic propositions to empirical test. In this case the dilemma is that a high level of unconscious self-esteem is seen as leading to the acceptance and positive evaluation of others, while a compensatory conscious sense of superiority (based on a low level of unconscious self-esteem) is said to require hostility toward and belittling of others. But how to distinguish groups with a truly (that is, unconsciously) positive self-evaluation from those with a manifestly positive self-evaluation in which they do not unconsciously believe?

One line of argument which helps solve this problem stems from a reexamination of what this theory states concerning attitudes toward others. The "mentally healthy" evaluation of others is not really conceived of as indiscriminately positive, that is, the person with a high level of unconscious self-esteem is not said to be a Pollyanna who loves everyone regardless of their actual qualities and their behavior toward him. He is conceived of as being relatively free of the unconscious need to increase his self-evaluation through indiscriminately hating and belittling others; this freedom allows him to perceive the attributes of others with relative accuracy and to evaluate and act toward them in a selective way which is related to their actual attributes. He will react positively to some, negatively to others, depending on their behavior, and one basis for these differential reactions will be the effects of their behavior on him. The person with a negative self-evaluation, however, has an unconscious need to increase his self-evaluation through hating and belittling; this need interferes with the accuracy of his perception of others and leads to his being indiscriminate in his rejection of them. Thus he may react negatively even to those who would wish to befriend him. Thus high self-esteem leads to selective behavior toward others based on accurate perception of their attributes; low self-esteem leads to generalized negative attitudes that are applied to others regardless of their attributes (and involves distortion of their actual attributes). It is also implied that low self-esteem requires a greater enhancement of contrast between self and others (because of the strength of the need for comparative evaluation).

Applied to the level of group interaction, this argument implies that we can distinguish the outgroup attitudes theoretically expected of groups high and low on self-esteem as follows: those high on self-esteem should differentiate to a high degree among outgroups in their environment (in terms of like-dislike, social distance patterns, stereotype content, and evaluation), and their images of outgroup should show a high degree of correspondence with the actual attributes of the groups. Those low on self-esteem should be extremely general in their rejection of outgroups (along the same dimensions), with a high degree of distortion in their images of groups.

However, to characterize groups as high and low on self-esteem in terms of the hypothetical correlates of self-esteem in outgroup attitudes does not allow us to examine the question of whether self-esteem and outgroup attitudes are empirically related. Thus we must return to the problem of operationalizing self-esteem itself at the group level.

First, it must be stated that there can be no exact counterpart of the self at the group level, because an ingroup is simply a collectivity whose members endow it with some properties of their selves, and an individual may belong to a number of such groups. The clear boundary between self and others that is so natural and pronounced in individual development is subject to numerous variations at the group level, shifts in identity incumbent on situational variations both within the lifespan and across differing groups. Furthermore, an ingroup is from the individual viewpoint comprised of others — admittedly others with whom he identifies himself, but nevertheless distinct selves — and this also serves to diminish the analogy between self and ingroup. The import of this is that the existence, maintenance, and enhancement of boundaries is much more central to discussions of ingroup and outgroup than to self and others.

Any ingroup is two kinds of stimuli to its members: an entity identified with self and an aggregate of others. When interaction with outgroups is in focus, the entity identified with self is salient; when internal relations are in focus, the members comprising the group are likely to be seen as external. In this sense, fission and fusion as discussed by Evans-Pritchard are universal properties of groups. When we speak of the self-esteem of a group we mean, in part, its internal solidarity or harmony, that is, the esteem (and other positive attitudes) which its members have for each other. In this sense, measures of internal solidarity are measures of group self-esteem. But what about the group with low self-esteem (or solidarity) which achieves such solidarity through ethnocentric activity? First, if the group really has low self-esteem by comparison with other groups, then this must manifest itself in some signs of less solidarity or more conflict than groups with high self-esteem. Second, it is likely that the group with low self-esteem whose solidarity is simply a response to outgroup challenge will tend to manifest its solidarity in terms of the specific challenge (usually military activity) and in terms of the conscious image of their ingroup entity but not in terms of the full range of intragroup relations that a total social system or community encompasses. In other words, we would expect a group low in self-esteem to react to outgroup threat by producing an ingroup image of superiority effective for military defense but not by wiping out the internal hostility generated by their routine functioning. They exalt their collectivity but are nevertheless aggressive to other members of it where this aggression does not seriously interfere with group survival. The conclusion of this discussion is that the proper way of operationalizing group self-esteem is in terms of measures of intragroup conflict: those groups with comparatively high frequencies of ingroup interpersonal aggression (for example, feuding, homicide, brawls, assault, litigation, and witchcraft accusations) will be considered low on group self-esteem; those with low frequencies on these indexes will be considered to have high group self-esteem. It should be observed, however, that this way of operationalizing group self-esteem refers only to the counterpart of unconscious self-esteem as conceived of in psychological theory; the compensatory conscious sense of superiority is measured through the explicit comparative evaluation of ingroups and outgroups and through the conscious images to which these evaluations are attached.

The propositions stemming from self-esteem theory can be stated as follows:

9.2.0   *The higher groups are on indexes of ingroup interpersonal aggression:*
9.2.1   *The stronger their hostility toward outgroups* (as measured by warfare, social distance customs, attitudinal expressions of dislike).
9.2.2   *The stronger their tendency to see outgroups as threatening and aggressive*.
9.2.3   *The stronger their tendency to see all the outgroups in their environment as similar* (that is, to make few discriminations on the basis of actual differences among the outgroups) *and contrasting sharply with the ingroup.*
9.2.4   *The lower their evaluation of outgroups generally*, that is, the greater their tendency in conscious statements to view the ingroup as superior to all other groups.
9.2.5   *The less their accuracy in intergroup perception;* the less their complementary agreement with the outgroup.

Exception might be taken to the implication in the first proposition that groups with more internal aggression or conflict are more likely to wage war against outsiders, on the grounds that their low internal solidarity would weaken their military capacity. However, if this is considered in conjunction with the second hypothesis, which states that the groups with internal aggression see outsiders as threatening and aggressive, this implication may be modified to the prediction that the internally aggressive groups are more likely to regard outsiders as military enemies and to adopt a defensive and hostile posture toward them, without necessarily engaging frequently in combat.

Protection of self-esteem through derogation of outgroups and enhancement of ingroup virtues may be augmented by the defense mechanism of "identification with the aggressor." At the individual level, this mechanism is described as a means of transforming oneself from the person threatened to the source of threat by impersonating the aggressor, assuming his attributes, or imitating his aggression (Anna Freud, 1946, p. 121). At the group level, identification with the aggressor might take the form of adopting the customs, values, success symbols, and military stance of a successful adversary, probably without conscious recognition of the origins of the imitated behaviors.

9.2.6   *The higher a group is on indices of ingroup interpersonal aggression (low self-esteem), the more likely it is to imitate, without recognition, the customs and values of successful military enemies.*

The equation proposed here between ingroup aggression and low group self-esteem suggests that aspects of social structure relating to the internal solidarity of ethnic units might be determinants of group self-esteem and thus also related to the outcome variables of ethnocentrism (See LeVine, 1965). In this regard, ethnic units might be rated along a solidary-divisive dimension, which would represent the source of the groups' self-esteem. At one end of the dimension would be those with social structures which, through central coordination or cross-cutting ties (or a combination of the two) maintain a high degree of internal solidarity, and at the other end would be those groups which not only lack central coordination (multicentric systems in Bohannon's terminology) but also manifest a high degree of internecine conflict. If degree of political centralization were held constant, these hypotheses would follow:

9.2.7   *The more divisive groups manifest more of the above outcomes of low self-esteem as well as being more defensive in military activity, while the more solidary groups show more of the outcomes of high self-esteem and also are more offensive in military activity.*

9.2.8   *Projection of hostility is more characteristic of divisive groups* (who assume that others are as hostile to them as they are to each other), *while displacement of hostility is more characteristic of solidary groups* (for whom ingroup members are friends but some outgroups are enemies).

Social-structural considerations of this kind suggest a further modification of the hypotheses derived from self-estem theory. The major consideration involved is the difference between aggression within the ethnic unit, which is organized along subgroup lines, and that which is purely interpersonal. Proposition 9.2.3 above, which predicts that groups with more internal conflict will differentiate more sharply between ingroup and outgroup at ethnic boundaries, makes sense if we are talking about interpersonal aggression in centralized political systems. Those politically centralized societies with more intragroup hostility at the personal level may very well be led to augment their flagging solidarity through emphasis on their boundary with outgroups. However, in the ethnic groups that lack political centralization and have violence between subgroups, the relationship may well be reversed. In these multicentric systems, greater internal violence would seem to lead to the sharpening of boundaries and loyalties at the subgroup rather than at the ethnic unit level. Furthermore, since their internecine conflict is organized in groups, it can serve as a model for intergroup conflict at the level of ethnic boundaries. With the absence of an ethnic boundary that in centralized societies separates militarily unified peace groups and promotes displacement of aggression outward against foreigners, there is the possibility of transferring military habits back and forth between local levels and wider ones, so that generalization becomes a more probable mechanism than displacement. This is particularly likely in segmentary lineage systems, where the shifting scope of military ingroups and the institutionalization of transferring military postures from one level to another favors a prediction of a single generalized tendency applied to outgroups of varying scope. Thus the hypotheses 9.2.1 to 9.2.8 must be considered to apply where the ingroup aggression (self-esteem measure) is interpersonal (homicide, assault, and witch-craft accusations), but not where it is intergroup (as in feuding and warfare).

9.3.   **Projection.**   Perhaps no concept has been more consistently applied to group stereotypes by psychoanalytic observers than that of projection, that is, the attribution to others of unacceptable impulses within one's self. Characteristic of this approach is Ackerman and Jahoda's (1950) dictum concerning anti-Semitism, "The Jew is a living inkblot." Taken in its most extreme form this approach argues that stereotypes of outgroups are simply fantasies wholly derived from the unconscious needs of ingroup members with no correspondence to the objective attributes of outgroups. The following propositions for comparative study derive from this position:

9.3.0   *Stereotypes of outgroups will correspond to motives that are being inhibited at the ingroup level.* Thus:

9.3.1   *The more a group inhibits aggression at the ingroup level, the more it will perceive outgroups as aggressive* (see Mack and Snyder, 1957: Proposition 39).

9.3.2   *The more a group inhibits sexuality, the more it will perceive outgroups as sexually immoral.*

9.3.3   *The more a group emphasizes cooperation and honesty at the ingroup level, the more it will perceive outgroups as dishonest, unregulated, anarchic, and stingy.*

9.3.4   *Stereotypes of outgroups correspond more to ingroup motives than to outgroup realities;* thus where inhibited motives vary among the groups of a region, there will be less cross-group agreement about outgroup attributes (particularly those related to inhibited motives).

9.3.5   *If only one group in a region is markedly high on inhibition of a given motive, it will deviate from the outgroup stereotypes of the other groups by attributing that motive more generally and intensely.*

9.3.6   *The general correspondence between outgroup stereotypes and any objective measure of outgroup characteristics will be low.*

An application of the concept of projection that might be more faithful to its original psychoanalytic form is in terms of guilt arising from the discrepancy between the repressive ideal and actual behavior: the greater the discrepancy, the greater the need to project the forbidden impulses outward, thereby reassuring the self (or in this case, the ingroup) that others are deviating further from the ideal. Thus,

9.3.7   *Those groups manifesting a greater discrepancy between cultural prohibitions on aggression and actual frequency and intensity of ingroup aggression will be more likely to perceive outgroups as aggressive.*

9.3.8   *Those groups manifesting a greater discrepancy between cultural prohibitions on sexuality and the frequency of sexual violations will be more likely to perceive outgroups as sexually immoral.*

9.3.9   *Those groups manifesting a greater discrepancy between ideals of cooperation and honesty and actual level of ingroup cooperation and honesty will be more likely to perceive outgroups as anarchic and dishonest.*

Bettelheim and Janowitz (1950) present an important development of this position involving the objective characteristics of outgroups selected as appropriate targets for projections of different parts of personality. Groups high on achievement like Jews are selected to be superego projections; that is, they are seen as representative of the demands made by the anti-Semite's superego, and become a medium for the expression of his resentment at failing to live up to these demands. Groups dark in skin color and of low social status like Negroes are selected to be id projections, that is, they are seen as representative of the racist's own repressed erotic impulses and become a medium for the expression of his resentment at not allowing himself gratification of those impulses. Some of the implications of this position for the relation between stereotype content and social role will be spelled out in Chapter 10. Some other propositions can be stated here:

9.3.10   *Groups seeing themselves as unsuccessful in living up to their own ideals* (for example, through defeat in interethnic warfare, subsistence failure in the face of famine) *will manifest their greatest hostility toward outgroups that are successful in those particular ways.*

9.3.11   *Groups seeing themselves as deprived of hedonistic gratification by their own ideals will manifest greatest hostility toward (a) groups viewed as having darker skin color, and (b) groups in the region with the least restrictive ideals.*

The concept of "contrast projection" reviewed by Campbell et al. (1964) can be derived in part from a Freudian version of complementary projection. In the latter, the inhibited individual exaggerates the expressiveness of his less inhibited fellows (because they seem to express his own repressed impulses), but there is no assumption that the more expressive individual exaggerates the inhibitedness of his less expressive fellows, since in Freudian theory he has no need to do so. From the standpoint of adaptation-level theory, however, Campbell et al. argue that individuals high or low on any personality dimension will enhance any existing contrast between themselves and others. Thus propositions of the following distinctive type can be generated:

9.3.12   *Groups that are most warlike will perceive others as weak.*

9.3.13   *Groups that are wealthiest will perceive their neighbors as impoverished.*

9.3.14   *Groups that have the most sociopolitical complexity or urbanism will perceive their neighbors as uncivilized.*

9.4   Authoritarian personality.   The theory of the authoritarian personality as developed by Adorno et al. (1950), is not independent of psychoanalytic ego and self-esteem theories, frustration-aggression-displacement theory, and cognitive theory, but is a complex precipitate of the three theoretical sources applied to one historical-cultural problem. The work of Melikian (1959) indicates that the concept as operationalized in the F-scale may have cross-cultural validity and not represent simply a twentieth century American or Western syndrome.

The authoritarian personality concept is particularly rich in testable hypotheses because it involves hypothetical links between ethnocentrism as a cluster of attitudes toward outgroups and (a) attitudes toward sociopolitical structures and relationships, (b) cognitive styles, that is, general modes of thinking, (c) child-rearing practices, and (d) family structure as it impinges on the developing child.

1.   **Attitudes Toward Sociopolitical Structures and Relationships**

Highly ethnocentric persons:

   a.   Have an emotional need for unconditional submission to authority which expresses itself in: family interaction, other interpersonal relations, political attitudes, and attitudes toward supernatural figures.

   b.   Desire the polity to be ruled by a powerful, autocratic leader to whom all would grant total allegiance, unquestioning obedience, and extreme deference.

   c.   Believe that obedience and respect for authority are paramount values and the most important virtues children should learn.

   d.   Believe in extremely severe punishment of deviants: not only those who defy leaders but also offenders against conventional mores such as sexual restrictions.

   e.   Perceive others as being deviant or committing violations against conventional morality even when they are not, and view mankind generally as being potentially anarchic and immoral when not under the control of a powerful leader.

   f.   Have a preoccupation with power, viewing all relations in terms like strong-weak and dominant-submissive, and admire displays of militancy, strength, and punitiveness ("toughness") by respected leaders.

2.   **Cognitive style**

Highly ethnocentric persons:

   a.   Avoid introspection, reflection, speculation, imaginative fantasy.

   b.   Believe in mystical or fantastic external determinants of individual fate, that is, the operation of large, unseen powers controlling one's destiny.

c. Think in rigid categories, believe oversimplified explanations of natural and social events, and dogmatically apply these categories and explanations to ambiguous phenomena (that is, cannot tolerate ambiguity). (Cf Rokeach, 1960.)

3. Child-rearing practices

Highly ethnocentric persons:

a. Experienced in childhood, fathers who were aloof, stern, and punitive.

b. Experienced in childhood a good deal of physical punishment or threat of physical punishment administered by mother or father or both.

4. Family structure

Highly ethnocentric persons:

a. Were raised in families in which husband-wife, parent-child, and sibling relations were organized along hierarchical lines, with idealization of the father as a powerful figure who is also feared.

b. Organize their own families as adults along hierarchical lines, emphasizing the subordination of women and children, and continue to prefer this organization to "modern" egalitarian arrangements.

The above propositions concern individual differences and involve preferences for kinds of structural arrangements rather than the structural arrangements themselves. By making two assumptions: that the relationships can be plausibly applied to *group* differences and that the individual preference for a structural pattern can be plausibly translated into the actual presence of that pattern in a group, we can recast the propositions into a form that is cross-culturally testable at the group level. The following propositions result from such a reformulation.

9.4.0 *The more ethnocentric the society:*
9.4.1 *The more authoritarian in family (or domestic group) structure, community structure, supracommunity structure* (that is, the greater the command power of leaders, the more total is loyalty, deference, and obedience to them).
9.4.2 *The more severe the sanctions against those who defy authority or violate cultural prohibitions and taboos of any kind.*
9.4.3 *The more persons in it tend to believe that deviance is widespread and anarchy an imminent possibility if autocratic leaders are absent.*

9.4.4   *The more fragile is integration at the societal level* (as evidenced by outbreaks of internecine warfare).

9.4.5   *The more persons in it indulge in malicious gossip and witchcraft and sorcery accusations against each other*, that is, against those of the same status as themselves.

9.4.6   *The more cultural approval for the leader who is punitive, frightening, possessed of great power* (physical, military, or supernatural).

9.4.7   *The less are its members willing to examine motives for the behavior of themselves or others or to speculate about other questions of causation.*

9.4.8   *The more its culture involves belief in supernatural powers controlling individual fate rather than mastery by the individual himself over his environment.*

9.4.9   *The fewer the cultural categories for natural and social events*, the more rigid adherence to previously held categories in the face of novel facts or situations, and the greater the reluctance of informants to admit that anything is indeterminate, unknowable, or complicated.

9.4.10   *The more punitive are fathers* (or other primary male authority figures) *to their preadolescent sons, and the more are sons afraid of their fathers.*

9.4.11   *The greater the emphasis on obedience to authority as a prime value to be inculcated in children.*

9.4.12   *The greater the reliance on physical punishment in child-training practices.*

9.4.13   *The greater the emphasis on subordination of wives to husbands, children to parents, junior siblings to senior siblings, in family groups.*

9.4.14   *The greater the emphasis on the subordination of women in the society and the greater the hostility to male homosexuals or any male manifesting behavior labeled as effeminate.*

9.5   Compensatory Masculinity.   Cross-cultural studies of crimes of violence from a psychoanalytic perspective produce propositions relevant to the aggressive aspect of ethnocentrism. Bacon, Barry, and Child (1963) present the basic position succinctly:

"In our society crime occurs mostly in men, and we have no reason to doubt that this sex difference characterizes most societies. Several writers have called attention to the sex role identification of males as especially pertinent to the development of delinquency in our society. It is assumed that the very young boy tends to identify with his mother rather than his father because of his almost exclusive contact with his mother. Later in his development he becomes aware of expectations that he behave in a masculine way and as a result his behavior tends to be marked by a compulsive masculinity which is really a defense against feminine identification" (Bacon, Child, and Barry, 1963, pp. 292-293).

"The hypothesis that crime is in part a defense against initial feminine identification would lead to the expectation that all factors which tend to produce strong identification with the mother and failure of early identification with the father would be positively correlated with the frequency of crime in the adult population" (Bacon, Child, and Barry, 1963, p. 293).

The assumption here is that crime (in effect, theft and crimes of violence) is universally perceived as an exaggeration of masculine aggressiveness and, therefore, universally available as an outlet for those men who need to prove their masculinity. In their cross-cultural study, Bacon, Barry, and Child include theft and personal crime, the latter defined by "intent to injure or kill a person; assault, rape, suicide, sorcery intended to make another ill, murder, making false accusations, etc. . . ." (1963, p. 292). In a sample of 48 societies, they found a correlation of +.46 between theft and personal crime but that these two types of crime have different correlates among factors of child training, socioeconomic variation, and cultural attitudes. Theft is correlated negatively with childhood indulgence and positively with socialization anxiety (the amount of punishment administered to children for failing to perform a particular form of behavior in the areas of responsibility, self-reliance, achievement, and obedience). The authors interpret this as evidence for the view that a high frequency of theft results, in part, from a love-deprived childhood, which leads to "symbolic gratification of an infantile demand for unconditional indulgence irrespective of other people's rights or interests" (Bacon, Child and Barry, 1963, p. 296). The correlates of personal crime are the mother-child household, mother-child sleeping arrangements, dependence socialization anxiety, and perception of the environment as hostile in folktales. This suggests to the authors:

". . . that the conditions in childhood leading to a high frequency of personal crime among adults are as follows: a mother-child household with inadequate opportunity in early life for identification with the father, mother-child sleeping arrangements which tend to foster a strong dependent relationship between the child and the mother, subsequent socialization with respect to independence training which tends to be abrupt, punitive, and productive of emotional disturbance in the child. . . . We would predict that this pattern of child training factors would tend to produce in the child persistent attitudes of rivalry, distrust and hostility, which would probably continue into adult life" (Bacon, Child, and Barry, 1963, p. 298).

They point out that some of their childhood antecendents for personal crime are the same as those of Whiting, Kluckhohn, and Anthony (1958) for male initiation rites at puberty, which were interpreted in the earlier study as attempts to control the disruptive behavior of adolescent boys who might compensate for an early closeness to mother by delinquent activity. Another convergence is with Whiting's (1959) study showing sorcery correlated with mother-child household and mother-child sleeping arrangements. Bacon, Barry, and Child remark that sorcery falls within their definition of personal crime and would be expected on theoretical grounds to have the same antecedents. Although Whiting's prediction, based on the Freudian concept of paranoia, that severe sex socialization would also be correlated, works for sorcery but not for personal crime, it does not appear essential as support for the paranoia hypothesis. In psychoanalytic theory, paranoia is a defensive position in which homosexual wishes are projected onto outside objects and transformed from love to hatred and fear. The authors speculate that severe treatment of the boy's intimate relation with his mother in dependency training would affect his sexual feelings in a broad sense. Thus there might be two converging paths between sex identity conflict and personal crime — one through the need for a boy to prove himself manly in an exaggerated way, and another through his paranoid suspicion that the world is full of enemies out to get him and he must strike at them first. Initiation ceremonies could be seen either as providing the boy with a culturally valued masculine defense, as Burton and Whiting (1961) argue, or as an attempt to control his defensive aggressiveness; perhaps it would be more plausible to view them as trying to direct the defensive masculinity of the boy into culturally approved channels of adult male aggressiveness such as warfare, feuding, and litigation.

Beatrice Whiting (1965) provides additional support for the Bacon, Child, and Barry findings from the *Six Cultures Study of Socialization*. Her basic hypothesis, however, is not identical to theirs; it posits a sex identity conflict leading to crimes of violence only where the relative absence of the father (or low salience of the father in the infant's perception) during infancy is followed by the child's entry into a world conspicuously dominated by males. Without male dominance, there is no need for the boy to defend himself against his feminine identity by exaggerated masculinity; in such societies it is permissible for him to express the feminine side, as in the custom of couvade (see Burton and Whiting, 1961). B. Whiting states:

"It would seem as if there were a never-ending circle. The separation of the sexes leads to a conflict of identity in the boy children, to unconscious fear of being feminine, which leads to "protest masculinity," exaggeration of the difference between man and woman, antagonism against and fear of women, male solidarity, and hence to isolation of women and very young children" (1965, p. 137).

She goes on to derive from this analysis four hypotheses about internal social control:

"1. I would predict that in those societies whose social structure engenders sex-identity conflict and 'protest masculinity' there will be more forms of violence that are considered lawful by the society than in societies that do not engender such conflict.

"2. There will be more conflict in the resolution of trouble cases in these societies because it will be considered unmanly to admit guilt and, hence,

"3. There will be more formalized legal codes and procedures and more litigation than in societies of equal size and integration that do not engender such conflict; and finally

"4. Punishment for what the society considers deviant behavior will be more severe in these societies and will be characterized by desire for revenge" (1965, p. 137).

This entire line of analysis is much more relevant to ethnocentrism than it might seem to be. Warfare between groups has most of the characteristics attributed to internal physical violence: it is aggressive, it is "masculine" in the extreme, it is conducted primarily by young men. Thus the hypotheses predicting internal violence might as well be predicting intergroup warfare. John Whiting (personal communication) has suggested that warfare as a form of "protest masculinity" should place great emphasis on the accumulation of visible, noneconomic symbols of success: the taking of trophies, ritual cannibalism, and headhunting. This would help distinguish it from the warfare that lacks that motivational source, where the emphasis might be on territorial conquest or economic plunder, or defense. The following field report from a missionary observer of the Asmat in New Guinea illustrates what Whiting has in mind:

"Headhunting is required for the bodily development of young men and for their sexual maturation. The Asmat is inclined to consider that things having a similarity in shape or otherwise (are) related . . . The decapitated head of a victim is laid between the out-spread legs of the initiate, almost touching the genitals of the boy who is about to mature sexually. I have repeatedly been told that after this ceremony the boys grow very fast . . . (As) the human head is associated with fruit, the Asmat expect that the germinative power of the head (fruit) will be transferred to the boy's genitals by the ritual of placing it between his legs, and thus that it will enable him to reproduce" (Zegwaard, 1959, p. 1039).

". . . In Asmat society all prestige, and therefore all authority, is ultimately derived from achievements in war. It is impossible to be a man of social standing without having captured a few heads. A bunch of skulls at the door post is a measure of status" (Zegwaard, 1959, p. 1040).

". . . An Asmat can marry without having acquired a single head, even without initiation, but he will be constantly reminded of his nothingness. His opinion will not be asked in the bachelor's house; his own wife will pay little attention to him . . . He is not considered a real man; he belongs to the category of women and children . . . As a result, he may work himself into a frenzy and go out and kill. Then he can look eye to eye with the other men and has the admiration of the women and children, for he has proven that he too has a soul . . . There is also a vague relationship between headhunting and sexual intercourse, which seems to follow from the manner in which headhunting contributes to manliness. Mention has been made of the cry of the headhunters at the beginning of the attack: "I am your husband from Sijuru." It seems to me that the enemy is called woman for more than one reason. But undoubtedly, headhunting is drawn into the sexual sphere. There is a story telling how some men were decapitated and how their heads were miraculously restored, but this was a secret the women were not to know. When the secret was given away by a child, the men were unmanned and transformed into dolphins (which have a hole in the nape of the neck and a skull that shows a striking resemblance to the human skull)" (Zegwaard, 1959, p. 1041).

The "protest masculinity" hypothesis may have even broader application to the phenomena of intergroup conflict. The cross-cultural formulations of the Whitings and Bacon, Child, and Barry are derived mainly from observations of delinquent youths in American society. These delinquents form themselves into gangs based on territorial boundaries, and the gang is responsible for upholding standards of aggressive masculinity. Much of the aggressiveness of delinquent gangs is directed toward other gangs, with a pattern of intergroup provocation and vengeance providing a major avenue for the display of masculine courage, strategic skill, fighting ability, and strength. The resemblances to feuding in stateless societies are many and striking. There, too, young men and adolescent males from a given territory form fighting groups and engage in intermittent conflict with other groups. Each group tries to prove itself more manly than those surrounding it, by tolerating no breach of its territory, property, or women without fierce retaliation designed to hurt and frighten the enemy rather than to conquer them. At the same time, each group plays a game of provocation in which the group or an individual member demonstrates masculine valor by raiding, trespassing, or abducting women in another group's territory. The conflict pattern seems more a semi-institutionalized game played for the benefit of the young men than a realistic assertion and protection of the interests of the group as a whole. Although it could be both, it is significant that the elders sometimes try to restrain the warriors (with varying degrees of success). Among both the American juvenile gangs and the feuding groups in stateless societies, intergroup alliances are formed that appear (impressionistically) to follow principles that may operate in international relations as well. One might speculate further that it is protest masculinity, with its heightened group narcissism, its hypersensitive, proud, prestige-conscious belligerence, that lies behind the ethnocentrism syndrome in its most extreme and irrational forms, not only in fighting gangs and feuding warriors but in the contemporary nationalistic leadership of competing states.

The following propositions can be generated from these studies of compensatory masculinity and related thinking:

9.5.0   *Societies in which father-infant contacts are reduced to a minimum because of customs maintaining a high degree of social distance between men and women* (as in polygynous families with separate mother-child households or the seclusion of women), *and in which men are dominant in social life* (as indexed indirectly by patrilocality-patrilineal inheritance and more directly by reported patterns of sex role behavior), *will, by contrast with societies in which father-infant contact is greater or male dominance less pronounced, show the following characteristics:*

9.5.1   *A higher frequency of internal violence.*

9.5.2   *A higher frequency of sorcery.*

9.5.3   *More legitimized forms of violence.*

9.5.4   *More overt hostility in litigation and the settlement of disputes.*

9.5.5   *More formalized legal codes and procedures.*

9.5.6   *More litigation* (ceteris paribus).

9.5.7   *More severe punishment for deviant behavior.*

9.5.8   *More emphasis on revenge in the punishment of deviant behavior.*

9.5.9   *In the absence of centralized political organization, a higher frequency of feuding among segments of the ethnic community; with political centralization, a higher frequency of inter-ethnic warfare.*

9.5.10   *A greater tendency to use as incentives for warriors the accumulation of visible, non-economic symbols of success* (trophies, scalps, enemy heads) *or the public practice of ritual cannibalism.*

9.5.11   *A greater tendency to view surrounding groups as hostile and strong.*

9.5.12   *A greater tendency to boast of ingroup superiority and maintain a jealous and hypersensitive attitude concerning territorial and other prerogataves of the ingroup vis a vis. outgroups.*

9.5.13   *As a consequence, a greater tendency to maintain a strongly defensive, quick-to-retaliate position vis a vis. outgroups.*

9.5.14   *A greater desire to humiliate enemies in warfare and feuding by showing them to be weaklings and cowards.*

9.5.15   *A greater emphasis on the continued display of courage verging on recklessness in military leadership.*

Chapter 10

PERCEPTION OF OUTGROUP ATTRIBUTES

Where customs or social roles differ between groups these differences tend to become reflected in the mutual stereotypes that groups hold for each other. This lawful process involves social and psychological principles not covered in our major theories of prejudice and intergroup conflict. This chapter approaches these principles in two ways: in the initial sections (10.1 to 10.3), they are inductively developed from ethnographic experience. In the last section (10.4) these same propositions are derived from technical aspects of psychological theory. Although this redundancy goes beyond the immediate needs of this propositional inventory, and involves details of psychological theory that are far removed from the level of discourse of other chapters, it is retained as an illustration of the potential for integration among social-science theories.

10.1.   Stereotypes Concomitant with Ethnic Differentiation in Socioeconomic Roles.   There is a qualitative difference between the ethnic stereotypes of each other held by ethnic groups that are integrated within a single economic and political order and the stereotypes of groups that are not only territorially discrete but also politically and economically autonomous. When ethnically heterogeneous groups that were autonomous become parts of a national (and international) economy and polity, their group stereotypes tend to become polarized along three dimensions: (1) urbanism, (2) occupation, and (3) political-technological dominance.

In the rural-urban polarity, the image of the rural group held by the urban ones is that of the "country bumpkin," unsophisticated, guileless, confused, and ill at ease when he comes to town. The urban groups are seen, in turn, as knowledgeable, mannered ("urbane"), avaricious, and as using their sophistication to take advantage of the countryman. In terms of process in the non-Western world, as Redfield (1953) discussed it, the development of this type of imagery is the cognitive counterpart and result of the transformation of a folk culture into a peasant culture. The once-autonomous tribesmen with their highly distinctive ways of life are increasingly evaluated in terms of their degree of urbanity, with the more conservative groups coming to be seen as backward bumpkins rather than as simply diverse.

A polarity emerging when there is even a moderate degree of occupational differentiation and stratification involves the distinction between manual and nonmanual occupations; there is some overlap in stereotype content with the rural-urban dichotomy but the images are not identical. The manual laborer is seen as strong but stupid, pleasure-loving, improvident — a childlike giant. Servility may also be part of the image. The trader or businessman is seen as grasping, haughty, cunning, exclusive, and domineering. Where the economy is expanding and upward mobility is possible, and where bureaucratic and technical occupations have developed, the image of the ambitious, hard-driving, industrious, aggressive person is likely to emerge as characteristic of those who are successful in achieving bureaucratic and technical positions.

The dimension of political-technological dominance involves an advanced-backward polarity growing out of colonialism and the distinction between the industrial nations of great military strength and the nonindustrial, militarily weak nations. The stereotype of the person from an advanced nation (in an underdeveloped area) endows him with omnipotence — through his manipulation of technology and political influence — and unlimited wealth. His image of the indigenous people combines elements of the stereotypes of rural persons and manual laborers, with some laziness and perverse conservatism added.

The rural-urban and occupational polarities are attitudinal products of a specialized division of labor which is rare (although not absent) among folk societies in their traditional form. When several of these societies, having been more or less hostile to one another in the past, are pacified and encompassed by a superordinate authority, the stage is set for their entry into a single economic system, involving what Durkheim (1947) referred to as "organic solidarity." Whatever their interaction in the past, they begin to interact increasingly as peasants and townsmen, employers and employees, traders and consumers, and civil servants and applicants. If any of these categories should happen to coincide with the "primordial ties" discussed by Shils (1957) and Geertz (1963) (that is, groups defined by race, language, descent, and religion), creating an equivalence between economic transaction and ethnic interaction, then content derived from their respective roles in the new division of labor permeates the images that the groups have of each other. Thus Ladino-Indian relations in Chiapas, as described by Colby and Van den Berghe (1961), are intensely colored by the rural-urban and occupational differences that correspond with cultural differences, and the stereotypes involved appear similar to the ones generated by these distinctions anywhere in the world. Even where ethnic groups and economic roles are not congruent, urbanism creates new modes of evaluating persons which may become more important than ethnicity. In Kenya and Tanzania, an area of folk societies until quite recently, the Swahili word, *shenzi*, meaning wild or uncivilized, has become widespread as a concept to denote the crudities of rural people lacking in urban sophistication; "bush" is the equivalent in West African pidgin and is also widely used to evaluate individuals and groups. Also in West Africa, the influx of persons from particular ethnic groups into technical, bureaucratic, and entrepreneurial occupations has given rise to the image of the "pushful" Ibo in Nigeria (for example, LeVine, 1966a), the ambitious and aggressive Ewe (Ghana) and Bamileke (Cameroun). The Kikuyu are similarly stereotyped in Kenya, where British travelers' accounts mention their reputation as the "Jews of East Africa." In fact, the stereotype of the Jew in Europe appears to recur for ethnic groups specializing in trade anywhere: the Indians in East Africa, the Chinese in Southeast Asia, the Syrians in the Middle East, the Arabs in Ethiopia, and the Lebanese in West Africa.

We would go so far as to assert that these intrasocietal ethnic stereotypes are not only recurrent but universal concomitants of a certain degree of socio-economic complexity and that they stem from the type of social perception occasioned by institutionalized role relations between ethnic groups within a social system characterized by this complexity. Institutionalized role relations constitute the most repeated and socially reinforced context for interaction and observation between groups varying in degree of urbanization and occupation. This context acts to *sensitize* persons to the role-relevant attributes of those groups, thus limiting the basis for stereotype content. This makes it possible to predict the stereotyped images that will develop where there are ethnic groups occupying particular positions in the socioeconomic system.

In line with this reasoning, we would argue that much of the content of the images held by white Christian Americans of Negroes and Jews is predictable simply from the facts that the Negroes are predominantly manual workers of immediately rural origins and that Jews are urban people in nonmanual occupations. Other physical and cultural characteristics (for example, dark skin, slave background, and jazz for the the Negroes; unique religion, physiognomy, and political activity for the Jews) heighten their visibility as distinctive objects to whom these general stereotypes may be attached as well as adding some special glosses to the image content. Nevertheless, the stereotypes of them resemble in broad outline the stereotypes of groups occupying similar positions in a complex social structure wherever such structures are found.

Crucial to this argument is the notion that the stereotypes resulting from institutionalized role relations have a certain "social validity." The rural person, new to the city, *is* lacking in relevant knowledge and is more gullible than urbanites. The latter *are* more sophisticated in the hard and impersonal ways of the city and are, at least, in a position to mislead, cheat, and otherwise take advantage of the peasant. The same type of validity holds true for the usual comparisons based on occupational differences. However, the context established by these role relations preselects a narrow sample of behavior for social participants to observe. The stereotypes they form on the basis of this observation represents an accentuation of the characteristics, that is, a generalization of the role-relevant attributes from the context in which the behavior was observed to all other contexts. Since the role relations set not only the most frequent opportunities for observation but also the most frequent opportunities for interaction, the stereotypes are likely to lead to socially adaptive, appropriate behaviors a large proportion of the time. A smaller proportion of the time they will be invalid and lead to inappropriate behaviors.

A hypothetical example is provided by a white Southerner, whose contacts with Negroes may be restricted to those who are servants and unskilled laborers. On the basis of these restricted observations, he forms a generalized image of Negroes that is similar to images of servants and unskilled laborers everywhere. In the life of this Southerner, his stereotype may be an adequate guide to behavior in nine out of ten contacts he has with Negroes. The tenth contact, where the stereotype is inadequate, can occur in two situations: (1) where he meets a Negro business or professional man of considerable urbanity and education, and (2) where he is called on to make a judgment concerning a Negro servant or laborer in one of the latter's other roles, for example, a family role. In these situations, which are rare in his life, the stereotypes may lead to inappropriate behavior which we would consider biased. The Southerner has been perceptually sensitized by the most familiar context of his interaction with and observation of Negroes to their role-relevant attributes, and this sensitization increases his tendencies to view Negroes as having these attributes in other role contexts where they do not necessarily have them. Thus the role context of group interaction within a social system is a powerful determinant of group stereotype content.

The phenomenon we have been discussing may be referred to as socially structured bias in intergroup perception. It may be conceptualized in terms of the following causal chain: superordinate socioeconomic system embracing several ethnic groups → institutionalized role relations between ethnic groups → perceptual sensitization to role-relevant attributes of out-groups → generalization of role-relevant attributes to unobserved behavior of outgroups. This hypothetical sequence appears to produce a transcultural set of socially structured biases in intergroup perception centered around urbanism, occupation, and political-technological dominance.

To summarize the principles of this section:

10.1.0   *When socioeconomic differentiation is concomitant with ethnic differentiation, ethnic images emerge that reflect the social and economic roles.*
10.1.1   *Rural groups are seen by urban groups as unsophisticated, guileless, gullible, and ignorant.*
10.1.2   *Urban groups are seen by rural groups as sophisticated, urbane, avaricious, dishonest, and immoral.*

10.1.3   *Groups doing manual labor are seen as strong, stupid, pleasure-loving, improvident.*

10.1.4   *Groups occupied as businessmen and traders are seen as grasping, haughty, cunning, and domineering.*

10.1.5   *Groups upwardly mobile in professions and in bureaucratic and technical occupations are seen as ambitious, aggressive, and industrious.*

These stereotypes are given local ethnic content, but are actually most characteristic of social role, recurring wherever ethnic concentration in these social roles occur.

10.2   Stereotypes between Autonomous Independent Groups.   How does the perception of group differences vary from this model when the ethnic groups are autonomous political and economic units with territorial boundaries? In thinking about this, we are immediately faced with the greater variability in stereotyped images possible because of more variability in the contexts and frequency of interaction between these groups. One aspect of autonomy is a degree of self-determination with respect to intergroup relations; another aspect is the possibility of breaches in relations between groups. Without the pressures of a superordinate system forcing them into institutionalized role relations, autonomous ethnic groups may organize themselves vis-a-vis each other in a variety of ways, ranging from no contact at all through military combat and diplomatic negotiations to close contacts in trade, military, and ritual alliances, intermarriage, intermigration, and friendly visiting. Almost by definition such autonomous groups are likely to have more spatial distance between them and less frequent contact (for the average group member) than groups within the same socioeconomic system. With fewer opportunities for mutual observation, the groups are more ambiguous stimuli for each other, and this allows more autistic perception, that is, the development of images that are detached from the actual attributes of the outgroups. These fantasies may represent the wishes or fears of the ingroup and may serve the group's needs for solidarity, dominance, or self-esteem or its members' individual motives. However, the amount of this autism in group perception should vary with the isolation and uninstitutionalized relations of the groups with one another. Thus the comparative study of autonomous groups provides a greater range of variability in factors affecting the perception of group differences than the study of groups coexisting in a superordinate socioeconomic structure. From this point of view, socially structured bias is inevitable in the latter situation and variable in the former, being contingent on structural integration of the groups.

In terms of modern nations, the contrast occurs between the individual's perception of ethnically distinct outgroups in his own nation, about whom he is likely to have partially valid stereotypes formed around the most salient aspects of his own interaction with them and strongly biased by the structural context of this interaction, and his perception of foreigners, about whom he has even less information and is thus freer to devise autistic fantasies. This is not to say that he may not project his own needs into perception of domestic outgroups or have some valid notions about foreigners but, instead, that the average difference in opportunities for observation of domestic and foreign outgroups will lead to more fantastic and varied imagery concerning the latter. It is assumed that the same perceptual-cognitive processes are operating for both but that the stereotype differences are produced by usual differences between the national and international environments as structural fields for intergroup perception. When a group is located at an unusual point in respect to these structural fields, for example, near an international boundary where the group has more regular interaction with "foreigners" than with some ethnic groups in its own nation, then it should not manifest the usual stereotype differences, being perhaps more autistic about the more remote "domestic" outgroups.

Insofar as the argument as presented above is valid, it provides a rationale for concentrating the attention of a wide-ranging comparative study of ethnocentrism which seeks maximal variance in intergroup stereotypes on autonomous ethnic groups rather than ones that are politically and economically amalgamated. Hence the search (in the Cross-Cultural Study of Ethnocentrism) for the imagery of folk societies prior to the advent of national administration and intensive westernization. Apart from this point of research strategy, however, this view of intergroup stereotype formation generates the following hypotheses:

10.2.1   *The greater the spatial proximity between groups, the greater the accuracy of their images of each other.*

10.2.2   *The greater the frequency of contact between groups, the more accurate their images of each other.*

10.2.3   *The greater the degree to which intergroup relations are institutionalized and patterned, the more accurate the intergroup images.*

10.2.4   *Insofar as outgroup images are accurate, they reflect the actual interaction of groups and are generalizations of attributes manifest in that interaction.*

Thus a group will perceive the outgroups that war against it as aggressive, hostile, and as strong or weak. A group will perceive those with whom it engages in trade in terms of dishonesty, gullibility, avarice, cleverness, and the like.

10.2.5   *The greater the degree to which any single activity dominates the interaction between two groups, the more intergroup imagery will be dominated by the attributes of that activity.*

10.2.6   *Interaction-based mutual images may be complementary* (as when sellers view buyers as gullible, while buyers view sellers as dishonest) *or similar* (as when warring groups view each other as hostile and aggressive) *without being contradictory.*

10.2.7   *Those conditions leading to low accuracy of stereotypes will produce images or stereotypes most reflecting projected ingroup motives, wishes, guilts, fears, and frustrations.*

Thus they will be more frequent for distant outgroups or those infrequently visited or observed.

10.3.   A Recurrent North-South Patterning in Intra-Ethnic Stereotypes.
U. R. Ehrenfels (1957; 1961) has called attention to a recurrent north-south polarization of mutual stereotypes between regions within the nation in countries lying north of the equator, citing evidence from 20 nations. The northerners are seen as hardworking and stolid, the southerners are seen as lazy and artistic, and so forth. He explains these differences as due to internal migration in response to climatic preferences, resulting in a polarization at the limits set by barriers to migration, such as national boundaries, language, and physical barriers. Thus by reputation, the southern Irish are more "southern" in personality than the northern French, the southern Germans and French more "southern" than the northern Italians and Spanish. Temperament differences in regions caused by such internal migration would, of course, be enhanced in reputation by environmentally produced differences in behavior and by the absolutistic polar reification of directional differences of small degree. Supporting the environmental factor is the fact that south of the equator (for example, Brazil), the more southerly regions receive the "northerly" reputations. In more detail, the recurrent self-images and stereotypes of the other are as follows:

Northerners see themselves as:

1. Of strong character
2. Powerful militarily
3. Economically vigorous
4. Good organizers
5. Industrious, hard-working
6. Reliable
7. Manly
8. Serious
9. Thrifty

Southerners see themselves as:

1. Eloquent
2. Artistic
3. Socially refined
4. Patient
5. Clever, intelligent
6. Obliging
7. Graceful
8. Amiable
9. Generous

Southerners see Northerners as:

1. Powerful economically
2. Powerful militarily
3. Hard working, energetic
4. Physically strong
5. Slow and heavy
6. Rough and dirty
7. Egocentric
8. Stingy
9. Pessimistic
10. Hard-hearted
11. Serious
12. Stupid
13. Fanatic

Northerners see Southerners as:

1. Economically weak
2. Militarily weak
3. Lazy
4. Weak
5. Quick and fast
6. Amiable and oily
7. Unreliable
8. Wasteful
9. Optimistic
10. Light-hearted
11. Crafty
12. Clever
13. Spineless

10.4   A Learning-Theory approach to the "Grain of Truth" and the Projective Content in Stereotypes.   The following analysis confirms rather than adds to the above presentation, but it derives the same principles from psychological instead of social science considerations. In particular, it is focused on demonstrating the way in which stereotyped images of outgroups can also reflect both the "true" nature of the group described, and "projected" preoccupations of the describing group.

A basic formula of Hull's (Hull, 1952; Spence, 1956) learning theory can be stated as follows (See Figure 10.1):

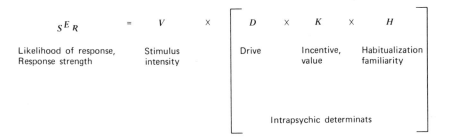

FIGURE 10.1

In relating this formula to perception, to "noticing" stimuli, or to selective awareness, it should be noted first that perception must be indicated and measured by responses. Any law of perception must be a law about a certain kind of response. It will be assumed that the basic law of Hull's shown in Figure 10.7 holds true for these responses. Thus in this diagram, one could add under $_sE_R$ tne phrases "Likelihood of perception of the stimulus," "Probability of the stimulus being noticed," "Apparent strength of the stimulus" (as opposed to stimulus intensity as physically measured, which determines V), "Vividness of the stimulus in conscious awareness," and "Accuracy of perception of the stimulus."

It may help to provide a crude neurological model. The order of events activated by an external stimulus S (the effective strength of which is presented by V) is first neural impulses reaching the brain, which there are mixed with neural impulses from drive stimuli D differing depending on which drives are strongest. These impulses activate neural trains going through the memory or association areas of the brain, and the routings resulting depend on the past association of reward or punishment K with similar stimuli and with the past frequency H with which these pathways to response have been activated.

Somewhere in this neural flow are neural activities that are isomorphic to conscious experience — in this region what we call "seeing" or "perception" has its counterpart. Were the ordinary "naive realism" or "phenomenal absolutism" (Segall, Campbell, and Herskovits, 1966) to be transferred into this picture, it would locate conscious experience prior to the mixing of sensory neural messages with drive and memory, since the ordinary man is totally unaware that his drives and values influence his perception, that his articulation of sense data into meaningful perceptions is dependent on past experience and memory. Although research shows clearly that each individual's motives and his life history contribute to what he sees, although research shows that perception is highly mediated and inferential — phenomenally none of this is present. We all feel we "see" directly things that are incorrigibly there, perceiving totally external objects perfectly known.

To reconcile the known facts of perception with the neurological picture, we must conceptualize the neural activity isomorphic to perception as *subsequent* to the mixing of the neural impulse train with drive and memory. This is also required to represent the contributions of cognitive or gestalt social psychologists (for example, Sherif, 1936; Krech and Crutchfield, 1948; Asch, 1952). If one wanted to put perception in Hull's formula, as *P*, it should be written

$$S \rightarrow V \rightarrow D \times K \times H \rightarrow (P) \rightarrow s\dot{E}_R \rightarrow R$$

or, still better, to represent the epiphenomenal point of view dominant in psychology today:

$$S \rightarrow V \rightarrow D \times K \times H \xrightarrow{\quad \nearrow (P) \quad} sE_R \rightarrow R$$

Certainly the *P* should not be placed right after the *V*. As Murphy (1947, p. 333) says:

"We do not really see with our eyes or hear with our ears. If we all saw with our eyes, we should see pretty much alike; we should differ only so far as retinal structure, eyeball structure, etc. differ. We differ much more widely than this because we see not only with our eyes, but also with our midbrain, our visual and associative centers, and with our systems of incipient behavior, to which almost all visual perceiving leads."

The brevity of the present analysis forces it to be more dogmatic than persuasive, but it will have to suffice. For more extensive argument, see Campbell (1963).

Returning to the basic formula,

$$sE_R = V \times D \times K \times H,$$

it can be seen as summarizing the results of dozens of researches on perceptual thresholds as affected by drive, value, and familiarity. Thus, the more drive-relevant the stimulus, the more associated value it has, and the more familiar one is with responding to it, the more likely it is to be perceived (the lower its perceptual threshold), and the more likely it will be misperceived as being present when it is not actually there. (See Postman, 1953, for a representative summary of this voluminous research.) This literature thus represents the "intra-psychic" or "personality" determinants of the formula, that is, D, K, and H, the contribution of the individual to his perceptions in any give instance.

The intrapsychic D, K, and H determinants may be regarded as "projections" of the personality of the perceiver. Notice first the more obvious case when the V comes not from the stimulus to which K and H are appropriately associated through past learning but, instead, from an actually irrelevant stimulus of sufficient similarity to activate, albeit weakly, some of the same sensory nerves as does the appropriate stimulus. If in this case D, K, and H are collectively very strong, then a "projective" perception (or a "projective" response) may occur even though V is very weak, or the stimulus is very inappropriate. In such cases the perception and the response are very clearly "projections." Aristotle (*On Dreams*, 460B) has very effectively described these effects:

"We are easily deceived respecting the operations of sense-perception when we are excited by emotions, and different persons according to their different emotions; for example, the coward when excited by fear and the amorous person by amorous desire; so that with little resemblance to go upon, the former thinks he sees his foes approaching, the latter that he sees the object of his desire; and the more deeply one is under the influence of the emotion, the less similarity is required to give rise to these illusory impressions."

So much for the clearly projective effects of D, K, and H. Let us now consider two people in the same stimulus field, for whom V is equal. One perceives or responds to the stimulus, and the other does not — the difference here, too, is explicable in terms of D, K, and H — the one with the strongest relevant D's, K's, and H's will be the more likely to perceive the relevant S. Thus perceiving the S is in this case also symptomatic or projective of personality. Consider a man and his wife walking downtown at the end of a long day — both exposed to the same myriad of stimuli; each having the same V's. The man shows exceptional acuity in accurating smelling the odors of a bakery shop two blocks away. The woman spots a pair of shoes across the street and up one block just the color to match her chartreuse suit, the selective perceptions of each accurately diagnosing their motivational dispositions. With external stimulation held constant, the diagnostic value of their valid perceptions is just as great as are those instances in which the husband mistakes the odors of a shoeshine parlor for those of a restaurant (they'd been shopping *so* long), and in which the wife guesses it must have been something else, but she felt sure that she saw such shoes in this window.

The experimental literature on perception shows that the same factors determine both lower perceptual threshold and "covaluant errors," that is, perceiving the stimulus to be present when it is not (for example, Postman, Bruner, and McGinnies, 1948; Postman, 1953; Campbell, 1963, pp. 115–117). Research relating the degree of anti-Semitism with accuracy in judging from photographs which persons are Jewish provides a relevant application. The cumulative result of a dozen studies indicates no difference in accuracy. However, anti-Semites judge more photos to be Jewish than do non-anti-Semites, both when the picture is, in fact, of a Jewish person, and when it is of a Gentile person (Allport and Kramer, 1946; Carter, 1948; Lindzey and Rogolsky, 1950; Elliot and Wittenberg, 1955; Scodel and Austrin, 1957). The diagnostic or projective nature of the response is equal under both circumstances.

Neglected in the discussion thus far — and neglected in the write-ups of the research cited — is the obvious fact that the perception (and the response) is also a function of the V, the stimulus strength. The stronger, more vivid the stimulus, the more apt it is to be perceived, to be noticed, to be selected for attention, and to be responded to. Whenever stimulus strength is varied, this law is confirmed. In the typical threshold study of the Bruner and Postman tradition (see Postman, 1953), V is varied by the *length* of exposure of the stimulus. Longer exposures lead to more frequent and certain perceptions of the stimulus. Although not usually done in this tradition, the result holds up when durations are presented in random order. Brightness of the stimulus (usually projected on a screen) increases frequency and certainty of perception also. Clarity of focus (for example, Wyatt and Campbell, 1951) shows this law, too, if clearer focus is interpreted as stronger V. Usually these effects are the strongest of factors varied, but usually they are tangential to the purposes of the study and are not reported. In the anti-Semitism studies, the non-Jewish photographs can be treated as lower in V for Jewishness than the Jewish faces. In this case, too, more Jewish faces are judged to be Jewish than non-Jewish faces are judged to be Jewish, a stronger effect than the effect of anti-Semitic attitude.

If we take the stereotypes or images that persons or groups have of each other, and regard them as perceptions or sE_R's for this analysis, we see that such stereotypes can at one and the same time reflect both the character of the group being described and, projectively, the character of the group doing the describing or holding the stereotypes. This frees us from either-or analysis of stereotypes in which, when interpreting stereotypes to be symptoms of the preoccupations of the stereotype holder, one implicitly regards the outgroup being stereotyped as a "living inkblot" (for example, Ackerman and Jahoda, 1950) whose characteristics, if any, are independent of the content of the stereotype. In the terms of Zawadski's (1942) analysis, the "well-deserved reputation" theory of prejudiced stereotypes and the "scapegoating" theory can both be appropriate in the same setting.

In many instances, the strength of various stimuli is obvious — in general, the more physical energy in a physical stimulus such as a sound wave or light beam the stronger the *V*. However, closer analysis shows that a still more appropriate statement of stimulus strength is in terms of *relative* physical energy in contrast to previous stimulations or stimuli from other parts of the stimulus field (Helson, 1964; Campbell and Kral, 1958; Krantz and Campbell, 1961). Helson has referred to this as the law of *adaptation level*. The effective stimulus strength depends on its degree of departure from the adaptation level for that stimulus modality established by prior stimulation or other parts of the contemporaneous stimulus field. A stimulus intensity below the adaptation level can be as stimulating as one above. Thus turning the light off in a room can be as striking a stimulus as turning the light on. Thus rats can be conditioned to jump to the turnoff of an otherwise continuous sound as well as to the turnon of a sound interrupting an otherwise continuous silence. Thus the same saline solution can taste salty on one occasion and sweet on another, depending on what saturation the mouth has previously been adapted to.

The upshot of this principle is that the greatest contrasts provide the strongest stimuli. When we consider the perceptions which one group will have of another, this prediction results:

10.4.1   *The greater the real differences between groups on any particular custom, appearance, item of material culture, the more likely that culture trait is to appear in the stereotyped imagery each group has of the other.*

Notice that this implies that attributes of a group which in some inter-group contexts would go totally unnoticed, may become the object of vivid disparaging imagery by other groups in a cultural context in which this stands out. Thus the Luo absence of circumcision is the prime content of vivid stereotyped imagery both for adjacent groups and groups living great distances away in Kenya, Uganda, and Tanzania, while it would go unnoticed on the part of a South American Indian tribe.

This prediction seems obvious when one starts from the anthropological position that groups, cultures, and the like do in fact differ, and asks then the question as to how these differences will be treated in mutual imagery. Sociology also provides an expectation of a "grain of truth" in stereotypes, in descriptions of social class differences, and the tendency for ethnic groups to become concentrated in one social class. Thus across-class ethnic stereotypes should involve the groups within one class accusing those of another class of its class-related traits. For example, popular American stereotypes of Negroes and Mexicans predominately attribute to them lower class attributes. Role specialization within class, as by trade or profession, provide further sociological basis for a "grain of truth" in stereotypes, as we have extensively analyzed above. Still more relevant is the extensive sociological analysis of the effects on personality, aspirations, achievement effort, and moral behavior caused by oppressed minority status, segregation, the lack of access to upward social mobility, and the exclusion from the larger moral community. If minority status has effects, if it produces differences, then these differences would be expected to appear in majority group stereotypes of these minority groups, These stereotypes would have the great unfairness of justifying segregation by "validly" accusing minority group members of having those very traits that segregation had produced. Nonetheless, taken as descriptions (rather than as justifications or causal explanations, as will be discussed below), they would have a "grain of truth."

In contrast to these anthropological and sociological bases for expecting real group differences that would, in some sense, provide "accurate" components for stereotypes, in social and educational psychology a literature and teaching practice has grown up which says that all stereotypes of group differences are false and, implicitly, that all groups are similar. This social-psychological literature was, perhaps, started by the excellent and classic study of Katz and Braly (1933) which showed that college students had stable and elaborate stereotypes of a wide variety of minority and nationality groups. They found no relation between the elaborateness and uniformity of these stereotypes and the amount of contact with the groups in question. For groups actually quite unknown, such as the Turks and the Japanese, there were as vivid stereotypes of as high concensus as there were for more familiar groups such as American Negroes. Other research of the 1930's showed that whites with no personal acquaintances with Negroes held, if anything, more elaborate and disparaging stereotypes of them than did whites who had Negro acquaintances (Minard, 1931; Smith, 1943; Horowitz, 1936). A classic study by La Piere (1936) showed that when checked, the stereotype held in Fresno, California about the local Armenian minority was point-by-point in error. Levinson and Sanford (1944) showed that anti-Semites accused Jews of such contrary traits as sticking to themselves and trying to force themselves into gentile society. (Harding, et. al., 1954, provide an extensive review of the many similar studies.)

Certainly this literature did demonstrate that stereotypes can be completely false and can be held in absence of validating contact with the group in question. But aside from the one La Piere study, there was little or no comparison of the content of stereotypes with the corresponding social statistics and anthropological data. Neglected were comparisons of the group data on intelligence test performance (for example, Klineberg, 1944, pp. 82—96) and the stereotypes about stupidity and shrewdness (relevant even though functional intelligence is recognized as poor evidence of innate intelligence). There was little or no recognition of the fact that predominately lower-class minority groups were being accused of the lower-class morality and the lack of achievement orientation also demonstrated in the sociologist's statistics. This summary is perhaps overdrawn, and certainly Gordon Allport (1954) and Krech and Crutchfield (1948, pp. 171—172) must be exempted, but it is probably an accurate description of most teachings about prejudice and stereotypes in social psychology courses offered in psychology and education departments between 1935 and 1954.

Although descriptively stereotypes may have a grain of truth, the social psychologists were, of course, right that the stereotypes and the larger context of prejudice in which they occurred were fundamentally in error. It is essential to explain in what sense all this can be true.

The first wrongness is in the phenomenal absolutism of the normal ingroup member's imagery of the outgrouper or minority group member. Naively, one assumes without question that the outgroup is as one perceives it, or as the ingroup informs one about it. Awareness that one's own preoccupations have projectively contributed to the content, that fallible communication and knowledge processes are involved, that the image can be totally wrong — all awareness of this kind is lacking. For many a social psychologist, his own overcoming of such an ethnocentric enculturation is a deeply experienced revelation, and one that he wants to communicate. In so doing, the message that stereotypes contain a large portion of error and projection becomes over-compensated into an implicit denial of group differences. The message that stereotypes of groups or images of specific others contain a projective contribution from one's own (or one's ingroup's) personality, either in fabricated content or selective attention to perjorative content, is an unsuspected lesson that every normal undergraduate needs to learn. But it must be taught without denying group differences.

A second wrongness is in the degree of difference perceived, the homogeneity with which either ingroup or outgroup members have the trait in question, and the amount of overlap between the groups on the trait in question. Thus, if in test results (for example, Klineberg, 1944), tested intelligence gives an average IQ of 95 for Negroes and 103 for Jews, to be compared with 100 for the general population, the corresponding stereotype is that all Negroes are dumb, and all Jews are smart. If one asked the average person what percent of all Negroes are brighter than he is, he probably would give an average reply of 0 to 4 percent, rather than the 38 percent to which the 95 IQ figure approximately corresponds.

Such effects correspond to pervasive cognitive processes, noted in perception research as the enhancement of contrast through homogenization of differences within gestalt boundaries and the exaggeration of differences across boundaries. The effect for a group learning situation follows directly (if tediously) from elementary considerations of stimulus generalization in learning theory (Campbell, 1956). In a classroom in which there is an average race difference in examination performance, when students know something of the performance levels of their individual classmates, and when skin color leads to greater generalization (or confusion) within racial groupings than between, the generalization effect predictably leads to the underestimation of the overlap between the two groups (Clarke and Campbell, 1955; Campbell, 1956).

Thus another contribution of learning theory is this law:

10.4.2   *Differences between ingroup and outgroup, if sufficient to be noted, will be exaggerated in the mutual stereotypes each holds of the other.*

It would seem from the standpoint of both perception and learning theory that this effect should hold true for all observers, not just prejudiced ones. Awareness of any such bias is, of course, absent phenomenally.

The third error is one of causal misperception (for example, Heider, 1944; Michotte, 1946) and is the most important although difficult to explicate. It concerns the relationship between the content of the stereotype and the hostility felt toward the outgroup. The naive ingrouper perceives the different characteristics of the outgroup as causing his hostility. He feels that were it not for these despicable traits, the outgroup would be loved. The outgroup's opprobrious characteristics seem to him to fully justify the hostility and rejection he shows toward it. The social scientist from most theoretical points of view sees the opposite causal direction: causally, first is the hostility toward the outgrouper, generated perhaps by real threat, perhaps by displacement, and the like. In the service of this hostility, all possible differences are opportunistically interpretated as despicable, and the most plausibly despicable traits are given most attention.

So flexible is our emotional language that a difference in almost any direction can be anathematized. An outgroup can be hated as too lazy or as too industrious, as too dumb or as too shrewd, as too forward or too reclusive, as too emotional or as too cold, as too generous or too thrifty (Merton, 1957). In southern legislatures in the last 100 years, the alleged intellectual inferiority of Negroes has played an important role. Removing the belief that Negroes are inferior would not, however, remove the hostility, although it would change the content of stereotypes. If the World War I test results showing northern Negroes to be more intelligent than southern whites had been effectively publicized in the South, opportunistic hostility could certainly have created an image of the northern Negro carpetbagger whose opprobrious traits included shrewdness, trickiness, and egg-headed intellectuality. Here again it can be seen that remedial education in race relations focused on denying or disproving stereotypes implicitly accepts the prejudiced ingrouper's causal conception instead of the social scientists', and is undermined where actual group differences are found.

A fourth wrongness in the naive ingrouper's stereotypes of outgroups is likewise an erroneous causal perception, predictable from the principles thereof. This is in the tendency to perceive racial rather than environmental causes for group differences. Perception of causality occurs most readily between stimuli that are spatially and temporally contiguous (Michotte, 1963; Heider, 1944). It centers around the stimuli that are strongest, most vivid, and striking. Again, contrast provides this V strength. To take a domestic American example, the white person in contact with uneducated Negroes might conceivably perceive the lack of education as caused by the environmental background, lack of opportunity, and motivation. But stimuli representing these environmental factors are not present and visible in the immediate situation. In addition, they are multiple, diffuse, and complex. On the other hand, the stimuli of race such as skin color, physiognomy, accent, and name, are visible and vivid. They are also spatially and temporally contiguous to the patent signs of ignorance. Thus the established principles of causal perception strongly favor the perception of race as the cause of the ignorance.

Reverting to our main theme, the preceding analysis predicts:

10.4.3   *There will be latent agreement in the reciprocal stereotypes of two groups.*

These stereotypes can be separated into components: the evaluative (representing the *D, K, H* components, especially the *K*) and the descriptive (representing the *V* component). The mutual stereotypes of self and other can be represented in the matrix shown in Figure 10.2, with the evaluative component indicated:

		Descriptions of	
		Group A	Group B
Descriptions by	Group A	Good	Bad
	Group B	Bad	Good

FIGURE 10.2

With an actual difference added, one might get the responses shown in Figure 10.3 as for the English vis-a-vis the Yankees

Bruner (1956) has described a similar situation in the Dakotas, between the Hidatsa Indians and the local ranchers of European extraction, whom we may call Yankees (see Figure 10.4).

As described by Bruner, the moral requirement of immediate sharing was fully as imperative for the Hidatsa as was the imperative to thrift and providence among

	Descriptions of	
Descriptions by	English	Yankee
English	(Good) Reserved, respect privacy of others	(Bad) Intrusive, forward, pushing
Yankees	(Bad) Snobbish, cold, unfriendly	(Good) Friendly, outgoing, open–hearted

FIGURE 10.3

the Yankees. Both were able to report "accurately" on a genuine cultural difference, and to sincerely judge the outgroup as evil. Mack (1954) reports a similar complementary (if not compl*i*mentary) set of reciprocal stereotypes between the Swedes and Italians of a mill town in the United States. Peabody (1967) has elaborated on this issue.

The above analysis deals with traits on which groups differ. Similar effects can occur for certain traits on which groups are similar, but for which the conditions of observation are such that the behavior on one's own part is

	Descriptions of	
Descriptions by	Hidatsa	Yankees
Hidatsa	(Good) Generous unselfish, share good fortune immediately with relatives and friends	(Bad) Stingy, selfish, hoarders
Yankees	(Bad) Spendthrifty, improvident	(Good) Thrifty provident

FIGURE 10.4

perceived in a different context than is comparable behavior on the part of an outgrouper. This will be particularly true of behavior directed toward the outgroup. Thus to take a historical example, a "defensive" act on the part of the United States, such as arming Turkey, was perceived as a hostile, aggressive, expansionist act by Russia. Bronfenbrenner (1961) and Merton (1957) have especially emphasized these mirror image reversals.

10.4.4   *If most or all groups are, in fact, ethnocentric, then it becomes an "accurate" stereotype to accuse an outgroup of some aspect of ethnocentrism.*

This generates a set of "universal" stereotypes, of which each ingroup might accuse each group, or some outgroup, or the average outgroup.

Self Description	*Stereotype of Outgroup*
1. We have pride, self-respect and revere the traditions of our ancestors.	1. They are egotistical and self-centered. They love themselves more than they love us.
2. We are loyal.	2. They are clannish, exclude others.
3. We are honest and trustworthy among ourselves, but we are not suckers when foreigners try their tricks.	3. They will cheat us if they can. They have no honesty or moral restraint when dealing with us.
4. We are brave and progressive. We stand up for our own rights, defend what is ours, and can't be pushed around or bullied.	4. They are aggressive and expansionistic. They want to get ahead at our expense.
5. We are a peaceful, loving people, hating only our vile enemies	5. They are a hostile people who hate us.
6. We are moral and clean.	6. They are immoral and unclean.

The general principle of this section has been stated:

10.4.1   *The more real contrast between groups on a given trait, the more likely is that trait to appear in the mutual stereotypes each has of the other.*

But a number of other implications of the basic formula $_sE_R = V \times D \times K \times H$ can be stated in agreement with the principles derived in Section 10.2.

10.4.5   *The more opportunities for observation* and
10.4.6   *the longer the exposure to the outgroup, the larger the role of real differences in the stereotypes.*

This occurs through increasing V strength and, hence, its role in determining $_sE_R$.

It implies that

10.4.7   *The nearer outgroups will be more accurately stereotyped.*

10.4.8   *Outgroups with which most interchange of persons and interaction occurs will be most accurately stereotyped.*

To state it in opposite terms:

10.4.9   *The more remote and less well known the outgroup, the more purely projective the content of the stereotype and the less accurate it is.*

An analogous principle recognizes that the content of intergroup interaction provides greatest V strength for those traits invoked in the interaction:

10.4.10   *Those trait differences involved in intergroup interaction will be most strongly represented, and most accurately represented in mutual stereotypes.*

Another important principle is:

10.4.11   *Among trait differences of approximately equal contrast, those which are drive and incentive relevant are most apt to be noticed and represented in stereotyped imagery.*

We assume from other analyses that there is a positive K or incentive for disparaging the outgroup; hence, those stimuli most offering opportunity for this response will be most represented in stereotypes. Thus of all of the innumerable real differences that might be represented in stereotypes, the subset chosen is symptomatic of the intrapsychic determinants, D, K, and H of the ingroup.

We have used D, K, and H rather loosely and collectively as intrapsychic determinants, leaving it to theories like the frustration-aggression-displacement theory to fill them out. It is probably best that it be left at this. H, or familiarity of making this response to this stimulus, has been least well represented at this global usage. For a given individual, it implies that the more familiar he is with making prejudiced statements, the easier such a statement will appear on any given occasion — or the more readily the stereotyped difference will be perceived. This does not provide a very useful prediction at the group level — except some sort of perseveration or inertia to stereotypes:

10.4.12   *Once a stereotype or perception of difference is established, less real difference is required to maintain or reevoke it.*

There is another way in which H and K components may be evoked, through stimulus generalization in another dimension.

10.4.13   *Those traits that have well-established rejection responses associated with them for within-ingroup usage will be most apt to be perceived in outgroup stereotypes.*

Thus if an outgroup shows a behavior for which ingroup members are regularly punished or despised, this behavior is much more apt to be noticed and made a part of the outgroup stereotype than some other trait for which responses are less ingrained. Thus the Gusii ridicule uncircumcized children for their childishness and accuse an older boy still uncircumcized of cowardice. This provides a familiar stimulus-response basis for their outgroup stereotypes of their uncircumcizing Luo neighbors. Similarly, the Gusii emphasis on body and elimination modesty in the training of older children provides a familiar association for stereotypes of both Luo and Kipsigis, since they differ on these factors.

Chapter 11

COGNITIVE CONGRUITY THEORIES[1]

Under this title we group a variety of theories that deal with congruence and disparity among beliefs and affective bonds. They include balance theory (Heider, 1958; Harary, Norman, and Cartwright, 1965; Davis, 1963), orientation system theory (Newcomb, 1961), psychologic (Abelson and Rosenberg, 1958), congruity theory (Osgood and Tannenbaum, 1955), dissonance theory (Festinger, 1957), belief-system theory (Rokeach, 1960), and others. They have much in common, along with subtle differences, and even a partial exposition of them is not possible here. Standard texts provide summaries (Cohen, 1964; Secord and Backman, 1964; Brown, 1964) and more ambitious integrations are available (for example, Abelson, Aronson, McGuire, Newcomb, Rosenberg, and Tannenbaum, 1968; McGuire, 1967). Here we present the theories only in the specific context of derivations from various aspects of them. Direct applications to ethnocentrism and intergroup relations are rare in the literature, but have been explicitly made by Harary (1961), and Rokeach (1960), and by Jaspars, van de Geer, Tajfel, and Johnson (1965). The theory has much more to say about which groups will like each other than about the attributes of ethnocentric ingroups, so we will begin with the former in this chapter.

Similarity and the Liking of Outgroups

Basic to balance theories (for example, Heider, 1958; Newcomb, 1959; 1961; Harary, Norman and Cartwright, 1965; Davis, 1963) is the triad,

where A and B are two actors, valuers, believers (ethnic groups in our setting, persons in Newcomb's analysis of friendship and values, which we parallel at the group level), and where X is some object, value, item of belief, and the like toward

[1] This chapter has been coauthored by Marilynn B. Brewer.

which A and B have evaluative attitudes or identifications. X can be another group (person, actor) in which case its reciprocal valuings can be considered, and this is discussed in the subsequent section on balanced relations. In the present section, X is to be regarded as an item of culture, as a custom, belief, or artifact. Liking between A and B occurs when their valuing of X is similar, that is, when both are positive toward it, or when both are negative toward it. Disliking accompanies dissimilar attitudes toward X. All of such instances of liking and disliking are balanced. In diagram form, they are as follows:

$$A + B \qquad A + B \qquad A - B \qquad A - B$$
$$+ + \qquad\quad - - \qquad\quad + - \qquad\quad - +$$
$$X \qquad\qquad X \qquad\qquad X \qquad\qquad X$$

Other possible relations are imbalanced, unlikely, and unstable:

$$A + B \qquad A + B \qquad A - B \qquad A - B$$
$$- + \qquad\quad + - \qquad\quad + + \qquad\quad - -$$
$$X \qquad\qquad X \qquad\qquad X \qquad\qquad X$$

In the pure balance form of the model, there is no causal asymmetry, the attitude of A toward B being as likely to "cause" his attitude toward X as his attitude toward X to cause his attitude toward B. Attention here focuses on the latter type however. Considering the many X's about which A and B both have attitudes, we can infer net degrees of liking as a product of likings induced by the many covalued X's. The resulting prediction is that, from the point of view of any ingroup:

11.1   *The more similar an outgroup is in customs, values, beliefs, and general culture, the more liked it will be.*

Social distance and friendly commerce may be included among symptoms of liking.

Rokeach (1960, pp. 293–331) has proposed this for intergroup relations, and has tested it for intergroup attitudes among religious bodies in the United States. He finds a strong relationship between dissimilarity and rejection. He further finds that shifts of church membership, choice of denomination, and of college, and frequency of interfaith marriages are directly related to similarity. In subsequent research he has sustained the claim that even in Negro-White relationships in the United States, it is belief-disparity rather than skin color or biological race that is the target of the hostility (for example, Rokeach and Mezei, 1966; Stein, Hardyck and Smith, 1965). In a study of the attitudes of Dutch children, Jaspers, van de Geer, Tajfel, and Johnson (1965) found the perceived similarity of another nation to The Netherlands to be strongly related to liking for that country. While perceived similarity rather than more independently assessed similarity was at issue, the same balance principle is involved.

In our own research arena, interethnic attitudes, strong confirmation is also already present. Mitchell (1956) studied social distance among workers from 20 groups in Zambia. Of several principles emerging, cultural similarity (matrilineal versus patrilineal organization) was the strongest factor, and Brewer (1968) confirmed this by using a more general index of intergroup similarity. We have done a secondary analysis of a study by Gordon Wilson (1961) that provides further evidence. He surveyed the attitudes of 12 ethnic areas of Kenya toward each other. Three pairs of questions have been selected for this purpose because they are presented in both positive and negative form: "Which of the above tribal groups do you feel will present the greatest (least) problem to internal security after independence?" "Which of the above tribal groups do you feel are the most friendly (unfriendly) people?" "If you were forced to leave your own tribal group for some reason, among which of the above tribal groups would you most (least) like to live, other than your own?" In each ethnic area there were interviewed 100 persons, 93 percent male, predominantly urban and small town, only 15 percent with no education, and only 7 percent self-employed in agriculture. As the main pooled index of attitude, the average percent giving the favorable response (Wilson, 1961, Tables 8B, 9A, 10A) less the average percent giving the unfavorable response (Tables 8A, 9B, 10B) has been used. These values are presented in Table 11.1.

Groups have been classified in three degrees of similarity. Thus for the Kikuyu, the Meru and Embu were judged similar, all other Bantu groups (Abaluhya, Coast, Kamba, Kisii, Taita) were judged as intermediate, and the Luo, Masai, Kalenjin, and Somali were judged as dissimilar. For the Luo and Somali, all other groups were classified as dissimilar, and they thus do not contribute as judges to this analysis. The Masai and Kalenjin were judged of intermediate similarity to each other, with no similar groups present for either. Among the other Bantu groups there were two similarity pairs: Coast and Taita, and Kisii and Abaluhya. From the viewpoint of the Kamba, the Meru, Embu, and Kikuyu were judged similar, other Bantu groups were judged intermediate, and the non-Bantu groups were judged dissimilar. Linguistic grounds and belief in common origin were primary bases of classification, other cultural factors supporting them.

Figure 11.1 portrays the outcome, with results that dramatically support the principal of liking and similarity. The "all outgroups" line is an average of averages. For each ingroup, the average percent of mentions for outgroups of each degree of similarity has been computed. These three values have then been averaged for the eight ingroups having outgroups of all three levels of similarity. The result is a strikingly consistent effect of similarity. Of the 24 opportunities for reversal (8 of $S < I$, 8 of $S < D$, 8 of $I < D$) only 1 occurs, (an $I < D$). There are two other comparisons available, $I > D$ for Masai and Kalenjin, and both of them are confirmatory.

Table 11.1 Net Favorability in Wilson's 1961 Survey of Interethnic Attitudes in Kenya (Adjacency is indicated by *, one degree removal by +)

Voting by						Groups Chosen						
	Kikuyu	Kamba	Meru	Embu	Luo	Kisii	Abaluhya	Kalenjin	Masai	Taita	Coast	Somali
Kikuyu		− 2*	9*	15*	8	3	− 8	−25+	−27*	15+	−10	−13+
Kamba	32*		2*	3*	2	0	− 2	− 6	−42*	11*	2+	−18+
Meru	28*	12*		22*	0	0	− 1	−13	−30*	22+	−16	−32+
Embu	34*	1*	21*		−	−	−	−13	−22*	28+	−13	−36+
Luo	18	3	0	0		10*	5*	−16*	−47+	14	2	− 9
Kisii	− 8	− 4	− 4	− 2	− 6*		28+	− 6*	−20*	6	2	− 4
Abaluhya	−69	4	1	0	−13*	9+		13*	− 1+	1	10	1
Kalenjin	−62+	0	− 1	− 1	−14*	2*	39*		2*	0	10	0
Masai	−18*	− 3*	0*	0*	− 8+	0*	10+	7*		3*	10+	− 7+
Taita	−37*	1*	− 1+	− 1+	−27	0	5	8	− 7*		32*	0+
Coast	−45	7+	0	0	−30	0	10	7	− 8+	40*		− 1*
Somali	−12+	− 2+	5+	5+	−19	− 1	12	2	−10+	5+	21*	

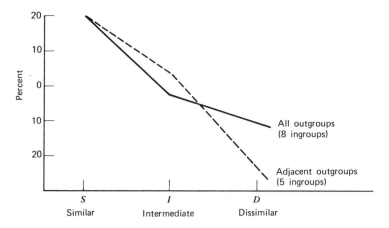

FIGURE 11.1. Average net favorability to outgroups as a function of cultural similarity (secondary analysis of data from Wilson, 1961).

Another prime interest in the analysis was the effect of proximity. Although degree of proximity produces no clear-cut trends when similarity is controlled, there is a special interest in adjacent outgroups, for which interaction should have made attitudes more stable. For five ingroups, all three levels of similarity were available in the adjacent outgroups, and Figure 11.1 presents these averages too, again confirming the principle.

A number of weaknesses in this analysis could obscure relationships or create spurious ones. Most conspicuous is the great variability in number of mentions received by various outgroups, due to fame, visibility, or generally shared beliefs. Thus on the first question the number of mentions received from the sum of all other tribes varies from zero to 454 (for the Kikuyu). In an effort to correct this, an analysis was done in terms of votes received, rather than votes given, so that in any given direct comparison, all attitudes were being expressed about the same outgroup. This analysis used columns from Table 11.1 whereas the net favorability analysis used rows.

The received votes analysis confirms, although with less clarity, the similarity-liking correlation, shown in Table 11.2, which also reports on the number of instances of inequalities in a given direction (including instances from ingroups having incomplete sets of outgroups). For adjacent outgroups, both analyses support a direct relationship. For the comparison between intermediate and dissimilar, the all groups analysis by received votes finds no difference, actually a slight reverse trend. For this analysis there is a trend toward an interaction between adjacency and similarity: remote groups are better liked if they are dissimilar. Probably this is a product of the then current political alliances, as discussed below, which produced favorable images of the Luo and Kalenjin (dissimilar to most judges) on the part of remote groups that would not otherwise have known of them at all.

Table 11.2   Similarity and Favorable Attitudes: Three Indexes

Index		Average Values			Inequalities		
		Similar	Intermediate	Dissimilar	$S>I$	$S>D$	$I>D$
Net favorable:	All	23	− 1	−10	$\frac{8}{8}$	$\frac{8}{8}$	$\frac{9}{10}$
Net favorable:	Adjacent	22	5	−26	$\frac{5}{5}$	$\frac{6}{6}$	$\frac{6}{7}$
Received votes:	All	22	− 1	0	$\frac{8}{8}$	$\frac{8}{8}$	$\frac{7}{10}$
Received votes:	Adjacent	22	10	− 4	$\frac{4}{5}$	$\frac{6}{6}$	$\frac{7}{7}$

Another potential weakness, although not one that we believe invalidates the clear-cut finding, is the recurrence of the same target group in the same location for a number of ingroups. Thus in the adjacent outgroups analyses, for those five ingroups having all three levels of similarity among adjacents, the dissimilar outgroup is always the Masai, due to the Masai's great geographical dispersion. The Masai, moreover, are generally disliked. This may be because they are so strikingly dissimilar, in which case no artifact is involved. But it might be for an irrelevant reason, here multiply represented. Certainly for statistical purposes there is a great reduction in effective degrees of freedom through this repetition. Because of the ambiguity on these points, we have not attempted the probability statements to which the tallies of inequalities point.

As to the political party alliances current at that time, they, of course, may be regarded as products of attitudes, but it is also clear to any Kenya expert looking at Table 11.1 that attitudes have been caused by them too. At this time, the KANU party was headed by the Kikuyu-Luo alliance, unpredictable on similarity grounds, but showing up in favorable attitudes. The competing KADU alliance was formed by smaller tribes out of fear of domination by the two largest, and it, too, cut across similarity lines, allying, in its leadership, the Bantu Abaluhya and Coast with the Nilo-Hamitic Kalenjin and Masai. Of the high similarity relations, only the Kisii (belatedly KANU) and Abaluhya fall into separate camps. In general, the effect of political alliance works more against the similarity-liking hypothesis than for it, accounting for the bulk of the exceptions.

Balanced Patterns of Intergroup Relations

One use of balance theory, particularly as developed in the signed graph tradition (for example, Harary, Norman, and Cartwright, 1965; Flament, 1963; Davis, 1963; 1967) is to predict patterns of interpoint relationships where the relationship can take the values of positive (for example, liking) negative (for example, disliking) and absent. Although such theory is usually applied to persons as points, it can readily be applied to relationships among groups, as Harary (1961) has done in a model prediction of international attitudes in the Middle East. The presentation here will be essentially nonmathematical, and depends heavily on Davis (1963).

The basic prediction is that:

11.2   *Regional patterns of intergroup relations will be "balanced."*

The concept of balance is in its mathematical statement, a complex one, that we shall not give fully but will, instead, illustrate. Here are some commonsense statements about triads:

11.2.1   *An ally of an ally will be an ally.*
11.2.2   *An enemy of an ally will be an enemy.*
11.2.3   *An ally of an enemy will be an enemy.*
11.2.4   *An enemy of an enemy will be an ally.*

To give further relevance to the problems this abstract algebra attempts to cover, we can quote from an amazing chapter on "Political Geometry" in Zimmer's survey of the philosophy of ancient India.

"The principal Hindu formula for the arrangement of foreign alliances and coalitions is based on a pattern of concentric rings of natural enemies and allies. Each king is to regard his own realm as located at the center of a kind of target, surrounded by "rings" (*mandalas*) which represent, alternately, his natural enemies and his natural allies. The enemies are represented by the first surrounding ring; these are his immediate neighbors, all alert to pounce. The second ring then is that of his natural friends, i.e., the kings just to the rear of his neighbors, who threaten them in turn through the very fact of being neighbors. Then beyond is a ring of remoter danger, interesting primarily as supplying reinforcement to the enemies directly at hand. Furthermore, within each ring are subdivisions signifying mutual natural animosities; for since each kingdom has its own *mandala*, an exceedingly complicated set of stresses and cross-stresses must be understood to exist. Such a plan of mutual encirclement is to be cast, carefully weighed, and then used as a basis for action. It delineates and brings into manifestation a certain balance and tension of natural powers, as well as touching off periodic, terrific outbursts of widely spreading conflict. Taken for granted as a universal social principle is the propensity of neighbors to be unfriendly, jealous, and aggressive, each biding his hour of surprise and treacherous assault. (The science of the *mandala*, 'the circle of states,' is discussed in Kautiliya Arthasastra 7.)" (Zimmer, 1951, pp. 114–115).

In this, an assumption that the relations of immediate neighbors are hostile is combined with balance considerations. They do not combine readily, as the middle sentences indicate, and under usual circumstances, the alternative rings of enemies and allies will not be balanced.

If we take from the mandala theory an ingroup, one of its immediate neighbors, and the group on the far side of that neighbor, balance holds, for the enemy's enemy is an ally and the ally's enemy is an enemy. But this balance does not hold for an ingroup and two adjacent immediate outgroups. For them, if the mandala ring is to hold for each in turn, the two outgroups being adjacent to each other would be enemies, and an unbalanced all negative triad would result, for the enemy's enemy would be an enemy.

The requirement for balance in a triangle (or any other circle) is that the product of the signs be positive.

Thus   o + o   and   o + o
                        + +   − −
                          o   o

are balanced, while   o − o   and   o − o
                            − −   + +
                              o   o

are unbalanced.

For larger sets of points, the most usable statement of balance for our situation is that all triangles be balanced. (Other statements require a complete set of points, whereas for any regional survey of intergroup relations, unrecorded relations will extend on all edges.)

There is, perhaps, only one regular pattern that provides both balance and mandala circles. This is one in which each ingroup has only four adjacent outgroups, contacts at the "corners" not counting as adjacency. Figure 11.2 provides such a diagram. Although a territorial pattern of this kind is unlikely, it may exist for street gangs organized around intersections, as in Figure 3.[2] For larger numbers of adjacent outgroups than four, balanced mandala circles seem to be unavailable.

Figure 11.4 illustrates the nearest that we have been able to come, with a balanced mandala-like ring pattern for six outgroups. In it, all A's are surrounded by hostile B's. The B's, twice as numerous, have as immediate neighbors half A's and half other B's (that is, half friendly, half hostile). For the A's, their closest allies (other A's) lie beyond the immediate ring of B's and conform to the enemy's enemy rule. One half of those in this second ring are, however, enemy B's. The very uneven sizes and shapes of actual group boundaries make these ideal types of little practical value.

[2] We are indebted to Robert Abelson for this point.

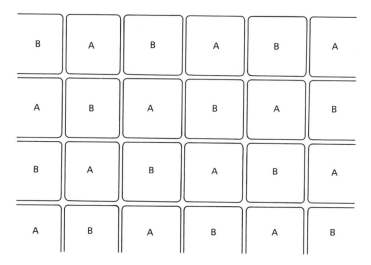

FIGURE 11.2. Balanced mandala of four-sided territories. Groups of type A are enemies of type B's, and allies of other A's.

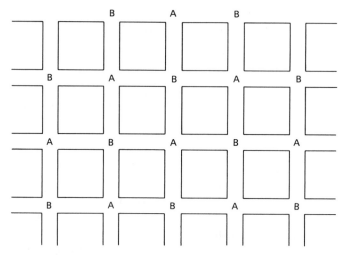

FIGURE 11.3. Balanced mandala of street gangs centered at intersections of city blocks. Type A gangs are enemies of type B gangs, and allies of other type A gangs.

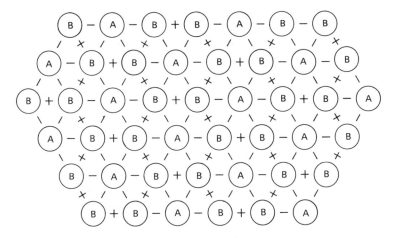

FIGURE 11.4. A quasi-mandala pattern of intergroup relations. (Pluses represent positive relations; straight lines are minuses, representing negative relations.)

Balance theory in its simple algebra predicts that all positive fields (that is, all ally fields in which every group loves every other) should be more likely than all negative fields (in which each group hates each other). The former are balanced, the latter are unbalanced. The prediction of all positive fields goes so much against common observation that balance theorists have not paid much attention to it. All negative fields, in which each ingroup distrusts all foreigners, seem more likely, and are even to be predicted in the standard presentations of ethnocentrism (for example, Sumner, 1906). Heider in his original presentation hedged on this point, and recent trends in modifications of balance theory are toward scoring such patterns as balanced (Davis, 1967).

Given a mixture of positive and negative valences between groups, the balance-theory prediction is that the *groups will fall into only two cliques*, with friendly relations within each and hostile relations between. This condition is illustrated in Figures 11.2, to 11.4, and in the mandala circles concept, in which the odd-numbered concentric circles would be one clique, the even-numbered and the ingroup would be another. Bipolar tendencies in world alliances provide anecdotal confirmation. But the rigidity of this prediction is something of an embarrassment to applied balance theory, and Davis (1967) is attempting to weaken the requirements so that several-clique outcomes can be incorporated.

In the work of Davis, and Abelson (1967) among others, statistics for the degree of approximation to balance for a set of points are being achieved. They have not been applied to the data of Table 11.1, but they could be. For Abelson's suggestion that balance be tested by extraction of a single bipolar factor, degrees of liking, such as provided in Table 11.1, could be used, although row and column asymmetry should be first achieved.

If there were perfect balance, then one could order the tribes of Table 11.1 so that the members of each clique were listed adjacent to fellow clique members, and so that there would be two areas straddling the diagonals that were all positive, with the away-from-diagonal quadrants all negative. We have tried to arrange Table 11.1 in this way, and with attention also to party. The first six tribal groups belonged in 1961 to KANU (Kikuyu, Kamba, Meru, Embu, Luo, and Kisii, with the Kisii present ambivalently because of their felt closeness to the KADU Abaluhya.) The KADU group are listed next, Abaluhya (late in joining), Kalenjin, Masia, Taita, and Coast. The uniformity of the pattern is reduced by the very general popularity of the Taita and the very general unpopularity of the Masai and the Somali. The degree of balance is somewhat increased if the Kisii are moved to the KADU group. If this is done, and if the Somali's are assimilated to that group too, about 76 percent of the signs are in accord with balance ($^{84}/_{100}$, omitting zeros).

In the simplest balance theory, the valence between two points is + or −, a single value relating A to B and B to A. In fuller treatments (for example, Harary, Norman, and Cartwright, 1965) A's valuation of B is treated separately from B's valuation of A. Such is actually the case for Table 11.1, where the valence of each tribe for the other is recorded separately. In this situation, balance theory predicts that:

11.3   *Reciprocal attitudes will tend to agree.*

Either both members of a pair like each other or they dislike each other. This prediction can be derived by assuming that each group likes itself. Thus there is a basic A to A bond, and when B dislikes A, balance is achieved by A disliking B, and so on.[3]

$$
\begin{array}{cc}
\text{A} + \text{A} & \quad \text{A} + \text{A} \\
+ \quad + & \quad - \quad - \\
\text{B} & \quad \text{B}
\end{array}
$$

When we examine Table 11.1 for this, eliminating pairs where either of the values is zero, 66 percent of the remaining 42 pairs are in agreement. Of the 23 pairs where both percentages are ± 5 or larger, 74 percent of the pairs agree.

From balance theory also comes predictions, illustrated by Harary (1961) that:

11.4.1   *Perceptions of intergroup relations will show more balance than will actual relations.*

---

[3] We are indebted to Dr. Jorge Garcia Bouza for this suggestion.

11.4.2   *Perceptual distortions will be in the direction of greater balance.*

One area of major differences among the various balance models is the relative emphasis on intrapersonal, perceived balance or interpersonal, objective structural balance. Heider's theory is purely intrapersonal, Cartwright and Harary's primarily interpersonal, and Newcomb's A—B—X model is presented in both forms, a distinction being made between intraindividual and collective "systems of orientation" (Newcomb, 1959; 1963). Newcomb emphasizes the role of communication in mediating the two types of balance. In the absence of communication, perceived similarity is likely to be distorted to agree with initial attraction, but after a period of interpersonal communication perceived similarity is more closely related to objective similarity, with attraction adjusted accordingly. Newcomb's extended longitudinal study of interpersonal attraction (Newcomb, 1961) confirmed this predicted development. The expected relationship between communication and accuracy of perceived similarity could account for the more direct relationship between similarity and liking among adjacent groups than among nonadjacent groups in the previously reported data.

Future developments will no doubt free balance theory from the unit valence assumption by substituting mathematics that use degrees of positive and negative valence, as Harary (1961) suggests. Further developments may also provide differential rules for induced valances. Writing on the subject of intergroup relations, MacCrone (1937, p. 253) suggests one:

"Furthermore, the existence of the outgroup as an object of hostility itself leads to an increased intensity of identification between members of the ingroup, since a common object of hate is, in some respects, a stronger bond between individuals than a common object of love."

Coalition and Balance of Power

In balance theory the relationship between liking and perceived similarity is a two-way bond. Just as ingroups are predicted to ally themselves with outgroups that they perceived as similar, so they are expected to perceive outgroups as more similar to themselves after entering into alliance than before. Thus, the conditions of alliance, or coalition-formation, are relevant to a consideration of balance theory. One approach to coalition formation has grown out of work in the mathematical theory of games (Luce and Raiffa, 1957). The analysis is based on Shapley's method for evaluating "pivotal power" of potential allies (cf; Shapley and Shubik, 1954), which is essentially the proportion of possible alliances a person (or group) could enter into in which his resources could change a losing coalition into a winning one. Prediction of alliances is based on the principle of "minimum power," that those coalitions will be formed which combine the least amount of pivotal power needed to gain control in a competition. Thus a moderately powerful group would be more likely to ally itself with a number of other moderately powerful groups in opposition to a single extremely powerful enemy, than it would be to enter into an alliance with the most powerful group in which its contribution to the coalition would be less perceptible. This reasoning leads to this proposition:

11.5.1   *In a region in which large differences in military or economic power exist, coalitions will be formed among the weaker groups, leaving the strongest group isolated from alliances.*

The consideration of the relationship between alliance and perceived similarity produces these derivations:

11.5.2   *Moderately powerful groups will perceive more similarity between themselves and other relatively unpowerful groups than between themselves and highly powerful outgroups.*
11.5.3   *The most powerful group in a region will recognize least similarity between itself and other groups.*

The preceding formulation of the conditions of coalition formation corresponds roughly to the "balance of power" model of international relations (Kaplan, 1957; 1962). The balance of power system is characterized by short-term alignments based on immediate security concerns. Maintenance of the system requires a relatively large number of independent states to provide potential coalition partners, since flexibility of alignment is necessary for the stability of balance of power. Thus the system creates pressures against the creation of supranational organizations and interference in internal affairs of other states, since they would reduce the flexibility of coalition formation on which the prevention of imbalance depends. In such a system, the use of force is restricted not by the enforcement of international law but by the existence of counterforce.

According to Kaplan (1962), in relations among modern nation-states the balance of power model has been replaced by a "loose bipolar" model characterized by blocs of nations organized on the basis of long-term interests, often at the sacrifice of many short-term interests that would be served by alignments that cross bloc lines. Under this system, norms against universal organizations and international intervention are no longer strong, and an important role in the maintenance of stability is played by uncommitted nations.

The propositions 11.5.1 to 11.5.3 are relevant primarily under balance-of-power conditions where alliances are flexible and short-term. Where a bipolar system of alignments has evolved, sentiment and perceived similarity would be expected to correspond to the pattern of long-term alignments.

Degrees of Ethnocentrism

A basic class of predictions we seek from social-science theories asks which group is, or what kinds of groups are, most ethnocentric. Such predictions do not come as directly from balance theory as do those of the previous sections, but they are available. In addition, dissonance theory, thus far not considered specifically, makes still other predictions.

Some such predictions come from the application of balance theory at the level of persons to clique formation (for example, Davis, 1963; 1967) and then translating "cliques" for our purposes as ingroups and outgroups. If all persons have some negative and some positive interpersonal valences, and with a pool of persons including ingroup and outgroup members, the following prediction results:

11.6   *The more mutual liking there is within the ingroup, the more ethnocentric the group will be*, defining ethnocentrism for this purpose as degree of hostile attitudes towards outgroups.

The causation could be in any direction. Thus the presence of threatening hostile outgroups, hated in parallel by all threatened ingroup members, induces positive interpersonal attitudes among ingroup members. In thus predicting more ingroup solidarity under greater outgroup threat, balance theory concurs in one of the most ubiquitous of social science predictions, one we have examined in Chapter 3.

In applying to persons the principles of balance theory that we have already applied directly to the group level, a parallel prediction emerges:

11.7   *The more homogeneous the belief-systems of the ingroup members, the more homogeneously hostile toward outgroups will be these members.*

Internal agreement on belief systems represent parallel valuing of a large number of "objects" or "X's." These parallel valuings induce balancing positive interpersonal bonds. These positive intragroup bonds force all the hostilities or negative valencings by ingroup members (given that there are some) on to outgroup members.

Shifting to group-level application again, we can predict that:

11.8   *In any local set of groups, the most dissimilar ingroup will show the most hostility toward outgroups.*

This is simply an application to the "which ingroup" question of the similarity-and-liking principles of the first section above. In that presentation we spoke as though similarity was causal of liking, but balance theory allows balance to be achieved through adjustments in any direction. Sumner hypothesizes a reverse causal relationship, from hostility to cultural uniqueness: "Ethnocentrism leads a people to exaggerate and intensify everything in their own folkways which is peculiar and which differentiates them from others. It therefore strengthens the folkways" (Sumner, 1906, p. 13). Leach (1954) has presented in detail a social system in which historically arbitrary linguistic differences are preserved for these purposes.

Congruity Model

Although it leads to similar conclusions about interpersonal perception, the congruity model of cognitive consistency (Osgood and Tannenbaum, 1955; Osgood, Suci, and Tannenbaum, 1957) developed from a very different conceptual background from the other balance models. Osgood equates cognitive elements with the affective meaning of concepts, particularly on the evaluative dimension as measured by the semantic differential. The semantic differential provides a scale of the evaluative meaning of a concept running from +3 (extremely good) through 0 (neutral) to −3 (extremely bad), the direction of evaluation referring to the sign (positive or negative) of a scale position, and polarization to its distance from 0, regardless of sign. Unlike the structural balance models already discussed, which define balance in terms of relations between cognitive elements, the congruity model deals with the direction of relation between two elements and the affective value of the elements themselves. The structural element of the theory is an *assertion* that relates two concepts, either associatively $(A + B)$ or dissociatively $(A - B)$. Assertions may be linguistic (*A approves of B; A is a friend of B; A refuses to support B*), behavioral (*A is seen holding hands with B*), or inferred (*A likes B which is related to C; therefore, A likes C*).

The basic assumption of the congruity model is that when two or more concepts occur near-simultaneously, only one cognitive reaction can be made to both or all of them. Thus, if A is positively associated with B, the evaluative meaning of both A and B must be the same, in both direction and polarization. If the evaluations of the two elements before association are unequal, the point of congruity (equal polarization) will be a compromise between the two original values. Evaluations of both elements will be modified, but the degree of modification of each will be in inverse proportion to its original polarization. The congruity formula predicts the point at which two associated elements will reach equality:

$$c = \frac{|p_1| \, (p_1) + |p_2| \, (p_2)}{|p_1| + |p_2|}$$

$|p_i|$ = absolute evaluative score of element i (that is, intensity of evaluation, ignoring direction).

where (p_i) = Algebraic evaluative score of element i (that is, intensity and direction of evaluation, with + for favorable, and − for unfavorable).

The point of congruity is a weighted average of the values of the component elements, where weights are determined by degree of polarization of the component values. The congruity formula is such that when a neutral element (evaluative score = 0) is associated with a polarized element (evaluative score $\neq$ 0), the point of congruity is equal to the value of the originally polarized element.

Although the formulation of the principle of congruity was based on interpersonal cognitions, Osgood points out that:

"We can at least hypothesize that laws governing the thinking and behaving of individuals also govern the 'thinking' and 'behaving' of groups . . . The analogue of a cognitive element for an individual is what we may call a *cultural meaning* (stereotype, public image, etc.) for a group" (Osgood, 1960, p. 363).

Applying the congruity formula to examples in intergroup perception, if ingroup A evaluates outgroup B as highly negative (-3) and the trait of generosity as moderately positive ($+2$), then the association "B is generous" will be incongruous and if believed, will be resolved by changing the evaluations of both B and "generosity" to -1 (slightly negative). On the other hand, if generosity ($+2$) is associated with an unknown group, C (for whom initial evaluation is neutral, 0), the resolution of incongruity will result in C being evaluated $+2$. The congruity principle also applies to associations between groups. If ingroup A evaluates outgroup B as highly negative (-3) and outgroup C as slightly negative (-1), then the knowledge that C has become associated with B in a military alliance will be incongruous. The congruity resolution will be such that both B and C are evaluated equally as -2.5.

Extending the congruity principle to intergroup relations leads to the following prediction:

11.9.1   *The direction and polarization of evaluation of outgroup X will be equal to the evaluation of all the groups with which X is associated.*

This prediction holds true whatever the nature of the associative bond between X and each of the other groups. Thus, the recognition that X, Y, and Z are military allies would require congruity of the evaluations of all these groups, but so would any other perception that brought them into a common cluster. The fact that it is perceived rather than objective association that determines congruity may provide an explanation of the apparent paradox of the mandala ring discussed previously. If, with respect to the circle of adjacent outgroups, it is not the incongruous fact that enemy X is an enemy of enemies Y and Z that is most relevant to the ingroup but, instead, the fact that X, Y, and Z are all enemies of the ingroup, which *implies* an associative bond among them, then the equal evaluation of X, Y, and Z is consistent with the congruity principle.

The equality of direction and polarization of evaluation of any perceived cluster of outgroups (or of outgroups and ingroup) follows from the fact that congruity is predicted to hold true no matter what the nature of the associative bond between the cognitive elements. The theory makes no distinctions in relative strength or degree of association. However, the congruity principle holds true only while two or more elements are relevant to each other. It is possible to make distinctions between sets of elements according to the relative *probability* that associations among them will be relevant at any point in time. Thus the fact that outgroup X is a military ally of outgroup Y may create a different probability of X being associated with Y than the fact that X and Y cooperate in an annual religious ceremony. With respect to any set of groups, some are more likely to be included in the same cluster more often than are others, depending on the nature and quantity of associative bonds among them.

The congruity model can also be extended to the prediction of the nature of intergroup stereotypes and attraction.

11.9.2   *The direction and intensity of evaluation of outgroup X will be equal to the weighted averaged of all the characteristics associated with that group, and, conversely,*

11.9.3   *Any characteristic associated with outgroup X will have the same evaluation as X.*

As Osgood points out, "if we are good, kind and fair and they are our enemy, then psycho-logic dictates that they must be bad, cruel, and unfair" (Osgood, 1960, p. 365). This leads to a contrast of perception of those groups that are associated with the ingroup (positive) and those that are dissociated (negative) such that:

11.9.4   *The similarity of liked groups will be exaggerated, as will the dissimilarity of disliked groups.*

The principle that association between two elements requires that they be equally evaluated also has implications for the extent to which stereotypes will be indiscriminately applied to all members of an outgroup:

11.9.5   *Hated outgroups will be seen as internally homogeneous, their individual differences neglected.*

Dissonance Theory

Many, perhaps all, of the above predictions could also have been derived from that specific cognitive congruity theory known as dissonance theory (Festinger, 1957). In these terms, it is a dissonant cognition to recognize that a liked and respected person disagrees with you about some third object, or about your valuation of self. Changing your attitudes toward the objects, or changing your valuation of the person, are obviously ways of reducing cognitive dissonance. Dissonance theory makes, in addition, other predictions which we might not arrive at from the balance model. They are given here in terms of the "which ingroups" or "what kinds of ingroups" question.

One aspect of dissonance theory is an emphasis on congruity between the valuation of an attitude object and the effort or sacrifice made in the service of the object. Thus a group is more valued the more cruel and painful the initiation rite, that high value being required to achieve congruity with the pain endured (for example, Aronson and Mills, 1959). This leads to the prediction that:

11.10.1   *The more suffering, cost, and effort that members have endured in association with their group membership, the more loyal and ingroup-esteeming they will be.*

This principle has been often noted. Hitler, for example, believed that World War I had "welded together" the German people (Walser, 1964, p. 38). The principle seems separate conceptually from the effects of external threat, although in actual situations external threat and subsequent suffering for the ingroup often will be confounded.

Even more frequent in dissonance research is the forced compliance, *fait accompli*, effect (for example, Brehm and Cohen, 1962). The anthropological evidence suggests that when economic and political conditions change so as to increase both the scope and intensity of coordinated activity, cognitive aspects of ethnocentrism (group labels and stereotypes) subsequently become consistent with the new boundaries implicit in the new forms of coordination; when economic or political conditions change in the reverse direction, however, group labels and stereotypes consistent with the wider coordination are retained.

Our own investigations in Kenya reveal that the territorially separate and autonomous peoples, whose only interethnic contacts were intermittent ones with the immediately adjacent peoples, did not develop full-blown stereotypes of most of the groups in their region, despite sharp discontinuities in language and culture, until they began to be incorporated into the superordinate economic and political system imposed by the British; they then developed rich stereotypes similar in many respects to those of modern societies like that of the United States. Other observations (for example, Mitchell, 1956; Colby and van den Berghe, 1961) indicate that the incorporation of diverse tribal peoples into a modern, urban occupational status system gives the formerly perceived labels and boundaries new stereotype content based on the new status categories. Moerman (1965) found that in northern Thailand, where linguistic and cultural variations are considerable but without sharp and mutually congruent boundaries, contemporary ethnic labels appear to be derived from a series of defunct states, each with its capital city, which once integrated (at the political level) diverse populations.

This type of evidence might be accounted for in terms of cognitive dissonance, as in the following two hypotheses:

11.10.2 *When a population has imposed on it economic or political structures that entail compliance to a new set of organizational demands entailing an alteration in boundaries between groups or statuses, then group labels and stereotypes will be altered so as to be concordant with the newly established boundary conditions.*
11.10.3 *When such economic or political structures decay without being replaced by organizations making new demands, group labels and stereotypes concordant with the defunct structures will persist.*

In terms of dissonance theory, the key point is the compliance involved. When a state develops in or is imposed on a formerly stateless polulation, the members of the population, whatever benefits of security they may derive from the new organization, find themselves having to comply with a whole new set of regulations concerning law and order, military service, taxation, and deference to authority. At the same time the state, or its leaders, have to define who must comply and who need not, that is, the boundaries of the state. Members of the new state are faced with the dissonance between their own compliance and the noncompliance of those who are not included. Why should *they* comply with the state's onerous demands when others need not, and when, in fact, they themselves did not in the recent past? They reduce this dissonance by defining themselves primarily as members of the state, diminishing the salience of their other group identities (for example, those based on kinship, language, and culture) and by exalting the state and membership in it so that nonmembership is seen as inferiority. If the state should disappear there is no need to alter the identity until it is replaced by another agency requiring similar compliance. The persistence of an identity based on former state membership is particularly likely where, as in northern Thailand, all other bases for identity are inconsistent with one another and would tend to raise the level of cognitive dissonance.

It also follows from this line of argument that once state boundaries are firmly established and the state is exalted as an entity, other bases of group loyalty (for example, those based on the primordial ties of language, kinship, religion) that are not congruent with state boundaries because they include outsiders, would come to be viewed as dissonant with the state membership as ethnic identity, and efforts would be made to eliminate them and to homogenize the population. This would predict that states would move more rapidly in the direction of linguistic and cultural homogenization than stateless societies.

If the imposition of a superordinate state on diverse ethnic groups occurs simultaneously with the introduction of a modern occupational system, however, it is possible to reduce the dissonance more easily by reinterpreting old linguistic and cultural differences in terms of occupational status, especially if ethnic groups have differential access to occupations (see Chapter 10). The boundaries that formerly defined ethnic identity come increasingly to define status differentiation within a single state-bounded nation. Since status differentiation is not dissonant with the modern state, on the contrary is, perhaps, even required by it, the simultaneous development of the state and the modern occupational system will promote the perpetuation of reinterpreted ethnic boundaries. In this situation, unless there is a rapid incorporation of the bulk of the population into the modern occupational structure, instability is likely to occur, since groups that find themselves rated low in the new status system before they have given up their traditional occupations will find it more dissonance-reducing to redefine themselves as autochthonous tribesmen desiring secession and a state of their own. When (and only when) they have complied with modern occupational demands to such an extent that there is no going back, will they look for a means of reducing the dissonance of their new-found low-status position within the new polyethnic state instead of in a tribalist retreat.

This cognitive dissonance between the traditional and modern evaluations of groups, and their political attempts to reduce it are dramatically illustrated in the phenomenon of nation-building in contemporary Africa. The rapid establishment of new states with boundaries embracing a multitude of recently autonomous tribes — all of whom are called on to participate in the national polity — has been accompanied by the slow and uneven incorporation of the population into modern occupations. It is typically those groups that have a strong traditional basis for high self-esteem but did not become educationally and economically modernized during the colonial period that experience the most intense dissonance between traditional self-evaluation and low evaluation by other groups in the new nation. These groups often become the dissident regionalists and secessionists in the African states and represent threats (of varying magnitude) to their fragile national integration.

The Masai of East Africa, for example, have long been noted for the pride they take in their own pastoral way of life, despising their agricultural neighbors and others who eat vegetable foods. In recent years, however, they have found themselves not only dominated by their more politically active agricultural neighbors in the new states of Kenya and Tanzania but also despised, in turn, as backward nonparticipants in national status systems based on literacy, education, and ability to take advantage of modern occupational opportunities. In a 1965 survey organized by the authors, the Masai were most frequently mentioned by other Kenya groups as being not only the most backward and uncivilized but also the most dirty and stupid. (In northern Tanzania, the Masai and Gogo — another pastoral group — were most frequently named.) By refusing to climb the new status ladders, they have — in the eyes of those who have climbed — come to occupy the bottom rung.

The Masai have not accepted this new evaluation of themselves. Despite the famine and impoverishment that have afflicted them in recent years, Masai respondents to the survey in both Kenya and Tanzania named their own group as "most wealthy." This judgment must be based on number of cattle owned, their traditional measure of wealth, in which they still exceed their more prosperous (by any other standard) neighbors. Thus they reduce the dissonance between their traditionally high evaluation of themselves and the low evaluation they receive in modern economic and social terms (which they can hardly fail to perceive) by adhering rigidly to traditional standards of evaluation by which they rank higher. The majority of Masai are still able to put this into action by remaining pastoralists and refusing to enter the modern occupational system, thus protecting themselves from dissonant self-evaluations. Those that have become educated and are more involved in the national life both economically and politically have given support to the regionalist KADU party (now defunct) in Kenya and have produced proposals for a Masai state, uniting the Masai of Kenya and Tanzania and reasserting the independence of the other ethnic groups. These proposals for opting out of a national unit in which a modernized status system prevails can be seen as efforts to reduce the extreme dissonance incurred by the contempt that the Masai and other pastoralists experience in the new states.

An even more striking illustration of this phenomenon can be found in Nigeria, where the refusal of certain groups to accept the political subordination that tends to go with the lack of educational and occupational modernization has dominated the politics of independence. The Hausa-Fulani of the northern states of Nigeria had strong sources of precolonial pride in their successful conquest states and their Islamic heritage. The colonial administration protected their high self-evaluation by governing indirectly through the traditional rulers and keeping Christian missionaries (virtually the only source of Western education) to a minimum. At the end of the colonial period the Hausa-Fulani were far behind Nigerians of the south in education and occupational modernization and were regarded by Christian southerners as unsophisticated, backward people. The dissonance between the subordinate status they would have in a society dominated by southerners and their own untarnished sense of religious and cultural superiority led the Hausa-Fulani rulers to refuse to go into a federation unless they could dominate it politically. Since they controlled a majority of the Nigerian population, their claims were stronger than those of minorities like the Masai in other African nations, and they did control the federal government from 1959 to 1966 (Coleman, 1958; Sklar, 1964; LeVine, 1966). In the 12-state federation proclaimed in 1967, they have less control over other groups but continue to enjoy sufficient autonomy to reduce the dissonance between their high evaluation of themselves and the low evaluation they experience when measured by the standards of southern Nigerians. The Biafran secession of the Ibo after 1966 indicates that this hypothesis requires a corollary to take account of situations of violence, in which ethnic conflict reaches the point at which group members that have been maximally committed to moving up *within* the national social structure feel so threatened and unsafe that secession appears to them to be the only means of restoring their group self-esteem.

It must be emphasized that, from the viewpoint of dissonance theory, the regionalist tendencies of groups like the Hausa-Fulani and Masai are not due simply to the dissonance in group evaluation but are also determined by these groups not having developed a strong commitment to modern occupational roles (even if low ones) prior to national self-government. Our interpretation of dissonance theory predicts that groups whose members have moved en masse into the modern structure (although in low positions dissonant with their traditional self-image) will attempt to reduce dissonance by efforts to move up *within* the structure rather than to secede from it. Hagen (1962) has developed an elaborate theoretical formulation based on this idea and gives many historical examples. In Nigeria, groups like the Ibo (prior to 1966) seem to exemplify this phenomenon, and other examples as well suggest the general hypothesis that when a relatively disadvantaged ethnic group experiences national self-government before modernization, they will choose secession or regional autonomy as a means of dissonance reduction, whereas if they experience occupational modernization first, they will attempt to reduce dissonant evaluations of group status by increased competition within the national framework.

Chapter 12

TRANSFER AND REINFORCEMENT THEORY[1]

We place under this heading the theories that concern the extension of behavioral dispositions from familiar contexts in which they were acquired and are regularly performed to novel or remote contexts, through mechanisms such as transference, habit transfer, and stimulus generalization. In the application of these theories to ethnocentrism, the central notion is that the ethnocentric dispositions of adults constitute repetitions on the wider group level of behavior patterns acquired through prior interpersonal experience in primary groups.

This theoretical approach can be seen most clearly in regard to aggression. Some behaviorists argue that aggressive social behavior is not an instinctive reaction to frustration but a set of habits established by trial-and-error or imitation and reinforced by reward (Buss, 1961; Bandura and Walters, 1963). The aggressive behavior of adults is viewed not as a manifestation of an acquired drive (as in the discussion in Chapter 8) but as the performance of habits acquired in childhood, and the intensity of adult aggression is proportionate to its reinforcement in childhood. The intensity of adult aggression directed toward any particular object is proportionate to that object's similarity to the objects in the child's environment for which particular aggressive responses were reinforced. Adults should be aggressive to outgroups in proportion to those outgroups' similarity to the ingroup, since the latter provide the environments in which aggressive habits are originally learned and in which they continue to be reinforced in adulthood. The same line of reasoning could be applied to positive social dispositions such as sociability or gregariousness, and to avoidance behavior.

AGGRESSION AND VICARIOUS LEARNING

As a habit, rather than a learned drive, aggressive behavior would be expected to be elicited as any other action potential, according to the model described in Chapter 10 (see page 163). The strength of two of the factors in this model, V and SH_R, may be acquired directly or indirectly (Campbell, 1961a):

[1] This chapter has been coauthored by Marilynn B. Brewer.

198

a. *Direct learning:*   The individual spontaneously emits aggressive responses and is reinforced (for example, with social praise, unpleasant drive reduction, acquisition of desired objects), thereby increasing the probability of reoccurrence under similar stimulus conditions.

b. *Imitative learning:*   The observation of aggressive *responses* of others is followed by response imitation and consequent reward or punishment.

c. *Vicarious reinforcement:*   The observation of the *consequences* of others' aggressive responses (learning the conditions of reward) affects the probability of response elicitation without direct reinforcement. (*Note*: linguistic instruction may be a substitute for direct observation among human beings.)

Generalization, or learning-transfer from one stimulus situation to another, is a function of stimulus similarity, habit strength, and drive and incentive conditions. The higher the drive (D) or greater the reward (K) for aggressive behavior, the more likely it is to generalize to a new situation and the less stimulus similarity is required to elicit it. Also, the more frequently the behavior has been elicited in the past, under diverse conditions, the more likely is generalization. For our purposes, two kinds of generalization, or transfer of learning, are relevant: generalization of responses learned in childhood to adult interpersonal behavior, and generalization of responses elicited among ingroup members to outgroups.

The propositions derived from this type of analysis are as follows:

12.1   *The more parents in a society reward aggressive behavior in children, the greater the tendency toward aggression among adult members of that society.*

12.2   *The greater the frequency of rewarded aggression among members of the ingroup, the more aggression against outgroups in general.*

12.3   *The more similar outgroups are to objects of ingroup aggression, the more likely they are to be targets of aggression from the ingroup.*

12.3.1   *The greater the frequency of rewarded aggression within the ingroup, the less ingroup-outgroup similarity required for aggression against an outgroup.*

This formulation views behavior toward outgroups as an extension of ingroup habits instead of as an outlet for tendencies inhibited at the ingroup level. The concept of habit transfer thus generates a prediction about ethnocentrism that is contradictory to the concept of displacement, at least with respect to aggression. This prediction can be elaborated further, as follows:

12.4   *All indexes of aggression* (physical, verbal, interpersonal, group) *will be positively correlated across societies: societies high on one form of aggression will be high on the others; those low on one will be low on the others.*

Here the contrast with hydraulic displacement and safety-valve concepts of aggression is sharpest. Some experimental evidence exists in favor of this cosymptom model over the hydraulic model. For example, people who express hostility toward outgroups on questionnaires tend to express hostility toward their ingroup on questionnaires (Sullivan and Adelson, 1954).

In this view, aggression is a habitual response repeated whenever the appropriate stimuli are presented; it is not discharged, drained off, or in any way reduced by performance. Socializing agents, however, may provide differential reinforcement for different kinds of aggression or other social behavior, or for behavior directed at different targets; in other words, discrimination learning may take place. Thus,

12.5   *The more parents in a society reward certain forms of aggression as opposed to others, the more the rewarded forms will be manifested among ingroup adults.*
12.6   *The more parents in a society make group distinctions in the aggression, sociability, and avoidance training of their children, the more adults are likely to make these distinctions in their behavior toward groups.*

On the basis of this latter proposition, the familiar syndrome of ingroup solidarity and outgroup hostility is possible, but other combinations are also theoretically possible, for example, ingroup hostility and outgroup friendliness. This is not as absurd as it might at first seem: Gusii parents are more alarmed at their children fighting strangers (whose parents might bring lawsuits) than siblings; Gusii adults seem nowadays to be more hostile to those close to them than to strangers. This phenomenon has also been noted in African witchcraft studies (for example, Middleton and Winter, 1963).

In the absence of specific discrimination training, however, stimulus generalization applies; that is, the degree to which adults behave toward outgroups as they do toward their fellow ingroup members is contingent on the degree of perceived similarity between a particular outgroup and the ingroup.

12.7   *Those outgroups perceived as similar to the ingroup, will be treated (in terms of aggression, sociability and avoidance) more like the ingroup than outgroups perceived as dissimilar.*

(This proposition is concordant with the doctrine that cultural and linguistic homogeneity provides a basis for political unity among the peoples.)

The psychoanalytic concept of transference makes a different but related prediction about the effects of information concerning a group on the possibility of extending ingroup behavior to it:

12.8   *Outgroups that are less known* (for example, those more *remote*) *will be treated more like the ingroup than those better known* (if the latter are known to contrast with the ingroup).

This last proposition is not necessarily contradictory to 12.3, since the stimulus-generalization principle does not cover situations in which there is no information. The Hullian habit hierarchy principle, however, would predict that in the absence of information to the contrary, the habit highest in the hierarchy would be applied, and this is consistent with psychoanalytic transference. It should be noticed that the spatial proximity implications of this proposition are concordant with the realistic-group-conflict-theory prediction that remote groups are more likely allies than neighboring ones, although only with the added assumption that ingroup behavior is not predominantly hostile.

These habit-theory formulations of aggression have had little influence on sociologists and anthropologists who are concerned with social conflict. This is probably because acquired-drive concepts of the frustration-aggression-displacement variety are so compatible with the prevailing functionalism of recent sociology and anthropology: displacement can be seen as operating between functional alternatives, and the process of displacing aggression from socially disruptive forms and targets to socially adaptive forms and targets can be plausibly viewed as eufunctional for the social system as well as gratifying to the individual (see Spiro, 1961). By contrast, habit-transfer notions appear to generate predictions of groups mechanically repeating previously acquired habits regardless of their functional or adaptive value in the new environment and, therefore, regardless of the positive or negative feedback from the environment. This seems, at best, irrational and possibly suicidal.

Such a view of habit-transfer theories, however, is not entirely accurate. Stimulus-generalization is itself a principle of adaptation, matching past experience against current environments to assess the degree to which the former is applicable to the latter. Even sheer habit transfer without stimulus-generalization is based on a principle of least effort: that it it easier to repeat well-established habits in new situations than to learn new ones. In applying this principle to intersocietal relations, the well-established habits are those that favor conformity to ingroup norms, while the new situation is the intersocietal environment. The least-effort arrangement, in which members of a society acquire a single set of dispositions oriented toward ingroup conformity but repeated in their behavior toward outgroups, might be highly adaptive for the society, since its habit structure is based on the most predictable part of the environment (ingroup norms) and since there are no potentially competing habits to impede ingroup conformity. The resultant gain in ingroup conformity would improve the stability (if not the solidarity) of such societies as social objects for their members and might have meant that over long periods of time they survived more frequently than societies differently arranged. According to this argument, habit transfer from the primary group to the intergroup level aids in the development of culturally coherent ingroups and might have been selectively retained in sociocultural evolution. Although this is, perhaps, stretching the argument beyond the bounds of plausibility, it does suggest that habit-transfer concepts are not totally incompatible with evolutionary and functional concepts of adaptation.

Another sociological application of habit-transfer thinking is that of LeVine (1965, partly recapitulated in Chapter 4 of this book), who sees generalization of ingroup habits to intergroup behavior as characteristic of a particular type of society rather than as a universal adaptive process. In this view, the displacement of aggression from ingroup to outgroup is characteristic of socially integrated societies, while socially divisive societies, in which ingroup behavior is alternately aggressive and peaceful, tend to transfer this same ambivalence to outgroups. Members of a socially divisive society (an ideal type based on cases of "segmentary societies") are in the peculiar situation of having to learn to be violent as well as solidary to their fellow ingroup members; consequently, they do not see sharp boundaries between members of their own society and foreigners, even if the latter are hostile. Lacking trust in their fellow men, they do not exalt the ingroup and hence denigrate outgroups less by comparison.

IMITATION AND AGGRESSION

Whatever the conditions of reward for aggression within the ingroup, the observation of successful aggression by outgroups should increase the probability of imitative aggression, through the principles of vicarious reinforcement:

12.9   *An ingroup surrounded by successfully aggressive outgroups will imitate the outgroup patterns of aggression.*
12.9.1   *The most successfully aggressive outgroup is most likely to be imitated by the ingroup.*

The above propositions may be compared with the psychoanalytic mechanism of identification with the aggressor (see proposition 9.2.6).

The principles of vicarious learning apply to imitative learning of outgroup characteristics other than aggression. The greater the reward associated with ingroup behavior, the less likely is the imitation of outgroup customs. But ingroups that are unsuccessful relative to powerful or wealthy outgroups are likely to adopt the behaviors of their more successful neighbors. Thus the principles of vicarious reinforcement produce propositions parallel to those of reference-group theory (Chapter 5):

12.10   *Of the groups in a region, those most likely to be taken as models for emulation are those which have a conspicuous advantage over the others in terms of survival or adaptation to the environment.*
12.10.1   *The group perceived as successful in warfare will be most admired and emulated.*
12.10.2   *Those groups having a superordinate political hierarchy, where other groups do not, will be the most admired and emulated.*
12.10.3   *Wealthier groups will be more admired and emulated.*
12.10.4   *Those groups recognized as higher in the regional occupational ranking system will be more admired and emulated.*

PART 4

Summary

Chapter 13

CONCORD AND DISCORD AMONG THE THEORIES[1]

The task of comparing the propositions stated in the foregoing chapters is not as simple as it might seem from the standpoint of a formal deductive approach to theory. It would be feasible to translate most of the propositions into symbolic logic and to compare them formally, even by machine, for identities and contradictions. The results would not make sense, however, for reasons that are fundamental enough to consider in detail.

THE COMPARABILITY OF THEORIES

Social scientists of widely divergent research specialties share a great many terms (for example, "group," "conflict," "hostility," and "cooperation") but use them in such different contexts that their meanings are often effectively restricted to the context most familiar to the particular theorist. There is no general consensus on what these terms refer to or how they may be operationalized in empirical research. To take them at face value as if they represented the identical concepts across theoretical orientations, disciplines, and research specialties would be to create spurious contradictions in abundance. Our propositional treatment, with its fairly uniform terminology and its extraction of general statements from formulations couched in specific contexts, will tend to amplify and multiply false contradictions unless we take account of the diverse referents for each term that we use.

This is a particularly acute problem for "ethnocentrism," "outgroup hostility," and related terms that are assumed to vary in strength across human populations. We pointed out in the introduction that "ethnocentrism" can refer to individual cognition and emotion, to cultural ideology and stereotype, and to collective action and institutional policy, or to all of them as a syndrome. This is equally true of "outgroup hostility," which can refer to individual behavioral dispositions involving hatred or the desire to attack, retaliate or avoid, to

[1] This chapter has been coauthored by Marilynn B. Brewer.

bellicose or derogatory ideologies, and to group combat and exclusions of various types. Where a theoretical formulation has clearly specified a form of action, attitude, or ideology to which its reference is restricted, we have followed suit in our propositions, but the restrictions are most frequently implied by the theorist's research context and usual frame of reference instead of explicitly stated. Although we could have respected his original intent with regard to the range of applicable generalization, this might have defeated our purpose in carrying out this survey, namely, to arrange a confrontation between theories of diverse origin. Furthermore, having pursued our exploration across the lines that divide specialists, we may well be in a better position to judge the plausible range of applicability of their propositions. We have, therefore, used our own judgment in deciding when two propositions are genuinely contradictory and when their apparent contradiction is plausibly qualified by differences in situational context so great that both propositions could be valid, each in its own context. The reader is invited to make his own comparison of propositions, to see if he agrees with our conclusions or finds points of concord and discord that we did not identify as such.

What are these differences in situational context that make terms like "ethnocentrism" and "outgroup hostility" so variable in meaning? One concerns the presence of armed combat as a realistic option in the relations between groups. Consider two situations in which ethnic communities are associated with territory and clearly defined in visible symbols. In one situation, all men are armed and are responsible for the defense of their territory, since there is no standing army, police force, or superordinate political authority. When another ethnic group is perceived to have violated the boundary between them, perhaps in an effort to gain territory, the ingroup men hastily get together and attack (or retaliate against) the others, engaging in assault, homicide, and the taking of property. In the second situation, men are not armed or are not allowed by higher authority to use their arms except in special circumstances. A boundary dispute between ethnic groups, both under a common political authority, leads to litigation in the courts, perhaps verbal dispute, social exclusion and rising suspicion, and possibly isolated acts of violence that may be tolerated or treated as crimes. In one situation, the response to threat is immediate organized violence; in the other, organized violence does not occur but other reactions do. Would it make sense to say that the threatened ingroup in the second instance is less ethnocentric, less hostile, or even less warlike? This would not take into account that armed combat is not a realistic option in their intergroup situation, whereas it is not only realistic but the easiest alternative in the first situation. If organized violence between groups were to occur in the second situation, it would be in spite of institutionalized controls unknown in the first, and probably the result of much greater provocation. It seems clear that characterizations of groups in terms of "ethnocentrism" and "outgroup hostility" will and must have different meanings depending on whether or not violence is an easily available alternative to other modes of responding to outgroup threat.

A second situational factor of similar effect is the number of boundary levels across which group combat can be conducted. Contrast a situation like that of the classic segmentary society described by anthropologists, in which armed combat is a realistic possibility at *several* levels of group differentiation in a pyramidal hierarchy of groups, with the more familiar situation in which, despite multiple levels of group differentiation, organized violence is present and (for the most part) possible at only one level (for example, the international). The temporal variability in boundaries between peace groups and potential enemies in the first situation and the permanence of such boundaries in the second, creates different contexts for assessing "ethnocentric" and "hostile" behavior. Where combat occurs at several intergroups levels, the ingroup-outgroup distinction varies, and it becomes difficult to decide whether an instance of combat should be regarded as an attack on an outgroup ("highly ethnocentric") or as a breakdown in ingroup solidarity ("low ethnocentrism"). Neither Sumner nor many of his nonanthropological followers anticipated this problem, although if one shifts the terms of reference from war and peace to group like and dislike or social inclusion and exclusion, the phenomenon exists to some degree in all societies. The distinction between multiplicity and singularity of peace-group boundaries is such an important one, however, that we might plausibly expect different principles of intergroup relations to hold true in the two different contexts (see Otterbein and Otterbein, 1965).

A third factor concerns whose behavior is being referred to when we characterize one society as more ethnocentric than another. Here we face the contrast between relatively unstratified sociopolitical structures, which allow wide participation in small group decisions about outgroups, and politically stratified structures in which a specialized ruling elite makes the military and diplomatic decisions, has better access to information about outgroups, and generates beliefs and commands concerning outgroups that are accepted by the nonparticipant majority. When we rank societies of the first type in order of ethnocentrism or outgroup hostility, we are usually referring to the behavior of the majority of adult males in their populations or, in some instances, to the majority of young warriors, whom the elders will not or cannot control.[2] When we make a similar ranking of societies of the second type, we are likely to base our assessment on the publicly expressed attitudes of the decision-making elite and the actions of the populace in carrying out their decisions, for example, their readiness to go to war. In the unstratified societies, the processes of

[2] Unstratified groups are not necessarily homogeneous, however; there can be important differences between subgroups at the outgroup boundary, who have more knowledge of and grievances against the outgroup, and subgroups more remote from that boundary, for whom the outgroup is less salient in realistic terms.

developing consensus about the perception of threat, the means of reacting to threat, and the conduct and termination of combat usually occur in autonomous local groups that can meet on a face-to-face basis. In the more stratified societies, there is a gap between the elite and the masses in information and participation concerning foreign affairs, and the larger the population and territory and the more specialized the elite, the greater the gap. Much of the theorizing about ethnocentrism in stratified societies has to do with this gap, and it is not surprising that some of the propositions thus generated are not applicable to unstratified societies.

The situational factors discussed thus far — the possibility of armed combat at the intergroup level and at subgroup levels, and differential elite-mass participation — are closely related to political development. A high level of political development, in terms of political institutions that are centralized, functionally specialized, and capable of large-scale coordination, involves the maintenance of intrasocietal peace, even where there are localized ethnic groups, restricting armed combat to one level defined by political boundaries, and a decision-making elite that takes responsibility for foreign and military affairs. Some of the anthropologists whose work we have surveyed generate propositions that are primarily, perhaps exclusively, applicable to situations found only at low levels of political development, while many of the other social scientists have assumed a high level in their thinking about group behavior. In other words, some of the propositions about cross-cultural variations in ethnocentric behavior assume certain political factors to be held constant, but they do not all assume them held constant at the same level or value.

Time span is another factor that varies across theories in a way that can generate spurious contradictions if it is not taken into account. For example, one of the major contradictions this survey reveals is in the causal direction posited for the hypothetical link between ingroup solidarity and hostility toward outgroups: Realistic-group-conflict theory states that actual threat from an outgroup generates hostility toward it, and that ingroup solidarity follows as a gathering of forces to meet the threat; frustration-aggression-displacement theory states that ingroup solidarity generates aggressive tension that seeks an outgroup target. Stated in this form, the contradiction is clear, but only because the time span involved is ambiguous. If one interprets the realistic-group-conflict hypothesis as referring to short-term response to threat, as in Leslie White's example of the United States armed forces after Pearl Harbor (Chapter 3), and the frustration-aggression-displacement idea as applying to institutionalized stabilities in sociopsychological functioning, then the contradiction disappears: those peoples whose social structures impose greater discipline and restraint on their impulses could be more ethnocentric over long periods of time than those under less institutional discipline, while all groups in the short run might respond to external threat with an increase in their respective levels of ingroup unity and coordination; and those groups most threatened at any point in time might exhibit more internal unity at that point than those less threatened. This statement incorporates features of both theories without distorting them. It demonstrates that they are not *necessarily* contradictory in their implications, or rather that not *all* of their implications contradict one another. It is possible to derive compatible as well as incompatible propositions from these "opposed" theories of ethnocentrism.

The ambiguity concerning the compatibility of the two theories involves conceptual vagueness beyond that of time perspective alone. The term "ingroup solidarity" can mean, among other things, "military unity sufficient to meet military threat" or "attachment and responsiveness of a people to their collective institutions and symbols." These two senses of "ingroup solidarity" are not identical. Social anthropology has given us many examples of groups that can unite militarily whenever it is called for without achieving a permanent functioning solidarity in the broader sense; we have sometimes referred to this as "threat-dependent solidarity" or "military alliance" (as opposed to political or administrative union). The basic question is not whether groups respond to threat by uniting for military action, but whether this process accounts for the evolution of wider and more effective political solidarities in the past and for the apparent connections between warlikeness and advanced political development in the present. When the propositions of realistic-group-conflict theory are put into evolutionary perspective, as in Chapter 6 (particularly in the discussion by Fried, 1961, quoted there at length), the points at which they genuinely contradict frustration-aggression-displacement notions become clear (and will be discussed below). This analytic separation of genuine from spurious contradictions is our major task in this chapter.

IMPLICIT PREMISES OF THEORETICAL ORIENTATIONS

Another obstacle to a direct empirical confrontation between theories of ethnocentrism concerns implicit premises or axioms that are not testable in themselves but that give theoretical formulations differing orientations and emphases that cannot be entirely reduced to propositional form. We can do little more than mention these orientations as creating theoretical divergences that may defy early resolution through empirical research.

One such divergence involves assumptions about the inevitability or constancy of human aggression. Theorists who assume that intergroup conflict stems from biologically based dispositions common to the human species or (as in frustration-aggression-displacement theory) universal conditions of human life, are predisposed to believe that aggressive tendencies may be directed toward more or less disruptive goals but cannot be eliminated as a major factor in group behavior. Those who assume intergroup conflict is a pattern of group behavior, developed and retained for its adaptive value in the course of man's sociocultural evolution from hunting band to nation-state, are predisposed to believe that it should disappear under environmental conditions in which it is maladaptive. This becomes not only a clash of pessimistic versus optimistic outlooks on the future of humanity but also a question of assessing disruption and adaptation through human history, which in the present state of the social sciences can be influenced by the predispositions of the investigator. In other words, there is no definite empirical solution in sight for the issue of whether ethnocentric behavior is primarily disruptive or adaptive, and proponents of both views can find abundant evidence to support their respective positions. The testing of the propositions set forth in this book, although shedding light on this problem, is unlikely to eradicate the convictions that lie behind these differing orientations.

The issue of how relevant and important psychological factors are in accounting for ethnocentrism represent another point of divergence in the underlying premises of theorists. We have given this problem a good deal of attention in the text and organization of this volume. Here we want only to emphasize that the inclusion or exclusion of psychological factors is often a matter of the inclinations of the particular theorist. Coser (1957), for example, is a realistic-group-conflict theorist who spells out psychological mechanisms involved in group response to threat, whereas others who share many of his views would want to exclude or deemphasize individual psychology. Dollard (1938) combined Sumner's formulation with Freudian premises of frustration-aggression and displacement without the sense of contradiction that other sociological theorists, including Sumner, would have experienced. We have made efforts to bring out in our propositions the genuine contradictions between "sociogenic" and "psychogenic" formulations, but we have the feeling that there remains an area of arbitrary choice for the interpretation of data in sociopsychological or nonpsychological terms.

A related but not identical point of divergence is the issue of whether to conceptualize intergroup relations in terms of objective conditions or subjective perception. Can intergroup behavior be predicted from an outside observer's assessment of the relative size, wealth, power, bellicosity, and the like, of groups and the advantage to them of war, peace, and alliance, or is it necessary to take special account of how the groups perceive each other? Some economic and ecological determinists emphasize objective conditions, which they see as operating with or without the awareness of those involved; other theorists lay the greatest weight on the group phenomenology, its collective definition of its situation vis-a-vis other groups. With respect to real versus perceived threat by an outgroup, for example, the two viewpoints represent merely optional ways of discussing those many situations in which real and perceived threats coincide. Wherever a real threat is not perceived by the threatened group or a perceived threat has no basis in reality as assessed by an outside observer, it becomes necessary to distinguish objective from subjective reality and to take both into account. Insofar as the noncoincidence of objective and subjectively perceived situations is frequent, it would seem that disregarding the group's subjective assessment of threat would lessen predictability and invalidate the "objectivist" position. But the matter is not so simple: "objectivists" can concentrate their attention on sociocultural situations in which external pressures are so strong as to be coercive; they can take a macroscopic view of intergroup environments, in which adaptive consequences invisible to participating groups can be seen as determining their interactions; and they can take a long-term historical view in which gaps between perception and reality appear as momentary aberrations from realistic adaptive behavior. "Subjectivists," on the other hand, can concentrate their attention on those situations in which the assessment of threat and other features of the external environment is sufficiently problematic (for example, because of inadequate information of outgroup intentions and capabilities) that the factor of perception by the group (or its decision-making elite) becomes paramount and is not reducible to objective conditions. In other words, theorists differing on this point are able to produce different orders of data supporting their own viewpoints.

Finally, there is the issue of consistency in social behavior. Some theorists and theories are particularly inclined to view the social objects of behavior as dichotomized according to distance from the self — self-other, friend-stranger, ally-enemy, ingroup-outgroup — with the assumption that behavior will be polarized accordingly. Sumner's concept of ethnocentrism and Freud's concepts of displacement and projection entail such an assumption. Other theories, notably those of a behavioristic cast, assume that behavioral dispositions are habitual tendencies that generalize from familiar and proximate objects to unfamiliar, remote ones unless special discrimination learning takes place. It is possible to generate from those opposed formulations, propositions that are genuinely contradictory and testable, and we have done so. Group behavior is sufficiently complex and multifaceted, however, to reveal both continuities and discontinuities from one level to another, providing a measure of support for the convictions underlying opposed viewpoints. Insofar as both similarities and differences are shown to be present, the manner of combining them and the emphasis given to one or the other is likely to reflect the investigator's nonempirical beliefs about behavioral consistency.

To summarize: we have sought in this section to indicate in detail our recognition that social science theories about ethnocentrism represent convictions of an axiomatic nature that go beyond the realm of empirical research but that are actively involved in designing, focusing, and interpreting research. We showed that beliefs concerning the nature of human aggression, the importance of psychological factors, the objective or subjective quality of determinants of intergroup behavior, and the consistency of social behavior are reflected in the theories surveyed, and that differing assumptions about these points may not be entirely resolved by testing the propositions we extract from those theories. This discussion, like the preceding one concerning genuine and spurious contradictions, brings to light another limitation on our goal of reducing theoretical dispute to its empirically testable core.

EXPLICIT CONTRADICTIONS

The propositions taken as a whole concern two types of variation. The first we consider is that of variation *between groups* in the relative strength of ethnocentrism, examining each of the "symptoms" of Sumner's syndrome separately and in relation to one another. At the between-group level there are propositions concerning the functional interrelatedness or interdependency of ethnocentrism symptoms, many of them generated by Sumner's original formulation, and other propositions concerning the sources, causes, or determinants of variations between groups in ethnocentrism. The second type of variation is *within each group* in the strength and quality of its ethnocentrism toward the several outgroups in its awareness; here we have propositions about differential relations and attitudes toward different outgroups and the selection of targets for ethnocentric hostility.

Between Group Variations

Four major areas of contradiction are present among propositions about between-group variations in ethnocentrism:

1. Viewing Outgroups as Weak or Strong   The first apparent contradiction occurs within the list of indexes derived directly from Sumner, between propositions 1.5 (*ethnocentric groups see outgroups as weak*) and 1.23 (*ethnocentric groups distrust and fear outgroups*), where perceptions that support ingroup self-regard seem to be at odds with perceptions that support the maintenance of a hostile, defensive, posture against outgroups. This same contradiction occurs among propositions derived in other chapters. Realistic-group-conflict theory places emphasis on perceptions that account for defensive militancy such that *ethnocentric groups perceive outgroups as strong and aggressive* (3.20), and *perceptions of threat from outgroups produces increased ingroup solidarity and outgroup hostility* (3.22). This is supported by the displacement aspect of frustration-aggression theory reflected in proposition 8.36, that *hated outgroups will be perceived as frustrating, inhibiting, and depriving*, but modified by the need to overcome inhibitions against aggression which leads to proposition 8.40, *hated outgroups will be perceived as weak, and unable to punish aggression.*

This contradiction, recurring within theoretical formulations rather than between opposing viewpoints, may represent a contradiction inherent in the uncertainty of intergroup competition or conflict, that is, no matter how much confidence you have in your own side, you cannot be sure enough of the outcome to avoid fearing failure. Thus even when you believe the other side to be weaker, you cannot rule out their turning out to be stronger, and the lack of definitive information causes you to vacillate between these poles.

Another possible explanation of this seeming contradiction is that it is based on the double-edged rhetoric leaders use to mobilize their followers in intergroup conflict — the other side is weak and we can beat them, the other side is strong and we had better redouble our efforts — the "carrot and stick" of encouragement and scare. This rhetoric is familiar to Americans, who are frequently told that their nation is the most powerful on earth and that it is falling behind the Soviet Union in military strength. There can be little doubt that this reasoning, no matter how contradictory it seems, effectively provides support for a policy of preparedness for war on an extremely large scale, which means it strikes a responsive chord in contemporary Americans. It is not clear how general such responsiveness is among other societies, but there is the possibility that this rhetoric can serve to maintain militancy anywhere by simultaneously (or alternatively) reducing self-doubts and overconfidence. To put the matter another way, the contradiction can also be seen as indicating that an ethnocentric position is best served by perceiving outgroups as moderately powerful — potentially threatening enough to justify hospitality, but weak enough (relative to the ingroup) to be successfully aggressed against. This implies a curvilinear, rather than directly positive, relationship between other measures of ethnocentrism and perceived outgroup strength.

2.   **Continuity and Discontinuity in Ingroup-Outgroup Behavior and Attitudes.**   The connection between ingroup solidarity and hostility toward outgroups, the heart of Sumner's syndrome and a fundamental tenet of much social-science thought, is also a major point of theoretical disagreement, especially insofar as it entails negative relationships between indexes of aggression or violence at different levels of grouping. This connection, proposed not only by realistic-group-conflict theory (3.4), and by frustration-aggression-displacement theory (8.16), represents a significant point of theoretical convergence, but it is incompatible with the propositions derived from theories that posit continuity in social behavior across group levels. In Chapter 4, for example, it is suggested that the connection holds true for some societies but not for others: (4.5.4) *frequency of inter-ethnic warfare and frequency of intra-ethnic feuding are positively related in stateless societies and negatively related in politically centralized societies,* and (4.5.5) *in societies lacking a superordinate political authority, situations of scarce resources cause intergroup conflict both within and between ethnic communities; thus internal feuding and external warfare covary with scarcity of resources and are positively correlated with each other.* Self-esteem theory proposes that (9.2.0) *the higher groups are on indexes of ingroup interpersonal aggression,* (9.2.1) *the stronger their hostility toward outgroups . . . ,* (9.2.2) *the stronger their tendency to see outgroups as threatening . . . ,* and (9.2.4) *the lower their evaluation of outgroups generally.*

Two other sociopsychological formulations posit cross-level continuity. Authoritarian-personality theory proposes that (9.4.0) *the more ethnocentric the society . . . ,* (9.4.4) *the more fragile is integration at the social level (as evidenced by outbreaks of internecine warfare),* and (9.4.5) *the more persons in it indulge in malicious gossip and witchcraft and sorcery accusation against each other.* Transfer theories, notably social-learning theory, propose that (12.2) *the greater the frequency of rewarded aggression among members of the ingroup, the more aggressive they will be to outgroups in general,* and (12.4) *all indexes of aggression will be positively correlated across societies: societies high on one form of aggression (physical, verbal, interpersonal, group) will be high on the others. . . .*

Thus the ethnocentrism syndrome, in its implications for the distribution of aggression across ingroup-outgroup boundaries, does not go unchallenged in the social-science literature. Although, impressively, the correlation of ingroup solidarity with hostility to outgroups can be derived from a psychological formulation like frustration-aggression-displacement theory as well as from purely societal theories, it must be observed that other formulations of psychoanalytic and behavioristic origin generate contradictory propositions. It is also remarkable that although Sumner intended his original concept to apply to primitive tribes, the recent anthropological literature (for example, Otterbein and Otterbein, 1965) indicates that it is least applicable to stateless societies. This is clearly an important area for future research. On the psychological side of this same issue, frustration-aggression-displacement theory and social-learning theory generate propositions concerning psychological determinants of variations in ethnocentrism that contradict one another in a manner parallel to their contradiction mentioned above. The former predicts that the severity of inhibition will be related to the probability of displacement so that *the greater the severity of punishment for fighting in childhood, the more ethnocentric the ingroup* (8.20). In contradiction, social-learning theory suggests a positive relationship between the expression of aggression in childhood and hostility toward outgroups such that *the more parents reward aggression in children, the more aggressive will ingroup adults be toward outgroups* (12.1). This is another important issue for investigation.

3.   **The Causal Direction of the Ingroup Solidarity-Outgroup Hostility Relationship.**   Although the correlation of ingroup solidarity with hostility to outgroups is consistent with both realistic-group-conflict theory and frustration-aggression-displacement theory, it is predicted from them on differing premises with contradictory implications. In the former theory, the correlation derives from a group's solidary response to real threat coming from outgroups, whereas the latter generates it from the frustrations of ingroup discipline leading to aggression displaced onto outgroups. The causal sequence is reversed, so that although both theories would predict identical results from a synchronic comparison of societies, they would make opposite predictions in a historical (diachronic) study of the development of the ethnocentrism syndrome. In the latter case, realistic-group-conflict theory would posit an intergroup environment of conflict over scarce resources as the antecedent condition, followed by the establishment of stronger and stricter ingroup cohesion, coordination, and

discipline; frustration-aggression-displacement theory proposes the establishment of ingroup cohesion, and the like, as the antecedent condition, followed by attack on, or heightened sensitivity to threat by, outgroups. This issue needs research, but it cannot be resolved by the usual synchronic cross-cultural comparison; only diachronic studies of change will indicate which of the contradictory implications is more valid.

   4.   Rewards and Costs of Ingroup Membership.   The question of how the rewards and costs of group membership relate to ethnocentrism elicits contradictory, or potentially contradictory, answers from the theories surveyed. On the one side are the propositions derived from reference-group-theory (5.6, 5.7) and group-narcissism theory (9.1), suggesting that groups giving their members more rewards, material and symbolic, that are visibly associated with group membership, engender more ingroup loyalty and are, therefore, more likely to be ethnocentric. Since wealthy and militarily successful groups have more rewards to distribute, they will be more ethnocentric than less successful groups, assuming that the rewards are well distributed throughout the population. On the other side are theories that attribute ethnocentrism to deprivation rather than to reward. The cognitive-dissonance theory of cost and effort justification suggests that *the more suffering, cost and effort endured in group membership, the more ingroup loyalty and esteem* (11.10.1). From a different set of premises, frustration-aggression-displacement theory predicts that *the more that ingroup norms place restraints on impulses, the more ethnocentric the group should be* (8.17). More simplistically, ethnocentrism can be viewed as economically motivated, as in 6.11, *the less self-contained and self-sufficient the economy (the greater its need for imports), the more warfare and ethnocentrism,* or as psychic compensation for poverty, as in 9.1.2, *the poorer the ingroup, the more it indulges as compensation in group narcissism.* Theorists have found plausible sources of ethnocentrism in wealth and success on the one hand, and poverty and deprivation on the other.

   Undoubtedly a kernel of genuine contradiction exists in this welter of propositions, but from the viewpoint of imagining decisive empirical research, it seems to be buried in ambiguity about which aspects of the group are most salient to its members and about which standards of comparison they are applying to it. Group membership can be both rewarding and frustrating, and the same group can be judged successful or unsuccessful, wealthy or poor, according to whom or what it is compared with. The most plausible theoretical solution to this problem has been recurrently found in giving prominence to what is perceived by the group members themselves instead of to the "objective" conditions as perceived by the scientific observer. The issue then becomes what conditions of group life are most likely to be perceived as frustrating or rewarding by the group members, and the emphasis is on *relative deprivation,* that is, the amount of perceived discrepancy between past and present conditions or among visible and comparable individuals and groups, and on the extent to which members are able to perceive relative deprivations and rewards as connected with the subjective image of the group. An analysis based on relative deprivation within the ingroup is that of Fried (1961), represented in proposition 6.12, which attributes more intense, economically motivated warfare to the greater differentiation between haves and have-nots in more complex societies. In the case of the clear division of a society into status groups with unequal access to resources, it can be safely assumed that the lower groups consider themselves to be deprived relative to the upper groups. Similarly, when a group has recently and repeatedly beaten its neighbors in armed combat and obviously has the resources to do so again, it may be assumed that the defeated groups consider themselves to be relatively militarily unsuccessful in the context of their intergroup environment. But when the contrasts are less sharp, the degree to which populations experience group membership as rewarding or depriving is an empirical question and requires investigation. When the experience of group reward and deprivation is directly and validly assessed, it should be possible to state with greater certainty whether the propositions considered here are in genuine contradiction, that is, whether they predict the same outcome from opposite conditions or are implicitly assuming different contexts for the assessment of reward and deprivation and are, therefore, complementary rather than contradictory.

It should also be noted that the propositions regarding the effects of rewards and costs associated with ingroup membership tend to be ambiguous and variable about their dependent variable, that is, group loyalty, esteem, and solidarity, which may have behavioral referents differing in assumed stability, intensity, and generality. The potential contradiction is obvious, however, and the issue should be clarified through comparative study.

Within Group Variation

Among the propositions about an ingroup's differential relations with and attitudes toward outgroups, what we have called within-group variations, we found three major areas of contradiction:

1. **Outgroup Strength, Wealth and Size.**   Just as the military prowess of the ingroup may affect its need or willingness to engage in intergroup hostility, so the strength of the outgroup may determine its appropriateness as an object of these hostilities. In terms of potential sources of real group conflict, *the strongest and most threatening outgroup should be the target of most ethnocentric hostility from the ingroup* (3.19). This proposition is partly supported by frustration-aggression theory in that strong, potentially frustrating outgroups provide an obvious object for displaced hostility such that *stronger, more frustrating outgroups will be most hated* (8.30.2), *and can more plausibly be blamed for ingroup troubles* (8.41). However, the fear of retaliation for hostility against powerful groups may make the level of inhibition against aggression greater than the level of evocation so that *outgroups with the power*

to retaliate will be least likely to be aggressed against and will be the object of the least unfavorable stereotypes (8.32). Thus it appears that the actual strength of the outgroup, as perceptions of its strength, should be related in a curvilinear way to ethnocentric hostility, so that the most overtly hated outgroups will be ones that are strong enough to be threatening but weak enough to be successfully aggressed against. From this point of view, it would be the *relative* power of an outgroup, not its absolute power, that would determine its likelihood of being selected as a target of hostility.

The predicted curvilinear relationship between outgroup strength and hostility is contradicted by an orientation toward the potential rewards and benefits of friendly association with militarily powerful outgroups. Reference-group theory predicts that *outgroups perceived as most successful in warfare will be most admired and emulated* (5.1.1) *and outgroups with successful military records will be most likely to be chosen as allies* (5.2.2). But this last proposition is contradicted by a balance-of-power coalition strategy which dictates that *in a region in which large differences in military or economic power exist, coalitions will be formed among the weaker groups, leaving the strongest group isolated from alliances* (11.5.1).

To the extent that the wealth of neighboring outgroups is associated with a sense of relative deprivation and potential threat for less affluent ingroups, realistic-group-conflict theory and frustration-aggression-displacement theory propositions regarding outgroup strength apply also to wealth. Those propositions are again contradicted by the potential reference-group status of economically successful groups, which suggests that *wealthier groups will be most admired and emulated* (5.1.3). Whether outgroup wealth is a source of threat or admiration may depend on whether the relative economic standing of the ingroup is perceived as one stage in a process of improvement or advancement, or as a permanent state of deprivation. This suggests the effect of a complex interaction between ingroup economic status and variations in outgroup wealth.

As with strength and wealth, the predicted effects of the relative size of different outgroups can vary, depending on whether large outgroups are seen in terms of a threat or potential advantage for the ingroup. Contrary to the implications of realistic-group-conflict and frustration-aggression-displacement theories, reference-group theory predicts that outgroups with large population size will be most likely to be chosen as allies (5.2.1). Insofar as population size is related to population density, however, its effect may be closely related to the distribution of land and other economic resources. Much may depend on whether large size is associated with strength or with desperation in the competition of scarce resources.

2. Proximity and Similarity. The potential effect of the physical proximity between two groups on the probability of ethnocentric relations and attitudes is a matter of considerable disagreement. Realistic-group-conflict theory and frustration-aggression-displacement theory suggest an emphasis on the potential for conflict inherent in close proximity so that *nearer outgroups will be targets of the most ethnocentric hostility* (3.18), and *nearer outgroups will be more hated* (8.30.1). However, as with outgroup strength, the capacity of near groups to retaliate against perceived aggression may produce inhibitory pressures whereby *outgroups most capable of retaliating and in a position to "overhear" ingroup expressions of ethnocentrism will be least hated or aggressed against* (8.32). Again, the conflicting forces of displacement and inhibition of aggression suggest a modification of the predicted effects of outgroup distance in favor of a curvilinear prediction in which the most hated groups are of intermediate distance from the ingroup — close enough to be salient but far enough to be "safe" targets of displaced hostility. This proposal is supported by proposition 4.1.4, that *most frequent military conflict occurs at a medium range of proximity.*

In contrast to the preceding emphasis on conflict between physically close groups, some theoretical positions suggest an emphasis on the potential for positive social contact between adjacent groups such that *adjacent groups will be most frequent allies in common defense and are, therefore, less likely to be targets of ethnocentrism* (4.1.4), and (from the emphasis on visibility in reference-group theory) *the nearer a group, the more likely it will be to serve as a military ally and model for emulation* (5.7.3). In addition, to the extent that physical proximity is related to cultural similarity among groups, the principle of consistency between similarity and affect (Chapter 11) predicts a positive relationship between nearness and friendship: *the more similar an outgroup is to the ingroup, the more liked it will be and the less the social distance at which it will be held* (11.1). In parallel with the position on proximity, the linearity of this relationship between similarity and liking is disputed by the implications of frustration-aggression-displacement theory. Since highly dissimilar outgroups are unlikely to evoke much generalization of the tendencies for expression or inhibition of aggression associated with the ingroup, this theory predicts that *outgroups that are intermediately similar to ingroup sources of frustration and inhibition will be most hated* (3.31).

The effects of similarity on generalization of ingroup responses are also emphasized by a learning-theory approach: *the more similar outgroups are to objects of ingroup aggression, the more likely they are to be targets of aggression from the ingroup* (12.3), but *the greater the frequency of rewarded aggression within the ingroup, the less ingroup-outgroup similarity is required for aggression against the outgroup* (12.3.1). Of course, the consistency principle is based on the assumption that the self-regard is positive, and in cases where this assumption does not hold true, as when groups are internally divisive, the effects of generalization of negative affect may appear to contradict the similarity-liking hypothesis. This qualification is somewhat indirectly supported by the reference-group theory proposition that *the more internally united an ingroup, the more similar an outgroup must be to the ingroup to be used as a positive reference group* (5.3.2).

Some of the potential contradictions to the principle of consistency may be attributed to an imperfect relationship between *actual* cultural similarity and *perceptions* of similarity by the two groups involved. Since several theoretical positions imply that intergroup perceptions may be distorted, or at least selected, to serve ethnocentric values, it can be predicted that the *liking of outgroups will correspond more to perceived similarity than to objective similarity* (11.4.1). Certainly, perceived similarity is not expected to be independent of actual similarity. Real group differences and similarities are consistently predicted to affect mutual perceptions, but there may be some influence of perceived similarity on actual objective similarity, as suggested by the following proposition: *outgroups perceived as similar to the ingroup will be treated more like the ingroup than outgroups perceived as dissimilar* (12.7).

We have considered propositions concerning proximity and similarity together under one heading because, for territorially based groups, proximity is one determinant of perceived similarity (in contrast with remote groups) and because the correlation of geographical proximity with cultural similarity appears to be empirically frequent among the peoples studied by anthropologists. We have found contradictions between theoretical viewpoints which predict that closeness promotes conflict, on the one hand, and common-defense and positive regard, on the other. Similarity is also viewed as a source of intergroup attraction by some theorists and of repulsion by others. As explicit as these contradictions are, the question remains of whether they would generate genuinely incompatible predictions in an empirical comparison of societies. The difficulty in arriving at a dependable answer stems from the problem of locating group boundaries and deciding whether to base judgments of similarity between groups on ingroup perceptions or on the investigator's assessment. Thus if several adjacent, culturally similar and mutually friendly groups are regarded as several groups, one theoretical position will be upheld, whereas if they are all regarded as one single group together interacting in a region with remote, dissimilar, and hostile groups, the opposite position could be upheld.

In the contemporary world of nations, this type of problem could arise in deciding whether to treat the Arabs as a single unit or as a dozen national units for purposes of comparison; obviously, the correlations of geographical proximity and cultural similarity with intergroup images and patterns of hostility and alliance would differ greatly according to what was decided. The problem is more pervasive and the possible alternatives greater in the world of prenational ethnic groups. Empirical generalizations could be biased by simply accepting the ingroup's subjective boundaries based on their tendency to make similarity and liking consistent with one another, that is, disliked groups might always be defined as different and liked groups as similar or even (if adjacent) as part of the ingroup, thus foreclosing the possibility of finding that similar groups could dislike each other. It is only when some critical research decisions have been made about the boundaries defining groups and about the group characteristics to be involved in determining similarity and dissimilarity that a confrontation between these apparently opposed theoretical formulations might be arranged. In Chapter 7 we consider the issues and evidence involved in the comparative study of group boundaries.

3.   Differential Information about Outgroups Based on Differential Intergroup Experience.   Theories about stereotyped images of outgroups are in contradiction over a major point of interest: whether they reflect outgroup actualities or project ingroup needs. The projective view of group stereotypes suggests that *stereotypes of outgroups correspond more to ingroup motives than to outgroup realities* (9.3) and that *general correspondence between outgroup stereotypes and objective outgroup characteristics will be low* (9.3.6), whereas the propositions of Chapter 11 predict that accuracy of perception will be related to opportunities for contact and observation between groups. From this latter point of view, it is predicted that *nearer outgroups will be more accurately stereotyped* (10.2.1; 10.4.7), while *the more remote and less well known the outgroup, the more purely projective and less accurate the stereotype content* (10.4.9). This potential for greater accuracy in perceptions of nearer outgroups suggests that the effect of proximity on ethnocentric hostility may be a function of an interaction with actual intergroup similarity such that *similar* groups are more *liked* if they are close, while *dissimilar* groups are more *disliked* when they are nearby and well known.

The effects of physical proximity on stereotypes may also be mediated by the nature and frequency of contact between group members. In particular, the type of contact is predicted to affect the content of intergroup perceptions: *the greater the frequency of contact between ingroup and outgroup, the more accurate the stereotypes each holds of the other* (10.2.2; 10.4.8); *accurate outgroup images reflect the nature of group interaction and involve generalizations of attributes manifest in interaction* (10.2.4; 10.4.10); *interaction-based mutual images are likely to be complementary* (10.2.6). None of these hypotheses proposes a direct relationship between contact and evaluation, since the latter will be determined by the type of contact and the corresponding perceptions. Presumably, friendly, equal-status contacts will produce concomitant positive evaluations, while hostile or competitive relations produce negative affect. Other types of contact, like economic role relations, may have no clear implications for affective reactions.

Thus in the pure projective viewpoint, stereotypes of all outgroups are predicted to be unrealistic constructions, whereas the social-perception viewpoint of Chapter 10 predicts a series of relationships between stereotype content and those factors in intergroup contact (proximity, frequency, and functional specialization) that determine the variations in information about outgroups available to the ingroup. This is a clear and genuinely contradictory issue, at least, when stated in extreme form, and one that calls for comparative research.

In summary, we identify seven areas of contradiction among propositions drawn from the preceding chapters which can be formulated as questions for investigation. The first four concern between-group variations in the strength of ethnocentrism: (1) Does the concept of ethnocentrism involve the ingroup's viewing its potential enemies as strong and, therefore, threatening, or weak, in support of the idea of ingroup superiority? Do groups that are more ethnocentric view their outgroup neighbors as stronger or weaker than less ethnocentric groups do? (2) Is ingroup solidarity associated with outgroup hostility, as originally posited by Sumner, or is there continuity in aggressive behavior across levels of group organization? Does ethnocentric hostility have its ontogenetic source in imposing inhibitory discipline on children or in encouraging them to be aggressive? (3) Is ingroup solidarity produced by external threat or does the frustration of ingroup solidarity generate hostility that is displaced onto outgroups? If groups with more internal solidarity are more hostile to outgroups, which behavioral pattern came first? (4) Is ethnocentrism intensified by reward or deprivation associated with group membership?

The other three areas of contradiction concern within-group variations, that is, differential behavior and attitudes toward outgroups and the selection of some and not others as targets of ethnocentric hostility: (5) Does the strength, wealth, or size of an outgroup generate attraction or hostility in the ingroup? (6) Does the greater proximity and similarity of an outgroup make it more or less likely to be a target of hostility? (7) Does the ingroup's amount of interaction with and knowledge of an outgroup affect the accuracy and other content of its stereotyped image, or are all such images projections of ingroup motives?

Despite the indicated semantic and operational ambiguities surrounding some of these questions, we believe that they represent significant issues which must be resolved through both empirical and theoretical work in this field. As contradictions in the strictly logical sense some of them may well turn out to be spurious or, at least more apparent than real, but as questions to which social-science theories provide different answers they are of high priority for comparative study.

AGREEMENTS: ACTUAL AND POTENTIAL

Our review of contradictions among the propositions also reveals several areas of agreement among diverse positions: in predicting a correlation between ingroup solidarity and outgroup hostility; in predicting the opposite, that is, continuity between ingroup and outgroup aggressive behavior; and in attributing the intensity of ethnocentric attitudes to rewards or deprivations associated with group membership. On these points, however, agreement across theories is limited by the opposition of other theories with contradictory implications. We now consider areas of agreement that not only represent implications of diverse theoretical formulations but that do not seem to be contradicted by other formulations surveyed in this book. These areas of unchallenged agreement may or may not be supported by research, but they are important as the possible basis for future theoretical developments.

   1.   Competition over Scarce Resources as a Source of Conflict and Ethnocentrism.   Although there is dispute about the *primacy* of realistic competition as a determinant of ethnocentrism, no other theory seriously challenges the basis tenet of realistic-group-conflict theory that the *greater the conflict of interests, the greater the ethnocentrism* (3.1), if one adds the assumption that the actual conflict of interests is perceived as such by the group involved. There is widespread agreement among theorists that if an intergroup conflict of interests over resources relevant to survival has been recognized by the groups, greater scarcity of those resources makes overt antagonism more likely.

   2.   Reciprocation of Hostility.   The agreement here concerns the tendency of groups to return hostility with hostility in behavior and attitude. Some of the most relevant propositions are as follows. *Overt, active, or past intergroup conflict will produce increased hostility toward the source of threat . . . and other symptoms of ethnocentrism* (3.2); *the outgroup with which warfare has been carried on most recently will be most hated* (8.30.4). *Outgroups with the most disparaging image and evaluation of the ingroup will be most hated* (8.30.5); *ingroups will return the perceived attitudes of outgroups toward themselves so that reciprocal attitudes (positive or negative) will tend to agree* (11.3). On this point, the implications of realistic-group-conflict theory, frustration-aggression-displacement theory and cognitive-balance theory converge. Although this may appear an obvious, common-sense principle, it has important implications regarding the course of intergroup conflict over time. If groups reciprocate hostility directed toward them, then retaliation is inevitable and escalation probable; thus the hostility of a single group will spread to its neighbors, perhaps engulfing a region in intergroup conflict. From this perspective, ethnocentrism once initiated becomes a compelling force in the interaction of groups.

   3.   Accentuation of Group Differences in Stereotypes.   This refers to a cognitive aspect of ethnocentrism, in which groups not only notice the real differences between them but magnify them in their beliefs: *perception of outgroups will involve exaggeration of the dissimilarity of the outgroup* (8.39); *real differences between the ingroup and outgroup are most likely to appear in the stereotype image of the outgroup* (10.4.1), and *differences between ingroup and outgroup will be exaggerated* (10.4.2). Contrast projection will occur in the stereotypes of outgroups such that *more warlike groups perceive others as weak*

(9.3.12), *wealthy groups perceive others as impoverished* (9.3.13), *and sociopolitically complex groups perceive others as uncivilized* (9.3.14).

   4.   Societal Complexity.   Several theories propose a positive relationship between complexity of social, economic and/or political structure and ethnocentrism in general: *groups with a superordinate political hierarchy (where surrounding groups have none) will be more ethnocentric* (5.6.2); (6.1) *groups at higher levels of societal complexity or social development are:* (6.1.1) *more ethnocentric and bellicose,* (6.1.2) *more developed in warfare institutions and tactics,* (6.1.3) *more predatory and expansive militarily,* (6.1.4) *more successful in warfare and military expansion. Regions with a longer history of intergroup warfare should have more complex and developed societies* (6.3.1); *the more politically organized the people, the more warfare and ethnocentrism* (6.7); *the more complex the division of labor, the more warfare and ethnocentrism* (6.9). These evolutionary propositions are complemented by ones derived from frustration-aggression-displacement theory and social-structural theories: *more ingroup coordination and discipline result in more outgroup hostility* (3.16); *the higher the level of political complexity, the less frequent internal feuding* (4.5.1). If these propositions are true, then the ethnocentrism syndrome as Sumner conceived of it is more likely to be found among the more politically centralized, social stratified, and economically differentiated societies of the modern world than among "primitive tribes."

   These four areas of agreement, viewed together, suggest a trend toward greater ethnocentrism as human society has developed over the last 10 thousand years, on the following grounds. The growth and expansion of human populations have increased conflicts of interest over resources for survival, particularly land and its products. Following the reciprocation and accentuation principles, intergroup conflict has proved contagious, and its cognitive basis has been stabilized in cultural beliefs that exaggerate group differences. Groups with greater societal complexity have needed to engage in war more (for a variety of reasons, depending on which theoretical premises are chosen) and, as larger and more efficient organizations, have been more successful at it, thus spreading ethnocentrism through conquest, extermination, and provoked relaliation. Whatever the social and psychological mechanisms involved, on which theorists disagree, this directional, perhaps irreversible, tendency toward ethnocentrism in sociocultural evolution appears compatible with most theories.

   This review of a rough theoretical consensus on a few major issues indicates the lines along which further research and theory in ethnocentrism and intergroup conflict might most fruitfully be pursued. This effort must involve a historical-evolutionary perspective, taking into account the vast differences in complexity and boundary conditions among human societies, and the developmental processes that account for them. The aim of this volume has been to provide a framework for these pursuits and, ultimately, for an integrated social science of intergroup relations.

REFERENCES

Abel, T. The element of decision in the pattern of war. *American Sociological Review,* 2, 853–859.

Abelson, R. P. Mathematical Social Psychology. In Berkowitz (ed.), *Recent advances in experimental social psychology,* III. New York: Academic Press, 1967.

Abelson, R. P., Aronson, E., McGuire, W. J., Newcomb, T. M., Rosenberg, M. J., and Tannenbaum, P. H. *Theories of cognitive consistency: A sourcebook.* Chicago: Rand-McNally, 1968.

Abelson, R. P., and Rosenberg, M. J. Symbolic psycho-logic: A model of attitudinal cognition. *Behavioral Science,* 1958, 3, 1–13.

Ackerman, N. W., and Jahoda, M. *Anti-semitism and emotional disorder.* New York: Harper, 1950.

Adinarayaniah, S. P. A research in colour prejudice. *British Journal of Psychology,* 31, 217–229.

Adorno, T. W., Frenkel-Brunswik, E., Levinson, D. J., and Sanford, R. N. *The authoritarian personality.* New York: Harper, 1950.

Alexander, F. The psychiatric aspects of war and peace. *American Journal of Sociology,* 1941, 46, *504–520.*

Alexander, F. *Our age of unreason.* (Rev. ed.) Philadelphia: Lippencott, 1951.

Allport, F. H. *Institutional behavior.* Chapel Hill: University of North Carolina Press, 1933.

Allport, G. W. *The nature of prejudice.* Cambridge: Addison-Wesley, 1954.

Allport, G. W., and Kramer, B. M. Some roots of prejudice. *Journal of Psychology,* 1946, 22, 9–39.

Allport, G. W., and Postman, L. *The psychology of rumor.* New York: Holt, 1947.

Almond, G. *The American people and foreign policy.* Rev. ed. New York: Praeger, 1960.

Aristotle. On dreams. Translated by J. I. Beare. In R. M. Hutchins (ed.), *Great books of the western world.* Chicago: *Encyclopaedia Britannica,* 1952, 8, 702–709.

Aronson, E., and Mills, J. The effect of severity of initiation on liking a group. *J. Abnormal Soc. Psych.,* 1959, 59, 177–181.

Asch, S. E. *Social psychology.* New York: Prentice-Hall, 1952.

Azrin, N. H., Ulrich, R. E., Hutchinson, R. R., and Norman, D. G. Effect of shock duration on shock-induced fighting. *Journal of the Experimental Analysis of Behavior,* 1964, 7, 9–11.

Bacon, M. K., Child, I. L., and Barry, H. H. III. A cross-cultural study of correlates of crime. *J. Abnormal Soc. Psych.,* 1963, 66, 291–300.

Bakan, D. *Sigmund Freud and the Jewish mystical tradition.* Princeton: Van Nostrand, 1958.

Bandura, A., and Walters, R. H. *Social learning and personality development.* New York: Holt, Rinehart and Winston, 1963.

Barnouw, V. *Culture and personality.* Homewood, Illinois: Dorsey Press, 1963.

Barry, H., Child, I., and Bacon, Margaret K. Relation of child training to subsistence economy. *American Anthropologist,* 1959, **61**, 51–63.

Barth, F. Ecologic relationships of ethnic groups in Swat, North Pakistan, *American Anthropologist,* 1956, **58**, 1079–1089.

Barth, F. (ed.) *Ethnic groups and boundaries: The social organization of culture difference.* Boston: Little, Brown, 1969a.

Barth, F. Introduction. In F. Barth (ed.) *Ethnic groups and boundaries.* Boston: Little, Brown, 1969b.

Barth, F. Pathan identity and its maintenance. In F. Barth (ed.), *Ethnic groups and boundaries.* Boston: Little, Brown, 1969c.

Bay, C., Bullvag, I., Ofstad, H., and Tonnessen, H. *Nationalism: A study of identifications with people and power.* Oslo: Institute for Social Research, mimeographed, 1950.

Beals, A. R. Cleavage and internal conflict: an example from India, *J. Confl. Resol.,* 1961, **5**, 27–34.

Beals, A. R. Pervasive factionalism in a south Indian village. In M. Sherif (ed.), *Intergroup relations and leadership.* New York: Wiley, 1962, pp. 247–266.

Beals, A. R., and Siegel, B. J. *Dirisiveness and social conflict: an anthropological approach.* Stanford: Stanford University Press, 1966.

Beidelman, T. O. Beer drinking and cattle theft in Ukaguru: intertribal relations in a Tanganyika chiefdom. *Amer. Anthropologist,* 1961, **63**, 534–549.

Beidelman, T. O. Intertribal insult and oppropruim in an East African chiefdom (Ukaguru). *Anthropological Quarterly,* 1964, **37**, 33–52.

Beidelman, T. O. Utani: Some Kaguru notions of death, sacrifice and affinity. *Southwestern J. Anthropology,* 1966, **22**, 354–380.

Benedict, Ruth. *Patterns of culture.* New York: Houghton-Mifflin, 1964.

Berkowitz, L. *Aggression: a social-psychological analysis.* New York: McGraw-Hill, 1962.

Bernard J. Parties and issues in conflict. *J. Confl. Resol.,* 1957, **1**, 111–121.

Bernard J. The sociological study of conflict. In J. Bernard et. al. (ed.) *The nature of conflict.* Paris: UNESCO, 1957, 33–117.

Berreman, J. V. Filipino stereotypes of racial and national minorities. *Pacific Sociological Review,* 1958, **1**, 7–12.

Berrien, F. K. *General and social systems.* New Brunswick: Rutgers University Press, 1968.

Bertalanffy, L. von. The theory of open systems in physics and biology. *Science,* 1950, **111** 23–28.

Bertalanffy, L. von. *General systems theory.* New York: Braziller, 1968.

Bettelheim, B., and Janowitz, M. *Dynamics of prejudice.* New York: Harper, 1950.

Blake, R. R., and Mouton, J. S. Competition, communication, and conformity. In I. A. Berg and B. M. Bass (eds.), *Conformity and Deviation.* New York: Harper, 1961, pp. 199–229.

Boas, F. Introduction. In F. S. Krauss, Sudslavishe Volksuberlieferungen. *Anthropophyteia,* 1, v–vi, 1904. (Cited on p. 4 in A. L. Kroeber et al., Frank Boas 1858–1942, Memoir 61, *American Anthropologist,* 1943, **45**, No. 3, Part 2.).

Boas, F. Some traits of primitive culture. *J. Amer. Folklore,* 1905, **17**, 243–254.

Boas, F. *The mind of primitive man.* New York: Macmillan, 1911.

Bogardus, E. S. *Measuring social distances.* J. Appl. Sociology, 1925, **9**, 299–308.

Bogardus, E. S. *Immigration and race attitudes.* Boston: D. C. Heath, 1928.

Bohannon, P. J. *Social anthropology.* New York: Holt, Rinehart and Winston, 1963.

Boulding, K. E. *Conflict and defense: a general theory.* New York: Harper, 1962.

Bramson, L., and Goethals, G. W. (eds.). *War: studies from psychology, sociology, anthropology.* New York: Basic Books, 1964.

Braunthal, J. *The paradox of nationalism.* London: St. Botolph, 1946.

Brehm, J. W., and Cohen, A. R. *Explorations in cognitive dissonance.* New York: Wiley, 1962.

Brewer, M. B. Determinants of social distance among East African tribal groups. *Journal of Personality and Social Psychology,* 1968, **10**, 279–289.

Bronfenbrenner, V. The mirror image in Soviet-American relations. *Journal of Social Issues,* 1961, **17**, 45–56.

Brown, P. Enemies and affines. *Ethnology,* 1964, **3**, 335–356.

Bruner, E. M. Primary group experience and the process of acculturation. *American Anthropologist,* 1956, **58**, 605–623.

Buckley, W. *Sociology and modern systems theory.* Englewood Cliffs, N. J.: Prentice-Hall, 1967.

Burton, R., and Whiting, J. W. M. The absent father and cross-sex identity. *Merrill-Palmer Quarterly,* 1961, **7**.

Bush, R. R., and Whiting, J. W. M. On the theory of psychoanalytic displacement. *Journal of Abnormal and Social Psychology,* 1953, **48**, 261–272.

Buss, A. *The psychology of aggression.* New York: Wiley, 1961.

Campbell, D. T. Adaptive behavior from random response. *Behavioral Science,* 1956a, **1**, 105–110.

Campbell, D. T. Enhancement of contrast as composite nabit. *Journal of Abnormal and Social Psychology,* 1965b, **53**, 350–355.

Campbell, D. T. Perception as substitute trial and error. *Psychological Review,* 1956c, **63**, 330–342.

Campbell, D. T. Common fate, similarity, and other indices of the status of aggregates of persons as social entities. *Behavioral Science,* 1958, **3**, 14–25.

Campbell, D. T. Methodological suggestions from a comparative psychology of knowledge processes. *Inquiry,* 1959, **2**, 152–182.

Campbell, D. T. Blind variation and selective retention in creative thought as in other knowledge processes. *Psychological Review,* 1960, **67**, 380–400.

Campbell, D. T. Conformity in psychology's theories of acquired behavioral dispositions. In I. A. Berg and B. M. Bass (eds.), *Conformity and deviation.* New York: Harper, 1961a.

Campbell, D. T. The mutual methodological relevance of anthropology and psychology. In F. L. K. Hsu (ed.), *Psychological anthropology: approaches to culture and personality.* Homewood, Illinois: Dorsey Press, 1961b, 333–352.

Campbell, D. T. Social attitudes and other acquired behavioral dispositions. In S. Koch (ed.), *Psychology: a study of a science.* New York: McGraw-Hill, 1963, **6**, 94–172.

Campbell, D. T. Ethnocentric and other altruistic motives. In D. Levine (ed.), *Nebraska Symposium on Motivation*: 1965. Lincoln, Neb.: University of Nebraska Press, 1965a, 283–311.

Campbell, D. T. Variation and selective retention in sociocultural evolution. In R. W. Mack, G. I. Blanksten, and H. R. Barringer (eds.), *Social change in underdeveloped areas: a reinterpretation of evolutionary theory.* Cambridge, Mass.: Schenkman, 1965b.

Campbell, D. T. Stereotypes and perception of group differences. *American Psychologist,* 1967, **22**, 812–829.

Campbell, D. T., and Kral, T. P. Transposition away from a rewarded stimulus card to a nonrewarded one as a function of a shift in background. *Journal of Comparative Physiological Psychology,* 1958, **51**, 592–595.

Campbell, D. T., and LeVine, R. A. A proposal for cooperative cross-cultural research on ethnocentrism. *Journal of Conflict Resolution,* 1961, **5**, 82–108.

Campbell, D. T., and LeVine, R. A. Ethnocentrism and intergroup relations. In Abelson, R. P., Aronson, E., McGuire, W. J., Newcomb, T. M., Rosenberg, M. J., and Tannenbaum, P. H. (eds.), *Theories of cognitive consistency: a sourcebook.* Chicago: Rand-McNally, 1968, 551–564.

Campbell, D. T., and LeVine, R. A. Field manual anthropology. In Naroll, R., Cohen, R. (eds.), *A handbook of method in cultural anthropology*. Garden City, N.Y.: The Natural History Press, 1970, Chapter 20.

Campbell, D. T., Miller, N., Lubetsky, J., and O'Connell, E. J. Varieties of projection in trait attribution. *Psychological Monographs*, 1964, **78**, No. 15 (Whole No. 592).

Carter, L. F. The identification of "racial" membership. *Journal of Abnormal and Social Psychology*, 1948, **43**, 279—286.

Catapusan, B. T. Social distances in the Philippines. *Sociology and Social Research,* 1954, **38**, 309—312.

Catton, W. R. The functions and dysfunctions of ethnocentrism: a theory. *Social Problems*. 1960, **8**, 201—211.

Chance, N. A. Factionalism as a process of social and cultural change. In M. Sherif (ed.), *Intergroup relations and leadership*. New York: Wiley, 1962, 267—273.

Clark, S. D. Canadian national sentiment and imperial sentiment. In H. F. Angus (ed.), *Canada and her great neighbor*. Toronto: Ryerson, 1938, 225—248.

Clarke, R. B., and Campbell, D. T. A demonstration of bias in estimates of Negro ability. *Journal of Abnormal Social Psychology*, 1955, **51**, 585—588.

Cohen, A. R. *Attitude change and social influence*. New York: Basic Books, 1964.

Cohen, R., and Middleton, J. *From tribe to nation in Africa: studies in incorporation processes.* Scranton, Pa.: Chandler, 1970.

Colby, B. N., and Van den Berghe, P. L. Ethnic relations in southeastern Mexico. *American Anthropologist*, 1961, **63**, 772—792.

Coleman, James S. *Nigeria: Background to nationalism*. Berkeley and Los Angeles: University of California Press, 1958.

Colson, E. Social control and vengeance in plateau Tonga society. *Africa,* 1953, **23**, 199—211.

Cooley, C. H. *Human nature and the social order*. New York: Scribner's, 1902.

Corbett, P., *The Individual and World Society,* Princeton University Center for Research on World Political Institutions, 1953.

Coser, L. A. *The functions of social conflict.* Glencoe, Illinois: The Free Press, 1956.

Coser, L. A. *Sociological theory: a book of readings.* In L. A. Coser and B. Rosenberg (eds.), New York: Macmillan, 1957.

Cronbach, L. J. Proposals leading to analytic treatment of social perception scores. In R. Tagiuri, and L. Petrullo (eds.), *Person perception and interpersonal behavior*. Stanford: Stanford University Press, 1958, 353—379.

Dahrendorf, R. The new Germanies. *Encounter*, 1964, **22**, 50—58.

Davie, M. R. *The evolution of war*. New Haven, Conn.: Yale University Press, 1929.

Davis, J. A. Structural balance, mechanical solidarity, and interpersonal relations. *American Journal of Sociology*, 1963, **68**, 444–462.

Davis, J. A. Clustering and structural balance in graphs. *Human Relations*, 1967, **20**, 181–188.

De Grazia, S. *The political community*. Chicago: University of Chicago Press, 1948.

Deutsch, K. *Nationalism and social communication*. New York: Wiley, 1953.

Deutsch, K. *Political community at the international level*. Garden City, New York: Doubleday & Co., 1954.

Devons, E., and Gluckman, M. Conclusions: modes and consequences of limiting a field of study. In M. Gluckman (ed.), *Closed systems and open minds*. Chicago: Aldine, 1964.

Dodd, S. C. A social distance test in the Near East. *American Journal of Sociology*, 1935, **41**, 194–204.

Dole, G. E. Tribe as the autonomous unit. In J. Helm (ed.), *Essays on the problem of tribe*. Seattle: University of Washington Press, 1968.

Dollard, J. Hostility and fear in social life. *Social Forces*, 1938, **17**, 15–25.

Dollard, J., Doob, L. W., Miller, N. E., Mowrer, O. H., and Sears, R. R. *Frustration and aggression*. New Haven: Yale University Press, 1939.

Dollard, J., and Miller, N. E. *Personality and psychotherapy*. New York: McGraw-Hill, 1950.

Durkheim, E. *The division of labor in society*. Glencoe, Ill.: The Free Press, 1947.

Ehrenfels, U. R. North-South polarization: a study in the typicality of attitudes. *Centenary Volume, University of Madras*, 1957, **28**, 85–103.

Ehrenfels, U. R. A trend in the development of national units. *Tamil Culture*, 1961, **9**, 1–12.

Ekvall, R. The nomadic pattern of living among the Tibetans as preparation for war. *American Anthropologist*, 1961, **63**, 1250–1263.

Elliot, D. N., and Wittenberg, B. H. Accuracy of identification of Jewish and non-Jewish photographs. *Journal of Abnormal and Social Psychology*, 1955, **51**, 339–341.

Erikson, E. H. Ontogen of ritualization in man. *Philosophical Transactions of the Royal Society of London*. Series B, Vol. 251, 1966, pp. 337–349.

Evans-Pritchard, E. E. *The Nuer.* London: Oxford University Press, 1940.

Fallers, L. *Bantu Bureaucracy*, Cambridge, England, Heffer, 1956.

Faris, R. E. L. Interaction levels and intergroup relations. In M. Sherif (ed.), *Intergroup relations and leadership*. New York: Wiley, 1962.

Festinger, L. *A theory of cognitive dissonance*. New York: Row Peterson, 1957.

Flament, C. *Applications of graph theory to group structure*. Englewood Cliffs: Prentice Hall, 1963.

Forde, D. *The Yoruba-speaking people of Western Nigeria*. London: Oxford University Press, 1951.

Forde, D., and Jones, G. I. *The Ibo and Ibibio-speaking people of Eastern Nigeria*. London: Oxford University Press, 1950.

Fortes, M. *The dynamics of clanship among the Tallensi*. London: Published for the International African Institute by Oxford University Press, 1945.

Fortes, M. The structure of unilineal descent groups. *American Anthropologist*, 1953, 55, 17–41.

Fortes, M., and Evans-Pritchard, E. E. *African political systems*. London: Oxford University Press, 1940.

French, D. Types of organization and change among North American Indians. Unpublished ms., 1961.

French, D. H. Ambiguity and irrelevancy in factional conflict. In M. Sherif (ed.), *Intergroup relations and leadership*. New York: Wiley, 1962, 232–243.

Fried, M. H. Warfare, military organization, and the evolution of society. *Anthropologica*, 1961, 3, 134–147.

Fried, M. H. *Evolution of political society*. New York: Random House, 1967.

Fried, M. H. On the concepts of "tribe" and "tribal society." In J. Helm (ed.), *Essays on the problem of tribe*. Seattle: University of Washington Press, 1968.

Fried, M. H., Harris, M., and Murphy, R. (eds.) *War: the anthropology of armed conflict and aggression,* Garden City, N.Y.: Natural History Press, 1968.

Freud, A. *The ego and the mechanism of defense*. New York: International University Press, 1946.

Freud, S. *Group psychology and the analysis of the ego.* Standard edition, vol. XVIII, London: Hogarth Press, 1955.

Freud, S. *Civilization and its discontents.* Standard Edition, Vol. XXI, London: Hogarth Press, 1961.

Fromm, E. *Escape from Freedom*. New York: Rinehart, 1941.

Fromm, E. The psychology of nationalism. Lecture, Friday October 25, 1963, at the Conrad Hilton Hotel, as a part of the Ninth National Conference of the United States National Commission for Unesco.

Fromm, E. *The heart of man*. New York: Harper & Row, 1964.

Geertz, C. The integrative revolution. In C. Geertz (ed.) *Old Societies and New States*. Glencoe, Ill.: Free Press, 1963, 105–107.

Gilbert, G. M. *The psychology of dictatorship*. New York: Ronald Press, 1950.

Gluckman, M. *Custom and conflict in Africa*. Glencoe: Free Press, 1955.

Gluckman, M. (ed.). *Closed systems and open minds: the limits of naivety in social anthropology*. Edinburgh: Oliver & Boyd, Chicago: Aldine, 1964.

Goody, J. R. *Social organization of the LoWiili*. London: Her Majesty's Stationery Office, 1956.

Goffman, E. *The presentation of self in everyday life*. New York: Doubleday Anchor, 1959.

Goldfrank, E. S. Historic change and social character: a study of the Teton Dakota. *American Anthropologist*, 1943, **45**, 67–83.

Goldschmidt, W. *Man's Way: A preface to the understanding of human society*. New York: Holt, Rinehart & Winston, 1959.

Gorer, G. *Himalayan village: an account of the Lepchas of Sikkim*. London: Michael Joseph Ltd., 1938.

Green, A. W. *Sociology*. 2nd ed. New York: McGraw-Hill, 1956.

Gregor, A. J. The dynamics of prejudice. *The Mankind Quarterly,* 1962, **3**, 3–12.

Gregor, A. J. Ethnocentrism among the Australian Aborigines: some preliminary notes. *The Sociological Quarterly*, 1963, 162–167.

Guetzkow, H. *Multiple loyalties: theoretical approach to a problem in international organization*. Princeton: Princeton University Press, 1955.

Gulliver, P. H. Land shortage, social change, and social conflict in East Africa. *Journal of Conflict Resolution*, 1961, **5**, 16–26.

Gulliver, P. H. *Social control in an African society*. Boston: Boston University Press, 1964.

Hagen, Everett E. *On the theory of social change*. Homewood, Ill: Dorsey Press, 1962.

Hamblin, R. L., Bridges, D. A., Day, R. C., and Yancey, W. L. The interference-aggression law? *Sociometry*, 1963, **26**, 190–216.

Harary, F. A structural analysis of the situation in the Middle East in 1956. *Journal of Conflict Resolution*, 1961, **5**, 167–178.

Harary, F., Norman, R., and Cartwright, D. *Structural models*. New York: Wiley, 1965.

Harding, J., Kutner, B., Proshansky, H., and Chein, I. Prejudice and ethnic relations. In G. Lindzey (ed.). *Handbook of social psychology.* Cambridge, Mass.: Addison-Wesley, 1954, **2**, 1021–1061.

Hayes, C. J. H. *Essays on nationalism*. New York: Macmillan, 1926.

Hayes, C. J. H. *The historical evolution of modern nationalism*. New York: Smith, 1931.

Heider, F. Social perception and phenomenal causality. *Psychological Review,* 1944, **51**, 358–374.

Heider, F. *The psychology of interpersonal relations*. New York: Wiley, 1958.

Helm, J. (ed). *Essays on the problem of tribe*. Seattle: University of Washington Press, 1968.

Helson, H. Adaptation level theory. In S. Koch (ed.), *Psychology: A study of a science*. Vol. 1. New York: McGraw-Hill, 1959, 565–621.

Helson, H. *Adaptation-level theory*. New York: Harper & Row, 1964.

Hemphill, J. K., and Westie, C. M. The measurement of group dimensions. *Journal of Psychology*, 1950, **29**, 325–342.

Henry, J. Homeostasis, society, evolution: a critique. *Scientic Monthly*, 1955, **81**, 305.

Herskovits, M. *Man and his works: the science of cultural anthropology*. New York: Knopf, 1948.

Hertz, F. *Nationality in history and politics*. New York: Oxford University Press, 1944.

Heyerdahl, T. *Aku-Aku*. Chicago: Rand McNally, 1958.

Hobhouse, L. T., Wheeler, G. C., and Ginsberg, M. *The material culture and social institutions of the simpler peoples: an essay in correlation*. London: Chapman & hall, Ltd., 1915.

Hofstadter, R. *Social Darwinism in American thought*. New York: Braziller, 1959.

Homans, G. C. *The human group*. New York: Harcourt, Brace, 1950.

Horney, Karen. *The neurotic personality of our time*. New York: Norton & Co., 1937.

Horowitz, E. L. The development of attitudes toward the Negro. *Archives of Psychology*, 1936, **28**, No. 194.

Hull, C. L. *A behavior system: an introduction to behavior theory concerning the individual organism*. New Haven: Yale University, 1952.

Hyman, H. H. The psychology of status. *Archives of Psychology,* No. 269, 1942.

Hyman, H. H. Reflections on reference groups. *Public Opinion Quarterly*, 1960, **24**, 383–396.

Hyman, H. H., and Singer, E. *Readings in reference group theory and research*. New York: Free Press, 1968.

Hymes, D. Linguistic problems in defining the concept of "tribe." In J. Helm (ed.), *Essays on the problem of tribe*. Seattle: University of Washington Press, 1968.

Ichheiser, G. Fear of violence and fear of fraud. *Sociometry*, 1944, **7**, 376–383.

Ichheiser, G. Misunderstandings in human relations: a study of false social perception. *American Journal of Sociology*, 1949, **55**, No. 2, Part 2, vii.

Jacobs, R. C., and Campbell, D. T. The perpetuation of an arbitrary culture through several generations of a laboratory microculture. *Journal of Abnormal and Social Psychology,* 1961, **62**, 649–658.

Jahoda, M. Race relations: a psychoanalytic interpretation. In *Symposium on man, race, and Darwin*. New York: Oxford University Press, 1960.

Jaspers, J. M. F., van de Geer, J. P., Tajfel, H., and Johnson, N. *On the development of international attitudes.* Leiden: Psychological Institute, University of Leiden, Report E.S.P. No. 001-65, 51, pp. mimeo, 1965.

Kaplan, M. *System and process in international politics.* New York: Wiley, 1957.

Kaplan, M. Bipolarity in a revolutionary age. In Kaplan, M. (ed.), *The revolution in world politics.* New York: Wiley, 1962, 251–266.

Katz, D. The psychology of nationalism. In J. P. Guilford (ed.), *Fields of psychology.* New York: Van Nostrand, 1940, 163–181.

Katz, D., and Braly, K. Racial stereotypes of one hundred college students. *Journal of Abnormal & Social Psychology*, 1933, **28**, 280–290.

Keith, A. *A new theory of human evolution.* New York: Philosophical Library, 1949.

Kelley, H. H. Two functions of reference groups. In G. Swanson, T. Newcomb, and E. Hartley (eds.), *Readings in social psychology.* New York: Holt, 1952, 410–414.

Klineberg, O. *Characteristics of the American Negro.* New York: Harper, 1944.

Klineberg, O. *The human dimension of international relations.* New York: Holt, Rinehart & Winston, 1964.

Kohn, H. *The idea of nationalism: a study in its origins and background.* New York: Macmillan, 1944.

Kopytoff, I. The "tribalisms" of southeastern Congo: the structure of reference groups. Unpublished manuscript, 1966.

Krantz, D. L., and Campbell, D. T. Separating perceptual and linguistic effects of context shifts on absolute judgments. *Journal of Experimental Psychology*, 1961, **62**, 35–42.

Krech, D., and Crutchfield, R. S. *Theory and problems of social psychology.* New York: McGraw-Hill, 1948.

Lack, D. *Darwin's finches.* Cambridge, England: Cambridge University Press, 1947.

Lambert, W. E. Comparisons of French and American modes of response to the Bogardus social distance scale. *Social Forces*, 1952, **31**, 155–164.

Lambert, W. E. A cross-national comparison of ethnocentrism, perception of similars, and affections vis a vis other peoples. *Proceedings of the Sixteenth International Congress of Psychology.* Amsterdam: North-Holland Publishing Co., 1962, 612–619.

Lambert, W. E., and Klineberg, O. A pilot study of the origin and development of national stereotypes. *Int. Soc. Sci. J.,* 1959, **11**, 221–238.

Lambert, W. E., and Klineberg, O. *Children's views of foreign peoples: a cross-national study.* New York: Appleton-Century-Crofts, 1967.

LaPiere, R. T. Type-rationalizations of group antipathy. *Social Forces*, 1936, **15**, 232–237.

Lasswell, H. D. *Propaganda technique in the world war.* New York: Knopf, 1927.

Leach, E. R. *Political systems of highland Burma.* London: G. Bell, 1954.

Lehman, F. Ethnic categories in Burma and the theory of social systems. In P. Kunstadter (ed.), *Southeast African tribes, minorities and nations.* Vol. II. Princeton: Princeton University Press, 1967.

LeVine, R. A. Anthropology and the study of conflict: an introduction. *Journal of Conflict Resolution*, 1961, **5**, 3–15.

LeVine, R. A. Witchcraft and co-wife proximity in southwestern Kenya. *Ethnology*, 1962, **1**, 39–45.

LeVine, R. A. Witchcraft and sorcery in a Gusii community. In J. Middleton and E. Winter (eds.), *Witchcraft and sorcery in East Africa.* London: Routledge, Kegan Paul, 1963.

LeVine, R. A. Socialization, social structure, and intersocietal images. In H. Kelman (ed.) *International behavior: a social psychological analysis.* New York: Holt, Rinehart, & Winston, 1965.

LeVine, R. A. *Dreams and deeds: achievement motivation in Nigeria.* Chicago: University of Chicago Press, 1966a.

LeVine, R. A. Outsiders' judgments: an ethnographic approach to group differences in personality. *Southwestern Journal of Anthropology*, 1966b, **22**, 101–116.

LeVine, R. A., and Sangree, W. The diffusion of age group organization in East Africa. *Africa*, 1962, **32**, 97–109.

Levinson. D. J. (with T. W. Adorno, E. Frenkel-Brunswik, and R. N. Sanford) (eds.), *The authoritarian personality.* New York: Harper & Row, 1950.

Levinson, D. J., and Sanford, R. N. A scale for the measurement of anti-Semitism. *Journal of Psychology*, 1944, **17**, 339–370.

Lewis, W. H. Feuding and social change in Morocco. *Journal of Conflict Resolution*, 1961, **5**, 43–54.

Likert, R. A motivational approach to a modified theory of organization and management. In M. Haire (ed.), *Modern organization theory.* New York: Wiley, 1959, 184–217.

Lindzey, G., and Rogolsky, S. Prejudice and identification of minority group membership. *Journal of Abnormal and Social Psychology*, 1950, **45**, 37–53.
Lipset, S. M. Some social requisites of democracy: economic development and political legitimacy. *American Political Science Review*, 1959, **53**, 69–105.

Lorenz, K. *Das sogenannte Bose: zur Naturgeschichte der Aggression.* Wein: Borotha-Schoeler, 1963. Trans. *On aggression.* New York: Harcourt, Brace & World, 1966.

Lorenz, K. A. Innate bases of learning. In K. H. Pribram (ed.), *On the biology of learning.* New York: Harcourt, Brace, & World, 1969, 13–93.

Luce, R. E., and Raiffa, H. *Games and decisions.* New York: Wiley, 1957.

MacCrone, I. D. *Race attitudes in South Africa.* London: Oxford University Press, 1937. [Reprinted 1957, 1965, Witwatersrand University Press.]

Machaivelli, N. *The prince.* New York: Crofts, 1947.

Mack, R. W. Ecological patterns in an industrial shop. *Social Forces,* 1954, **32,** 351–356.

Mack, R. W. The components of social conflict. *Social Problems,* 1965, **12,** 388–397.

Mack, R. W., and Snyder, R. C. The analysis of social conflict — toward an overview and synthesis. *Journal of Conflict Resolution,* 1957, **1,** 212–248.

Mahar, P. M. A multiple scaling technique for caste ranking. *Man in India,* 1959, **39,** 127–147.

Mahar, P. M. A ritual pollution scale for ranking Hindu castes. *Sociometry,* 1960, **23,** 292–306.

Malinowski, B. *Argonauts of the Western Pacific.* New York: Dutton, 1922.

Malinowski, B. An anthropological analysis of war. *Amer. Journal of Sociology,* 1941, **46,** 521–550.

Mayer, P. The lineage principle in Gusii society. *International African Institute Memorandum 24.* London: Oxford University Press, 1949.

McNeil, E. B. Psychology and aggression. *Journal of Conflict Resolution,* 1959, **3,** 195–293.

Meggitt, M. J. *Desert people.* Sydney: Angus & Robertson, 1962.

Melikian, L. H. Authoritarianism and its correlates in the Egyptian culture and in the United States. *Journal of Social Issues,* 1959, **15,** 58–68.

Melson, R., and Wolpe, H. Modernization and the politics of communalism: a theoretical perspective. *American Political Science Review,* 1970, **44,** 1112–1130.

Melson, R., and Wolpe, H. (eds.) *Nigeria: modernization and the politics of communalism.* East Lansing: Michigan State University Press, 1971.

Merton, R. K. *Social theory and social structure.* Glencoe, Ill.: The Free Press, 1949, 1957.

Merton, R. K., and Rossi, A. Contributions to the theory of reference group behavior. In Merton, R. K. *Social theory and social structure.* New York: Free Press, 1957.

Michotte, A. *La perception de la Causalite.* Louvain: l'Institut superieur de Philosophie, 1946.

Michotte, A. *The perception of causality.* London: Methuen, 1963.

Middleton, J. *Lugbara religion.* London: Oxford, 1960.

Middleton, J., and Tait, D. (eds). *Tribes without rulers: studies of African segmentary systems.* London: Kegan Paul, 1958.

Middleton, J., and Winter, E. (eds). *Witchcraft and sorcery in East Africa*. New York: Praeger, 1963.

Miller, D. The study of social relationships: situation, identity and social interactions. In S. Koch (ed.), *Psychology: the study of a science,* Vol. 5, New York: McGraw-Hill, 1959, 639—737.

Miller, J. G. Living systems: basic concepts. *Behavioral Science,* 1965a, **10**, 193—237.

Miller, J. G. Living systems: structure and process. *Behavioral Science*, 1965b, **10**, 337—379.

Miller, J. G. Living systems: cross-level hypothesis. *Behavioral Science*, 1965c, **10**, 380—411.

Miller, N. E. Experimental studies of conflict. In J. McV. Hunt (ed.), *Personality and the behavior disorders*. New York: Ronald Press, 1944, **1**, 431—465.

Miller, N. E. Theory and experiment relating psychoanalytic displacement to stimulus-response generalization. *Journal of Abnormal & Social Psychology,* 1948, **43**, 155—178.

Minard, R. D. Race attitudes of Iowa children. *University of Iowa Studies of Character*, 1931, **4**, No. 2.

Mitchell, J. C. *The Kalela dance*. Rhodes-Livingstone Institute, Paper No. 27, Manchester: Manchester University Press, 1956.

Moerman, M. Ethnic identification in a complex civilization: who are the Lue? *American Anthropologist*, 1965, **67**, 1215—1230.

Moerman, M. Being Lue: uses and abuses of ethnic identification. In J. Helm (ed.), *Essays on the problem of tribe*. Seattle: University of Washington Press, 1968.

Moreau, R. E. Joking relationships in Tanganyika. *Africa*, 1944, **14**, 386—400.

Morgan, L. H. *League of the Ho-De-No-Sau-Nee or Iroquois*, Vol. I. New York: Dodd, Mead, & Co., 1901.

Mukerjee, R. *Intercaste tensions*. University of Luknow, 1951. (Cited in *Social Forces*, 1952, **31**, 279.)

Murdock, G. P. Ethnocentrism. In E. R. A. Seligman (ed.), *Encyclopedia of the Social Sciences*, Vol. V. New York: Macmillan, 1931, 613—614.

Murdock, G. P. *Social structure*. New York: Macmillan, 1949.

Murdock, G. P. *Outline of world culture*. New Haven: HRAF, 1953.

Murphy, G. *Personality*. New York: Harper, 1947.

Murphy, R. F. Intergroup hostility and social cohesion. *Amercan Anthropologist,* 1957, **59**, 1018—1035.

Murphy, R. F., and Kasdan, L. The structure of parallel cousin marriage. *American Anthropologist*, 1959, **61**, 17—29.

Myers, A. Team competition, success, and the adjustment of group members. *Journal of Abnormal & Social Psychology*, 1962, **65**, 325–332.

Myrdal, G. *An American dilemma*. New York: Harper, 1944.

Nadel, S. F. *A black Byzantium: the kingdom of Nupe in Nigeria*. London: Oxford University Press, 1942.

Nadel, S. F. *The Nuba: an anthropological study of the hill tribes in Kordofan*. London: Oxford University Press, 1947.

Naroll, R. Two solutions to Galton's problem. *Philosophy of Science*, 1961, **28**, 15–39.

Naroll, R. *Data quality control: a new research technique*. Glencoe, Ill.: The Free Press, 1962.

Naroll, R. On ethnic unit classification. *Current Anthropology*, 1964, **5**, 283–312.

Naroll, R. Warfare, peaceful intercourse, and territorial change: a cross-cultural survey. Unpublished ms., n.d.

Newcomb, T. M. Individual systems of orientation. In Koch, S. (ed.), *Psychology: a study of a science. Vol. 3.* New York: McGraw-Hill, 1959, 384–422.

Newcomb, T. M. *The acquaintance process.* New York: Holt, Rinehart & Winston, 1961.

Newcomb, T. M. Stabilities underlying changes in interpersonal attraction. *Journal of Abnormal and Social Psychology*, 1963, **66**, 376–386.

Newcomb, W. W. Toward an understanding of war. In G. E. Dole and R. L. Carneiro (eds.), *Essays in the science of culture*. New York: Crowell.

Noberini, M. *Ethnocentrism and feuding: a cross-cultural study*. Unpublished MA thesis, University of Chicago, 1966.

Osgood, C. E. Cognitive dynamics in human affairs. *Public Opinion Quarterly*, 1960, **24**, 341–365.

Osgood, C. E., Suci, G. J., and Tannenbaum, P. H. *The Measurement of Meaning*. Urbana, Ill.: Univ. of Illinois Press, 1957.

Osgood, C. E., and Tannenbaum, P. H. The principle of congruity in the prediction of attitude change. *Psychological Review*, 1955, **62**, 42–55.

Otterbein, K. F. Internal war: a cross-cultural study. *American Anthropologist*, 1968a, **70**: 277–289.

Otterbein, K. F. Cross-cultural studies of armed combat. *Buffalo Studies, 1968b*, **4**, 91–109.

Otterbein, K. F. *The evolution of war: a cross-cultural study*. New Haven: HRAF Press, 1970.

Otterbein, K. F., and Otterbein, C. S. An eye for an eye, a tooth for a tooth: a cross-cultural study of feuding. *American Anthropologist*, 1965, **67**, 1470–1482.

Parsons, T. *The social system.* Glencoe, III.: Free Press, 1951.

Parsons, T. *Essays in sociological theory.* Glencoe, III.: The Free Press, 1958.

Parsons, T., and Shils, E. A. *Toward a general theory of action.* Cambridge: Mass.: Harvard University Press, 1951.

Peabody, D. Trait inferences: evaluative and descriptive aspects. *Journal of Personality and Social Psychology Monograph,* 1967, **7** (4, Whole No. 644).

Pepper, S. C. *The sources of value.* Berkeley: University of California Press, 1958.

Peristiany, J. G. *The social institutions of the Kipsigis.* London: Routledge and Sons, 1939.

Phillips, H. P. Problems of translation and meaning in field work. In R. N. Adams, and J. J. Preiss (eds.), *Human organization research: field relations and techniques.* Homewood, III.: Dorsey Press, 1960, 290–307.

Pillsbury, W. B. *The psychology of nationality and internationalism.* New York: Appleton, 1919.

Pitts-Rivers, J. *The people of the Sierra.* London: Weidenfeld and Nicolson, 1955.

Platt, J. Theorems on boundaries in hierarchical systems. In Whyte, L. L., Wilson, A. G., and Wilson, D. (eds.) *Hierarchical structures.* New York: American Elsevier, 1969, 200–213.

Postman, L. The experimental analysis of motivational factors in perception. In J. S. Brown et al., *Current theory and research in motivation.* Lincoln, Nebraska: University of Nebraska Press, 1953.

Postman, L., Bruner, J. S., and McGinnies, E. Personal values as selective factors in perception. *Journal of Abnormal & Social Psychology,* 1948, **43**, 142–154.

Prothro, E. T., and Melikian, L. Social distance and social change in the Near East. *Sociology and Social Research,* 1952, **37**, 3–11.

Ranulf, S. *Moral indignation and middle-class psychology.* Copenhagen: Munksgaard, 1938.

Ray, V. *Primitive pragmatists: the Modoc Indians of northern California.* Seattle: University of Washington Press, 1963.

Redfield, R. *The primitive world and its transformations.* Ithaca: Cornell University Press, 1953.

Richardson, L. F. *Statistics of deadly quarrels.* London: Stevens, 1960.

Riecken, H. W., and Homans, G. C. Psychological aspects of social structure. In G. Lindzey (ed.), *Handbook of social psychology.* Vol. 2. Cambridge, Mass.: Addison-Wesley, 1954, 786–832.

Rokeach, M. *The open and closed mind.* New York: Basic Books, 1960.

Rokeach, M., and Mezei, L. Race and shared belief as factors in social choice. *Science,* 1966, **151**, 167–172.

Rogers, C. R. *Client-centered therapy*. Boston: Houghton-Mifflin, 1951.

Rose, E. The English record of a natural sociology. *American Sociological Review*, 1960, Vol. 25. [Reprinted in N. F. Washburne (ed.), *Decisions, values and groups*. New York: Macmillan, 1962, 131–153.]

Rosenblatt, P. C. Origins and effects of group ethnocentrism and nationalism. *Journal of Conflict Resolution,* 1964, **8**, 131–146.

Royal Institute of International Affairs. *Nationalism*. London: Oxford University Press, 1939.

Sahlins, M. The segmentary lineage as an organization of predatory expansion. *American Anthropologist,* 1961, **63**, 322–345.

Sahlins, M. D., and Service, E. R. (eds). *Evolution and culture*. Ann Arbor: University of Michigan Press, 1960.

Salzman, P. Political organization among nomadic peoples. *Proceedings of the American Philosophical Society*, 1967, **3**, 115–131.

Sapir, E. The unconscious patterning of behavior in society. In E. S. Dummer (ed.), *The unconscious: a symposium*. New York: Knopf, 1928, pp. 114–142. [Reprinted in D. G. Mandelbaum (ed.), *Selected writings of Edward Sapir in language, culture, and personality*. Berkeley: University of California Press, 1958, 544–559.]

Schapera, I. The political organization of the Ngwato of Bechuanaland Protectorate. In M. Fortes and E. Evans-Pritchard (eds.), *African Political Systems*. London: Oxford University Press, 1940, 56–82.

Scodel, A., and Austrin, H. The perception of Jewish photographs by non-Jews and Jews. *Journal of Abnormal & Social Psychology*, 1957, **54**, 278–280.

Scrivenor, T. V. Some notes on *Utani*, or the vituperative alliances between clans in the Masai district. *Tanganyika Notes and Records*, 1937, **4**, 72–74.

Secord, P. F., and Backman, C. W. *Social psychology*. New York: McGraw-Hill, 1964.

Segall, M. H., Campbell, D. T., and Herskovits, M. J. *The influence of culture on visual perception*. Indianapolis: Bobbs-Merrill, 1966.

Shafer, B. C. *Nationalism: a myth and reality*. New York: Harcourt, Brace, 1955.

Shapely, L. S., and Shubik, M. A method for evaluating the distribution of power in a committee system. *American Political Science Review*, 1954, **48**, 787–792.

Sherif, M. *The psychology of social norms*. New York: Harper, 1936.

Sherif, M., and Sherif, C. W. *Groups in harmony and tension*. New York: Harper, 1953.

Sherif, M., Harvey, O. J., White, B. J., Hood, W. R., Sherif, C. W. *Intergroup conflict and cooperation: the robbers' cave experiment.* Norman, Oklahoma: University of Oklahoma Press, 1961.

Sherif, M., and Sherif, C. W. *Reference groups: exploration into conformity and deviation of adolescents.* New York: Harper & Row, 1964.

Shibutani, T. Reference groups as perspectives. *American Journal of Sociology,* 1955, **60**, 562–570.

Shils, E. Primordial, personal, sacred and civil ties. *British Journal of Sociology,* June, 1957.

Siegel, B. J., and Beals, A. R. Conflict and factionalist dispute. *Journal of the Royal Anthropological Institute,* 1960, **90**, 107–117.

Siegel, B. J., and Beals, A. R. Pervasive factionalism. *American Anthropologist,* 1960, **62**, 394–417.

Simmel, G. *Conflict and the web of group affiliations.* K. H. Wolff and R. Bendix (translators) Glencoe, Ill.: The Free Press, 1955.

Simpson, G. E., and Yinger, J. M. *Racial and cultural minorities.* Rev. ed. New York: Harper, 1958.

Singer, J. D. The political science of human conflict in E. B. McNeil (ed), *The nature of human conflict.* Englewood Cliffs: Prentice Hall, 1965.

Singer, J. E., Radloff, L. S., and Work, D. M. Renegades, heretics, and changes in sentiment. *Sociometry,* 1963, **26**, 178–189.

Skinner, G. W. The nature of loyalties in rural Indonesia. In G. W. Skinner (ed.), *Local, ethnic, and national loyalties in village Indonesia.* New Haven: Yale University Southeast Asia Studies, 1959, 1–11.

Sklar, Richard. *Nigerian political parties.* Princeton: Princeton University Press, 1964.

Smith, M. G. *The economy of Hausa communities of Zaria.* London: Her Majesty's Stationery Office, 1955.

Smith, M. G. On segmentary lineage systems. *Journal of the Royal Anthropological Institute,* 1956, **86**, 39–80.

Smith, R. S. *Kingdoms of the Yoruba.* London: Methuen, 1969.

Smith, T. *An experiment in modifying attitudes toward the Negro.* New York: Teachers College, Columbia, 1943.

Smythe, H. H., and Kono, S. A social distance test of the Eta caste of Japan. *Sociology and Social Research,* 1954, **38**, 309–312.

Southall, A. W. Lineage formation among the Luo. *International African Institute Memorandum XXVI,* 1952.

Southall, A. W. *Alur society: a study in processes and types of domination.* Cambridge: W. Heffer, 1956.

Southall, A. W. Ethnic incorporation among the Alur. In R. Cohen and J. Middleton (eds.), *From tribe to nation in Africa.* Scranton, Pa.: Chandler, 1970.

Spence, K. *Behavior theory and conditioning.* New Haven: Yale University Press, 1956.

Spiro, M. E. Social systems, personality and functional analysis. In B. Kaplan (ed.), *Studying personality cross-culturally*. Evanston, Ill.: Row, Peterson, 1961.

Stein, D. D., Hardyck, J. A., and Smith, M. B. Race and belief: an open and shut case. *Journal of Personality and Social Psychology*, 1965, **1**, 281–289.

Stenning, D. *Savannah nomads.* London: Oxford University Press, 1959.

Steward, J. H. (ed.) *Irrigation civilizations: a comparative study*. Washington, D.C.: Pan American Union, 1955a.

Steward, J. H. *Theory of culture change: the methodology of multilinear evolution*. Urbana: University of Illinois Press, 1955b.

Sullivan, H. S. *The collected works of Henry Stack Sullivan*. New York: W. W. Norton, 1955.

Sullivan, P. L., and Adelson, J. Ethnocentrism and misanthropy. *Journal of Abnormal & Social Psychology, 1954*, **49**, 246–250.

Sulzbach, W. *National consciousness.* Washington: American Council on Public Affairs, 1943.

Sumner, W. G. *Folkways.* New York: Ginn, 1906.

Sumner, W. G., Keller, A. G., and Davie, M. R. *The Science of society*. New Haven, Conn.: Yale University Press, 1927.

Swartz, M. J. Negative ethnocentrism. *Journal of Conflict Resolution*, 1961, **5**, 75–81.

Sweet, Louise E. Camel raiding of North Arabian Bedouin: a mechanism of ecological adaptation. *American Anthropologist*, 1965, **67**, 1132–1150.

Terhune, K. W. Nationalism among foreign and American students: an exploratory study. *Journal of Conflict Resolution*, 1964, **8**, 256–270.

Thoden van Velzen, H. U. E., and van Metering, W. Residence, power groups, and intrasocietal aggression. *International Archives of Ethnography,* 1950, **49**, 169–200.

Triandis, H. C., and Triandis, L. M. A cross-cultural study of social distance. *Psychological Monographs*, 1962, **76**, No. 21, 1–21.

Turner, R. H. Role-taking, role standpoint, and reference group behavior. *American Journal of Sociology*, 1956, **61**, 316–328.

Turney-High, H. H. *Primitive war.* Columbia, S. C.: University of South Carolina Press, 1949.

Ulrich, R. E., and Azrin, N. H. Reflexive fighting in response to aversive stimulation. *Journal of the Experimental Analysis of Behavior*, 1962, **5**, 511–520.

Ulrich, R. E., and Craine, W. H. Behavior: persistence of shock-induced aggression. *Science*, 1964, **143**, 971–973.

Vayda, A. Expansion and warfare among swidden agriculturalists. *American Anthropologist*, 1961, **63**, 346–358.

Waddington, C. H. *The ethical animal*. London: George Allen & Unwin, 1960.

Wagner, G. *The Bantu of North Kavirondo*, Vol. I. London: Oxford University Press, 1949.

Wallace, A. F. C. Revitalization movements. *American Anthropologist*, 1956, **58**, 264–281.

Walser, M. A German mosaic. *Encounter*, 1964, **22**, 33–38.

Warner, W. L. *A black civilization*. New York: Harper & Brothers, 1937.

Washburn, S., and Howell, F. C. Human evolution and culture. In S. Tax (ed.), *Evolution after Darwin, Vol. II*. Chicago: University of Chicago Press, 1960, 35–56.

Watson, J. B. (ed). *New Guinea: the central highlands*, special publication. *American Anthropologist*, 1964, **66**, No. 4, part 2.

Wechsler, J. A. The brothers Alsop and Adlai Stevenson. *The Progressive*, 1963, **27**, No. 3, 14–18.

Were, G. S. *A history of the Abaluyia of Western Kenya*. Nairobi: East African Publishing House, 1967.

Wesley, J. P. Frequency of wars and geographical opportunity. *Journal of Conflict Resolution*, 1962, **6**, 387–389.

Westermarck, E. *Ritual and belief in Morocco*. London: Macmillan & Co., 1926.

White, L. A. *The science of culture: a study of man and civilization*. New York: Farrar, Straus, 1949.

White, L. A. The concept of evolution in cultural anthropology. In *Evolution and anthropology: a centennial appraisal*. Washington, D.C.: The Anthropological Society of Washington, 1959a.

White, L. A. *The evolution of culture: the development of civilization to the fall of Rome*. New York: McGraw-Hill, 1959b.

Whiting, B. B. Sex identity conflict and physical violence: a comparative study. In L. Nader (ed.), *The ethnography of law*, special publication, *American Anthropologist*, 1965, **67**, No. 6, part 2, 123–140.

Whiting, J. W. M., and Child, I. L. *Child training and personality: a cross-cultural study*. New Haven, Conn.: Yale University Press, 1953.

Whiting, J. W. M., Kluckholm, R., and Anthony, A. A. The function of male initiation ceremonies at puberty. In E. E. Maccoby, I. M. Newcomb, and E. L. Hartley (eds). *Readings in Social Psychology*. New York: Holt, 1958.

Whiting, J. W. M. Sorcery, sin and the superego: a cross-cultural study of some mechanisms of social control. In M. R. Jones (ed.), *Nebraska symposium on motivation*. Lincoln, Neb.: University of Nebraska Press, 1959.

Williams, G. C. *Adaptation and natural selection*. Princeton: Princeton University Press, 1966.

Williams, R. M., Jr. *The reduction of intergroup tensions.* New York: Social Science Research Council, 1947, No. 57.

Wilson, G. *Tribalism in Kenya.* Nairobi: Marco Surveys, Report No. 8, 1961, mimeographed.

Wolff, H. Intelligibility and inter-ethnic attitudes. *Anthropological Linguistics,* 1959, 1, 34–41. [Reprinted in D. Hymes (ed.), *Language in culture and society.* New York: Harper & Row, 1964.]

Wright, Q. *A study of war, Vols. I and II.* Chicago: University of Chicago Press, 1942.

Wyatt, D. F., and Campbell, D. T. On the liability of stereotype or hypothesis. *Journal of Abnormal & Social Psychology,* 1951, 46, 496–500.

Yates, A. J. *Frustration and conflict.* New York: Wiley, 1962.

Yinger, M. Social forces involved in group identification or withdrawal. *Daedalus: Proceedings of the American Academy of Arts and Sciences,* 1961, 90, 247–260.

Young, D. *American minority peoples: a study in racial and cultural conflicts in the United States.* New York: Harper, 1932.

Zawadski, B. Limitations of the scapegoat theory of prejudice. *Journal of Abnormal and Social Psychology,* 1942, 43, 127–141.

Zegwaard, G. A. Head hunting practices of the Asmat or Netherlands New Guinea. *American Anthropologist,* 1959, 61, 1020–1041.

Zimmer, H. *Philosophies of India.* J. Campbell (ed.), New York: Pantheon Bollinges, 1951.

Znaniecki, F. *Modern nationalities.* Urbana: University of Illinois Press, 1952.

Appendix

ETHNOCENTRISM FIELD MANUAL

The field manual is designed to represent, in the form of an ethnographic procedure, the theoretical orientation that is surveyed in this book and is translated into a worldwide comparative hypothesis-testing study. As such, it was the means of coordinating the data-collection activities of the anthropologists who participated in the Cross-Cultural Study of Ethnocentrism, directed by the authors and supported by a grant from the Carnegie Corporation of New York to Northwestern University. Insofar as it fails in its original goal of translating theoretical propositions into research operations, it is not only because of difficulties inherent in the description and comparison of cultures and interethnic situations but also because our theoretical reviewing and thinking has had an additional five years to develop since 1965, when the field manual assumed final form

The field manual had a considerable history (some of it reviewed in the preface to this book) before the 1965 version which is presented in the following pages. Our original approach to the problem of ethnocentrism was to imagine interview questions that might be asked of peoples around the globe who were not yet dominated by Europeans or their forms of government; this was a prominent part of our published proposal (Campbell and LeVine, 1961). An explicit survey of theories for cross-culturally testable propositions came later. The interview questions were tried out in the field even before the 1961 article, and in 1962 after the awarding of the grant that made the study possible, we expanded the interview into a field manual that was used during the years 1963 to 1964 by Nelson Graburn among Canadian Eskimos and Indians, by James and Virginia Watson in the northeast highlands of New Guinea, and by Satish Saberwal and ourselves in Kenya. We all discussed our field experiences in Chicago during November 1964, and those discussions provided the basis for the final version of 1965. A major change was the omission of "regional ethnography," which required the fieldworker to investigate several adjacent ethnic groups, in favor of work with a single group. This was done in recognition of the tedium of the standard tasks assigned by the manual, making the replication by one fieldworker unlikely, but it meant that propositions regarding the reciprocality or complementarity of group stereotypes could not be tested unless fieldworkers worked in adjacent groups. The methodology of investigation using field manuals of this type is discussed by Campbell and LeVine (1970).

Twenty sets of ethnographic field notes based on this manual are or will soon be available as *Hraflex Books*, Ethnocentrism Series, through the Human Relations Area Files, P.O. Box 2054, Yale Station, New Haven, Connecticut 06520. The groups and ethnographers are as follows:

1. The Gusii of Kenya, Robert A. LeVine and Donald T. Campbell
2. The Embu of Kenya, Satish Saberwal
3. The Luo of Kenya, William Sytek
4. The Kofyar of Nigeria, Robert Netting
5. The Manga of Niger, Michael Horowitz
6. The Guge of Ethiopia, John Hinnant
7. The Gola of Liberia, Warren d'Azevedo
8. The Irakqkiah of New Guinea, Phillip Newman
9. The Siassi of New Guinea, Michael Freedman
10. The Dani of New Guinea, Karl Heider
11. The Batainabura of New Guinea, James Watson
12. The Pitjindjara of Australia, Aram Yengoyan
13. The Tausug of Philippines, Thomas Kiefer
14. The Bajau of Philippines, Harry Nimmo
15. The Nukuoro Atoll, Vern Carroll
16. The Nauthars of Nepal, Ed Kahn
17. The Lhassa of Tibet, James Downs
18. The Amdo of Tibet, Edward Parmee
19. The Shuswap of Canada, James Brow
20. The Eskimos of northern Canada, Nelson Graburn

ETHNOCENTRISM FIELD MANUAL

by

Robert A. LeVine
University of Chicago

Donald T. Campbell
Northwestern University

April, 1965

The Cross-Cultural Study of Ethnocentrism, supported by a grant from the Carnegie Corporation of New York to Northwestern University.

247

CONTENTS

..

I.   FIELDWORK PROCEDURE

A.   Selection of the Groups of Reference

This field manual is designed for use by an ethnographer who has already done extensive fieldwork in a given group of nonindustrial people inhabiting a region where the political-military units were free of superordinate control until 1880 or later. The tasks described here do not involve his working outside of that group, although in some cases he will have collaborators doing the same work among neighboring groups. In some areas there will be ambiguity concerning the type of boundary or level of grouping to be employed for defining the "ingroup," that is the group on which the ethnographer and his informants are reporting, and the "outgroups," that is the groups of which the informants report traditional ingroup images and relations. For example, in some stateless societies, the ingroup could (from the viewpoint of political autonomy, social distance, and military conflict) be a village, and the outgroups could be surrounding villages, even though those villages are very similar in language and culture, and even though beyond them there are pronounced linguistic and cultural boundaries. Such an ingroup-outgroup definition would mean that the results of the ethnocentrism inquiry schedule (Section IV) would not be descriptions of "intertribal," "intersocietal," "intercultural," or "interethnic" relations and images in the usual senses of those terms but, instead, intergroup relations at an "*intra*cultural" level. On the other hand, another ethnographer in the same situation could take the local boundaries designated by ethnographic and linguistic convention — the "tribes" or "cultures" of the region — as distinguishing ingroup from outgroup and have his informants report on the entire cultural or ethnolinguistic entity and its relations with and images of the other such distinct entities in the region, disregarding intergroup relations at lower levels (except insofar as they come up in Section IV as internal inter-community aggression). In this case, the images of culturally similar enemy groups would not be included in the data. Both alternatives are arbitrary and have disadvantages from the viewpoint of comparative study.

In Section III.A. an interview strategy is given for finding the levels of grouping most salient to informants from the local group with which work is started. It is not anticipated, however, that this will solve the problem for the ethnographer, for informants may well produce long lists of outgroups defined by various criteria, some being more inclusive than others. In III.A.8. there is a procedure for reducing the list of outgroups — and for defining the ingroup for purposes of the study. In applying this procedure to his specific case, the ethnographer should be guided by the principle that it is as undesirable to focus entirely on the relations of small, culturally similar groups when dissimilar groups were known to the people traditionally as it is to focus entirely on intercultural relations and images when culturally homogeneous segments were independent military groups with sharp social boundaries. Where the situation is this ambiguous, the principle dictates that both culturally similar *and* dissimilar groups be included in the list of outgroups and that the ingroup be defined at a level lower than that of the cultural-linguistic boundary. If there is a multitude of culturally similar groups in the immediate vicinity (for example politically autonomous villages or "subtribes") but a relatively small number of culturally or linguistically distinct groupings in the whole region, it would be preferable to include only a few of the similar groups and all of the more dissimilar recognized entities.

B.   Selection of Communities within the Ingroup

Since the final working definitions of the ingroup under study and the outgroups referred to may come out of the preliminary interviewing itself, the selection of a community or area in which to begin interviewing is crucial. If the first informants are from a marginal area located unusually near a linguistic boundary, they might give quite a different list of local groupings than would centrally located informants. A similar problem arises if the first subgroup worked with has a peculiar history of migration or of political dominance or subordination that sets it apart in terms of intergroup experience from other subgroups of the ethnographically designated unit. Considerations of personal convenience will undoubtedly play a part in the ethnographer's decision as to where to start work, but he may have options and the following principles will be a guide:

1.   Unless the ingroup is so small that all of its segments are very near ethnolinguistic boundaries, central communities are preferable to peripherally located ones.
2.   A community or segment with a history of intergroup experience (for example, migration) which appears in advance to be typical of that for the ingroup as a whole is preferable to one deemed atypical in this regard.
3.   All information the ethnographer has or acquires concerning peculiar factors which might have influenced the segment's relations with or perceptions of the intergroup enviornment should be explicated in detail in the materials that he provides the project.
4.   If the segment chosen for initial work is atypical, a special effort (apart from subsequent work described in the following section) should be made to do, at least, one ethnocentrism interview (Section III) with an informant in a different subgroup that is more typical in its intergroup experience of the ethnic group as a whole;
5.   If the ethnic group is highly centralized, for example a monarchy with a royal court, then the first informants should be chosen from the politically dominant sector without regard to typicality.

C.   Selection and Description of Informants

On the basis of the responses of initial informants to the survey outgroups (III.A), a series of final working definitions of the ingroup and outgroups should be arrived at. Where the ingroup unit decided on (according to the procedure outlined in III.A.) is a segment of the ethnographically defined unit rather than the whole unit, then informants should be chosen *exclusively from that segment*, apart from any special effort to compensate for atypicality (mentioned above). If the ingroup unit decided on coincides with the ethnographically defined unit, then informants may be chosen from any of its segments, and the greater the diversity of segments they come from, the better. Thus we are saying that although the ethnographer may use differing levels of ingroup-outgroup boundaries in *questioning* his informants, he must *select* informants on the basis of a single ingroup boundary consistently adhered to.

The cross-checking of informants' accounts represents a major methodological interest of the CCSE (Cross-Cultural Study of Ethnocentrism) as well as an important control on the reliability of the data; it is, therefore, essential that the informants be interviewed independently, with no informant having prior knowledge of another's responses to the questions he is about to be asked. This does *not* rule out group interviews, with notes on degree of consensus among multiple informants, but it does mean that anyone present at such a session cannot be used as a full independent source of information on the same topics (subsequent reports of disagreement with the group's consensus should, of course, be welcome). In selecting *informants*, the ethnographer should use the following desiderata as a guide:

1. *Expertness on the Traditional Culture.*   The informants are *not* to be selected per se as a representative cross section of the population but, instead, as experts on the traditional culture. Thus if there are official or semiofficial trained custodians of the oral history, they may be ideal.

2. *Articulateness, Willingness, and Perspective.*   Not all persons who fully participated in a culture can report on it fluently. Articulateness and willingness obviously are required. Interest in the content of history, in the contrast of cultures and in culture change, may all be requisite to a willingness to talk in detail, to search old memories, and the like. We cannot blanketly rule out the use of marginal persons as informants, although the source of bias and limitation that may accompany this should be noted. (In interview Section III.H we suggest a deliberate supplementary use of interethnic migrants.)

3. *Age.*   Insofar as articulateness and willingness are not jeopardized, the older the informant, the better for our purposes. Every informant should have reached adulthood before the group came under colonial or national administration.

4.   *Role and Status in the Community.*   First priority should be given to old persons who once occupied central political positions in the community. Persons who currently are politically active may be suspected of distorting past beliefs and actions so as to better justify current political stands and alliances. Although past political responsibles have top priority, if useful informants are sufficiently available, the four replications should be spread over social roles and statuses. Thus traditional followers and soldiers, as well as leaders, should be used. If religious, military, peacetime, and judicial leaders were differentiated, some use of all types would seem desirable. Notice that although we aim at four or more complete replications of the interview content, these may be spread over 10 or 20 informants, as it is not expected that one informant will go through all interview content.

5.   *Sex.*   Males should be used exclusively for all sections except Section M, for which there should be two female and two male informants.

The ethnographer is likely to find that it is easier to use numerous informants, breaking the interview up into parts, rather than getting all of the material from only four or five. The main advantages are the reduction of informant fatigue and the elimination of the insult of asking for information the informant feels he has already given.

The evaluation of the informant interviews will be greatly facilitated if the ethnographer makes notes concerning relevant aspects of each informant's background, interview performance, and local reputation. The following points should be covered.

1. Age and Travel Experience.   This can be obtained from — or in the case of age, laboriously worked out with — the informant himself, and has proved in some field situations to be a good way of beginning with an old informant. Dating his age by a local event calendar is essential for assessing his reliability in reporting memories of particular occurrences and customs. The details of his travel experience are indispensable for understanding the extent to which his accounts are based on idiosyncratic experience, including direct contact with foreign peoples, or on secondhand information and conventionalized folk beliefs. Obtain a crude life history of the informant in terms of where he has lived from childhood onward, who he saw there, etc. Allow him to elaborate at any length he chooses on his contact experiences, without directing him to use group names that he does not spontaneously mention.

2. Interview Performance.   An anthropologist develops a way of judging the honesty, frankness, and capability of his informants in a particular culture, and these intuitive judgments, even if closer to impressions than demonstrable evaluations, are extremely important to record. In recording them, the ethnographer should keep in mind the following informant qualities: (a) the comprehension of questions; (b) the fluency of answers; (c) the memory for detail; (d) the ability to distinguish what he knows from what he does not know or, conversely, the tendency to fabricate in the absence of knowledge; (e) the internal consistency of answers; (f) the tendencies to distort, exaggerate, or conceal any or all types of information; (g) the general willingness or unwillingness to talk or to continue after a short period of time (for example, does he become bored and then give short answers?).

   3. Local Reputation.   This involves judgments by others who know the informant which bear on the reliability of his answers. For example, is he known as honest or dishonest, a man who knows much or little about the past? Do his family, kin group, or other connections and loyalties make him more likely to bias answers in particular ways? The ethnographer will probably obtain this kind of information in the course of selecting his informants, and it is essential to record it.

   In addition to these general evaluations of informant characteristics, insertions should be made in parenthesis in the interview text concerning particular replies that are dubious, biased, or based on misunderstanding.

D.   Selection of Interpreters.

   The considerations of competence and absence of bias mentioned for the choice of informants are also relevant to the choice of interpreters. He should be a native speaker of the local language, this being more important (because less obvious to the ethnographer) than his English competence. If he is a local outgrouper, his own ethnicity may affect the informant's answers and his own translations, especially for a content such as ours. Even so, each interpreter is a biased vehicle, and for this reason, in the replication of interviews, a replication through different interpreters each time is desirable. This may not be feasible in all cases, but should be striven for. (The double-translation procedure, described below, will provide some feeling for how important this requirement is.)

E.   Data Collection Procedure.

   Although most of the data will be collected through informant interviews, with only the background material in Section V derived from observation by the ethnographer and from documentary records, several different procedures will be followed for informant interviewing. On some topics (indicated below) there are set interview schedules that are to be translated into the vernacular (and then translated back into English by a different bilingual as a check on the original translation) as accurately as possible. On other topics the ethnographer will be free to devise his own interviewing strategy and schedule, so long as he obtains data to answer the questions that are asked of him in this manual. In either event he is to record the responses (or their English translation) in detailed field notes.

II.   INTERVIEWS WITH BILINGUAL INFORMANTS ON RELEVANT VERNACULAR TERMINOLOGY

As background to the translation of the Ethnocentrism Inquiry Schedule, two special explorations of conceptual structure are desirable: on concepts of social organization, and on concepts of aggression. These explorations should be done in two steps: first English-vernacular, with one informant, then vernacular-English, with another informant.

A.   Concepts of Social Organization

The aim is to map out the meanings of the terms that refer to group organization and membership by getting a starter vocabulary of local language terms in this domain and by using them as points of departure for learning the range of their application. Although the task is similar to the investigations of folk taxonomies in other domains, we do not aspire to the exhaustive or axiomatized goals represented by componential analysis.

A.1.   Elicit all of the vernacular equivalents (and their literal meanings if they are idiomatic) for the following English words (or their English equivalents most likely to be understood by the bilingual):

A.1.1.   Mankind

A.1.2.   Human being

A.1.3.   Animal, nonhuman

A.1.4.   People

A.1.5.   Persons

A.1.6.   Group (in the generic sense as a reified aggregate of people)

A.1.7.   Family, domestic group

A.1.8.   Home, homestead

A.1.9.   House, household, compound

A.1.10.   Descent group(s)

A.1.11.   Territorial unit: village, community

A.1.12.   Larger territorial unit: subtribe.

A.1.13.   Tribe, people, those speaking the same language or with the same customs, etc. (Find actual basis for the term and explore whether it applies equally to allies and enemies)

A.1.14.   Kingdom

A.1.15.   Nation (with modern nations as examples). This is, of course, an arbitrary list expressing the range of concepts in which we are interested. The ethnographer will find it necessary to improvise but should not omit any of the above It is particularly important to record the absence of near equivalents for the English terms, as an introduction to the folk conceptual scheme which seems to be operating.

A.2.   Add to the resulting list of vernacular terms any other generic terms used in describing the hierarchy of local membership groups. For each of them, get from another bilingual all of the English equivalents. Probe to find conceptual boundaries, distinctions, conditions of usage, and.

B.   Concepts of Aggression.

The aim here is to obtain data on the categories most commonly used by group members in speaking about behavior that we label aggressive, the scope and content of each category in terms of the discrete acts and/or subjective experiences to which it refers, the use of the categories as dispositional constructs for designating tendencies of persons and/or situations, and the beliefs concerning what gives rise to the acts, experiences, and tendencies covered by each category. The list below is arbitrarily ordered according to Western categories.

Elicit the vernacular equivalents (and their literal meanings if they are idiomatic) for the following English words (or their English equivalents most likely to be understood by the bilingual):

B.1.   Physical aggression:
B.1.1.   Strike, hit, attack, assualt, fight (verb)
B.1.2.   Injure, hurt
B.1.3.   Kill, murder
B.1.4.   Brawl, combat, fight (noun)
B.1.5.   Violence
B.2.   Verbal aggression:
B.2.1.   Insult, abuse, swear at
B.2.2.   Scold, chastise
B.2.3.   Threaten
B.2.4.   Argue, quarrel (mutual)
B.2.5.   Slander, speak ill of (privately)
B.3.   Emotional states of aggression:
B.3.1.   Dislike, hatred, wishing ill to someone
B.3.2.   Anger, rage
B.3.3.   Irritability, quickness of temper
B.3.4.   Envy, jealousy
B.4.   Aggression (that is, the English word for a general concept covering physical and verbal manifestations of emotional hostility)
B.5.   Character traits:
B.5.1.   Violent, combative
B.5.2.   Quarrelsome (verbally)
B.5.3.   Abusive
B.5.4.   Slanderous, backbiting
B.5.5.   Belligerent (unprovoked)
B.5.6.   Irritable, easily angered

B.5.7.   Secretly hostile, ill-wishing

B.5.8.   Envious, jealous

B.5.9.   Violently insane, mad. As with the group terminology, so with these vernacular terms, translation back into English by another bilingual informant should be performed. Explore for distinctions, conditions of usage, etc.

B.6.   At least one of the bilingual informants should be asked concerning each category of aggression elicited: "Is_____(category name) always good, always bad, or sometimes good and sometimes bad? Why?"

III.   ETHNOCENTRISM INQUIRY SCHEDULE

(Methodological Introduction)   In this section and Section IV, which follows, the ethnographer is asked to obtain the information indicated. It is intended that he ask the questions and use the approaches that are required to achieve this goal. Public opinion poll procedures are neither feasible nor sufficient. The job is not done when a specified question has been asked and an answer given, if the required information has not been obtained. Similarly, if this informant has already provided the information required, there is no need to ask the question. (But notice that, at least, four independent reports on each topic are wanted).

Because of this, in a previous version of this section, the questions were addressed to the ethnographer rather than to the informant or respondent. The present version differs in providing suggested wordings in English for starter questions to be asked of the informant. This is done for two purposes. On the one hand, for most topics the ethnographer has at some point to frame a question for his interpreter to relay, and in the haste of the face-to-face situation may employ a colloquial, elliptical, or ambiguous English. It may, therefore, be convenient to have a ready-worded statement in English.

Second, a specific English wording is needed for the *Double-Translation Task,* to provide the original version with which to compare the English back-translation. Even where one is using a tried-and-true interpreter, this procedure is highly desirable, if only because of the often forgotten ambiguity of colloquial English, and because of the often subtle distinctions required in the inquiry. For such a concentrated and focused inquiry there are lacking the opportunities to cross-check and to learn by listening and observation that normal ethnography provides. Thus it is particularly important to be sure that when new topics are introduced, the starting question is as close to that intended as is possible.

In what follows, those portions in quotes are for use in the double-translation task. They are to be translated by one interpreter into the local language, and then independently translated back into English by a second interpreter. If the interpreters are literate, both of these steps can be done in writing. If they are not, the first translation into the local language (but not the original English) can be spoken into a tape recorder, and this record subsequently played to a second interpreter who then interprets into English. The oral process is much more disappointing in outcome than is the written process and is not to be preferred. However, fifteen-minute samples of the oral process provide an enlightening screening test for potential interpreters, and one that has face validity to the candidates involved.

As a supplementary project, the process of double translation is being studied in its own right. For this purpose, where feasible, the records of the process are desired. Most important is a copy of the first English back-translation, no matter how poor it may be. As this back translation is used in discussion with the interpreters in revising the local language version, it will help if the English back-translation is red-penciled to indicate the nature of its errors. If the error seems to have occurred in the initial step from English to local-language, mark it I.E. (in error); if the error is in the translation from the local language back into English, mark it O.E. (out error).

With two interpreters doing written translations, the double-translating and the subsequent corrective editing will probably take from five to seven days. The original English questions can be divided between the two for in-translation, and they can then back-translate each others' in-translations. It may be found helpful in achieving adequate translations to substitute the actual name of the ingroup, and the name of some specific outgroup where (ingroup) and (outgroup) are indicated in the version here presented, before turning the original English questions over to the interpreter. For field use, however, the local language version should make easy and clear the substitution of different outgroups from phase to phase of the inquiry. A final edited local-language version can be usefully used in the actual interviewing of informants, if the interpreter is literate. The interpreter can keep a copy in front of him to refer to for the agreed on starter wording, for use as indicated by the ethnographer who may be able to start an inquiry by merely designating the question number. Of course, once any given topic has been started, the follow-up questioning must be extemporized by ethnographer and interpreter until proper comprehension and response is achieved.

For many of the topics that follow, more alternative wordings and probes are offered than will actually be needed in many interviews. On other topics, there is only a sampling of possible probes that might prove useful.

The English wordings provided are often stilted, awkward, and childish. In part, at least, this is because of the efforts to provide a completely explicit English, as through repeating nouns instead of using pronouns which are so often ambiguous in their reference. Even so, in double-translation task there will occasionally be a need to provide altered English wordings before the interpreter can make his first in-translation. Where this is so, a note of these changes is needed for the double-translation study.

Before the comparison of the two English-language versions and the subsequent editing of the local-language versions of Sections III and IV, the ethnographer should conduct the II.A. and II.B. interviews on concepts of social organization and aggression, to sharpen the ethnographer's awareness of available terminology in the local language for these conceptual domains. For example, among the Gusii, the II.B. interview uncovered the common usage of the same verb for "injure" and "kill" and led to the insertion in the Gusii-language questions of explicit reference to death where "killing" rather than "injury" was the intended meaning.

In conclusion, we emphasize again that while specific queries to the informant are provided throughout, it is important to regard them as topic indicators addressed to the ethnographer, who is to use the tactics and wordings that seem to him optimal in achieving the information required.

A.   Survey of Outgroups

The effort in this section is to get from the informant in an as unprejudiced manner as possible a traditional vocabulary of groups. No uniformly successful approach has been found, and it may be expected that some of the entries into the problem will draw a blank. The first few questions approach the problem in an open-ended manner, from several diverse starting points. Later questions are more specific and directive. If previous questions have elicited partial or complete answers to subsequent ones, the questioning should be modified accordingly. Terms for outgroups and ingroup should be recorded in the vernacular.

A.1.   *Original people.*
A.1.1.   "According to the beliefs of your ancestors before the Europeans arrived; who were the first human beings in the world?"
A 1.2.   "Where did the first human beings live?"
A.1.3.   "What language did the first human beings speak?"
A.1.4.   "What other parts of the world were there?"
A.1.5.   "Where did the other peoples (groups) come from?"
A.1.6.   "Where did these other peoples live?"
A.2.   *Language.*
A.2.1.   "According to the beliefs of your ancestors in the time before the Europeans, what peoples spoke different languages from each other?" (If this draws a blank, then ask:)
A.2.2.   "Did all the peoples speak the same? Which ones spoke differently from one another?"
A.2.3.   "Which peoples could not understand one another?"
A.2.4.   "Which peoples spoke differently but were able to understand one another?"
A.2.5.   (If not previously given)
"Which peoples could your ancestors understand?"
A.2.6.   "Which ones could they not understand?"
A.2.7.   "Among the peoples your ancestors *could* understand, which ones

spoke differently (said words differently, had a different way of talking) from your ancestors?''

A.3.   (*Groupings by warfare*)

A.3.1.   "In the days of your fathers and grandfathers, which peoples (groups) fought wars with which other groups?''

A.3.2.   "Against which peoples (groups) did your ancestors go to war?''

A.4.   (*Groups that have disappeared*).

A.4.1.   "Were there any tribes or peoples known to your ancestors long ago that have since disappeared?'' (For each such;)

A.4.2.   "Where did they live?''

A.4.3.   "What language did they speak?''

A.4.4.   "What caused them to disappear?''

A.4.5.   "Where did they go?''

A.5.   (*Migration of ingroup*)

A.5.1.   "When did the (ingroup people) come to this land?''

A.5.2.   "Where did they come from?''

A.5.3.   "What people lived on this land before the (ingroup people) came?''

A.5.4.   "Why did those people leave?''

(In this question and following ones, the ethnographer must choose a vernacular term for the ingroup. The decision will often be an arbitrary one, but one which is important for the study. If there was a traditionally centralized political organization, the term should be for the most inclusive continuous political organization. If not, it should be for the most inclusive designation carrying feelings of belonging, group membership, loyalty, pride, and the like. Language-group designations are acceptable in the absence of political structures, if the feeling of membership is present.)

A.6.   *Neighboring peoples.*

A.6.1.   "Before the coming of the Europeans, what groups lived next to the (ingroup) people?'' (Probe for neighbors in all directions.) For each of the immediately adjacent groups:

A.6.2.   "What group lived beyond the (specific outgroup)?'' (By asking what group lived beyond each mentioned group, a map of the area should be filled out with names of groups for three levels of adjacency, if possible. More remote groups should be learned of if known. It is important, however, for the informant to distinguish between his present knowledge and the knowledge had by his people at the time of the first European contact.)

A.7.   When the informant's ready inventory of outgroup names has been exhausted, ask about knowledge of and names for other outgroups that you, as an ethnographer, know to have existed in the area.

A.7.1.   "Did the (ingroup) know about the _____ in those days?''

A.7.2.   "By what names did they know them?''

A.8.   *Reducing the list of outgroups.*

In some inquiries, the same groups will be mentioned again and again in the preceding questions, and the ethnographer therefore, will, have little problem in selecting ten or more outgroups, about which to conduct the basic inquiry. In other areas, the names dredged up will differ greatly from question to question, and a much larger list of potential outgroup names will result. In this instance, a process of selecting and combining names will be necessary. In some cases, several subgroup names will have been obtained, and an inclusive name may be found that can be used instead. In other cases of strong similarities among groups but inclusive name lacking, one typical group might be taken as a representative, the similars being omitted on the presumption that the stereotypes and attitudes evoked would be essentially the same. If there are centralized state organizations among potential outgroups, these should certainly be employed. Lacking them, warfare groupings should be given high priority. Linguistic units territorially compact are also acceptable.

There may be instances in which ambiguity exists as to whether a given segment should be regarded as an outgroup neighbor or as a part of the ingroup. In such instances, it is well to remember that one of the goals of the inquiry is the testing of hypotheses dealing with the effect of cultural similarity on ethnocentric hostility. For this reason, it is desirable to have among the outgroups as much diversity as possible, including some highly similar to the ingroup. From this point of view, it would be desirable to have one of the outgroups a neighboring people sharing the same language and culture.

With these critieria in mind, the ethnographer should select some ten to fifteen outgroups for the subsequent inquiry. They should include all of the adjacent outgroups and those one degree removed. If cutting is needed, representative samples from more remote outgroups can be used.

A.9.   Masterlist of Outgroups.   In accordance with the guiding principles set forth above, prepare a master list of outgroups to be asked about in subsequent questioning. Sections B and C, which follow, are to be repeated asking about each outgroup in turn. There may be 10, 15, or more of these outgroups in some areas. Even if spread over several sittings, fatigue and boredom may very well lead to more perfunctory responses to the outgroups asked about last. If the order of inquiry were systematic, this fatigue would be confounded with factors such as proximity, size, and importance, leading to spurious relationships. For this reason the order in which outgroups are treated should be changed for each informant, and should ideally be random with regard to nearness, size, and the like. It is recognized, however, that the requirements of salience in maintaining informant rapport at crucial stages may require deviations. However, we are providing a randomization plan that should help. With the A.9. master list of outgroups are sets of random numbers to be used in ascertaining interview order where feasible. The outgroups can be listed in any order, for example, as mentioned by the informant. Not all rows will be filled, of course For the rows filled, interview first about the outgroup that has the

A.9.   Master list of Outgroups   Ingroup _____

	Name Used by Informant	*Other Names for Same Group*	Suggested Interview Order						
			1	2	3	4	5	6
1.	_____	_____	5	11	4	10	4	18
2.	_____	_____	4	13	9	9	10	1
3.	_____	_____	8	17	19	14	11	19
4.	_____	_____	18	14	20	7	17	5
5.	_____	_____	3	9	15	8	18	7
6.	_____	_____	10	6	6	11	12	2
7.	_____	_____	17	5	12	1	16	4
8.	_____	_____	11	4	3	16	2	6
9.	_____	_____	7	15	11	6	5	14
10.	_____	_____	1	10	7	3	6	8
11.	_____	_____	9	1	16	15	7	3
12.	_____	_____	14	2	2	12	9	20
13.	_____	_____	6	18	5	4	13	16
14.	_____	_____	12	20	8	19	15	11
15.	_____	_____	2	8	18	2	19	15
16.	_____	_____	20	7	13	17	20	17
17.	_____	_____	16	12	14	20	3	13
18.	_____	_____	15	3	1	13	8	12
19.	_____	_____	13	16	17	5	14	9
20.	_____	_____	19	19	10	18	1	10

Informant's Name

263

lowest number in the column corresponding to the informant being interviewed. Outgroup order should be recorded in the field notes. If there are more than 20 outgroups, randomly select 15 for inquiry. They should include all of the immediately adjacent outgroups, and a random selection at each of the further removes. Where the remoteness of the outgroup, and the informant's general denials of knowledge make it foolish to ask some of the very specific questions, they can be eliminated at the ethnographer's discretion. The general evaluative and introductory question should not be skipped, however.

OPTIONS FOR DISTRIBUTING SECTIONS B AND C AMONG INFORMANTS

It may seem too tedious to give both sections to the same informants about each outgroup. In this case, each of these sections (preceded by Section A) should be given to separate informants, running through all of the outgroups on one section with this same informant. (An alternate division of content in which one informant would answer B and C for part of the outgroups, while a second would do the same for the rest of the outgroups, would be undesirable because it would reduce the comparability among outgroups, confounding it with informant differences.) Use of both Sections B and C for all outgroups with a single informant is acceptable if informant patience is sufficient.

Where B and C are used separately, not only should *each* informant be asked A, but each should also be asked D. The informants asked about B should also be asked about F. This is for reasons of comparability between ingroup and outgroup trait descriptions.

B.   Imagery of the Outgroup

(B and C to be asked about each outgroup in turn. Use the traditionally commonest specific designation. If there are two terms of equal currency, use the more proper, less abusive term.)

B.   "For a while now, our questions will all be about the (specific outgroup) people."

B.1.   "What were all the names and nicknames used by the (ingroup) to refer to the (specific outgroup)?"

(For each name:)

B.1.1.   "What other meanings does that name have?"

B.1.2.   "Why were they called that name?"

B.1.3.   "Were there other peoples called by the same name?"

B.2.   "Did the (ingroup) like or dislike (the specific outgroup)?"

B.3.   "What did the (ingroup) people think were the virtues and good characteristics of the (outgroup) people?"

B.4.   "What did the (ingroup) people think were the sins, the weaknesses, and the bad characteristics of the (outgroup) people?"

B.5. "In what ways were the (specific outgroup) people different from the (ingroup) people?" (Record the spontaneous ordering of topics, then probe especially as indicated in B.5.1. to B.5.18. For the first few we explore alternative wordings of the basic comparisons, and then essay a standard question form. (When the respondent gives an answer that characterizes only one of the groups under comparison, ask him how the other group was on this trait.)

B.5.1. "In what ways did the (outgroups men) dress differently from the (ingroup men)?"

B.5.2. "In what ways did the (outgroup women) dress differently from the (ingroup women)?"

B.5.3. "In what ways were the (outgroup people) different from the (ingroup people) in their physical appearance?" (Probe for skin color, physiognomy, body build, bodily mutilations, etc.)

B.5.4. "In what ways was the (outgroup) language different from the (ingroup) language?" "In what ways were the (outgroup) people different from the (ingroup) people in_____?"

B.5.5. "Ways of getting food to eat?" (farming, livestock, hunting, fishing, collecting)

B.5.6. "Customs of eating?"

B.5.7. "Rules about marriage?"

B.5.8. "Circumcision of boys?"

B.5.9. "Circumcision of girls?"

B.5.10. "Rules and prohibitions about lovemaking between boys and girls?"

B.5.11. "Rules about sexual relations?"

B.5.12. "Customs of urination and defecation?"

B.5.13. "Ways of teaching children?"

B.5.14. "Customs of fighting in wars?"

B.5.15. "Political organization?"

B.5.16. "Drinking alcoholic beverages?"

B.5.17. "Crafts, manufactures, artisans?"

B.5.18. "Their houses and how they were built?"

B.5.19. , "How they treated foreigners?"

B.5.20. "Pride in themselves?"

B.6. "Were the (outgroup) people ever used as good examples in teaching (ingroup) children? Did (ingroup) people ever say to their children, 'Be like the (outgroup) people'? For what things, ways of acting, was this done?"

B.7. "Were the (outgroup) people ever used as a bad example in the teaching of (ingroup) children? Did the (ingroup) people ever say to their children, 'Don't be like the (outgroup) people'? For what things, ways of acting, was this done?"

B.8. "When (ingroup) parents were trying to frighten their children into being good, did they ever mention the (outgroup) to their children? Did the (ingroup) people ever say to their children, 'The (outgroup) will get you if you don't stop being bad' or 'I will give you away to the (outgroup) if you are bad'?"

B.9.   "Did the (ingroup) people fear the (outgroup)?"

B.10.   "Were there any of the (ingroup's) troubles or problems which (the ingroup) blamed the (outgroup) for?"

B.11.   (This shifts to the knowledge of reciprocal stereotypes, to the ingroup's knowledge of the outgroup's view of the ingroup.)

B.11.1.   "What did the (outgroup) people say about the (ingroup)?"

B.11.2.   "Did the (outgroup) people like the (ingroup)?"

B.11.3.   "Were the (outgroup) people afraid of the (ingroup)?"

B.11.4.   "Did the (outgroup) people blame the (ingroup) for troubles of the (outgroup)?"

B.11.5.   "What names did the (outgroup) have for the (ingroup) people? What did these names mean?"

C.   Traditional Relationships with the Specific Outgroup

(Asked about each outgroup, just as B. This should be modified insofar as a given informant has already provided the information.)

C.1.   *Peaceful relationships with the specific outgroup.*

C.1.1.   (If needed.) "What types of contacts and relationships did the (outgroup) people have with the (ingroup) people?"

C.1.2.   (To be asked for adjacent outgroups only.) "In those long ago days before the Europeans came, where was the boundary between (outgroup) land and the (ingroup) territory? How could one recognize this boundary? How had this boundary been decided upon?"

C.1.3.1.   "Did the (ingroup) have any common organizations with the (outgroup) people, such as clans, religious societies, age groups, blood-brother-hoods?"

C.1.3.2.   "Did the (ingroup) ever have military alliances with the (outgroup)?"

C.1.4.   "What things did the (outgroup) trade with the (ingroup)?"

C.1.5.   "Did any of the (ingroup) wizards, prophets, diviners, healers, priests, or sorcerers practice among the (outgroup) people, in the days before the Europeans came? Did any (outgroup) persons come to learn sorcery, witchcraft, divination, or other kinds of magic from (ingroup) experts?"

C.1.6.   "Did any (outgroup) wizards, prophets, diviners, healers, priests, or sorcerers practice among the (ingroup) people?" "Did any (ingroup) persons visit among the (outgroup) to get help from (outgroup) wizards, prophets, diviners, healers, priests, or sorcerers?" "Did any (ingroup) persons go to learn sorcery, witchcraft, divination, or other kinds of magic from (outgroup) experts?"

C.1.7.   "Did the (outgroup) people have any of the same religious beliefs as the (ingroup) people? Did they worship any of the same spirits and gods?"

C.1.8.   (If conceivable.) "Did people from the (ingroup) ever work together with people from the (outgroup)? On what sorts of activities?"

C.1.9.   "Did (ingroup) people ever join (outgroup) people for feasts or celebrations?"

C.1.10. "Were there games, contests, or competitions between (ingroup) people and the (outgroup) people? What were these?"

C.1.11. "Did the (outgroup) people provide gifts, tribute, slaves, children, brides, or services to the (ingroup) people? Were these obligatory or voluntary?"

C.1.12. "Did the (ingroup) provide gifts, tribute, slaves, children, brides, or services to the (outgroup)? Were these obligatory or voluntary?"

C.1.13. "How many of the (ingroup) could understand the (outgroup) language?"

C.1.14. "How many of the (outgroup) could understand the (ingroup) language?"

C.1.15. "Did the (ingroup) regard any of the (ingroup's) laws, customs, gods, tools, crops, domesticated animals, handicrafts, songs, words, methods of divination and sorcery, and the like to have originated among the (outgroup)? Were these regarded as good or bad?"

C.2. *Migration and intermarriage with the specific outgroup.*

C.2.1. "Were there any men or women who lived with the (ingroup) in those long ago days who were born as one of the (specific outgroup)? What were they called? What was their position? Were they slaves, servants, or just like other (ingroup) members? Were they given land? Were these migrants treated the same as (ingroup) members under (ingroup) laws? Were their children treated as (ingroup) members? Why did they move? How many such migrants were there?"

C.2.2. "Were there men or women born (ingroup) members who lived with the (outgroup) people? What was their position? Were they slaves or servants or like other (outgroup) persons? Why did they live there? How many such migrants were there?"

C.2.3.1. "Could (ingroup) men marry (outgroup) women? Where would such a couple live, among the (ingroup) or among the (outgroup)?"

C.2.3.2. "Could an (outgroup) man marry an (ingroup) woman? Where would they live?"

C.2.4. "Could a man be a member of both the (ingroup) and the (outgroup) at the same time?"

C.2.5. "Did the (ingroup) allow (outgroup) people to come as visitors into (ingroup) territory?" "Did the (outgroup) allow (outgroup) people to come as visitors into (ingroup) territory?" "Were there certain places in (ingroup) territory where (outgroup) visitors were not allowed to go?" "Were such (outgroup) visitors allowed into (ingroup) houses?" "Were such (outgroup) visitors allowed to eat or drink with (ingroup) people?

C.2.6. "Did the (ingroup) allow (ingroup) persons to go as visitors to (outgroup) territory?" "Did the (outgroup) allow (ingroup) persons to go as visitors into (outgroup) territory?" "Were there certain places in (outgroup) territory where (ingroup) visitors were not allowed to go?" "Were such (ingroup) visitors allowed into (outgroup) houses?" "Were such (ingroup) visitors allowed to eat or drink with (outgroup) persons?"

C.3.   *Hostile and predatory individual acts toward the outgroup.*

C.3.1.   "Did the (ingroup) in those days encourage or prohibit (ingroup) men to steal, raid, or take cattle, food, and tools from the (outgroup) persons?"

C.3.2.   "Did the (outgroup) in those days encourage or prohibit (outgroup) men to steal, raid, take cattle, food, and tools from the (ingroup)?"

C.3.3.   "Did the (ingroup) people encourage or prohibit (ingroup) men to rape, seduce, or steal women from the (outgroup)?"

C.3.4.   "Did the (outgroup) people encourage or prohibit (outgroup) men to rape, seduce, or steal women from the (ingroup)?"

C.3.5.   "Did the (ingroup) people encourage or prohibit (ingroup) men to kill (outgroup) persons?"

C.3.6.   "Did the (outgroup) people encourage or prohibit (outgroup) men to kill (ingroup) persons?"

C.3.7.   "Did (ingroup) persons use witchcraft or sorcery against (outgroup) persons?"

C.3.8.   "Did (outgroup) persons use witchcraft or sorcery against (ingroup) persons?"

C.4.   *Warfare relationships with the specific outgroup:*

In addition to the general questions outlined below, the ethnographer should use this opportunity to encourage the informant in describing specific encounters (particularly major ones or typical ones) as fully as possible and in outlining a chronology of intergroup conflicts which will help in the military history of the region, as described in Section IV.E. below.

C.4.1.   (If necessary by this time.) "Was there ever fighting between the (outgroup) people and the (ingroup) people?" (Ask even if no tradition of formal warfare exists.)

C.4.2.   "What were the causes of these fights, these wars?"

C.4.3.1.   "What were the goals for which the (ingroup) people fought? Did they fight for defense? For revenge? For wrongs? For trophies? To prove manhood? For booty and plunder? For captives? For slaves? For political control of the region?"

C.4.3.2.   "What happened when an (ingroup) man killed an (outgroup) man in war? Were there rituals he had to perform? Were there special honors awarded him? Were body parts of the dead enemy taken as trophies?"

C.4.4.   "What were the goals for which the (outgroup) fought?"

C.4.5.   "What weapons were used? How were they used? Were spears thrown from a distance? or was the fighting close in, hand-to-hand? Were attacks announced to the enemy? or was stealth and ambush used?"

C.4.6.   "What did the (ingroup) do with (outgroup) war captives?"

C.4.7.   "What did the (outgroup) do with (ingroup) war captives?"

C.4.7.1.   "In these fights, was there anything a man could do to keep from being killed when enemy warriors had him surrounded?"

C.4.8.1.   "In such fights did any of the (ingroup) men or women help the (outgroup)?"

C.4.8.2.   "In such fights, did any of the (outgroup) men or women help the (ingroup)?"

C.4.9.   "How many men were killed in such a war? What damage did wars cause? Were houses destroyed, crops ruined, and the like?"

C.4.10.   "How did such wars end? How was peace made?"

D.   Rankings of Outgroups

In this section, for up to ten of the most important groups (if more than this have been covered in Sections A, B, and C), we aspire to a complete ranking of groups on a few particularly important features. For all topics, D.1. to D.8. a complete ranking is wanted, although tied ranks will be accepted. The sample wording provided is illustrative rather than complete. For D.1. to D.5. be sure that the ingroup is included in the ranking.

D.1.   "We have talked of many tribes or groups, the_____, the_____, the_____(etc., specific outgroups) and the (ingroup). Of all of these groups, which one had the most land, the largest territory?"

"Which group had the next most land?"

"Which group ranked third in land?"

"Which group had the least land?"

"Did (outgroup A) have more land or less land than (outgroup B)?"

"Of these groups, which ones had less land than the (ingroup)?"

D.2.   "Of all of these groups, which one had the most people?"

D.3.   "Of all of these groups, in which one was there the largest city or village? What was the name of that city? How many people lived in that city?" (Get the name, if known, and population of the largest city in each group, as of the days before Europeans, as well as the rankings of these cities.) If specific known cities are not available, ask: "Which group had the largest villages? How many people lived in one of the largest villages?" and secure ranks in terms of largest village size.

D.4.   "Of all of these groups, which one was strongest in political power and war strength?"

D.4.1.   "Of all of these tribes, which one was wealthiest?"

D.5.   "Of all of these tribes, which one was the most virtuous, moral, and good?"

For the following, D.6., D.7., and D.8., the ingroup is not to be included in the ranking, but is instead an external referent.

D.6.   "Of all of these tribes, which one was the most similar to the (ingroup) in customs and ways of life?"

D.7.   "Of the languages of all of these groups, which language was the most similar to the (ingroup) language? Which most different?" Crude bases of ranking are provided previously in the several coverings of B.3.3.

D.8.   "Of all of these groups, which group did the (ingroup) people like the best in the days before the Europeans came? Which did they dislike the most?" (Etc.)

E.   Bipolar Trait Inquiry for Groups Collectively

In this section, the inquiry centers about traits that may or may not have been spontaneously mentioned by the respondent in Section B, thus serving as a cross-check and, more particularly, as an attempt to move the respondent into a language of character traits. The ethnographer should have in front of him (and the interpreter in front of him in the decided local-language usage) a list of the groups for which B and C have been done. The goal will be to get the informant to consider the status of *all* of the tribes or outgroups on the trait in question. The basic language will be bipolar: thus we shall first ask a question like, "Of all of the tribes that we have been talking about including the (ingroup), which ones did the (ingroup) regard as Dirty, and which ones did they regard as Clean?" If some tribes are mentioned in each class, then ask about the unmentioned ones, "Were the (specific outgroup) regarded as Dirty or Clean?" An intermediate category of "neither" or "in between" or "average" is acceptable if the tribe has been specifically mentioned. Full record should be made of the informant's responses, and restatements of the trait in his own words are to be recorded. If the informant states that all are Dirty, this should be recorded as such and, indeed, certain theories predict that all outgroups will be perceived in the same way on certain traits. However, in these instances follow-up questions should ask: "Which tribe was thought to be the most hardworking," and so forth. Even if the initial questions have provided two or three groups, it is desirable, where informant interest and discrimination permit, to follow up by asking for the extremes: "Which tribe was the dirtiest?" "Which tribe was the cleanest?"

Order effects, fatigue effects, attention, and recency of reminder effects, all create bias in such an inquiry, particularly in a section like this where abstractions are involved. This bias as it affects differential attention to groups can be reduced if the ethnographer's inquiry and reminder list is in the different order specified in Section A.9. for each separate informant and if in reminding on different traits, the groups are offered in changing orders. To prevent order and fatigue effects from uniformly piling up on certain traits, we request the ethnographer to *reverse the order of items E.1. to E.17. every other* time he administers them, *keeping the numbers the same* regardless of order. To assure accuracy in analysis, the interview record should spell out the trait name.

For items E.1. to E.17. use this general stem:

"Of all the groups we have mentioned, including the (ingroup), which groups did the (ingroup) in those old days believe to be_____?"

The only exceptions for the use of this general stem are items E.5., E.6., E.11., and E.12., which have "men" or "women" beside them. For these items use one of the following stems with the appropriate sex:

"Of all the groups we have talked about, which groups did the (ingroup) believe to have_____ men/women ?" Or if that does not translate smoothly, "Of all the groups we have been talking about, which groups did the (ingroup) think to have men/women who were _____ , and which men/women who were _____ ?"

E.1.	"Peaceful among themselves	or	Quarrelsome among themselves"
E.2.	"Peaceful with neighboring tribes	or	Quarrelsome with other tribes"
E.3.	"Honest and trustworthy among their own people	or	Dishonest and treacherous among their own people"
E.4.	"Honest and trustworthy dealings with foreigners and strangers	or	Dishonest and treacherous in dealings with foreigners and strangers"
E.5.	"Hardworking men	or	Lazy men"
E.6.	"Hardworking women	or	Lazy women"
E.7.	"Brave	or	Cowardly"
E.8.	"Dirty, filthy	or	Clean, sanitary"
E.9.	"Stupid	or	Intelligent, clever"
E.10.	"Weak physically (muscle strength)	or	Strong muscled"
E.11.	"Handsome, beautiful men	or	Unattractive, ugly men"
E.12.	"Handsome, beautiful women	or	Unattractive, ugly women"
E.13.	"Had strong magical powers	or	Had weak magical powers"
E.14.	"Friendly, warm, hospitable	or	Unfriendly, cold, inhospitable"
E.15.	"Sexually restrictive, controlled	or	Sexually immoral"
E 16.	"Cruel	or	Not cruel"
E.17.	"Distrusting of others, suspicious	or	Trusting, gullible"

F.   Questions about the Ingroup Parallel to Section B

F.1.   "What names did the (ingroup) people use in naming themselves? What did they name their own tribe?" For each name: "What was the meaning of that name? What other meanings did that name have? In what ways would the (ingroup) use that name?"

F.2.   "What did the (ingroup) people think were the good characteristics of the (ingroup) people?"
F.3.   "What did the (ingroup) people think were the sins, weaknesses, and bad characteristics of the (ingroup) people?"

G.   Evaluation of Trait Pairs Used in Section E

(Ask for each of the Pairs in E).

"Did the (ingroup) people in those long ago times think it better (more virtuous) to be_____ or _____?" Explain if necessary that groups differ in what things they regard as good. Get explanations on unlikely or puzzling responses. In records use numbers G.1. to G.17. in parallel to E.1. to E.17.

H.   Special Interview

This is to be used with an old outgrouper dwelling among the ingroup. Such persons are not to be used as regular informants, unless rules of exogamy and residence make no other males available. If these migrants are numerous, restrict to migrants from the major outgroups, as used in D, or from the basic cluster. These interviews focus only on the comparison of and relationship between the two groups involved.

H.1.   "How did you happen to come to live here? Why did you leave your original people?"
H.2.   "How have you been treated here? What is your position here? In what ways are you treated differently from other (ingroup) men? In what ways are you restricted from full membership as an (ingroup) member? What things are you not allowed to do? Was there any initiation or naturalization ceremony making you an (ingroup) member?"
H.3.   "Are you still regarded as a member of the (outgroup) in which you were born? Would the (original outgroup) allow you to return there to live?
H.4.   "What would you do in case of war between the (ingroup) and the (original group)?"

Then do B. C, D, and E using the two groups only.

IV.   INTERVIEWS ON INTERNAL FEATURES OF THE GROUP

(N.B. The subsection's index letters here follow those of Section III rather than replicating them.)

This section covers a wide range of variables that appear in various theories as causes or correlates of ethnocentric hostility and imagery. The data requirements are stated as questions to informants for the most part, although supplementary information will be welcome.

It appears altogether likely that the interview questions set forth below will not be sufficient to elicit the desired information from informants in all of the diverse areas of the world covered by this study. The ethnographer should feel free to *supplement* these questions as necessary to obtain the data.

I.   Aggression

1. Interpersonal Aggression within the Local Community   So many social science theories emphasize a relationship between "internal" order and conflict, on the one hand, and "external" war and peace, on the other, that the reliable assessment of amount or degree of conflict at various structural levels in all known human societies would naturally assume the highest priority among types of information required to further the comparative understanding of the subject. Central to this goal would be the measurement of the extent to which violent acts occur *within* self-regulating social units, such as local communities tend to be in stateless societies. In societies without records, assessments of this type are exceedingly difficult to make with any reliability, unless the kind of behavior is unusually frequent or practically nonexistent. The importance of the information, however, compels persistence in its pursuit by whatever means we have available.

The procedure outlined below is an attempt to overcome the various difficulties inherent in obtaining rates of homicide and other aggressive behaviors from informants. It may be unworkable in many areas, but the ethnographer should regard it as representing problems for which he may be able to find better solutions in the context of his particular group. It is hoped that after trying the recommended procedure, he will experiment with strategies for the estimation of rates and will adopt one that works best. *Some* estimations, if accompanied by a description of the procedure used to obtain them, are much preferable to none in this important area of investigation.

Locating the Local Community Boundary of Reference   For Sections I to N the ethnographer should decide on some local unit of unambiguous reference, territorially contiguous, and of a determinate population. For Kisii Highlands (southwestern Kenya) where no villages exist but where there is a high degree of localized lineage organization, the unit chosen was a localized medial lineage in which cattle had been traditionally herded together, and which represented the maximal scope of everyday social intercourse. These units were eponymous, commonly used designations and were traditionally the minimal units of common defense, organized around the common herd of cattle. In other areas the unit chosen might be a village, a cluster of hamlets if given a common name and with recognized boundaries. However, if the population of the unit is smaller than say 300, the murder rates, and so forth will be unstable, and a larger unit would be preferred. Thus it would be better if a cluster of villages can be unambiguously designated with a name in local currency, and which ideally functioned as a political unit or segment of the ethnic group. Another desideratum is that the unit have such internal communication that any alert member would hear the details of any conspicuous act of violence such as murder occurring within the unit.

By using a population unit of concrete reference and acquaintance, and by getting, where possible, recollections of specific instances, we hope to achieve approximate frequency data for cross-cultural comparison. Thus we are seeking informant reports on total frequency for a specified population segment of his acquaintance during a specified period of time. Although the estimates will be crude, we expect the cross-cultural variations in a large sample of societies to be great enough to justify exploratory analyses on this type of measure. For example, the variations of homicide rates of modern nations, from less than 1/100,000 per year to more than 10/100,000 per year, might well represent a narrower range than that found in traditional tribal societies. For an informant discussing a population segment of 10,000, the first figure would be reported as about once in ten years, while the second figure would be reported as approximately one homicide a year. If, however, the population segment had a population of 1000, the first rate would be reported as once in 100 years — a figure probably indistinguishable from never or from once in 50 years. In such a case, it would seem well to use in addition a larger designatable population unit *for this event*: probably rare but dramatic events such as murder are uniformly known about for a much larger population area than would be a commoner event, for example, drunken brawling short of murder.

Where, in the following questions in Sections I to N frequency of occurrence is asked for, the following questions and probes may be of use:

a.   "How frequent was (specific crime or deviant behavior) in your (specified population segment) in the days before the Europeans came?"
b.   "How many times did it happen in a lifetime of a man who lived to be fifty?"
c.   (If answer to b is more than 5) "How many times did it happen in a ten-year period?"
d.   (If answer to c is more than 10) "How many times in a year?"
e.   (If answer to d is more than 12, etc.) "How many times in a month?"

In some areas it may be found — at least, for homicide—that informants will more readily enumerate specific instances in a remote period than they will generalize about average frequencies. This is a highly desirable situation if properly exploited. It requires three steps: (1) an estimate of population size of the group being reported on at a particular period; (2) the establishment of a reporting period by relative or absolute dating; (3) the enumeration and description of each case of homicide for the given group during the given period.

1.   Estimate of Population Size.   The exact technique to be employed by the ethnographer will necessarily vary from one area to another, but the following procedure used among the Gusii of Kenya can serve as an illustration: (a) focus the informant's attention on a particular stage in his life, for example, the time of his initiation or the time of his first marriage; (b) ask him to enumerate all the persons actually living in his own domestic group at that time; (c) having obtained a total figure for his own domestic group, ask him to compare its size with others in the local segment: were there larger ones, smaller ones, what was about average and so on? (d) ask him to enumerate all of the domestic groups in the local segment as of that period, and at the end inquire how many he thinks he has missed; (e) multiply the average domestic group size by the number of domestic groups in the local segment to get a population estimate for one local segment at one time period; (f) ask the informant to compare the size of adjacent local segments with that of his own; (g) if the informant's local segment is so small that he claims to remember all of the homicide cases in adjacent segments, go through the above procedure with a suitable informant from, at least one of the adjacent segments, in order to estimate population size for the whole cluster of segments.

2.   **The Reporting Period.**   Dating pre-European events in a nonliterate society can be difficult. However, frequently the ethnographer can gain access to reliable records of a few local events — wars, epidemics, famines, eclipses, vocanic eruptions, the arrival of specific groups of Europeans, and the like — that are clearly remembered by his informants and that can be used as a marker for recollection. In addition to these absolute dates, there may be indigenous methods of establishing the passage of years through annual events or other regular cycles, so that it would be possible to know how many years there are between events x and y without knowing exactly when they occurred. By absolute or relative dating, or some combination of the two, the ethnographer can establish two points in time that are meaningful markers for the informant (for example, his initiation, first marriage, father's death, plus a later public event) or a determinate period of years. This period is to be used for the reporting of homicide cases.

3.   **Enumeration of Homicide Cases.**   Ask the informant to mention each instance of homicide during the reporting period for his own local segment and hopefully (if his memory is good enough) for the other segments in the cluster as well. For instance, ask him to report the sex and age of the killer and victim, the relationship between them, the motive (even if in general terms) and whether intoxication, insanity, witchcraft and sorcery, and so forth, was involved. Any other details he is willing and able to provide are welcome. When his enumeration is finished ask him if he thinks he has really remembered all of the homicides occurring in the segment during that period, and to estimate the number he has missed.

This procedure results in (1) a figure representing the number of homicide cases in an estimated population during a specified number of years — which can be used to compute a crude homicide rate; (2) case material that provides the relative frequency of types of homicide probably still more validly comparable with current and European data than are the absolute total rates.

The same enumerative procedure can probably be followed for certain other rare and memorable events such as suicide and violent insanity, using the same population bases and reporting periods.

I.1.   "In the old days, before the Europeans came, to what (local community) did you belong?" (Use the specific community name where appropriate in the questions that follow.) "In those days, how many families (or other domestic groups) were there in that (local community)? Approximately how many persons, including children were there in each family?"

I.1.1.   "What sorts of quarrels, physical fighting, and violence took place within (informant's local community)?"

I.1.2.   "Were there lawless killings among the people of (local community)? Who killed whom? Were the killer and killed related to each other? (Probe for tendencies for it to be members of the same domestic group or neighborhood, landlord-tenant, nephew-uncle, father-son, co-wives, specific age-sex groups, etc.) "Why did people kill each other?" (Distinguish lawless murder from execution.)

I.1.3.   "In those days before the Europeans came, how frequent were lawless killings among the people of (local community)?"

I.1.3.1.   "Since the Europeans came, are there more or fewer of such lawless killings among the (local segment)?"

I.1.4.   "In those days before the Europeans came, what happened when one person killed another? Did the treatment or settlement vary depending on how the killer and killed were related? How?"

I.1.4.1.   "In those days, how frequently were people killed by group decision because of some crime they had committed, or because some god or spirit has requested it? What were the causes of these executions? How were they carried out?"

I.1.5.   "Were there fights, assaults, injurious physical violence short of killing, among the people of (local segment)? Between whom?" (Probe for relationship of parties involved, as in I.1.) "What were the usual situations in which these fights occurred? Were the people who fought usually drunk?"

I.1.6.   "How frequent were such injurious fights among the people of (local segment)?"

I.1.7.   "What happened when someone was injured in such a fight? What punishment or settlement would occur?"

I.1.7.1.   "Since the Europeans came, are there more or fewer of such injurious fights among the (local segment)?"

I.1.8.   "What about arson and deliberate destruction of property among the people of (local segment)? Between what persons? What were the usual situations in which it occurred? Were the persons who did it usually drunk?"

I.1.9.   "How frequent was such arson and deliberate destruction of property among the people of (local segment)?"

I.1.10.   "What punishment or settlement would occur in the case of arson or other deliberate destruction of property?"

I.1.10.1.   "Since the Europeans came, is there more or less arson and destruction in (local segment)?

I.1.11.   "What about serious quarrels with words but without physical fighting? Between what persons? What were the usual situations in which it occurred? Were the persons who did it usually drunk?

I.1.12.   "How frequent were such quarrels without physical violence?"

I.1.12.1.   "Since the Europeans came, are there more or fewer quarrels without physical violence in (local segment)?"

I.1.13.   "Was there 'back-biting' (serious accusations made when the person is not present, slanderous, malicious gossip) among the people of (local segment)?"

I.1.14.   "How frequent was such 'back-biting'?"

I.1.14.1.   "Since the Europeans came, has there been more or less 'back-biting' in (local segment)?"

(Intracommunity aggression in the form of witchcraft and sorcery is covered in Section L.4. below.)

I.2.   Aggression between Communities within the Ingroup.   This section deals with aggression between the members of different communities. For his coverage of sociopolitical structure the ethnographer will have collected data on supracommunity political organization and other interterritorial and intersegmental bonds (including intermarriage) within the ethnic unit. This background will enable him to identify the several levels of segmentation between the local community and the ethnic units (the "ingroup" of our questions). For example, in a pyramidal territorial structure, whether lineage-based or not, one would speak of intervillage relations, relations between recognized clusters of villages, and between recognized and named groups of such clusters.

For *each* traditional level of segmentation within the ethnic group, the ethnographer should get the following information:

I.2.1.   "What types of unfriendly, hostile, action occurred between one (specific segment at one level) and another (at the same level)?" (For each segmentation level, probe for intergroup theft, abduction of women and children, witchcraft and sorcery, litigation, encroachment on land, murder, organized fighting, and warfare. Where warfare occurred comparable to that between outgroups, get the information to compare their liking and disliking of an opposing segment with that for outgroups. See I.2.11. below.) (For each type of unfriendly action, at each level): "What were the rules regarding such action? What about punishment and restitution?"

I.2.2.   (For each) "How frequent?" (Use I.1. scale.)

I.2.3.   (If killing as isolated murder or warfare is mentioned, get frequency rates of actual incidence between the informant's own segment and specific adjacent segments for a specified time period, as in I.2., above.) (For those segmentation levels at which there is group fighting, battles, warfare, ask the following:)

I.2.4.   "What were the causes of these fights, these wars?"

I.2.5.   "What were the goals for which people fought?" (Probe for: defense, revenge, trophies, to prove manhood, booty, and plunder, captives, slaves, territory, and political control.)

I.2.6.   "What weapons were used? How used?" (thrown weapons versus close-in fighting) "Were attacks announced to the enemy, or was there stealth and ambush?" (Probe for any differences in the rules for such warfare and that between ingroup and outgroups as reported in the repetitions of Section C.4. above.)

I.2.7.   "What was done with captives?"

I.2.8.   "Were there any things a man could do to prevent being killed?" (surrender signs, etc.)

I.2.9.   "How many men were killed in such a war? How much damage did such wars cause?" (houses destroyed, crops ruined, etc.)

I.2.10.   "How did such wars end? How was peace made?" (Probe for differences with outgroups wars.)

I.2.11.   (If intensity of warfare is comparable to that with outgroups, get the segment in question ranked among outgroups for liking, as in D.8.) "Did the (local segment) like better the (enemy segment of the ingroup) or (the specific outgroup)?"

I.3.   *Suicide.*

I.3.1.   "How frequent was self-killing (record vernacular term for suicide) in your (local segment) in the days before the Europeans came? Was it more or less frequent than killing others in (local segment)?"

I.3.2.   "How did people kill themselves?"

I.3.3.   "Why did people do it?"

I.3.4.   "What did people say when someone killed himself in those days? Was the funeral for such a person different?"

I.3.5.   "What did people do if they saw someone trying to kill himself? How did they treat him?"

I.3.6.   "Since the Europeans came, is suicide more or less frequent?"

I.4. ,   *Other symptoms of aggression.*

I.4.1.   "When persons became insane, crazy, did they ever try to hurt or kill other people? Explain."

I.4.2.   "Sepaking of your own (local segment) in the days before Europeans came, how frequent were such insane persons?"

I.4.3. ,   "In your whole lifetime, how many insane persons of this type have you known personally? How many have you heard about?"

I.4.4.   "In the days before Europeans came, were there any ceremonies performed by your people in which persons were killed, attacked, hurt, insulted, or teased?'' (Probe on funerals, weddings, birth or naming rites, initiations, religious festivals, etc.) ''How frequent were such ceremonies?'' (The ethnographer should cover the major ceremonies he knows to have been practiced and give examples if the informant does not understand.)

I.4.5.　''Tell me about the sports or games played by the (ingroup) before Europeans came. Were there games in which one person could hurt another? Were there games of intense competition, in which persons tried very hard to win? Describe such games and tell how often they were played.''

I.4.6.　(Using his local knowledge to provide concrete phrasing, the ethnographer should frame questions to reveal possible aggressive sadistic aspects in the killing of animals.) ''How were animals killed? Who did the killing? In what ceremonies were animals killed? What was the largest number of animals that would be killed in a single ceremony?''

I.4.7.　''What was the attitude of the (ingroup) people toward teasing, kicking, beating, animals? Were there any animals which they enjoyed tormenting? What did they do when children tormented animals?'' (*Note.* The ethnographer should record his own contemporary observations on aggression toward animals.)

I.4.8　''Did people ever eat human beings? Who? When? How frequently did it happen?''

J.　Sexual Behavior

The focus of this section is on the traditional restrictiveness of formal rules concerning sexual behavior, the probable frequency of several categories of behavior (whether formally prohibited or not) and the severity of sanctions on the violation of rules.

J.1.　*Premarital sexual behavior.*

J.1.1.　''In the old days before the Europeans came, what were the rules young man do when he wanted to have sexual relations with a woman? How difficult was it to arrange? How frequently during a week or month would he do it?''

J.1.2.　''Were any girls virgins at marriage? What proportion of girls?''

J.1.3.　''Were there girls who had sexual relations frequently with many men?''

J.1.4.　''What happened to boys and girls who broke these rules concerning sexual relations between unmarried persons?''

J.2.　*Extramarital sexual behavior.*

J.2.1　''In the old days before the Europeans came, what were the rules restricting husbands and wives having sexual relations with other persons? Were there different rules for husbands than for wives?''

J.2.2.　''What proportion of husbands had sexual relations with other women than their wives? For such husbands, how frequently would they do so?''

J.2.3.   "Did such husbands attempt to conceal these extramarital affairs? Why?"

J.2.4.   "What proportion of wives had affairs with men other than their husbands? How frequently would such a wife do so?"

J.2.5.   "Did such wives attempt to conceal these extramarital affairs? Why?"

J.2.6.   "What happened to husbands and wives who violated the rules concerning adultery? Were men and women treated differently?"

J.3.   *Homosexuality, transvestism, and attitudes toward women.*
(If the local language has a word for homosexuality, record this and use in J.3.1., etc.)

J.3.1.   "In the old days, were there any men who had sexual relations with other men or boys?" (Record any affective response by informant as well as answer) "Was it kept secret or not?"

J.3.2.   "How many men of this sort would you say there were in your (local segment) in the days before the Europeans came? How many in your (larger segment)?"

J.3.3.   "How frequent was homosexuality?" (Use scale recommended for I.)

J.3.4.   "What happened to such homosexual men? How were they treated?"

J.3.5.   "In the old days, were there any women who had sexual relations with other women? Etc. Was this kept secret?"

J.3.6.   "How frequent were such women in your (local segment)? How many in your (larger segment)?"

J.3.7.   "What happened to such homosexual women? How were they treated?"

J.3.8.   "In the old days, did men ever put on women's clothing or act like women in other ways? Describe."

J.3.9.   "What happened to men who did that?"

J.4.   *Bestiality.*

J.4.1.   'Did men or boys have sexual relations with animals?" (If yes) "How frequently?"

J.4.2.   "What happened to a person who did this? What happened to the animals?"

J.5.   *Necrophilia.*

J.5.1.   "Did men or boys have sexual relations with dead persons?" (If yes) "How frequently did this happen?"

J.5.2.   "What happened to a person who did this?"

J.6.   *Impotence.*

J.6.1.   "Were there men who were unable to have sexual intercourse with women?" (If yes) "Why were they unable? How frequently did this happen?"

J.6.2.   "What happened to such a man?"

K.   Other Behavior Patterns

This section deals with the incidence and treatment of forms of deviant behavior not already covered in previous sections.

K.1.   *Theft.*

K.1.1.   "What kinds of things did one person steal from another in those days?" (Probe for likely types of property.)

K.1.2.   "What things were stolen most often? What next most often?" Etc.

K.1.3. ,,   "How frequent was theft in your. (local segment)?"

K.1.4.   "Were people afraid of theft? How did they guard their property?"

K.1.5.   "What did people do when a theft occurred?"

K.1.6.   "How were thieves treated when caught?"

K.2.   *Intoxication.*

K.2.1.   "Did people in those days drink anything that made them drunk?" (Probe for men, women, and children.)

K.2.2.   (If yes) "How often did most people drink such beverages? Were there some people who did not drink them?"

K.2.3.   "Did some people get very drunk and out of their senses? How did people act when they were drunk?"

K.2.4..   "What proportion of men got drunk like that? How about women? How often would men get drunk? Women?

K.2.5.   "How did other people treat someone who was very drunk?"

K.2.6.   (This question seeks to ascertain the frequency of chronic alcoholism of an incapacitating extent. Because the synonyms of a single word such as "drunkard" vary so much in the severity connoted from language to language, it seems better to utilize a more extensive descriptive phrase in translation.) "Were there people who were drunk every day, so much that they could not do useful work or participate in community activities?"

K.2.7.   "How many such persons were there in your (local segment) in the days before the Europeans came?" (Probe for men, women.)

K.2.8.   "How many such persons have there been in your (local segment) since the Europeans came?" (Ethnographer should record his own observation on this as well.)

K.2.9.   "How did people treat such persons in the days before the Europeans came?"

K.3.   *Narcotics addiction.*

K.3.1.   "Did people in those days smoke or eat anything that made them feel particularly happy or feel dizzy, or see visions, or act strangely, or prevent them from sleeping? What was it? (Probe for opiates, marijuana, betel, kola, coffee, tea, etc.) When was it smoked or eaten?"

K.3.2.   "What proportion of people used such substances? What types of persons used them?" (Probe for sex, age, and economic differences.)

K.3.3.   "How frequently did they use these substances?"

K.3.4.   "Were there some people who used them all the time?" (Probe so that addiction is ascertained.)

K.3.5.   "How many such people (addicts) were there in your (local segment) in the days before the Europeans came?"

K.3.6.   "How many such persons have there been since the Europeans came?"

K.3.7.   "What did people say about such persons? How were they treated?"

K.4.   *Stuttering.* (Discuss with interpreters and other bilinguals the problem of a word for stuttering and/or stammering, and if there is a word, whether it is a traditional one or a recent loan word. The linguistic situation is in itself an indication of the presence or absence of the behavior problem in the pre-European culture.)

K.4.1.   (If there is no wrod for stutterer.) "Have you ever seen or heard of a person who speaks in jerks, who has trouble getting words out and says the first part of a word over and over again?" (Ethnographer and interpreter may have to imitate stuttering.)

K.4.2.   "How many stutterers were there in your (local segment) in the days before the Europeans?"

K.4.3.   "How many stutterers have there been in your (local segment) since the Europeans came?"

K.4.4.   "What did people say about stutterers? What was believed to cause stuttering? How did people treat stutterers? How did they cure stuttering?"

K.5.   *Litigation.*

K.5.1.   "In the old days before the Europeans came, were there trials, sessions to settle, mediate, or arbitrate disputes, judges, or courts of law? What kinds of trials were there? How were disputes settled? How were judges selected?"

K.5.2.   "How long did such trials take?" (How much of a day, or how many days; typical and extreme lengths.)

K.5.3.   "In your (local segment) how many times a year (how often) were such trials in the days before the Europeans came?"

K.5.4.   "Has the frequency of such cases increased or decreased since the Europeans came? How frequent are such cases now?"

K.5.5.   "In the days before the Europeans came, what sorts of cases were most frequently brought to trial? What kinds of cases are brought nowadays?"

L.   Beliefs and Rituals

L.1.   *Roster of supernatural beings.* The aim of this section is to achieve at least an outline of the personified and impersonal images which the group has of the invisible beings whose action might be relevant to their own lives. The cross-cultural variability of beliet systems is such that no single set of questions is likely to work everywhere, even as a preliminary checklist. If the ethnographer finds that these questions do not achieve their aim, he should devise ones that do or provide a sketch of the religion from his previous interviewing. In any event, ask specifically about L.1.8.

L.1.1.   "What gods did your ancestors worship or believe in in the days before the Europeans came?" (Get a description of each.)

L.1.2.   "Was there one god who was above the other gods, or ruled the other gods?" (Probe for relationship.)

L.1.3. "Did any of these gods care what human beings did, or how human beings acted? How did they show this concern?"

L.1.4. (For each god or class of gods.) "Did this god bring harm to human beings or did this god help human beings?" (How, when, etc.)

L.1.5. "In what ways did your people send messages to the gods, or seek the favor of the gods? How did the gods send messages to people, let them know what the gods wanted the people to do?"

L.1.6. "What other spirits were there that people believed in or worshipped, in those days?" (Probe for helpful, malevolent, feared; ancestral, and animal.)

L.1.7. (For each spirit or class of spirits.) "Tell me about these spirits? What did they do? What relationships did they have with human beings? How did human beings try to control them?"

L.1.8. "Of all of these gods and spirits we have talked about, did any of them concern themselves with how (ingroup members) acted toward other peoples (outgroups, tribes)?" (Probe for nature of behavior required, types of sanctions.)

L.2. *Taboos.* The aim here is to obtain data on the degree to which the life of the group was permeated with prohibitions, and the degree to which violation of these prohibitions was thought to result in dire consequences of a group-enforced or super-natural nature. For each area of possible taboo, ask these questions:

a. "Were there prohibitions dealing with_____?"

b. (Where appropriate) "How long did the prohibition last?"

c. "Was the prohibition demanded by a god or a spirit? Why?"

d. "Did people ever violate this prohibition? How frequently did such violation occur?"

e. "What happened to someone who violated the prohibition?" (Probe for group and supernatural sanctions.)

L.2.2. "Marriage between certain types of kin?"

L.2.3. "Sexual relations between certain types of kin?" (Probe for degrees of taboo: on coitus alone, on sexual joking, on seeing each other naked, on being alone in same room together, etc.)

L.2.4. "Social contact between certain types of kin?" (for example, mother-in-law speaking prohibition; father and son sleeping under same roof, etc.)

L.2.5.1. "Women when pregnant?"

L.2.5.2. "Women when menstruating?"

L.2.5.3. "A woman who has just given birth to a child?"

L.2.5.4. "A woman who is breast-feeding her baby?"

L.2.6. "Eating certain types of foods? When? Who?"

L.2.7. "Kinfolk of a person who has just died?"

L.2.8. "Speaking or laughing on certain occasions or in front of certain people?"

L.2.9.   "A man having sexual relations with his wife at certain times?"

L.2.10.   "Were there other important prohibitions not yet asked about?"

L.3.   *Theories of disease.*

L.3.1.   "When someone died, what did people say caused it? How did people explain death? Was the death thought to result from something the dead person had done? or had failed to do? What were these acts or failures?"

L.3.2.   "Which explanations of death were most frequent?"

L.3.3.   "If they thought death was due to_____ , what did they do about this?"

L.3.4.   "In the days before the europeans came, what different types of sickness were known among the (ingroup) people?" Probe to achieve a list of five or ten illnesses. For each:

L.3.4.1.   "What did they believe caused_____?"

L.3.4.2.   "What did they do to cure_____?" (Probe on disease therapy to the extent that ingestion of medicine, cessation of eating, emetics, laxatives, sacrifice, sorcery, and the like can be distinguished. There is no desire for ethnopharmacology per se.)

L.3.5.   "Of the causes for disease you have mentioned (above), which were most frequently mentioned by people as causing specific deaths?"

L.4.   *Witchcraft and sorcery.* The previous section will probably have elicited reference to witchcraft and sorcery (black magic, evil eye, bad medicine, poisoning, etc.) In the present section there is also wanted information on the social aspects of witchcraft and sorcery, beliefs and practices.

L.4.1.   "In the days before the Europeans came, could one person make another ill? How?" (Probe for distinction between physical poisoning and magic acting at a distance.) "What types of witches and sorcerers were there?" (If the local language lacks such terms, explain as bad women and men who could cause harm such as sickness and death to happen to others. If no actual cases reported, probe for common belief and scope of particular vernacular terms for such persons.)

L.4.2.   "What types of persons were witches and sorcerers?" (Age, sex, social status, etc.)

L.4.3.   "How did people get to be witches and sorcerers?"

L.4.4.   "In your (local segment) in the days before the Europeans came, how many witches and sorcerers were there?" (Get breakdown by type and sex.)

L.4.5.   "How many sorcerers and witches are there in your (local segment) nowadays?"

L.4.6.   "In the old days, how did people treat sorcerers and witches?"

L.4.7.   "What did people do to protect themselves against sorcerers and witches? What did people do to retaliate, fight back, against sorcerers and witches?"

L.4.8.   "Were sorcerers and witches ever punished? Under what circumstances? How?"

L.4.9. "How frequently did such punishments take place in your (local segment)?"

L.4.10. (The following question deals with *accusations* of witchcraft and sorcery, as distinct from persons generally accepted to be witches and sorcerers.) "How frequently did people accuse other people of using witchcraft and sorcery, including cases that probably were not correct, in the days before the Europeans came? What proportion of illness and death were believed due to witchcraft and sorcery? Would a person accuse someone in his own family? Give examples." (Probe for more remote relatives, co-wives, etc.) "Would a person accuse someone in his own local community? Would a person accuse someone of another tribe?"

L.4.11. "How frequently do people accuse other people of using witchcraft and sorcery nowadays?"

L.4.12. "Was there magic that an ordinary man could use to harm or kill an enemy?"

L.4.13. "What would cause him to do it?"

L.4.14. "How would he do it?" (for example, would he hire a professional sorcerer or use his own charms, etc.)

M. Child-Rearing Practices

This section shares with the previous one the problem of attacking a highly variable and elusive subject with questions that cannot be appropriate everywhere and will seem coarse and clumsy to an ethnographer making a thorough study of the subject. Since so few ethnographers concentrate on child-rearing practices, however, the questions may be welcome as something more than a checklist of topics to be covered. It should be emphasized that the extent to which CCSE can test a large number of psychological hypotheses regarding ethnocentrism and aggression is dependent on data obtained in response to this section.

M.1. *Stages and transitions.* The object here it to get the outline of the life cycle as seen in the traditional culture, with the emphasis on (a) the named stages of life from birth onward for both males and females, (b) the defining criteria for each stage and for movement to the next one, and (c) the ways of marking transition from one stage to another. Where actual age is not a criterion for transition, try to work out the average age at which each transition took place. The vernacular names for stages of life will have to be initially obtained from the bilingual translators in order to put the questions into the vernacular, but should be asked of the informants as well because of the possibility of multiple terms and concepts. Questions:

M.1.1. "How did people speak of newborn children? Was it the same for boys and girls?"

M.1.2.   "When did they stop speaking of them as_____(term for newborn or infant) and call them something else?"

M.1.3.   "What was the difference between a _____(term for newborn or infant) and a_____ (term for next stage)?"

M.1.4.   "What did people do when a_____ (newborn or infant) became a (next stage)?" Use the same approach for the whole life-span, probing more deeply when necessary and being especially sensitive to the gender of terms.

M.2.1.   "In the days before the Europeans came, what made little babies cry?" (If a term for preweaning or prewalking is used, this designates the appropriate age group.)

M.2.2.   "What was most often done when a baby cried?"

M.2.3.   "Did they feed a baby every time as soon as he cried, or did they make him wait?"

M.2.4.   "What were all the things that would make little boys cry?" (Use term covering age-span from weaning to approximately 6 or 8, insofar as available.)

M.2.5.   "What was done when a little boy cried?"

M.2.6.   "What made little girls cry?"

M.2.7.   "What was done when little girls cried?"

M.2.8.   "What made little babies happy and laugh?"

M.2.9.   "What made little boys happy and laugh?"

M.2.10.   "What made little girls happy and laugh?"

M.2.11.   "What games did boys play?"

M.2.12.   "What games did girls play?"

M.2.13.   "What toys were used by boys or girls?"

M.2.14.   "Where did fathers sleep?" (Was there a separate house? A separate room? A separate bed?)

M.2.15.   "Where did mothers sleep?"

M.2.16.   "Did fathers and mothers sleep together?" (The same room? The same bed?)

M.2.17.   "Where did baby boys (girls) sleep?" (With whom, shared or separate bed, etc.) "How long did they sleep there? What happened when a new baby was born?"

M.2.18.   "Where did boys sleep?" (Follow through all stages from infancy to adulthood, getting any intrastage transitions as well.)

M.2.19.   "Where did girls sleep?" (Through all stages, as for boys.)

M.3.1.   "When or at what age did mothers begin weaning a child from the breast? Why did they begin weaning? Was it when the mother was pregnant again? Or when a baby was big enough to eat by himself?"

M.3.2.   "What means were used to wean a baby? Did they send the baby to stay with other persons, away from the mother? Did they put bitter substances on the mother's breast?"

M.4.1. "At what age was a baby or child expected to control urination? Defecation?"

M.4.2. "Were children ever punished for uncontrolled urination or defecation? After what age?"

M.4.3. "Were there children as old as six years old who still wet their beds at night? How many such children were there in your (local segment) in the days before the Europeans came? Were these mostly girls? Or mostly boys? Did parents try to stop this? How?"

M.4.4. "Were there children who persisted in sucking their thumbs or fingers? When did they do this? To what age did this continue? How frequent were such children in your (local segment)? Were these mostly girls or mostly boys? Did parents try to stop this? How?"

M.4.5. "Were there children who persisted in biting their fingernails? To what age did this continue? How many such children were there in your (local segment)? Were these mostly girls or mostly boys? Did parents try to stop this? How?"

M.5. "What persons took care of babies and small children?"

M.5.1. "What persons disciplined little boys?" (Probe: Who else?) "What persons disciplined boys past adolescence?" (Or boys past initiation?")

M.5.2. "What persons disciplined little girls? Girls past adolescence?"

M.5.3. "Which persons were responsible for teaching a boy as he was growing up? A girl?"

M.6.1. "Did a boy (use term or terms for stages after infancy and before adolescence) fear his father?"

M.6.2. "Did a boy (use same terms) fear his mother?"

M.6.3. (Where social structure makes it appropriate, ask regarding other relatives, for example, "Did a boy fear his mother's brother?" etc.)

M.7. "Toward which persons did a boy have to show the most respect? Which other persons did he have to show respect to?"

M.8.1. "What were boys punished most for?"

M.8.2. "What were girls punished most for?"

M.9.1. "How were boys punished?" (Beaten by hand or switch, reprimanded, deprived of food, ridiculed, isolated, etc. Get relative frequency.) "How were girls punished?"

M.9.2. "Were persons other than parents ever used to punish children? Did chiefs, elders, medicine men, or wizards ever punish children instead of the children's parents?"

M.9.3. "Were children threatened with punishment by spirits or by gods?"

M.10.1. "What would happen to a child who engaged in sex play with other children?"

M.11. "At what age were boys required to conceal their genitals from public view? What age for girls?"

M.12.   "At what age did a boy have to dress differently and act differently from a girl?"

M.13.   "Describe the ceremonies (initiation rites) that used to be done for boys when they became men. At what age were these ceremonies done?"

M.14.   "Describe the initiation ceremonies for girls. At what age were they performed?"

M.15.1.   "What was done when boys fought with each other and with girls?"

M.15.2.   "What was done when girls fought with each other or with boys?"

M.15.3.   "What kinds of fights would a child's parents try to stop? Did the mother and father act differently about these fights?"

M.15.4.   "How would the parents stop it?"

M.15.5.   "What kinds of fights would a child's mother or father encourage?"

M.16.1.   "What happened when a child hit or insulted his father?"

M.16.2.   "What happened when a child hit or insulted his mother?"

M.16.3.   "What happened when a child hit or insulted some other adult?"

M.17.1.   "Did children play together in groups that had the same members each day?" (Stable organized gangs, etc.)

M.17.2.   "What was the rule for deciding which children belonged to which gang?" (for example, kinship, age grade, residential proximity, etc.)

M.17.3.   "Did such groups (gangs) have recognized regular leaders?"

M.17.4.   "Did mothers and fathers encourage children to belong to such a play group?"

M.18.   "Did mothers and fathers tell their children not to play with certain other children? Which other children?"

M.19.   "Were children taught to share things with others? What was done with a child who was greedy about food? Playthings?"

N.   Authority Patterns

N.1.1.   "Were married sons expected to obey their fathers?"

N.1.2.   "Was such obedience enjoyed or resented by the sons?"

N.1.3.   "What could happen if a married son disobeyed or was disrespectful to his father?"

N.1.4.   "Were there men other than fathers whom sons were expected to obey?"

N.1.5.   "Was there an age at which old men had to obey their sons or other young men?"

N.2.1.   "What could the headman (chief, elders) command other men to do?"

N.2.2.   "Could they refuse to do some things he would have wanted them to do?"

N.2.3.   "What would happen if a man disobeyed the headman (under prohibited conditions)?"

N.2.4.   "Did men enjoy obeying leaders or did they resent it?"

N.3.1.   "What were the attitudes of men toward women in those days? What respect were women given? What say did they have in the affairs of the community?"

N.3.2.   "Did a wife have any property or income which her husband could not control?"

N.3.3.   "Were women expected to obey every command of their husbands?"

N.3.4.   "Did women enjoy obeying their husbands, or did they resent it?"

N.3.5.   "Under what conditions could a woman refuse to do something her husband wanted?"

N.3.6.   "What could happen to a woman who was disobedient to her husband?"

N.3.7.   "Could a wife divorce her husband? Under what conditions?" How?"

N.3.8.   "Could a husband divorce a wife? Under what conditions?" How?"

N.3.9.   "Did a wife eat with her husband?"

N.3.10.   "Did a wife sit beside her husband?"

N.3.11.   "Did a wife have to show her respect for her husband? In what ways?"

N.3.12.   "Did a man's mother dominate (rule) his wife?"

N.3.13.   (If there is polygyny) "Among the wives of one husband, were some considered higher or better than others? What power did one wife have over the others?"

N.4.1.   "Among the sons of one man, were some considered higher than others? Did younger sons have to obey and respect their older brothers?"

N.5.1.   "How much of the average man's working time was spent in preparing for war in the days before the Europeans came?"

N.5.2.   "Were there full-time soldiers who did no other work?"

N.5.3.   (If so) "What prestige did this occupation have? How did people consider such soldiers?"

N.5.4.   "How were young men trained so as to be brave in fighting and warfare?"

N.6.1.   "Was it all right for a man to run away to save his own life in a fight or battle? Were there other things a man might do to save his life in battle?"

N.6.2.   "What actions in war were regarded as cowardly?"

N.6.3.   "How was cowardice in war punished?"

N.7.1.   "Were there special gifts, praises, or ceremonies for a man who had killed an enemy in battle or otherwise shown skill or courage in war?"

N.7.2.   "Were there men who were so brave that it seemed they sought to die in battle?"

N.7.3.   "How were those who died in battle honored? Did the gods or spirits honor those who died in battle? Were funerals for such men different?"

N.7.4.   "Were there men who were so brave and fearless in war that others thought them crazy and ridiculed them?"

N.8.1.   "When plans for wars were being talked about, were there some men who advocated peace? Were such men criticized by others?"

N.8.2.   "Were leaders who advocated war ever criticized for this by others?"

N.9.1.   "How did the (ingroup) people act when there was a war going on?"

N.9.2.   "When a war with another tribe was going on, did this increase or decrease the quarreling or conflict between different families, groups, or clans within the (ingroup)?"

N.9.3.1.   (Where this is conceivable) "What happened when a man was asked to fight in war against people who were his relatives (or affines or friends)?"

N.9.3.2.   "How many men had this happen to them?"

N.10.1.   "Did those men who fought like or enjoy fighting in wars? What about those men who did not actually fight; did they enjoy wars?"

N.10.2.   "Did women enjoy wars?"

N.10.3.   "Did men fear wars?"

N.10.4.   "Did women fear wars?"

V. GEOGRAPHIC AND ETHNOGRAPHIC BACKGROUND MATERIALS

In order for the cross-regional comparisons to be made with an adequate degree of validity by analysts who have not visited each of the regions, contextual data are needed on the intersocietal region and on the particular group studied. The following materials should be provided.

A.   Sketch Map of Region

A sketch map of the intersocietal region in which the fieldwork is done should be provided. This map should include (1) the names and territorial boundaries (or, at least, locations, if boundaries are difficult to acquire) of adjacent and more remote groups which are known to the people under study and discussed with them in the interviews, and (2) the locations of features that are believed by the ethnographer to have retarded or facilitated contact and communication between the groups in their precontact situation. Examples of retarding features would be mountains, unnavigable bodies of water, deserts, swamps, and other physiographic characteristics; facilitating features would include traditional centers of trade, urban development, or other attractive characteristics (for example, oases in a desert) which draw persons from several ethnic units together even if only for transient purposes. It will ordinarily be necessary for the ethnographer to supplement the map with an explanation of the extent to which each feature did act to facilitate or retard contact. For example, he should state if a range of mountains was or was not impassable for the local peoples and whether alternative routes were available, and whether the maritime technology of the area allowed bodies of water to be traversed. A rough scale of miles should be supplied on the map.

B.   Report on Geographical and Ecological Setting and Features of the Region.

1.   What is the overall physiography and ecology (that is, subsistence adaptations) of the region? Are there definable zones created by

elevation, rainfall, vegetation, proximity to bodies of water, and if so, how do these correspond to the ethnic units?

2. What is the population size and approximate density of the region as a whole and each of its component groups? Cite the source of data.

3. How discrete are the several groups territorially? Are there (for example) uninhabited spaces between them or are they intermingled at their boundaries? Do some groups have offshoot enclaves within others?

C.   Report on "Objective" Group Differences within the Region.

The ethnographer as a curious outsider who has prior experience of the region is in as good a position as anyone to make an unbiased statement about the realities of the group differences which may enter into the stereotypes the groups have of each other. Such a statement is essential if an estimate is to be made of the degree to which stereotypes represent distortions or accurate judgments of reality. The following is a checklist (not exhaustive) of possible group differences. The ethnographer might stimulate himself to provide a basis for these estimates by answering the questions of Section B.3. (Imagery of the Outgroup) in the Ethnocentrism Inquiry Schedule from the viewpoint of "objective reality."

1. Physical-racial. Noticeable group differences in stature, skin color, hair form, physiognomy, bodily proportions, and deformities due to disease (for example, eye conditions resulting from trachoma, skin conditions due to yaws).

2. Body mutilations. Scarification or cicatrization of face or body, nose piercing, elongation of ear lobes or lips (with or without wood or bone insertions), tooth removal, genital operations, tattooing, and the like.

3. Material culture.
   a. House type: shape of building, size of building, materials, type of roof, windows, wall decorations, arrangement of building in homestead or compound.
   b. Settlement pattern: clustered or dispersed, presence or absence of central plaza and communal buildings, and so forth.
   c. Tools and implements associated with subsistence or recreation.
   d. Art and decoration styles, presence or absence of types of craft objects such as masks, and human figurines.
   e. Food preparation: staples, other foods commonly or occasionally eaten, type and amount of cooking, use of hot spices, and the like.
   f. Clothing and bodily adornment.

Add to this any other distinctive or sharply discontinuous customs, whether actually visible or not, that are likely to be noticed by a visitor from a foreign group. These would include value differences such as variations in sexual mores, deference patterns and sociability; economic differences such as occupational specialization (for example, farmers, hunters, fishers, and traders) and wealth; magico-religious and ceremonial differences; and differences in social organization. Please notice that, unless these characteristics are asked for elsewhere in this manual, they are only to be noted here if the ethnographer, sensitized to such possible variations, notices that they distinguish one group in the region from another. An attempt should be made to find out if traits ascribed by one group to another are in fact characteristic of them, although in some cases it may be impossible to ascertain this in the time available.

D.   Report on Linguistic Differences in the Region.

These are also objective differences between the groups, but they are uniquely important, in terms of defining the units of study and in their role as features that might direct or retard communication between the groups. These questions are of primary importance:

1.   What is the relative and absolute degree of mutual intelligibility among the languages spoken by peoples in the region? This question may be answered by:
   a. Ranking each *pair* of related languages in the region for mutual intelligibility (in a region of five groups there are ten such pairs)
   b. Indicating for each pair whether it falls into one of the three following categories:
       (1)   Complete mutual intelligibility without practice.
       (2)   Complete and obvious mutual unintelligibility (as when the languages are totally unrelated).
       (3)   Some intermediate condition.

For pairs of the last category, try to find out if the other dialect can be understood and spoken with some limited practice, and how long this practice is on the average for persons in intensive and intermittent contact with speakers of the other dialect.

2.   What is the contemporary situation with respect to multilingualism in the area? Do most people know a second language, or is this knowledge restricted to certain persons with unusual opportunities for intercultural contact? Which languages do people tend to learn? Is there a lingua franca? If so, what relation does it have to the vernaculars, how old is it in the region, and how widespread is it in the area? Estimate the proportion of persons in each of the groups who speak a language understood by members of other groups in the cluster.
Note. In seeking to answer these questions about the contemporary interlinguistic situation (as distinct from the past situation, which is covered in one of the interviews below), it is not expected that the ethnographer will conduct an intensive linguistic inquiry but, instead, that he will have acquired this information in the course of his previous and current research in the area.

E.   Report on Military History.

Evidence independent of informants' accounts on the basic military history of the region is valuable and should be supplied by the ethnographer if available: historical works, travelers' accounts, district records, other documentary records or even oral retrospection by foreign witnesses. Where these materials are available. a summary account by the ethnographer, with citations, would be highly desirable. In scanning and summarizing the records, the following points are most important:

1.   The groups involved on each side.
2.   The duration, frequency, and severity (number involved and killed) of conflicts, and their relative chronological sequence.
3.   The goals and outcomes of conflicts.
4.   The offensive or defensive posture adopted by groups involved.

F.   Background Data on the Group Studied.

1.   Subsistence Base. Numerous and diverse theoretical positions emphasize several aspects of the subsistence economy as relevant to ethnocentrism and intergroup relations: frustrations generated by food scarcity, self-sufficiency of food production (or collection) versus the necessity to import food from outgroups, the movement of population generated by the food quest, and the like. Consequently, the ethnographer should try to supply answers to the following questions:

a.   What was the economic basis of the society? How adequate was the usual food supply, in terms of the prevention and alleviation of hunger, not in terms of nutritional content? How close to bare survival were people living in terms of food intake? Were there periodic famines, and if so, how frequent and how severe were they? Was there a "hungry season" each year? If so, how long did it last and how severe was it in terms of decrements of average diet? At what age did children begin experiencing cutbacks in food intake during this season?

b.   How extreme were economic differences within the society? Did everyone have enough for basic needs? Were there persons conspicuously or locally regarded as impoverished and if so, what approximate proportion of the total population did they constitute? Were there persons conspicuously or locally regarded as wealthier than average and if so, what approximate proportion of the population did they constitute? How much wealthier would you say they were than the average person in the society? To what extent were differences in wealth leveled through redistribution in feasts or culturally patterned obligations to help those who have less? What was the pattern of inheritance of property?

    c. Was the society or ethnic unit dependent on an outgroup for imports of food? To some extent this will be covered in the interview questions on intergroup trade, but here the ethnographer is to estimate the importance of the food imported for survival in terms of usual diet or at times of famine.

    d. Did economic pursuits involve the movements of persons, particularly in such directions as to increase their contacts with outgroups? What was the frequency and range of these movements? What proportion of the population is involved? How common was it for these movements to involve contacts with outgroup members, and under what circumstances? (For example, was the group nomadic or seminomadic? Did the men regularly go afar in hunting, fishing, or herding?)

2. Sociopolitical Structure. It is recognized that the ethnographer using this field manual is experienced in the collection and analysis of data on the social structure of peoples in the area he knows best. However, because the summaries needed for comparative analysis of his interview data will not allow him to meet his own high standards of sociological description, it is imperative that we make explicit which social-structural data are required.

    a. Brief sketch of sociopolitical system. The ethnographer is asked to provide an *introductory*, overall view of the traditional socio-political system of the ethnic group, stressing the basic principles of organization and its outstanding structural features as he sees them, including descent, inheritance, group organization, territorial organization, and the like. This may be as short as two double-spaced pages, or even shorter if he feels he can summarize it adequately in less space, and may be in technical anthropological language. This request for a summary is made so that the data analysts can have an informed view of the total system to work from rather than just an assemblage of the traits on which information is requested below.

    b. Territorial units. Four levels of territorial organization are likely to be involved, although a particular society may have more or less:

        (1) Domestic group. This includes households, residential family units whether nuclear or extended, homesteads and other compound units of joint residence. A simple diagram of a typical unit of this type, with indications as to the utilization of space, is desirable.

        (2) Neighborhood. A spatially demarcated set of contiguous domestic groups which forms a segment of a local community, for example, hamlets, neighborhoods, wards, barrios, or household clusters. If there were several levels of

territorial organization between the domestic group and the local community, then this level should be expanded to include these units of intermediate scope.

(3)   Local community. Normally the largest unit of frequent face-to-face interaction in folk societies, this unit may be a village or band.

(4)   Supra-community levels. In some folk societies, local communities are the highest level of organization and are autonomous; in others, territorial groupings of local communities exist. Where there were one or more levels above that of the local community, then this category should be expanded to include these superordinate units. Centralized states are included here.

For the typical unit *at each level of territorial organization*, the following information is desired:

(a)   Average population size.

(b)   Average area occupied and degree of clustering or compactness.

(c)   Composition. For the domestic goup, this means kin relationships of residents and marital forms (that is residence and plurality of spouses). At other levels it means the number and type of component groups and their degree of localization within the territorial unit. Some of these component groups are themselves territorial units of a lower level, while others are groups founded on other than territorial principles: descent groups, age groups, cult groups, cooperative work groups, sex-exclusive groups, and other associational organizations.

(d)   Functions. These include economic, ritual, adminstrative, judicial, military activities. The ethnographer should indicate which of these functions were assigned to a territorial unit at any particular level, and whether or not they were performed by component non-territorial groups. This will necessarily be fairly crude data.

(e)   Solidarity. The impression of the ethnographer, not merely of the absence of conflict within the unit, but of its positive, cohesive tendencies as manifested in cooperation, sociability, mutual dependence.

(f)   Leadership and authority. The following leadership characteristics should be attended to: number of leadership positions within a typical unit (for example a single leader, a hierarchy of several, a council of elders); functional specialization of leaders (religious, judicial, military, unspecialized, etc.); the manner in which leaders are appointed and the ease with which they can be deposed; apparent stability of leadership and of leadership positions; degree of command and enforcement power (sanctions) possessed and exercised by leaders. It is particularly important that information sufficiently relevant to the authoritarianism of leader-follower relations be provided so that a judgment can be made of the relative degree of authoritarianism at each level in the territorial system. For this purpose the ethnographer might want to include data on the deference and docility of members of unit vis-á-vis their leaders.

c. Societal complexity. The following indexes of societal complexity will probably have been reported on above, but should be specifically included.

(1) Size of the largest city, in pre-European times

(2) Types of craft and skill specialties, designating the degree to which each had full-time practitioners. (Including adminstrative military and religious roles.)

(3) Number of subordination levels in military organization, religious organization, judicial organization, administrative organization, economic organization (that is, number of levels in table of organization, who reports to whom, for example, a typical United States university has these seven levels: president, vice-presidents, deans, chairmen, professors, teaching assistants, and students, with the service personnel not adding levels, since they are a separate chain of command through president, vice-president, superintendent of buildings and grounds, single building superintendents, janitors, etc).

The ethnographer should add to this outline any type of information that he regards as essential to an adequate understanding of the traditional sociopolitical structure of the ethnic group. Some ethnographers will be working in a group that has been previously described in publication by competent professional ethnographers. Where this is the case, a bibliography on the group and an evaluation of the sources should be provided.

INDEX